Everyday Project Management Solutions

Questions and Answer

Suresh K Basandra

Ex Associate Professor & Head, Computer Center,
Management Development Institute, Gurgaon, Haryana, India
Ex Vice President of Engineering, Marble Security Inc., California, USA
Alumni, University of California, Berkeley, California, USA
M. Tech., Computer Technology, Indian Institute of Technology, Delhi, India
Ex Research Engineer, Electrical Engineering, Indian Institute of Technology, Kanpur, India
B.Sc. in Electronics Engineering, Delhi College of Engineering, Delhi, India

Everyday Project Management Solutions
Questions and Answers

Edition / Latest Update: 2026

Layout, Cover, and Illustrations Design by Karuna Basandra,
https://www.linkedin.com/in/karunabasandra/

Contact Author:
Email: sureshbasandra@cal.berkeley.edu
LinkedIn: https://www.linkedin.com/in/sureshbasandra/
@sureshbasandra
https://www.facebook.com/basandra

Dedication:
For Karuna Basandra - my wife, my best friend, and the love of my life

About Author

Suresh K Basandra is a software engineering executive with over 40+ years' research, development, management, and teaching experience in hardware, software, and information systems, 25 years in software development management, people management, and program management experience in early-stage start-ups to large global organizations as founding member/principal software engineer/software architect/senior manager/director/vice president.

He graduated in Electrical and Electronics Engineering from Delhi College of Engineering (Delhi Technological University), Delhi, India. He obtained his M. Tech. in Computer Technology from Indian Institute of Technology, Delhi, India, and Masters in Computer Science Courses from University of California, Berkeley, California, USA.

He successfully led multi-million dollars and multi-location software development products in his career. Recently he worked at Elo Touch Solutions, CDK Global (acquired by Brookfield Business Partners), LivePerson, Centrify (acquired by Thoma Bravo), Proofpoint (acquired by Thoma Bravo), Marble Security (acquired by Proofpoint), Meltwater, Good Technology (acquired by Motorola), Motorola (acquired by Google), Siebel Systems (acquired by Oracle).

Earlier, he worked as Research Engineer at Advanced Centre for Electronic Systems (ACES), Indian Institute of Technology (IIT), Kanpur, Executive Officer at Indian Ports Association (IPA), New Delhi, Senior Software Engineer at Centre For Development Of Telematics (C-DOT), New Delhi, Associate Professor and Head, Computer Center at Management Development Institute (MDI), Gurgaon, Project Manager, Computer Division, at Howe (India) Pvt. Ltd., New Delhi, Consultant at Digital Equipment (India) Ltd., New Delhi, a subsidiary of Digital Equipment Corporation (DEC), USA, Senior Project Leader at InfoGain, Inc., California, USA, and Project Manager at TCSI Corporation, California, USA.

He brought Mobile Threat Defense and Intellectual Property Protection products from concept to global markets and Social Media and Marketing products to next generation being part of the initial teams. Products he has personally led have generated over $200 million revenue per year. Based on the innovation and product and process enhancements, he has 7 patents in Analytics, Machine Learning and Application Security granted by the United States Patent and Trademark Office (USPTO) and European Patent, and two highest possible Bravo Awards from Motorola, Inc.

He has over fifty research papers and articles in the area of hardware, software, and information systems to his credit. These have appeared in various reputed journals and magazines like Information Processing Letters (Netherlands), CSI Communications, Dataquest, Information Technology (IT), Instruments and Electronics Developments, Indian Ports, and Electronics For You (EFY). He was contributing editor to Information Technology magazine from June 1991 to August 1994.

He has several books to his credit which are available globally in print as well as eBook: 'Computers Today', 'Computer Science Question Bank', 'Computer Systems Today', 'Advanced Computer Science Question Bank', 'Understanding Computers Through Common Sense', 'Local Area Networks', ' Object Oriented Software Engineering', 'Management Information Systems', 'Computers For Managers',

‘Everyday Management Solutions’, ‘Everyday Project Management Solutions’, ‘Everyday Software Development Solutions’.

Few of his books have been used as text book and reference by various accredited colleges and universities in their degree courses like B.Sc., BA, BBA, BCA, MCA, MBA, PGDCA, etc. in following 29 countries - Argentina, Bangladesh, Bhutan, Brazil, Denmark, Ecuador, Ethiopia, Ghana, India, Indonesia, Iran, Iraq, Jordan, Kenya, Malaysia, Nepal, Nigeria, Pakistan, Palestine, Russia, Singapore, Sri Lanka, Sultanate of Oman, Sweden, Tanzania, Tonga, Uganda, United Kingdom, Zimbabwe, etc.

His books, research papers and articles have been referred in various international research publications.

He has been guest faculty to State Bank of India (SBI) Staff Training College, Indian Institute of Materials Management (IIMM), and Indira Gandhi National Open University (IGNOU). He guided B.Tech. students at Indian Institute of Technology, Kanpur, India, and M.B.A. students of IGNOU for their projects. He was involved in the development of Computer Science Courses conducted by IGNOU and All India Management Association (AIMA).

His biographical details have been included in 'Reference Asia: Asia's Who's Who of Men and Women of Achievement', Vol. V, published by Rifacimento International, Delhi and 'Biography International', Vol. 3, published by Biography International, Delhi.

He is quoted in https://www.bos.com/inspired/75-quotes-on-integrity/, https://www.wow4u.com/saturdayquotes/, https://www.wow4u.com/encouraging-poems-page-4/, https://imammi.com/saturday-morning-quotes-see-the-best-collection-of-saturday-quotes, https://www.inspirationalstories.com/integrity/, https://www.womenspodium.com/quotes-on-integrity.html, https://www.360legal.net/news/360legal-blog.php, https://brontecollege.ca/wp-content/uploads/2022/04/Welcome-April.pdf, https://www.quote.cc/integrity-quotes/, https://www.goodreads.com/author/quotes/4723630.Suresh_Basandra, https://www.consultclarity.org/post/top-650-perseverance-quotes-never-give-up, https://nichequotes.com/code-reuse-quotes, https://quotessayings.net/topics/this-which/, https://quotessayings.net/authors/suresh-basandra-quotes/, https://www.consultclarity.org/post/happy-thursday-morning-quotes-and-wishes, https://alumnius.net/university_of_califo-7940-167, https://expandetumente.com/105-importante-frases-sobre-la-integridad/,

His professional affiliations include: Senior Life Member, Computer Society of India (CSI), India; Life Member, The Institution of Electronics and Telecommunication Engineers (IETE), New Delhi, India; Life Member, Indian Institute of Materials Management (IIMM), India; Life Member, Indian Science Congress Association (ISCA), Calcutta, India, Member, American Management Association (AMA), Member, Project Management Institute (PMI), Member, American Society for Quality (ASQ).

Preface

"If you would not be forgotten as soon as you are dead, either write something worth reading, or do something worth writing." - Benjamin Franklin

Today's problems cannot be solved with the same level of thinking that created them. - Albert Einstein

Numerous individuals find themselves in leadership roles such as team leads, project managers, or coordinators either by chance, due to their expertise, or because of situational factors. Often, they are appointed based on their subject matter knowledge without consideration for formal project management training.

However, lacking the specific skills and techniques necessary for effective leadership can turn the endeavor into a disaster. Fortunately, resources are available for those without formal backgrounds in project management or leadership who wish to acquaint themselves with these disciplines.

Managing a team or project is more than just delegating tasks; it requires the ability to lead, motivate, communicate clearly, mentor, evaluate performance, navigate office politics, and balance multiple responsibilities simultaneously.

Continuous improvement is crucial for all leaders, regardless of experience. This book addresses common challenges faced by project managers and leaders, providing practical solutions based on real-world scenarios.

Covering essential skills and concepts in about 300 questions and answers, this guide is invaluable for project managers and human resource professionals seeking solutions to everyday challenges. It offers practical advice based on the author's leadership experience in a format that is easy to understand and apply.

Arranged by topic, the book facilitates quick access to relevant information, making it suitable for both reference and in-depth study. It emphasizes that effective project management is a combination of various skills, each contributing to overall success.

The book also acknowledges the importance of gender equality and welcomes feedback for continuous improvement. Readers are encouraged to share their questions, insights, and success stories directly with the author.

Overall, this book serves as a comprehensive resource for anyone involved in project management or leadership roles, offering practical guidance and solutions for navigating the complexities of modern workplaces.

Forward

Suresh Basandra is a keen student of human nature who understand what makes a person effective and efficient in the workplace. He has a genius for communicate insights in simple, clear, and helpful language through various challenges managers and leaders face day to day.

Table of Contents

Everyday Project Management Solutions
1. Project Management Core Concepts
1.1. What is project management?
1.2. What is a project?
1.3. What is a project manager?
1.4. What are the rewards and stresses of project management?
1.5. What advice do you have for companies about the role of project management in a down economy?
1.6. What is the project life cycle?
1.7. What is the project management triangle or the triple constraint?
1.8. What are the project baselines?
1.9. Who are the project stakeholders?
1.10. How do you identify key players in your project?
1.11. What do you do about, handle, or manage stakeholders?
1.12. How to manage a client who is too busy to focus?
1.13. Do you think projects succeed or fail due to technical issues or user and management issues?
1.14. What are some of the classic people-related mistakes?
1.15. What are some of the classic process-related mistakes?
1.16. What are some of the classic product-related mistakes?
1.17. What are some of the classic technology-related mistakes?
1.18. What is silver-bullet syndrome and how and when does it occurs?
1.19. What is the single most important network feature in your project management communication system?
1.20. Which aspect of your project management processes needs the most improvement?
1.21. Which project documentation do you find most vital for success?
1.22. What do you need most often from executive sponsors?
1.23. What is the first thing you would do as a project manager?
1.24. Why is it important for project managers to understand the strategy of the organization that uses their services?
1.25. How would you deal with "if it is not broke" syndrome?
1.26. How would you work in an environment that implies that if you are not coding you are not working?
1.27. How would you divide your time between employee relations, project management, and paperwork?
1.28. List tips for successful project management.
1.29. What are the most urgent improvements your IT organization needs to make to support your business?
1.30. Describe a time when you implemented a new idea without being asked or pursued a new opportunity that could improve the project or company.
1.31. Describe a scenario where you had to balance competing customer demands with project constraints. How did you ensure customer satisfaction while maintaining the goals of the project?
1.32. What are some of the things a technical lead can do that a project manager cannot?
1.33. Provide summary of project management knowledge areas.
1.34. Why what happens what "After the Project" is sometimes more important than the project?
1.35. How does your management view projects? Do they view projects as being rooted in technology or focusing on business results?
1.36. What are the different project management "Level of Maturity"?
1.37. How do you manage project sponsors and stakeholders?
1.38. Why do developers sometime dislike project managers?
1.39. What is the future of project management?

1.40. How involved should the leadership be in projects?
1.41. What are the primary goals of every project?
1.42. Why is not good project management enough?
1.43. How do you manage a project?

2. Project Scope and Requirements Management

2.1. What is competitive advantage?
2.2. What is gap analysis?
2.3. What is the importance of requirements gathering?
2.4. What should you know about requirements?
2.5. How do you test the requirements?
2.6. What are the reasons for investing in requirements?
2.7. What are some of the risks related to investing in requirements?
2.8. What are the project groups' major concerns about stakeholders in discovering and specifying the requirements?
2.9. What is scope or feature creep? What are the causes of scope creep? How can you control scope creep?
2.10. What are the top five frustrations of requirements and the tips to avoid them?
2.11. What is a project charter?
2.12. How do you go about creating a project charter?
2.13. What are some of the tips for writing a project charter?
2.14. What is a deliverable? What are different types of deliverables? What are internal and external deliverables?
2.15. What is a project justification? What are the different ways of describing the cost-benefit ratio for a project in order to justify it?
2.16. What is the requirements process of a project? What are the different ways to find out the deliverables of a project?
2.17. What is a scope statement? What should a project scope statement include?
2.18. What is a work breakdown structure?
2.19. How do I do a work breakdown structure?
2.20. How do I test the work breakdown structure?
2.21. What is task list?
2.22. Why there is a need to manage diverse objectives and perspectives?
2.23. What is silo mentality, when and how does it happen, and how would you overcome it in your project team?
2.24. What are functional requirements or specifications?
2.25. How do you go about obtaining requirements from your customer?
2.26. What structure you will follow to obtain requirements from stakeholders, key managers, and end users?
2.27. How do you validate the requirements you got from customer? How do you make certain you understand what they want?
2.28. Once you have the requirements, what do you do with them?
2.29. How do you request a project scope change?
2.30. How do you communicate project scope changes?
2.31. How do you go about developing a feasibility study for a project?

3. Project Estimation

3.1. What is a project estimate? What are the major things that we estimate in a project? What are the various approaches or estimating methods used to estimate for a project? What are the various pitfalls in producing a good estimate for a project?
3.2. Why do project estimate at all for a project?
3.3. What terms are used in estimating?
3.4. What are the key steps in project estimation?

3.5. What factors are we concerned with when doing estimation for projects?
3.6. How does productivity and utilization factors play a role when doing estimating for projects?
3.7. What is life cycle cost?
3.8. What is life cycle cost as relates to software development projects?
3.9. What is statistical cost estimating?
3.10. What is Program Evaluation and Review Technique? Provide practical examples.
3.11. What is the difference between estimated cost and price of completing a project?
3.12. What is the law of diminishing returns? How this concept relates to project management?
3.13. What is a cost improvement curve?
3.14. What approach you follow for software estimation? Why use more than one estimating processes?

4. Project Planning

4.1. What is the point of planning in organizations?
4.2. Why is the project plan so important?
4.3. What should be in a project plan?
4.4. Why would you build a project plan?
4.5. How would you go about planning a project?
4.6. How would you go about building a project plan?
4.7. What is the distinction between planning and scheduling?
4.8. How do you determine staffing requirements?
4.9. Which planning method have you found yields the most accurate results?
4.10. How and why would you build dependencies into the project plan?
4.11. How would you incorporate a person's work pace into the plan?
4.12. How would you incorporate training, holidays, and individuals' education schedules?
4.13. How do you spread a task that occurs throughout the project requiring little time and effort, such as status meetings?
4.14. What value does metrics add to the project?
4.15. How would you incorporate the use of a new technology into a project plan?
4.16. How are actuals supplied to a project plan and what is the value of comparing the original estimates to actuals?
4.17. Describe what development project life cycle phases, activities, and deliverables you would include in a project plan for a software application product.
4.18. What are the most important considerations in planning a major capital project?
4.19. How do you use data to make project decisions?
4.20. What is the purpose of the project plan memorandum?
4.21. How do you write the project plan memorandum for the executive team and what does it look like?
4.22. How do develop communications plan for a project and what does it look like?
4.23. How do you develop an operations integration plan?
4.24. How do you respond to a question: "Tell me about a time... You had to proceed on a project with little information, etc."
4.25. How do you respond to a question: "Tell me about a time... You disagreed with the project design but had to deliver ..."
4.26. How do you ensure that projects are delivered on time and with high quality?

5. Project Cost Management

5.1. How do you go about cost estimation through the life cycle of a project?
5.2. What is the cost baseline?
5.3. How do you plan for and create a cost baseline in a project?
5.4. Why should we be concerned with cost budgeting or setting the cost baseline for a project?
5.5. What are the key elements to include in your cost management plan, what kind of information should be in each section, and how to do it?

5.6. What is the most difficult aspect of controlling project costs?
5.7. What steps companies can take to optimize the efficiency of its business processes?
5.8. What are some of the tips on managing and reducing project costs?
5.9. Why do we need to have two separate reserves like the contingency reserve and the management reserve set up to budget for risks?
5.10. What is the time value of money?
5.11. What is depreciation as relates to projects? How is it used as an accounting method? What are the different methods of depreciation?
5.12. What is the fundamental accounting equation?

6. Project Time Management
   6.1. What are dependencies?
   6.2. What is a lag?
   6.3. What is a milestone?
   6.4. What do you mean by resource constraint?
   6.5. What is the difference between duration and work effort?
   6.6. What is a network diagram? What are the different kinds of network diagrams and their usage?
   6.7. What is a network diagram as relates to projects? Describe, compare and contrast ''activity on arrow'' network diagram and the ''activity on node'' network diagram. What are the various logical relationship between the activities?
   6.8. What are the early start, early finish, late start, and late finish dates of a project schedule?
   6.9. How do I make a project schedule?
   6.10. What is float or slack in a project schedule? What are the different kinds of float? How do you calculate various floats? What concerns can arise when using various floats? Clarify using examples.
   6.11. What is a Gantt chart?
   6.12. What is a critical path?
   6.13. What is the critical path method? How is it used in projects?
   6.14. How do you manage critical path in projects?
   6.15. What is PERT?
   6.16. What is a milestone chart?
   6.17. What is a summary or hammock activity?
   6.18. What is a resource histogram?
   6.19. What is crashing and fast-tracking a project schedule?
   6.20. What is a buffered schedule?
   6.21. What is the Monte Carlo process? What and where are its applications specifically in project management?

7. Project Control
   7.1. What is Project Control?
   7.2. Why do you need to establish controls?
   7.3. Which project control functions need the most improvement?
   7.4. Why sometimes staying the course seems better option when your project is in trouble?
   7.5. What are some of the decisions a project manager must make as part of project control?
   7.6. What are the benefits of project control? Why do it?
   7.7. What are the various project control processes and how to formalize these project control processes?
   7.8. What does Project Control Officer mean? What are its roles and responsibilities? Why do we need this role?
   7.9. What are some of the tips for keeping IT projects under control?
   7.10. What are some of the steps to regaining project control if the project with issues or high priorities goes out of control?
   7.11. How much control and reporting do we need in project management? To make a success of the project control processes, what are the key objectives a project manager needs to achieve?

7.12. Why are project communications so important?
7.13. How do you control change requests in a waterfall project?

8. Risk Management
 8.1. Why projects fail?
 8.2. Why should you manage risk?
 8.3. What does risk management involve? Or What activities does an organization practicing risk management performs?
 8.4. What are some of the tips to manage project risks?
 8.5. How does project management help the company better manage risk?
 8.6. Do you plan to produce a risk management plan? And how often do you intend to update the plan?
 8.7. What is the best time to manage risks in your project?
 8.8. How do you approach risk management? How does formal risk analysis and risk management can help you?
 8.9. What is a project risk? What are its effects, whether positive or negative, on the prospects of achieving project objectives?
 8.10. How can I detect risks?
 8.11. How should we analyze risks?
 8.12. How should we prioritize risks?
 8.13. What is a risk class?
 8.14. What is the essence of risk management?
 8.15. What role do project partners have in managing project risks?
 8.16. What are the things you do to get projects back on track?
 8.17. Your team is primarily junior-level people and you are behind schedule with a drop-dead deliverable date. What would you do?
 8.18. Describe a time when you had a difficult situation working with a vendor or another peer. What was your approach to resolve the issues while maintaining a positive relationship?
 8.19. When managing a project, when do you know the project is off-track?
 8.20. How to spot a failing project before it becomes a famous failure?
 8.21. What are the steps to saving troubled projects?
 8.22. What is risk management?
 8.23. What are the basic steps in risk management?
 8.24. What is risk identification? What areas of the project should be recognized where the risks can occur? What process and/or techniques you should follow for risk identification?
 8.25. What is risk quantification?
 8.26. What are few statistical techniques for risk quantification?
 8.27. What is risk tolerance?
 8.28. What are risk response strategies?
 8.29. What is risk control?
 8.30. How to spot your weakest link in your project team?
 8.31. What are some of the tips for handling your weak link in your project team?
 8.32. How do risk management approaches correlate with the other parts of project management methodology?
 8.33. What are the most common mistakes to avoid which lead to project failure?
 8.34. If a project has more than one critical path, which critical path should the project manager focus on and why?
 8.35. What options do managers have when a project cannot be completed on time?
 8.36. How do you manage business risks through communications?
 8.37. What happens if you ignore project communications?
 8.38. How do you respond to a question: "Tell me about a time when a project failed and how you recovered?"

8.39. Suppose you are solving a problem but ran into some trouble. You do not have a lot of time and think you can solve it on your own. A friend suggests you work with someone you do not know to help. What are you MOST likely to do?

9. Project Closure
   9.1. Why project closure phase is important or critical?
   9.2. What are the benefits of project closure?
   9.3. What are the different reasons for premature project closure?
   9.4. What sources can be used for identifying lessons learned for a project?
   9.5. How do you allocate resources for project closure?
   9.6. How do you go about writing a project close-out report?
   9.7. Provide a project closure checklist.
10. Project Evaluation
   10.1. What is project evaluation?
   10.2. How do you evaluate a project?
   10.3. What are some of the ways to measure the success of any project?
   10.4. What is the most important success criterion for a project and why?
   10.5. How do you define project success?
   10.6. What are the top ten reasons projects fail or slip in time?
   10.7. What are the top ten project management challenges?
   10.8. What are the toughest challenges to the success of customer relationship management projects?
   10.9. What are the major issues and challenges you face in implementing business process management?
   10.10. What are the top reasons projects succeed in your organization?
   10.11. What are the dos and do nots for software project success?
   10.12. How to capture lessons learned?
   10.13. When do you complete lessons learned during your project?
   10.14. Tell me about a project that you were involved in that did not go well? What did you learn?
   10.15. How do software engineering teams measure their success?
   10.16. How do you measure your project team's performance?
   10.17. What can be the reasons why senior management is not as happy as you expected even when your latest project is nearly on time, under budget, and with scope?
   10.18. What can be the possible reasons project teams keeps on putting out one fire after another?
   10.19. How do you respond to a question: "Tell me about your most exciting project."
11. Project Management Organization
   11.1. Why do organizations do projects?
   11.2. Why program management office?
   11.3. What are the most significant benefits of creating and maintaining a project management office?
   11.4. What are the critical elements for a successful project office?
   11.5. What are the pros and cons of outsourcing project management?
   11.6. What are the differences between functional management and project management?
   11.7. How should we organize for project management? What all to consider to setup a project organization? What are the different types of project organization, and pros and cons of each type?
   11.8. What is a balanced matrix organization? What are the pros and cons of matrix organization comparing other types of organizations?
   11.9. Why would we want to use an unbalanced matrix organization?
   11.10. What does move toward matrix management require?
   11.11. How do organizations affect the projects and how does project management influence organizations?
   11.12. On a multinational project, which factor is most critical to efficient work?
   11.13. What are the typical delivery execution challenges that haunt the management with a project

team setup across geographies?

12. Program Management
    12.1. What is a project team?
    12.2. What is common in a project team?
    12.3. What is a program?
    12.4. What is program management?
    12.5. What is project management vs. program management vs. portfolio management?
    12.6. How do you matrix manage?
    12.7. How do you manage multiple projects?
    12.8. How would you handle multiple priorities that are all equally urgent?
    12.9. How do you manage competing change requests from stakeholders?
    12.10. What does managing complex programs involve?
    12.11. How often you should review your project portfolio?
    12.12. What is the role of a project manager?
    12.13. What is the responsibility of a technical project manager?
    12.14. What does upper management look for in a project manager?
    12.15. How important are people management skills for a project manager?
    12.16. What characteristic do you value most in project team members?
    12.17. Who are program managers?
    12.18. What are the key qualities of a good program manager?
    12.19. What are the responsibilities of a program manager?
    12.20. What are the typical duties of a lead project manager?
    12.21. What are some of the things that make a good project manager great?
    12.22. Describe your program management experience.
    12.23. Describe a recent project where you were responsible for managing multiple people or teams. What were some of the key challenges and how did you handle those challenges?
    12.24. What is the difference between project manager, program manager, and product manager roles?
    12.25. Why do companies need both product managers and product owners?
    12.26. How do you distinguish between project management and program management?
    12.27. How do project management and program management complement each other? How do you choose between them? How do you learn and improve them?
    12.28. How to become a program manager?
    12.29. How do you plan and conduct an effective program kick-off meeting and a program review meeting?
13. Framework, Methodology, and Process
    13.1. What do you mean by best practice?
    13.2. What is brainstorming?
    13.3. What is a methodology?
    13.4. Why use a methodology?
    13.5. What is a process?
    13.6. What is a procedure?
    13.7. What is a technique?
    13.8. What is the difference between method, methodology, technique and standard?
    13.9. What is a life cycle and why do you need one?
    13.10. Where does prototyping fit in to the project life cycle?
    13.11. How does object-oriented development differ in project management techniques from traditional development?
    13.12. What is the P-CMM?
    13.13. What is standard deviation?
    13.14. What is segmentation?

13.15. What is a flowchart?
13.16. Define metrics.
13.17. What are KPI measurement techniques?
13.18. What are some of the most useful program management techniques and frameworks that you would recommend?
13.19. What project management framework is best for leadership?
13.20. How can you manage agile vs waterfall projects more efficiently?
13.21. Compare and contrast SAFe with Agile Scrum.
13.22. Project Issues and Risks Template

1. Project Management Core Concepts

Project management is not just important to individual projects. Project managers are the key to achieving business and profitability goals - even more so now given the current economic situation. If projects overrun their timelines or budgets, not only does the project suffer, but the business also suffers too because of the impact on customer satisfaction, customer retention, customer relationships and/or business profitability at large.

Following strong project management methodologies has become more important than ever. Companies today are looking for ways to gain operational and organizational efficiencies, and project management can drive that. Project management is the key to customer satisfaction, which is the most important element of company's success. When projects meet the customers' satisfaction, it links directly to company's bottom line.

Mastering project management skills equips you to complete projects on time, within budget, and aligned with objectives. The field of project management offers tested strategies for clarifying project goals, avoiding critical oversights, and preventing costly errors. It also covers essential interpersonal skills needed to secure cooperation, support, and resources to ensure project success.

Project management is not just for dedicated project managers. Team members must understand how to effectively contribute to projects, while business executives need to know how to support project management initiatives within their organizations.

Pursuing a career in project, program, or functional management provides opportunities for advancement while allowing you to apply your existing expertise. These roles require individuals who are committed to making a positive impact on the organization, who are strong and influential leaders with a people-oriented approach, and who possess a solid technical background. Common sense, confidence, active listening, and sound decision-making are also essential qualities for success.

This section will help you grasp the fundamentals of project management and distinguish it from traditional functional or operational work. It also highlights the importance of project management in today's business and non-profit environments.

1.1. What is project management?

Project Management involves the strategic application of skills, tools, techniques, and knowledge to meet stakeholder expectations and achieve project goals. It is an iterative process that includes estimating, planning, reorganizing, integrating, measuring, and revising until the project's business objectives are fulfilled. Success in project management is driven by effective people management, active user involvement, and timely issue resolution. Key components of this process include feasibility studies, defining scope, creating plans and estimates, allocating resources, managing budgets and schedules, and addressing issues, risks, and changes.

While this definition might seem straightforward, mastering these skills and techniques requires extensive education and hands-on experience. The project management process typically involves forming a small organizational structure - a project team - that mirrors the larger organization. Once the project objectives are met, this team is generally disbanded.

What sets project management apart from general management is its focus on a final deliverable and a defined timeline, as opposed to the ongoing nature of general management. As a result, a project manager must possess a diverse skill set, including technical expertise, people management, and strong business acumen.

Project management principles and techniques are crucial for completing projects on time, within budget, and according to specifications. They also support the broader organizational goals of productivity, quality, and cost-effectiveness. The primary aim of project management is to optimize the balance between project cost, time, and quality.

1.2. What is a project?

A project is a temporary endeavor undertaken to create a unique product, service, or result. It is characterized by the following key attributes:

1. Temporary Nature: Projects have a defined beginning and end. They are initiated to achieve specific goals and are completed once those goals are accomplished.
2. Unique Output: Each project delivers a unique outcome, whether it is a new product, service, process, or result. This distinguishes projects from ongoing operations or routine activities.
3. Defined Objectives: Projects are guided by specific objectives and requirements that are established at the outset. These objectives drive the planning and execution phases of the project.
4. Resource Constraints: Projects operate within the constraints of limited resources, including time, budget, personnel, and materials. Effective resource management is crucial for successful project completion.
5. Progressive Elaboration: Projects often undergo progressive elaboration, meaning their scope and details become clearer and more refined as the project progresses and more information is gathered.
6. Stakeholder Involvement: Projects typically involve various stakeholders, including project sponsors, team members, customers, and other interested parties. Effective communication and stakeholder management are essential for project success.

Examples of projects include constructing a building, developing a new software application, launching a marketing campaign, organizing a conference, and designing a new product. Each of these activities has specific goals, a finite timeline, and produces a unique result.

1.3. What is a project manager?

A project manager is a professional tasked with overseeing the planning, execution, and successful completion of a project. Serving as the central point of contact, they coordinate all project aspects, including managing resources, timelines, budgets, and tasks. Their responsibilities include setting clear objectives, defining the project scope, assigning roles, managing risks, and ensuring the project achieves its goals within the established constraints. Strong communication, organizational, problem-solving, and leadership skills are essential for effective project management.

Project managers are responsible for delivering the project on time and within budget while meeting the business's requirements. They operate across all industries and organizations, whether as contractors, managers, employees, or independent consultants.

As a project manager, you must be adept at responding quickly to shifting business priorities, evolving expectations, and ongoing leadership changes, ensuring that everyone involved stays informed and aligned throughout the project.

1.4. What are the rewards and stresses of project management?

The role of a project manager is a double-edged sword, offering both rewards and challenges. Once you step into this position, you must be ready to handle both.

While everyone benefits from the successful implementation of a system, a project manager's unique reward lies in helping their team members reach their full potential. People are the most critical factor in achieving goals, and there is great satisfaction in seeing a well-motivated team thrive under your leadership and management skills.

However, people also present the greatest challenges. As human beings, they are influenced by factors beyond your control. Personal issues and conflicts among team members must be managed with diplomacy and objectivity by the project manager.

The project manager is also the first to be held accountable when anything goes wrong with the application, project, or team. Upper management and business users will look to the project manager to answer for delays, missed requirements, system bugs, or any team misconduct.

Advantages of Becoming a Project Manager:

1. It can serve as a steppingstone to promotion.
2. It provides a strong sense of accomplishment.
3. The role offers considerable variety - no two days are the same.
4. There is significant freedom to make choices.
5. It allows you to influence change across the organization.

Disadvantages of Becoming a Project Manager:

1. It requires a high tolerance for office politics.
2. It demands comfort with ambiguity and uncertainty.
3. The role comes with significant responsibility but often little authority.
4. You may feel disconnected from your technical expertise.
5. Some may perceive your role as lacking substance.

1.5. What advice do you have for companies about the role of project management in a down economy?

Companies today are looking for ways to gain operational and organizational efficiencies, and project management can drive that. Project managers historically have not been linked to the financial health of the organization, and they do not always see their relationship to business success. But, when project managers are made aware of how crucial they are to the business process, they will perform better, they will pick the best people for their teams, and they will use the tools and processes available to them to achieve greater productivity.

In a down economy, effective project management becomes even more critical for companies. Here is some advice:

1. Prioritize Projects Wisely: Evaluate all ongoing and potential projects, and prioritize them based on their potential return on investment (ROI), alignment with strategic goals, and feasibility in the current economic climate.
2. Resource Optimization: Utilize project management methodologies like Agile or Lean to optimize resource allocation and minimize waste. This includes efficiently managing both human and financial resources to ensure maximum output with minimum input.
3. Risk Management: Conduct thorough risk assessments for each project and develop mitigation strategies to address potential challenges and uncertainties. In a down economy, risks may be heightened, so it is crucial to proactively identify and manage them.

4. Cost Control: Implement robust cost control measures to ensure projects stay within budget constraints. This may involve renegotiating contracts, seeking cost-saving alternatives, or reevaluating project scope to align with available resources.
5. Stakeholder Communication: Maintain open and transparent communication with stakeholders throughout the project lifecycle. Keep them informed about any changes, challenges, or adjustments to project plans, particularly in light of economic conditions.
6. Focus on Deliverables: Emphasize the timely delivery of project milestones and deliverables to demonstrate value and maintain stakeholder confidence. This may require streamlining processes and eliminating non-essential activities to stay on track.
7. Agility and Adaptability: Remain flexible and adaptable in response to changing economic conditions. Project managers should be prepared to adjust plans, reallocate resources, and pivot strategies as needed to navigate uncertainties and capitalize on emerging opportunities.
8. Invest in Talent Development: Despite economic challenges, investing in the professional development of project management teams can yield long-term benefits. Well-trained and skilled project managers are better equipped to navigate complex situations and drive successful project outcomes.
9. Continuous Improvement: Foster a culture of continuous improvement within the organization. Encourage project teams to reflect on past experiences, learn from mistakes, and identify areas for enhancement to optimize project management practices.
10. Strategic Alignment: Ensure that project objectives align with the company's overarching strategic goals and objectives. Projects should contribute to long-term sustainability and competitiveness, even during economic downturns.

By emphasizing effective project management practices, companies can better navigate challenging economic environments and position themselves for success in the long term.

1.6. What is the project life cycle?

The project life cycle is a series of phases that a project goes through from its initiation to its closure. It provides a structured approach to planning, executing, and completing a project. The life cycle typically consists of the following phases:

1. Initiation: This is the first phase where the project is conceptualized and its feasibility is evaluated. Key activities in this phase include:
   a. Defining the project's purpose and scope.
   b. Identifying stakeholders.
   c. Conducting a feasibility study.
   d. Developing a project charter or project initiation document (PID).
   e. Securing initial approval and funding.
2. Planning: In this phase, detailed planning is conducted to outline how the project will be executed, monitored, and controlled. Major tasks include:
   a. Developing a detailed project plan, including timelines, resources, and budget.
   b. Defining project objectives and deliverables.
   c. Creating a work breakdown structure (WBS).
   d. Identifying risks and developing risk management strategies.
   e. Establishing communication and quality management plans.
3. Execution: This phase involves putting the project plan into action and carrying out the work required to complete the project. Key activities include:
   a. Coordinating people and resources.
   b. Managing stakeholder expectations and communications.
   c. Implementing project plans and schedules.
   d. Monitoring project performance and making adjustments as necessary.

    e. Ensuring quality assurance.
4. Monitoring and Controlling: This phase occurs simultaneously with the execution phase. It involves tracking, reviewing, and regulating the progress and performance of the project. Key activities include:
    a. Measuring project performance against the project plan.
    b. Identifying any variances from the plan and implementing corrective actions.
    c. Managing changes through a formal change control process.
    d. Ensuring that project objectives are being met and that risks are being managed.
5. Closure: This final phase marks the completion of the project. It involves finalizing all project activities and formally closing the project. Key activities include:
    a. Completing and delivering the final project deliverables.
    b. Obtaining formal acceptance from the stakeholders.
    c. Conducting a project review to identify lessons learned.
    d. Closing all project documentation and archiving project records.
    e. Releasing project resources.

The project life cycle provides a systematic framework for managing projects, helping to ensure that projects are completed efficiently, on time, and within budget. It also helps in managing risks, improving communication, and ensuring that project objectives align with organizational goals.

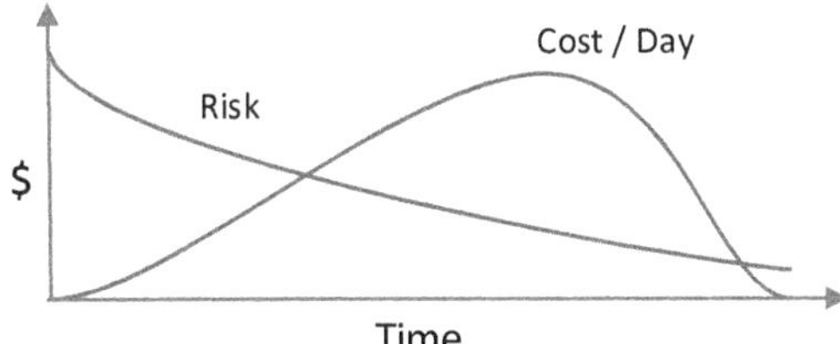

Figure 1.6.1 Project Life Cycle

The project life cycle, as shown in Figure 1.6.1, begins with the project charter and concludes once all deliverables, including closeout and cleanup, are completed. According to Figure 1.6.1, projects typically start with a low daily cost and a small team. As the project advances, spending and team size increase until they reach a peak. After this peak, both spending and team size gradually decrease as tasks are completed. Eventually, the project finishes, spending ceases, and all deliverables are provided. Throughout this process, the total risk associated with the project diminishes from start to finish.

1.7. What is the project management triangle or the triple constraint?

The project management triangle, also known as the triple constraint, is a fundamental model in project management that illustrates the interdependent constraints of project management. It consists of three key elements:

1. Scope: This defines the work that needs to be done to deliver a product or service with the specified features and functions. It encompasses all the tasks, deliverables, and objectives that need to be achieved to complete the project.
2. Time: This refers to the schedule for completing the project, including the deadlines for each phase and the final delivery date. It involves planning the timeline for project tasks and managing any deviations from the planned schedule.
3. Cost: This represents the budget allocated for the project. It includes all financial resources required, such as labor, materials, equipment, and other expenses necessary to complete the project.

The project management triangle illustrates that these three constraints are interrelated, meaning that changing one constraint will inevitably impact the others. For instance:

1. If the scope is increased (adding more features or tasks), it will likely require more time and cost to complete.
2. If the time allocated for the project is reduced (faster completion), it might lead to increased cost (overtime, additional resources) or a reduced scope (fewer features or lower quality).
3. If the cost is cut (budget reductions), it might result in a reduced scope (fewer features) or extended time (longer project duration due to limited resources).

Balancing these three constraints is a critical task for project managers to ensure project success. Effective project management involves continuously managing and negotiating these constraints to meet the project's goals and stakeholders' expectations.

The project management triangle (Figure 1.7.1) is a common tool used to demonstrate that project management success is determined by the project team's ability to deliver the expected results while effectively managing time and cost. The triangle, also known as the triple constraint, has three sides representing cost, scope, and schedule. Customer satisfaction can be thought of as the area within the triangle, as customers are always concerned with scope, time, and cost. To achieve customer satisfaction, we must fulfill the entire scope as promised, within the agreed budget, and deliver it on time.

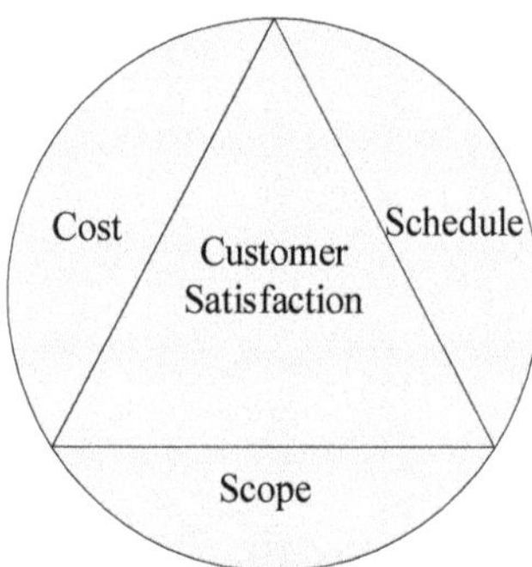

Figure 1.7.1 Project Management Triangle

1.8. What are the project baselines?

Project baselines are reference points in project management used to track and measure project performance. They are established at the beginning of the project and are crucial for managing and controlling the project as it progresses. The main types of project baselines include:

1. Scope Baseline: This baseline includes the project's scope statement, the work breakdown structure (WBS), and the WBS dictionary. It defines the project's deliverables and the work required to complete them. It serves as a reference for what is included in the project, helping to manage scope changes and prevent scope creep.
2. Schedule Baseline: This baseline consists of the project's approved timeline, including start and end dates for project activities, milestones, and dependencies. It provides a timeline against which actual progress can be measured, helping to identify schedule variances and manage time effectively.
3. Cost Baseline: This is the approved budget for the project, including all planned expenditures. It serves as a benchmark for measuring financial performance, allowing the project team to track actual costs against planned costs and manage budget variances.
4. Quality Baseline: This baseline outlines the quality objectives and criteria for the project. It includes standards and metrics for measuring quality, ensuring that the project meets the required

quality standards and customer expectations.

5. Performance Measurement Baseline (PMB): This is an integrated baseline that includes scope, schedule, and cost baselines. It provides a comprehensive view of project performance and is used for Earned Value Management (EVM) to track and control project performance and progress.

Establishing these baselines is essential for effective project management as they provide a clear point of reference for measuring project progress and performance. They help identify deviations from the plan, enabling timely corrective actions to keep the project on track.

1.9. Who are the project stakeholders?

Project stakeholders are individuals, groups, or organizations that have an interest in the outcome of a project or are affected by its execution and completion. Here are the common categories of project stakeholders:

1. Project Manager: The person responsible for planning, executing, and closing the project. They ensure the project meets its goals and objectives.
2. Project Team Members: Individuals who actively work on project tasks. Their expertise and efforts are critical to the project's success.
3. Project Sponsor: Typically a senior executive who provides resources and support for the project and is accountable for its success.
4. Customers or Clients: The individuals or organizations that will use the project's final deliverables or services. They are the primary beneficiaries of the project.
5. End Users: Those who will directly interact with and use the project's deliverables. They can provide valuable feedback on functionality and usability.
6. Suppliers and Vendors: External entities that provide goods, services, or materials necessary for the project. Their timely and quality contributions are essential.
7. Functional Managers: Managers within the organization who oversee departments that will be impacted by the project or whose resources are needed for project activities.
8. Steering Committee: A group of senior stakeholders who provide strategic guidance, resolve issues, and make decisions that affect the project's direction.
9. Regulatory Bodies: Government agencies or industry organizations that impose regulations and standards the project must adhere to.
10. Investors: Individuals or entities that provide financial backing for the project. They are interested in the project's financial returns.
11. Communities and the Public: Local communities or the general public that might be affected by the project's outcomes, especially for large infrastructure projects.
12. Media: Can influence public perception and inform about the project's progress and impacts.
13. Internal Stakeholders: Other departments or groups within the organization that might be affected by the project's outcome.
14. Competitors: Although not directly involved, competitors might have an interest in the project's outcome as it can impact market dynamics.
15. Board of Directors: In larger organizations, they oversee major projects and ensure alignment with the organization's strategic goals.

Effective stakeholder management involves identifying all stakeholders, understanding their interests and influence, and engaging with them appropriately throughout the project lifecycle.

1.10. How do you identify key players in your project?

Identifying key players in a project is a critical step to ensure successful planning and execution. Here are some systematic steps to identify these key players:

1. Understand the Project Scope and Objectives
    a. Review the project charter: This document typically outlines the project's goals, scope, and objectives. Understanding these elements helps identify who might have a significant influence or stake in the project.
    b. Identify deliverables: Knowing what needs to be delivered can help pinpoint the individuals and teams responsible for those deliverables.
2. Stakeholder Analysis
    a. List potential stakeholders: Start by listing everyone who is directly or indirectly involved in the project. This includes team members, managers, clients, suppliers, and anyone affected by the project outcomes.
    b. Categorize stakeholders: Group them into categories such as internal (within the organization) and external (clients, suppliers, regulatory bodies).
    c. Assess influence and interest: Use a stakeholder matrix to map stakeholders based on their level of interest and influence. Those with high influence and high interest are typically key players.
3. Consult with Senior Management
    a. Interview project sponsors and executives: They can provide insights into who the key decision-makers and influencers are.
    b. Leverage organizational charts: These charts can help identify the hierarchy and the key departments involved.
4. Identify Roles and Responsibilities
    a. Define key roles: Identify roles such as project sponsor, project manager, team leads, and key functional experts.
    b. RACI matrix: Develop a Responsibility Assignment Matrix to clarify who is Responsible, Accountable, Consulted, and Informed (RACI) for each task and deliverable.
5. Review Past Projects
    a. Analyze similar projects: Look at previous projects of similar scope and size to see who the key players were.
    b. Seek lessons learned: Past project documentation often highlights key players and their contributions.
6. Engage with the Project Team
    a. Conduct team meetings and workshops: These sessions can help surface key contributors and influential team members.
    b. Identify informal influencers: Sometimes, individuals without formal authority can have significant influence due to their expertise or relationships.
7. Consider External Factors
    a. Regulatory requirements: Identify key players who ensure compliance with legal and regulatory standards.
    b. Client representatives: For customer-facing projects, client liaisons or account managers are crucial.
8. Validate with Stakeholders
    a. Feedback loops: Confirm your identification of key players with other stakeholders to ensure no critical individual or role is overlooked.
    b. Stakeholder interviews: Directly ask identified stakeholders about their views on key project influencers.

Tools and Techniques

1. Stakeholder Mapping Tools: Software like Microsoft Project, Jira, or specialized stakeholder management tools can help visualize and track key players.

2. SWOT Analysis: Understanding the strengths, weaknesses, opportunities, and threats (SWOT) related to project roles can help identify key players.
3. Communication Plans: These plans often highlight key stakeholders and their information needs, indirectly identifying key players.

Key Criteria for Identifying Key Players
1. Authority: Who has decision-making power?
2. Influence: Who can impact project outcomes through formal or informal means?
3. Interest: Who stands to gain or lose the most from the project?
4. Expertise: Who has the critical knowledge or skills necessary for the project?

By systematically analyzing these factors, you can accurately identify the key players essential for the success of your project.

1.11. What do you do about, handle, or manage stakeholders?

Managing stakeholders involves several key activities to ensure their needs and concerns are addressed, and their influence on the project is effectively managed. Handling stakeholders effectively is crucial for the success of any project or organization. Here are some key steps and strategies for managing stakeholders:
1. Identify Stakeholders
    a. List all potential stakeholders: Identify everyone who is affected by the project or can influence its outcome. This includes internal stakeholders (e.g., employees, managers) and external stakeholders (e.g., customers, suppliers, regulatory bodies).
2. Analyze Stakeholders
    a. Assess their influence and interest: Use tools like stakeholder mapping or power-interest grids to categorize stakeholders based on their level of influence and interest in the project.
    b. Identify their expectations and needs: Understand what each stakeholder expects from the project and what they need to be satisfied.
3. Prioritize Stakeholders
    a. Classify stakeholders: Prioritize stakeholders based on their influence and importance. Focus on key stakeholders who have the most impact on the project's success.
4. Develop a Stakeholder Management Plan
    a. Define engagement strategies: Develop tailored engagement strategies for each stakeholder or group of stakeholders. This includes communication plans, meeting schedules, and feedback mechanisms.
    b. Set objectives: Clearly define what you aim to achieve with each stakeholder, whether it is gaining support, managing expectations, or mitigating risks.
5. Communicate Effectively
    a. Use appropriate communication channels: Choose the best methods to communicate with each stakeholder, whether it is email, meetings, reports, or informal conversations.
    b. Be transparent and honest: Provide accurate and timely information to build trust and credibility.
    c. Listen actively: Pay attention to stakeholders' concerns and feedback, and show that you value their input.
6. Engage Stakeholders
    a. Involve them in decision-making: Engage key stakeholders in important decisions to ensure their buy-in and support.
    b. Collaborate and negotiate: Work together with stakeholders to find mutually beneficial solutions and manage conflicts.

7. Monitor and Review
    a. Track stakeholder engagement: Regularly review and assess your stakeholder management strategies and adjust them as necessary.
    b. Measure satisfaction: Use surveys, interviews, and other tools to measure stakeholder satisfaction and identify areas for improvement.
8. Build Relationships
    a. Foster long-term relationships: Build and maintain positive relationships with stakeholders beyond the project. This helps in gaining their support for future initiatives.
    b. Show appreciation: Recognize and acknowledge the contributions of stakeholders to build goodwill and loyalty.

Tools and Techniques

1. Stakeholder Analysis Matrices: Tools like power-interest grids, influence-impact grids, and stakeholder engagement assessments.
2. Communication Plans: Detailed plans that outline how and when to communicate with each stakeholder.
3. Feedback Mechanisms: Surveys, suggestion boxes, or regular meetings to gather stakeholder feedback.
4. Conflict Resolution Strategies: Techniques to address and resolve conflicts among stakeholders.

Best Practices

1. Active Listening: Show stakeholders that you value their input by listening actively and responding thoughtfully.
2. Empathy and Respect: Treat all stakeholders with empathy and respect, recognizing their unique perspectives and contributions.
3. Building Relationships: Foster strong, positive relationships with stakeholders through consistent and meaningful engagement.

Effective stakeholder management can significantly impact the success of a project by ensuring that all parties are aligned, engaged, and supportive throughout the project lifecycle. By following these steps and strategies, you can effectively manage stakeholders, ensuring their support and mitigating potential risks to your project or organization.

1.12. How to manage a client who is too busy to focus?

Managing a client who is too busy to focus can be challenging, but there are several strategies you can employ to keep things on track and ensure that necessary work is completed efficiently:

1. Schedule Regular, Short Meetings
    a. Keep Meetings Short and Focused: Aim for 15-30 minute meetings. Shorter meetings are easier to fit into busy schedules and help maintain focus.
    b. Set a Regular Schedule: Establish a consistent meeting schedule (e.g., weekly, or bi-weekly) to create a routine.
2. Prioritize and Simplify Tasks
    a. Break Down Tasks: Divide large projects into smaller, more manageable tasks.
    b. Prioritize Tasks: Help the client prioritize tasks based on urgency and importance. Use tools like the Eisenhower Matrix to categorize tasks.
3. Use Efficient Communication Tools
    a. Project Management Tools: Utilize tools like Trello, Asana, or Monday.com to keep track of tasks and deadlines.
    b. Shared Documents: Use shared documents (e.g., Google Docs, Microsoft OneDrive) for easy collaboration without the need for constant meetings.

4. Prepare Thorough Agendas
    a. Detailed Agendas: Send a detailed agenda before each meeting. Clearly outline the topics to be discussed, decisions to be made, and any materials the client needs to review.
    b. Action Items: Highlight specific action items and decisions required from the client.
5. Asynchronous Communication
    a. Email Updates: Send concise email updates summarizing progress and any actions needed from the client.
    b. Recorded Messages: Use recorded video messages (e.g., Loom) to provide updates and explanations that the client can watch at their convenience.
6. Delegate and Automate
    a. Delegate Tasks: Encourage the client to delegate tasks to their team or to you, if appropriate.
    b. Automate Processes: Identify and automate repetitive tasks using tools like Zapier or automated email responders.
7. Be Flexible and Adaptable
    a. Adapt to Their Schedule: Be willing to adjust your schedule to accommodate the client's availability.
    b. Understand Their Priorities: Be aware of the client's most pressing priorities and align your work accordingly.
8. Follow Up Diligently
    a. Regular Follow-Ups: Send regular reminders and follow-ups to ensure tasks are not forgotten.
    b. Track Progress: Maintain a clear record of agreed-upon tasks and deadlines, and review them in each meeting.
9. Leverage Deadlines
    a. Set Clear Deadlines: Clearly define deadlines for each task and project milestone.
    b. Use Gentle Reminders: Send reminders as deadlines approach to help the client stay on track.
10. Build a Strong Relationship
    a. Build Trust: Establish a strong working relationship based on trust and reliability.
    b. Understand Their Needs: Take the time to understand the client's business and personal pressures to better support them.

By implementing these strategies, you can help a busy client stay focused and ensure that your projects progress smoothly despite their hectic schedule.

1.13. Do you think projects succeed or fail due to technical issues or user and management issues?

Project success or failure often hinges on a combination of technical, user, and management issues rather than being solely attributed to one factor. Here is a breakdown of how each aspect can influence the outcome:

1. Technical Issues: These are problems related to the technology being used in the project. They could include bugs, performance issues, scalability issues, integration challenges, or inadequate infrastructure. Technical issues can certainly lead to project delays or failure if not addressed promptly and effectively. However, even the most technically sound project can fail if user needs or management expectations are not met.
2. User Issues: Projects ultimately exist to serve users, whether they are end customers or internal stakeholders. User issues encompass factors like poor user experience, mismatched expectations, resistance to change, or inadequate user training. Neglecting user needs or failing to engage users throughout the project lifecycle can result in products or solutions that are rejected or

underutilized, leading to project failure.

3. Management Issues: Effective project management is crucial for guiding a project from inception to completion. Management issues could include inadequate planning, unclear objectives, scope creep, poor communication, ineffective leadership, or resource mismanagement. These issues can significantly impact project timelines, budgets, and overall success.

In reality, successful projects often require a balance between technical excellence, user satisfaction, and strong management practices. Projects that prioritize all three aspects tend to have a higher chance of success. Additionally, addressing challenges in one area often requires consideration of the others. For example, a technical solution might require user feedback to ensure it meets their needs, and effective project management ensures that resources are allocated appropriately to address technical and user concerns.

Projects mostly fail due to user and management issues as one can always work around technical problems. Here are some dos and do nots of project management:

Dos of Project Management:

1. Remember that projects are about change.
2. Get top management support.
3. Ensure that there is a sensible business case for a project.
4. Support project management with an electronic filing system.
5. Remember that quality does not look after itself.

Do nots of Project Management:

1. Exclude the customer from project status reports.
2. Skimp on training project managers.
3. Assume project management can be handled simultaneously with a technical job.
4. Assume everyone has the same enthusiasm for the project underway.
5. Have the project manager assume all responsibility for successful implementation.

1.14. What are some of the classic people-related mistakes?

Classic people-related mistakes in projects often stem from communication, leadership, and team dynamics. Here are some common ones:

1. Poor Communication: Ineffective communication can lead to misunderstandings, delays, and conflicts. This includes unclear instructions, lack of updates, and failure to listen to team members.
2. Inadequate Leadership: Weak or absent leadership can result in lack of direction, demotivated team members, and disorganization. Leadership should provide guidance, support, and motivation to keep the project on track.
3. Unclear Roles and Responsibilities: When team members are unsure of their roles or responsibilities, it can lead to confusion, duplication of efforts, and tasks being left undone.
4. Mismatched Skills and Tasks: Assigning tasks to team members without considering their skills and experience can result in inefficiency and poor-quality work.
5. Micromanagement: Micromanaging undermines trust and autonomy, leading to demotivation and resentment among team members. It also wastes the manager's time and prevents team members from fully utilizing their skills.
6. Poor Conflict Resolution: Ignoring or mishandling conflicts within the team can escalate tensions and disrupt productivity. It is important to address conflicts promptly and constructively to maintain a positive working environment.
7. Lack of Team Cohesion: A lack of cohesion within the team can hinder collaboration and

teamwork, leading to missed deadlines and subpar outcomes.

8. Failure to Recognize and Reward: Failing to recognize and reward the contributions of team members can result in decreased morale and motivation. Recognition and rewards are important for fostering a positive work environment and encouraging continued effort.
9. Ignoring Stakeholder Input: Neglecting to involve key stakeholders or dismissing their input can lead to misunderstandings and dissatisfaction with the project outcomes.
10. Underestimating Human Factors: Projects often encounter unforeseen challenges due to human factors such as illness, turnover, or personal issues. Failing to account for these factors in project planning can lead to delays and disruptions.

By addressing these common people-related mistakes, project managers can improve team effectiveness, morale, and ultimately the success of the project.

1.15. What are some of the classic process-related mistakes?

Classic process-related mistakes in projects often revolve around communication, planning, and execution. Here are some common ones:

1. Poorly Defined Objectives: Not having clear, measurable objectives can lead to confusion and misalignment among team members.
2. Inadequate Planning: Rushing into a project without thorough planning can result in missed deadlines, budget overruns, and low-quality deliverables.
3. Lack of Stakeholder Involvement: Failing to involve key stakeholders from the beginning can lead to misunderstandings, scope creep, and dissatisfaction with the final product.
4. Unclear Roles and Responsibilities: When team members are unsure of their roles and responsibilities, tasks may fall through the cracks, leading to delays and inefficiencies.
5. Ineffective Communication: Poor communication can result in misunderstandings, duplication of efforts, and missed deadlines. This includes both verbal and written communication within the team and with stakeholders.
6. Ignoring Risks: Not identifying and addressing potential risks early in the project can lead to costly issues later on.
7. Scope Creep: Allowing the project scope to continuously expand without proper evaluation can lead to delays, increased costs, and a final product that does not meet the original objectives.
8. Micromanagement: Micromanaging team members can lead to decreased morale, reduced productivity, and stifled creativity.
9. Insufficient Resources: Not allocating enough resources, whether it is time, budget, or personnel, can hinder the project's success.
10. Failure to Learn from Mistakes: Not conducting post-project reviews or retrospectives to identify areas for improvement can result in repeated mistakes in future projects.

Avoiding these common process-related mistakes requires careful planning, effective communication, and a commitment to continuous improvement throughout the project lifecycle.

1.16. What are some of the classic product-related mistakes?

Classic product-related mistakes in projects often stem from misaligned goals, poor planning, or insufficient understanding of the market. Here are some common ones:

1. Insufficient market research: Failing to thoroughly research the target market can lead to developing a product that does not meet customer needs or address existing pain points.
2. Ignoring user feedback: Neglecting to gather and incorporate user feedback throughout the development process can result in a product that does not resonate with its intended audience.
3. Scope creep: Allowing the project scope to expand beyond its original boundaries can lead to

delays, budget overruns, and a final product that lacks focus.

4. Over-engineering: Adding unnecessary features or complexity to the product can not only increase development time and costs but also make the product harder to use and maintain.
5. Underestimating resources: Failing to accurately estimate the resources (time, money, personnel) needed to complete the project can result in missed deadlines and budget overruns.
6. Poor communication: Ineffective communication among team members, stakeholders, and other parties involved in the project can lead to misunderstandings, delays, and ultimately a subpar product.
7. Lack of testing: Insufficient testing, both during development and before launch, can result in undetected bugs, usability issues, and overall dissatisfaction among users.
8. Ignoring scalability: Neglecting to design the product with scalability in mind can lead to difficulties in accommodating growth and adapting to changing market demands in the future.
9. Disregarding competition: Failing to analyze and understand the competitive landscape can result in developing a product that does not differentiate itself or offer unique value compared to existing solutions.
10. Not having a clear value proposition: If the product's value proposition is not clearly defined and communicated, it can be challenging to attract and retain customers.

Avoiding these common mistakes requires careful planning, continuous feedback loops, effective communication, and a deep understanding of both the target market and the project's objectives.

1.17. What are some of the classic technology-related mistakes?

Classic technology-related mistakes in projects often revolve around common pitfalls in development practices. Some of the classic technology-related mistakes are:

1. Poor Requirements Gathering: Failing to understand and document the project requirements accurately can lead to misunderstandings between stakeholders and developers, resulting in a product that does not meet user needs.
2. Lack of Planning: Inadequate project planning, including unclear goals, timelines, and resource allocation, can lead to delays, budget overruns, and scope creep.
3. Ignoring User Feedback: Neglecting to gather feedback from end-users throughout the development process can result in a product that does not align with user expectations or needs.
4. Overlooking Testing: Insufficient testing, including inadequate unit testing, integration testing, and user acceptance testing, can lead to bugs, vulnerabilities, and performance issues that degrade the user experience.
5. Poor Communication: Communication breakdowns between team members, stakeholders, and clients can result in misunderstandings, delays, and rework.
6. Ignoring Scalability and Performance: Failing to consider scalability and performance requirements early in the development process can lead to performance bottlenecks and system failures as user demand grows.
7. Technical Debt: Taking shortcuts or implementing quick fixes to meet deadlines can accumulate technical debt, making it harder to maintain, update, and extend the software in the future.
8. Not Following Best Practices: Ignoring industry best practices, coding standards, and design patterns can lead to code that is difficult to maintain, debug, and scale.
9. Scope Creep: Allowing the project scope to expand without proper evaluation and control can result in project delays, resource overruns, and a product that lacks focus.
10. Inadequate Documentation: Failing to document code, design decisions, and project processes can make it difficult for developers to understand and maintain the software over time.
11. Silver-bullet syndrome.
12. Overestimated savings from new tools or methods.
13. Switching tools in the middle of a project.

14. Lack of automated source code control.

By addressing these classic mistakes and adopting best practices in software development, teams can improve the quality, efficiency, and success of their projects.

1.18. What is silver-bullet syndrome and how and when does it occurs?

Silver-bullet syndrome refers to the mistaken belief that a single, simple solution (a "silver bullet") can effectively address a complex problem. This term is often used in the context of software development and project management, but it can apply to any field where complex problems arise. Here is a detailed look at what Silver-bullet syndrome entails, including how and when it occurs:

Silver-bullet syndrome is characterized by:

1. Over-Simplification: Believing that a single technology, tool, or methodology will solve all problems.
2. Over-Reliance: Relying too heavily on this single solution without considering other necessary components or potential issues.
3. Disappointment and Failure: Often leading to disappointment when the "silver bullet" fails to deliver the expected results because it cannot address the complexity of the problem on its own.

How and When Does Silver-bullet Syndrome Occur?

1. Desire for Quick Fixes
    a. Urgency: In situations where there is a high pressure to solve problems quickly, teams may look for quick fixes rather than comprehensive solutions.
    b. Management Pressure: Managers or stakeholders may push for rapid results, leading teams to adopt solutions that promise quick success.
2. Lack of Understanding of Complexity
    a. Inexperience: Teams or individuals with limited experience might not fully understand the complexity of the problem they are trying to solve.
    b. Misjudgment: Even experienced professionals can misjudge the complexity of certain problems, leading them to overestimate the effectiveness of a single solution.
3. Marketing and Hype
    a. Vendor Promises: Software and technology vendors often market their products as comprehensive solutions, which can lead to unrealistic expectations.
    b. Industry Trends: Following industry trends without critical evaluation can lead to adopting so-called "best practices" that may not fit the specific context.
4. Cognitive Biases
    a. Confirmation Bias: Once a team commits to a solution, they may ignore evidence that contradicts its effectiveness.
    b. Availability Heuristic: The tendency to rely on readily available solutions or those that are most easily recalled, even if they are not the best fit.
5. Inadequate Problem Analysis
    a. Surface-Level Analysis: Not digging deep enough to understand the root causes of a problem can lead to superficial solutions.
    b. Neglecting User Needs: Failing to consider the needs and contexts of the end-users or stakeholders can result in adopting inappropriate solutions.

Examples in Software Development

1. Technology Stack Choices: Believing that adopting a new programming language or framework (e.g., switching to microservices architecture) will solve all performance and scalability issues without considering the broader system implications.

2. Agile Methodologies: Assuming that simply adopting Agile methodologies will resolve all project management issues, without proper training, cultural change, or understanding of Agile principles.
3. Security Solutions: Implementing a single security tool and expecting it to provide complete protection without a comprehensive security strategy.

Preventing Silver-bullet Syndrome

1. Comprehensive Analysis: Conduct thorough problem analysis and understand the complexity before choosing a solution.
2. Diverse Solutions: Combine multiple approaches and solutions tailored to different aspects of the problem.
3. Continuous Learning: Stay updated with industry knowledge and best practices but evaluate them critically.
4. Manage Expectations: Set realistic expectations with stakeholders about what any single solution can achieve.
5. Iterative Approach: Implement solutions iteratively and be prepared to adapt based on feedback and results.

In summary, Silver-bullet syndrome occurs when there is an over-reliance on a single solution to solve complex problems, often driven by a desire for quick fixes, a misunderstanding of the problem's complexity, or external pressures. Recognizing and addressing this syndrome involves adopting a more nuanced and multifaceted approach to problem-solving.

1.19. What is the single most important network feature in your project management communication system?

The single most important network feature in a project management communication system is real-time collaboration. This feature enables team members to work together seamlessly regardless of their physical location, ensuring that updates, feedback, and critical information are shared instantly. Real-time collaboration tools include chat, video conferencing, shared document editing, and instant notifications, which help in maintaining effective communication, quick decision-making, and keeping everyone on the same page.

The most important network features in a project management communication system in the decreasing order of importance are:

1. Online collaboration
2. Transparent scheduling/timelines
3. Risk mitigation
4. Clear financial budgeting.

1.20. Which aspect of your project management processes needs the most improvement?

Improvement priorities in project management processes can vary depending on the specific context and challenges faced by your team or organization. However, here are some common areas where improvement is often needed, listed in decreasing order of importance:

1. Communication: Effective communication is vital for successful project management. Improving communication processes can involve enhancing clarity in project goals, ensuring timely dissemination of information, fostering open and transparent communication channels, and addressing any barriers to communication that may exist within the team or with stakeholders.
2. Risk Management: Identifying, assessing, and mitigating risks is crucial for minimizing potential

negative impacts on project outcomes. Improvements in this area may include conducting more comprehensive risk assessments, implementing proactive risk management strategies, and regularly reviewing and updating risk registers throughout the project lifecycle.

3. Resource Management: Optimizing resource allocation and utilization can help ensure that projects are completed efficiently and within budget. This may involve improving processes for tracking and managing resources such as personnel, equipment, and finances, as well as identifying opportunities to streamline workflows and eliminate unnecessary bottlenecks.
4. Quality Management: Delivering high-quality results is essential for meeting project objectives and satisfying stakeholders. Improvements in quality management may involve establishing clear quality standards and metrics, implementing quality assurance processes to prevent defects or errors, and implementing quality control measures to identify and address issues promptly.
5. Stakeholder Management: Engaging and managing stakeholders effectively is critical for gaining support, managing expectations, and ensuring project success. Improvement efforts in this area may include identifying key stakeholders and their interests, establishing regular communication channels, soliciting feedback, and addressing concerns or conflicts in a timely manner.
6. Change Management: Projects often involve changes to processes, technologies, or organizational structures, which can impact stakeholders and require careful management. Improvements in change management may involve developing clear change management plans, communicating changes effectively, addressing resistance to change, and providing support to stakeholders throughout the change process.
7. Scheduling and Time Management: Ensuring that projects are completed on time requires effective scheduling and time management practices. Improvement efforts may include developing realistic project schedules, identifying, and addressing potential scheduling conflicts, monitoring progress against deadlines, and implementing strategies to mitigate delays.
8. Scope Management: Managing project scope effectively is essential for preventing scope creep and ensuring that projects deliver the intended outcomes within the agreed-upon boundaries. Improvements in scope management may involve defining clear project scopes, establishing change control processes to manage scope changes, and regularly reviewing and updating project scopes as needed.

By assessing your specific project management processes against these areas, you can identify opportunities for improvement and prioritize actions to enhance overall project performance.

1.21. Which project documentation do you find most vital for success?

The importance of project documentation can vary depending on the nature and scope of the project. However, generally speaking, the following documentation is often considered vital for project success, listed in decreasing order of importance:

1. Project Charter: This document outlines the project's objectives, scope, stakeholders, risks, and high-level timeline. It sets the foundation for the project and aligns stakeholders on its purpose and expected outcomes.
2. Project Plan: A comprehensive project plan includes details such as tasks, resources, timelines, dependencies, and milestones. It serves as a roadmap for the project team to execute tasks efficiently and manage resources effectively.
3. Requirements Documentation: This includes the functional and non-functional requirements of the project, capturing what the end product or service should accomplish and any constraints or quality standards it must meet.
4. Risk Management Plan: Identifying, assessing, and managing risks is crucial for project success. A risk management plan outlines potential risks, their impact, mitigation strategies, and contingency plans to minimize their impact on the project.
5. Communication Plan: Effective communication is essential for project coordination and

stakeholder engagement. A communication plan defines communication channels, frequency, stakeholders, and protocols for disseminating project information.

6. Change Management Plan: Projects often encounter changes in scope, requirements, or resources. A change management plan outlines how changes will be identified, evaluated, approved, and implemented while minimizing disruption to the project.
7. Quality Management Plan: Ensuring deliverables meet quality standards is vital for customer satisfaction and project success. A quality management plan defines quality metrics, processes for quality assurance and control, and responsibilities for maintaining quality throughout the project lifecycle.
8. Issue Log: An issue log tracks and documents any problems or obstacles encountered during project execution, along with their resolution status. It helps the project team identify recurring issues, trends, and areas for improvement.
9. Lessons Learned Documentation: Documenting lessons learned throughout the project provides valuable insights for future projects. It captures successes, failures, and best practices, enabling continuous improvement and knowledge sharing within the organization.
10. Closure Documentation: As the project concludes, closure documentation summarizes project outcomes, final deliverables, lessons learned, and any outstanding tasks or issues. It provides a formal record of project completion and facilitates a smooth transition to ongoing operations or subsequent projects.

While these documents are essential, their importance may vary depending on the project's complexity, size, and specific requirements. It is crucial for project managers to adapt documentation practices to suit the needs of each project while ensuring key information is adequately captured and communicated.

1.22. What do you need most often from executive sponsors?

Executive sponsors play a crucial role in project success by providing support, guidance, and resources. Here are some key things that project managers often need from executive sponsors in decreasing order of importance:

1. Clear Objectives and Vision: It is crucial for executive sponsors to provide a clear understanding of the project's objectives and the overall vision. This ensures alignment with organizational goals and helps guide decision-making throughout the project lifecycle.
2. Resource Allocation: Executive sponsors play a pivotal role in allocating necessary resources, including budget, manpower, technology, and time. Adequate resources ensure that the project team can execute tasks effectively and efficiently.
3. Support and Advocacy: Executive sponsors need to actively support the project team by advocating for the project within the organization. This involves removing barriers, resolving conflicts, and providing political support when needed.
4. Risk Management: Executive sponsors should be involved in identifying potential risks and mitigating strategies. Their support in addressing risks and uncertainties helps in maintaining project momentum and minimizing disruptions.
5. Decision-Making Authority: Executive sponsors should have the authority to make critical decisions related to the project. Timely decision-making ensures that the project stays on track and avoids unnecessary delays.
6. Communication and Stakeholder Management: Executive sponsors should facilitate effective communication among stakeholders, ensuring that everyone is informed about project progress, milestones, and changes. They also play a role in managing stakeholder expectations and addressing concerns.
7. Continuous Engagement: Executive sponsors need to stay engaged throughout the project lifecycle, providing guidance, feedback, and direction as necessary. Their ongoing involvement reinforces the importance of the project and its alignment with organizational priorities.

8. Celebrating Success and Learning from Failure: Executive sponsors should acknowledge and celebrate project successes, recognizing the efforts of the team. Additionally, they should foster a culture that encourages learning from failures and using them as opportunities for improvement.

By prioritizing these aspects, executive sponsors can effectively support project success and ensure that initiatives are completed on time, within budget, and with the expected outcomes.

1.23. What is the first thing you would do as a project manager?

In addition to attending corporate orientation and familiarizing myself with the building, it is crucial to understand the priorities of the project manager, which include the business, company, project, team, individuals, and changes in environment, technologies, and methodologies. Therefore, I will arrange a meeting with my manager to identify these priorities. Schedule meetings with users and staff to obtain status reports and appraisals of all team members. Hold regular meetings to stay informed. The key is to quickly get up to speed on the business, the project, and the team members.

As a project manager joining a new company, the first thing I would do is familiarize myself with the project scope, objectives, and stakeholders. This involves:

1. Reviewing Project Documentation: I would thoroughly review all project documentation, including the project charter, scope statement, requirements documents, and any existing plans or schedules.
2. Meeting Stakeholders: I would schedule meetings with key stakeholders to introduce myself, understand their expectations, and gather insights into their needs and priorities for the project.
3. Assessing Team Resources: I would assess the availability, and skill sets of team members assigned to the project to understand their strengths and areas for development.
4. Understanding Organizational Processes: I would familiarize myself with the organization's project management processes, methodologies, and tools to ensure alignment with best practices and compliance with any relevant standards.
5. Identifying Risks: I would conduct an initial risk assessment to identify potential threats and opportunities that could impact the project's success.
6. Setting Clear Expectations: I would communicate with the project team to establish clear roles, responsibilities, and expectations, ensuring everyone understands their contributions to the project's success.

By taking these steps, I can lay a solid foundation for effective project management and build rapport with stakeholders and team members, setting the stage for a successful project delivery.

1.24. Why is it important for project managers to understand the strategy of the organization that uses their services?

It allows the project to be viewed in the context of the business's objectives. This clarity helps in understanding and managing the connections between this system and others that are either in development or already in use. It also enables the project manager to assess the project's value and identify new opportunities for additional value.

Understanding the strategy of the organization is crucial for project managers for several reasons:

1. Alignment: Knowing the organization's strategy ensures that project goals are aligned with broader organizational objectives. This alignment ensures that the project contributes meaningfully to the organization's overall mission and vision.
2. Resource Allocation: Understanding the organization's strategy helps project managers anticipate resource needs and allocate them effectively. They can prioritize resources based on strategic

goals, ensuring that projects with the highest strategic importance receive adequate attention and resources.

3. Risk Management: Awareness of the organization's strategy enables project managers to anticipate potential risks and challenges that may arise during project implementation. They can proactively address these risks and develop contingency plans to mitigate their impact, thus safeguarding the organization's strategic interests.
4. Stakeholder Engagement: Project managers need to engage with various stakeholders throughout the project lifecycle. Understanding the organization's strategy allows them to communicate effectively with stakeholders, demonstrating how the project contributes to strategic objectives and gaining their support and commitment.
5. Decision Making: Knowledge of the organization's strategy provides a framework for making informed decisions throughout the project. Project managers can evaluate alternatives based on their alignment with strategic goals and choose the most appropriate course of action to maximize the project's impact on organizational success.
6. Performance Measurement: By understanding the organization's strategic priorities, project managers can establish relevant performance metrics and benchmarks to assess project success. This ensures that project outcomes are evaluated in the context of broader strategic objectives, providing meaningful insights for future planning and decision-making.

In essence, understanding the organization's strategy empowers project managers to effectively plan, execute, and monitor projects in a way that maximizes their contribution to organizational success.

1.25. How would you deal with “if it is not broke” syndrome?

Implementing technology solely for its own sake is not sufficient to convince users or upper management of its value. However, if you can demonstrate how the technology delivers real business benefits, users will be more likely to support your proposal. Highlighting specific, well-known issues with the current system and citing concrete past incidents can effectively illustrate the need for change.

Dealing with the "if it's not broke" syndrome, where team members resist change because they believe the current system is working fine, can be challenging but manageable. Here is how I would approach it as a project manager:

1. Communication: Start by openly discussing the benefits of potential changes with your team. Clearly articulate why the proposed changes are necessary and how they align with the project goals. Encourage team members to voice their concerns and offer their perspectives.
2. Data-driven Approach: Use data and metrics to illustrate why the current system may not be as effective as perceived. Present evidence that supports the need for change, such as customer feedback, performance metrics, or industry benchmarks. Objective data can help overcome resistance based on subjective opinions.
3. Incremental Changes: Instead of proposing drastic changes all at once, consider implementing small, incremental changes. This approach allows team members to gradually adapt to new processes and systems without feeling overwhelmed or resistant. It also provides opportunities to gather feedback and make adjustments along the way.
4. Highlight Benefits: Emphasize the benefits that the proposed changes will bring to the team and the project as a whole. Whether it is increased efficiency, improved quality, or better alignment with organizational objectives, highlighting the positive outcomes can help motivate team members to embrace change.
5. Address Concerns: Take the time to address any concerns or objections raised by team members. Listen actively to their feedback and acknowledge their perspectives. Work together to find solutions that address their concerns while still achieving the project goals.
6. Lead by Example: Demonstrate your commitment to change by being open to feedback, adapting

to new processes yourself, and actively participating in the implementation of proposed changes. Your willingness to embrace change will set a positive example for your team.

7. Celebrate Successes: Recognize and celebrate the achievements that result from the implemented changes. Acknowledge the contributions of team members and highlight how their efforts have contributed to the project's success. Positive reinforcement can help reinforce a culture of continuous improvement.
8. Provide Training and Support: Ensure that team members have the necessary training and support to successfully transition to new processes or systems. Offer workshops, resources, and one-on-one assistance as needed to help mitigate any challenges they may encounter during the change process.

By employing these strategies, you can effectively address the "if it's not broke" syndrome and foster a culture of innovation and continuous improvement within your team.

1.26. How would you work in an environment that implies that if you are not coding you are not working?

Working in an environment that heavily values coding as the primary measure of productivity can be challenging, especially if your role involves tasks that are not directly related to coding but are still important for the overall success of the project or company.

Users exhibit greater patience when they sense a genuine grasp of their business goals. Articulating requirements in a comprehensible manner fosters transparent communication and instills confidence in your competence. Progress updates via project plans, status reports, prototypes, and demonstrations further reinforce this assurance. Sustain user engagement by actively involving them in the review of requirements, prototypes, and status reports.

Here are some strategies you can consider:

1. Communicate Your Value: Clearly communicate the value of your non-coding tasks to your team or manager. Help them understand how your contributions contribute to the larger goals, even if they might not involve writing code directly.
2. Quantify and Document: Whenever possible, quantify the impact of your non-coding tasks. Use data to demonstrate the positive outcomes of your work, even if it is not coding-related. Keep a record of your accomplishments to showcase your contributions during performance evaluations.
3. Educate and Advocate: Educate your colleagues about the importance of tasks beyond coding. Advocate for a more holistic understanding of productivity that includes various roles and responsibilities within the team.
4. Collaborate with Developers: Find opportunities to collaborate closely with developers. By actively participating in discussions, planning, and problem-solving, you can showcase your expertise and demonstrate how your work complements theirs.
5. Show Initiative: Look for ways to bridge the gap between your non-coding tasks and coding activities. Are there processes that could be automated or streamlined? Demonstrating an understanding of coding-related processes can enhance your credibility.
6. Skill Enhancement: Consider learning some basic coding skills. This does not mean you have to become a full-fledged developer, but having a foundational understanding of coding can help you communicate better with your coding-focused colleagues.
7. Highlight Efficiency Gains: If your non-coding tasks contribute to making the development process smoother or more efficient, emphasize how your work ultimately saves time and resources for the coding team.
8. Flexibility and Adaptability: Embrace a flexible mindset and be open to adapting your skills and tasks to align more closely with the coding-centric environment when necessary.

9. Focus on End Goals: Remind your team that the ultimate goal is to deliver high-quality products to customers or clients. Highlight how your work contributes to this goal, regardless of whether it involves coding.
10. Lead by Example: If you consistently deliver excellent results and showcase the importance of your non-coding tasks, you may influence a shift in the overall perception of productivity within the organization.

Remember that a diverse range of skills and roles contribute to the success of a project or company. It is important to foster an environment where all contributions are acknowledged and valued. Over time, by effectively demonstrating your contributions, you can help reshape the perception of productivity in your workplace.

1.27. How would you divide your time between employee relations, project management, and paperwork?

While people are invaluable and often require significant time, a project manager's priorities should be as follows:

1. Business objectives
2. Company objectives
3. Project goals
4. Team dynamics
5. Individual contributions
6. Adaptations to environmental, technological, and methodological changes.

Balancing time effectively as a project manager is crucial for success. Here is a general guideline on how to divide your time between employee relations, project management, and paperwork:

1. Employee Relations (30% of time):
   a. Build strong relationships with your team members. Spend time understanding their strengths, weaknesses, and career aspirations.
   b. Conduct regular one-on-one meetings to provide feedback, support, and guidance.
   c. Address any conflicts or issues promptly and fairly.
   d. Foster a positive team culture and encourage collaboration.
2. Project Management (50% of time):
   a. Plan and prioritize tasks and milestones to ensure the project stays on track.
   b. Hold regular team meetings to discuss progress, address challenges, and adjust plans as necessary.
   c. Monitor project timelines, budgets, and resources closely to prevent delays or overruns.
   d. Communicate effectively with stakeholders to manage expectations and keep them informed of progress and changes.
3. Paperwork/Administrative Tasks (20% of time):
   a. Allocate time for administrative tasks such as documenting project plans, status reports, and meeting minutes.
   b. Keep project documentation organized and up to date to facilitate easy access and reference.
   c. Handle any necessary paperwork related to budget approvals, procurement, or contractual agreements.
   d. Automate routine administrative tasks whenever possible to save time and reduce manual effort.

Remember, these percentages are just a guideline and may vary depending on the specific requirements of your project and organization. Flexibility and adaptability are key traits for effective project management.

Adjust your time allocation as needed to address emerging priorities and challenges.

1.28. List tips for successful project management.

Successful project management involves a combination of organizational skills, effective communication, strategic planning, and adaptability. Here are some detailed tips to help you manage your projects effectively:

1. Define Clear Objectives: Start by outlining specific, measurable, achievable, relevant, and time-bound (SMART) objectives for your project. Make sure everyone involved understands the goals and deliverables.
2. Create a Detailed Plan: Develop a comprehensive project plan outlining tasks, timelines, resources, and dependencies. Break down the project into smaller, manageable tasks to facilitate better tracking and control. Use project management tools like Gantt charts or Kanban boards to visualize and track progress.
3. Set Realistic Timelines: Be realistic about the time required to complete each task and the project as a whole. Factor in potential delays and allocate buffer time where necessary.
4. Allocate Resources Wisely: Identify the resources required for each task and allocate them effectively. This includes human resources, equipment, and budget.
5. Build a Competent Team: Assemble a team with the right skills and experience for the project. Foster collaboration.
6. Establish Clear Roles and Responsibilities: Clearly define who is responsible for each task and decision within the project team to avoid confusion and streamline workflow.
7. Establish Clear Communication Channels: Communication is key to successful project management. Maintain open and transparent communication channels among team members, stakeholders, and clients. Regularly update everyone on project progress, milestones, and any changes.
8. Manage Risks Proactively: Identify potential risks early on and develop strategies to mitigate or manage them. Regularly review and update your risk management plan throughout the project lifecycle.
9. Monitor Progress Regularly: Track progress against the project plan regularly to identify any deviations or delays. Use key performance indicators (KPIs) to measure progress and identify and address any issues promptly to keep the project on track.
10. Adapt to Changes: Be flexible and adaptable in response to changes in project scope, requirements, or external factors. Have a change management process in place to assess and implement changes effectively.
11. Manage Stakeholder Expectations: Keep stakeholders informed and engaged throughout the project lifecycle. Understand their needs and concerns and address them proactively to maintain their support. Seek feedback and incorporate it into project decisions where appropriate.
12. Quality Assurance: Implement processes for quality assurance to ensure that deliverables meet the required standards. Conduct regular reviews and inspections to identify and address any quality issues.
13. Document Everything: Maintain thorough documentation throughout the project, including plans, meeting minutes, decisions, and changes. This helps ensure transparency and provides a reference point for future projects.
14. Allocate Resources Wisely: Ensure that resources, including budget, personnel, and equipment, are allocated efficiently and effectively to support project goals.
15. Encourage Collaboration: Foster a collaborative environment where team members feel comfortable sharing ideas, providing feedback, and working together towards common objectives.
16. Celebrate Achievements and Milestones: Recognize and celebrate milestones and achievements throughout the project to boost team morale and motivation.

17. Conduct Post-Project Reviews: Once the project is complete, conduct a comprehensive review to evaluate what went well, what could be improved, and lessons learned for future projects.
18. Continuous Improvement: Use insights from post-project reviews to continuously improve your project management processes and practices.

By incorporating these tips into your project management approach, you can enhance your ability to deliver successful outcomes consistently.

1.29. What are the most urgent improvements your IT organization needs to make to support your business?

Prioritizing improvements in an IT organization depends on various factors like the current state of infrastructure, business objectives, customer needs, and industry trends. However, some common areas that IT organizations often need to improve include:

1. Cybersecurity: Enhancing cybersecurity measures is typically the highest priority due to the increasing frequency and sophistication of cyber threats. This includes implementing robust firewalls, intrusion detection systems (IDS), regular security audits, employee training on security best practices, and ensuring compliance with data protection regulations like GDPR (General Data Protection Regulation) or CCPA (California Consumer Privacy Act).
2. Disaster Recovery and Business Continuity: Developing and testing comprehensive disaster recovery (DR) and business continuity plans is crucial to minimize downtime and data loss in the event of natural disasters, cyber-attacks, or other emergencies. This involves implementing redundant systems, data backups, failover mechanisms, and establishing clear protocols for restoring operations.
3. Infrastructure Modernization: Upgrading outdated hardware and software infrastructure to improve performance, scalability, and reliability is essential. This may include migrating to cloud-based services, adopting virtualization technologies, upgrading networking equipment, and optimizing data center operations.
4. IT Service Management (ITSM): Implementing or improving IT service management processes and tools can enhance the efficiency and quality of IT services. This includes adopting ITIL (Information Technology Infrastructure Library) best practices, implementing a service desk system for incident management and service requests, and establishing clear service level agreements (SLAs) with stakeholders.
5. Data Management and Analytics: Improving data management practices and analytics capabilities can help organizations derive valuable insights from their data and make informed decisions. This involves implementing data governance frameworks, ensuring data quality and integrity, investing in advanced analytics tools, and fostering a data-driven culture within the organization.
6. User Experience (UX) and Digital Transformation: Enhancing user experience by providing intuitive interfaces, responsive support services, and efficient troubleshooting processes of internal systems and customer-facing applications can drive productivity, customer satisfaction, and competitive advantage. This may involve redesigning user interfaces, implementing self-service portals, improving helpdesk capabilities, conducting user training sessions, optimizing application performance, adopting agile development methodologies, and embracing digital transformation initiatives to streamline business processes.
7. IT Governance, Compliance, and Strategy Alignment: Strengthening IT governance frameworks and ensuring alignment with business goals and priorities and compliance with regulatory requirements is critical for mitigating risks and maintaining the trust of customers and stakeholders. This includes establishing clear policies and procedures for IT governance, conducting regular compliance audits, addressing any gaps or vulnerabilities identified, and performance metrics to measure IT effectiveness and value contribution to the organization.
8. Integration and Interoperability: Streamlining integration between different systems and

applications to enable seamless data flow and communication across the organization. This might involve adopting standardized protocols, APIs, and middleware solutions.

9. Compliance and Regulatory Requirements: Ensuring compliance with industry regulations and data protection laws by implementing appropriate controls, policies, and procedures. This includes staying updated on evolving regulatory requirements and adapting IT practices accordingly.
10. Resource Optimization and Cost Reduction: Identifying opportunities to optimize IT resources, such as consolidating servers, optimizing software licenses, and automating routine tasks to reduce operational costs and improve efficiency.
11. Mobile and Remote Access: Facilitating mobile and remote access to corporate resources for employees, clients, and partners. This may involve implementing secure mobile device management (MDM) solutions, virtual private networks (VPNs), and collaboration tools. Skills Development and Talent Acquisition: Investing in the training and development of IT staff and recruiting top talent with relevant skills and expertise is essential for building a high-performing IT organization. This includes providing opportunities for continuous learning, fostering a culture of innovation, and staying abreast of emerging technologies and industry trends.

Prioritizing these improvements will depend on the specific needs and priorities of the business, available resources, and budget constraints as well as the potential impact on overall operations and competitiveness. Regular assessment and alignment with business goals are essential to ensure that IT initiatives deliver maximum value and support the overall success of the organization.

Based on a survey by Project Management Institute (PMI) and International Data Corporation (IDC), here is the list in the decreasing order of importance or needs:

1. How applications better fit our business processes
2. Improve access to relevant information or data
3. Better systems for communications or collaboration
4. Lower cost to develop or deploy applications
5. Improved security of information
6. Lower costs of underlying IT infrastructure
7. Faster development or deployment
8. Near real-time monitoring of business processes
9. Visibility of applications' underlying IT infrastructure

1.30. Describe a time when you implemented a new idea without being asked or pursued a new opportunity that could improve the project or company.

Exhibiting courage and proactive initiative stands as a vital hallmark of proficient project managers. Entrusting the project's objectives, finances, and even their own standing, sponsors rely heavily on these managers. Sponsors acknowledge their limitations and depend on astute, self-driven individuals to tackle challenges, unearth fresh prospects, and drive progress without constant prompting.

When responding to that question, you want to provide a specific example that demonstrates your initiative, creativity, and positive impact. Here is a structured way to respond:

1. Briefly introduce the situation: Start by setting the context for your example. Mention the project or company you were involved in and the general circumstances that prompted your initiative.
2. Describe your idea or opportunity: Explain the new idea or opportunity you identified. What was it, and why did you believe it could improve the project or company? Provide enough detail to help the interviewer understand the significance of your proposal.
3. Discuss how you implemented it: Outline the steps you took to put your idea into action. Did you collaborate with others or work independently? How did you overcome any challenges or

resistance?

4. Highlight the results: Share the outcomes of your initiative. What impact did it have on the project or company? Be specific about any measurable improvements or positive changes that resulted from your actions.
5. Reflect on what you learned: Conclude by reflecting on what you gained from this experience. Did it teach you anything about leadership, problem-solving, or innovation? What would you do differently next time?

By following this structure, you can provide a comprehensive and compelling response that showcases your proactive approach and ability to drive positive change.

1.31. Describe a scenario where you had to balance competing customer demands with project constraints. How did you ensure customer satisfaction while maintaining the goals of the project?

Balancing a customer-centric mindset with timely project completion is a nuanced task. Often, business partners lack full comprehension of the technical intricacies involved in translating business operations into software solutions. Their primary concern lies in having a functional system that adapts to evolving business demands. Skilled project managers establish strong relationships with their partners, striving to grasp their core needs and preemptively tackle any issues. However, this equilibrium proves challenging, as project managers must uphold their commitment to project scope while accommodating the dynamic requirements of business customers.

Here is one possible response:

In a previous role as a project manager, I encountered a situation where we had tight project deadlines and limited resources, while simultaneously facing diverse and sometimes conflicting requests from different customers. One particular instance comes to mind where we were developing a software solution for a client within a strict timeline, but during the process, they requested several additional features that were not initially scoped out in the project plan.

To address this challenge, I employed a multi-faceted approach. First, I initiated transparent and open communication channels with all stakeholders involved, including the clients and my project team. I facilitated discussions to prioritize the newly requested features based on their impact on the project timeline, budget, and overall objectives. Through this process, we identified the most critical features that aligned with both the clients' needs and the project constraints.

Next, I utilized agile project management methodologies to adapt to changing requirements while maintaining project momentum. We implemented iterative development cycles, allowing us to incorporate essential features incrementally without derailing the project timeline. This approach enabled us to deliver tangible value to the client early in the process while continuing to address their evolving needs.

Additionally, I ensured that any compromises made to accommodate customer requests were clearly communicated and documented, along with their potential impacts on the project scope, schedule, and budget. By maintaining transparency and managing expectations effectively, we fostered trust and collaboration with our clients, which ultimately contributed to their satisfaction with the project outcomes.

Overall, by prioritizing effective communication, leveraging agile methodologies, and managing expectations proactively, I successfully balanced competing customer demands with project constraints, ultimately achieving customer satisfaction while meeting the goals of the project.

1.32. What are some of the things a technical lead can do that a project manager cannot?

A technical lead and a project manager play distinct but complementary roles in a project. While there may be some overlap in their responsibilities, there are certain tasks that a technical lead typically handles that a project manager may not be as well-equipped to handle due to differences in expertise and focus. Here are some examples:

1. Technical Architecture and Design: A technical lead often takes the lead in defining the technical architecture of the project and making key design decisions. This involves understanding the technical requirements, selecting appropriate technologies, and architecting the system to meet those requirements. While a project manager may have some understanding of the technical aspects, they may not possess the depth of knowledge required to make critical technical decisions.
2. Code Review and Technical Guidance: Technical leads are usually deeply involved in code reviews, ensuring that the codebase adheres to best practices, coding standards, and architectural guidelines. They provide technical guidance to the development team, helping them overcome challenges and improve their skills. While a project manager may participate in code reviews to some extent, the technical lead typically has a deeper understanding of the codebase and can provide more detailed feedback.
3. Hands-on Technical Work: Depending on the size and nature of the project, a technical lead may be actively involved in writing code, debugging issues, and resolving technical challenges. They may prototype solutions, conduct feasibility studies, or perform performance optimizations. While project managers may have some technical background, they are generally more focused on managing the project's overall progress, resources, and stakeholders.
4. Technical Roadmap and Innovation: Technical leads often contribute to the project's technical roadmap, identifying opportunities for innovation, evaluating new technologies, and proposing improvements to the existing system. They stay abreast of industry trends and emerging technologies, ensuring that the project remains technically competitive and aligned with strategic goals. While project managers may contribute to high-level planning and decision-making, the technical lead typically drives the technical direction of the project.
5. Resolving Technical Challenges and Risks: When technical challenges arise during the project, such as performance bottlenecks, scalability issues, or compatibility problems, the technical lead is responsible for resolving them. They diagnose the root cause of the problem, propose solutions, and coordinate with the development team to implement fixes. While project managers may facilitate communication and provide support, the technical lead is often the primary driver in addressing technical risks and issues.

Overall, while both technical leads and project managers play crucial roles in the success of a project, the technical lead's expertise lies in the technical domain, allowing them to take on tasks and responsibilities that leverage their deep understanding of technology and software development processes.

1.33. Provide summary of project management knowledge areas.

Project management knowledge areas are the key facets of project management that encompass various processes, activities, and skills necessary for successful project execution. According to the Project Management Body of Knowledge (PMBOK) guide, there are ten knowledge areas:

1. Project Integration Management: This involves coordinating all aspects of a project, ensuring that various elements work together seamlessly to achieve project objectives. It includes developing project charters, plans, and executing and monitoring project activities.

2. Project Scope Management: This knowledge area involves defining, managing, and controlling what is included and excluded from the project. It includes processes such as collecting requirements, defining scope, creating a Work Breakdown Structure (WBS), and controlling scope changes.
3. Project Schedule Management: This focuses on developing, managing, and controlling the project schedule. It includes activities such as defining activities, sequencing them, estimating durations and resources, and developing and controlling the project schedule.
4. Project Cost Management: This involves estimating, budgeting, and controlling costs throughout the project lifecycle. It includes processes such as cost estimation, budgeting, and controlling costs.
5. Project Quality Management: This knowledge area encompasses ensuring that project deliverables meet the required quality standards. It includes processes such as quality planning, assurance, and control.
6. Project Resource Management: This involves identifying, acquiring, and managing the resources needed for the project, including human resources, equipment, and materials. It includes processes such as resource planning, acquiring, developing, and managing the project team.
7. Project Communications Management: This involves planning, managing, and controlling project communications. It includes processes such as communication planning, distribution of information, performance reporting, and managing stakeholder expectations.
8. Project Risk Management: This encompasses identifying, analyzing, and responding to project risks to minimize their impact on the project's objectives. It includes processes such as risk identification, qualitative and quantitative risk analysis, risk response planning, and monitoring and controlling risks.
9. Project Procurement Management: This involves acquiring goods and services from external sources to support project execution. It includes processes such as procurement planning, solicitation, source selection, contract administration, and contract closure.
10. Project Stakeholder Management: This focuses on identifying stakeholders, understanding their needs and expectations, and managing their engagement throughout the project lifecycle. It includes processes such as stakeholder identification, stakeholder analysis, stakeholder engagement planning, and stakeholder engagement monitoring.

Each of these knowledge areas plays a crucial role in ensuring that projects are completed successfully, meeting their objectives within constraints such as time, cost, scope, quality, and stakeholder expectations.

1.34. Why what happens what "After the Project" is sometimes more important than the project?

"What happens after the project" often becomes more important than the project itself for several reasons:

1. Long-term Impact: While the project may have immediate goals and deliverables, its true value lies in its long-term impact. What happens after the project determines whether the initial investment of time, money, and resources was worthwhile.
2. Sustainability: Projects are often initiated to bring about positive change or improvement. However, sustainability is key. If the project's outcomes cannot be sustained or if they create unintended negative consequences in the long term, its success is questionable.
3. Integration: Projects are often part of larger initiatives or organizational strategies. What happens after the project determines how well its outcomes are integrated into existing systems, processes, or policies.
4. Lessons Learned: The post-project phase is an opportunity to reflect on what went well and what could be improved for future projects. It is where lessons learned are documented and shared, contributing to organizational learning and improvement.

5. Stakeholder Satisfaction: Ultimately, the success of a project is judged by its ability to meet stakeholders' needs and expectations. What happens after the project affects stakeholders' perception of its success and their satisfaction with the outcomes.

In essence, the "after the project" phase is where the true test of the project's success lies. It determines its lasting impact, sustainability, and contribution to organizational learning and stakeholder satisfaction. Therefore, paying attention to this phase is crucial for maximizing the value derived from the project.

1.35. How does your management view projects? Do they view projects as being rooted in technology or focusing on business results?

My management views projects as strategic initiatives that align with our overall goals and objectives. They prioritize projects based on factors such as their potential impact on the organization, resource requirements, and alignment with our core values. They emphasize effective planning, clear communication, and collaboration among teams to ensure successful project execution. Additionally, they value innovation and encourage teams to think creatively when approaching projects to drive continuous improvement and achieve optimal results.

In the grand scheme, my management sees projects as a fusion of both technology and business goals. They understand that technology is a means to an end, a tool to achieve specific business outcomes. Thus, while they value technological advancements and innovation, they always prioritize aligning these advancements with overarching business objectives.

Projects are often initiated with a clear understanding of the desired business results or outcomes. From there, technology comes into play as the enabler, helping to streamline processes, enhance efficiency, or create new opportunities for growth. Throughout the project lifecycle, there is a continuous evaluation of how technological solutions contribute to the bottom line and overall business strategy.

In essence, while my management appreciates the importance of technology, they ultimately gauge the success of projects by their impact on business results.

1.36. What are the different project management "Level of Maturity"?

Project management maturity refers to the organization's capability to effectively manage projects throughout their lifecycle. There are several models used to gauge project management maturity, but one common framework is the Project Management Maturity Model (PMMM), which defines different levels of maturity. Here they are.

1. Initial Level: At this level, there is a lack of standardized processes and procedures for managing projects. Project management is typically ad hoc, and success largely depends on individual effort rather than systematic approaches.
2. Repeatable Level: At this stage, organizations start to develop standardized processes and procedures based on past experiences. There is a recognition of the importance of project management, and basic project management practices are established and followed, although they may not be consistently applied across all projects.
3. Defined Level: Here, the organization has documented its project management processes and procedures. There is a clear understanding of roles, responsibilities, and workflows. Project management practices are standardized and consistently applied across the organization.
4. Managed Level: At this level, organizations actively monitor and measure their project management performance. Metrics are used to track progress, identify issues, and make data-driven decisions. Continuous improvement is emphasized, and there is a focus on optimizing processes and increasing efficiency.

5. Optimized Level: This is the highest level of maturity, where project management processes are fully integrated into the organization's culture and strategy. Best practices are systematically applied, and there is a culture of innovation and learning. The organization is agile and adaptable, able to quickly respond to changing conditions and opportunities.

These levels represent a progression from an immature, ad hoc approach to project management to a mature, systematic, and integrated approach that drives consistent project success and organizational performance.

1.37. How do you manage project sponsors and stakeholders?

Managing project sponsors and stakeholders is crucial for the success of any project. Here are some steps and strategies to effectively manage them:

1. Identify key stakeholders: Begin by identifying all the individuals and groups that have an interest in or will be affected by the project. This includes project sponsors, clients, end-users, team members, executives, and any other relevant parties.
2. Understand their expectations: Once stakeholders are identified, gather information about their expectations, needs, and concerns regarding the project. Conduct interviews, surveys, or meetings to gain insights into their perspectives and ensure their expectations are aligned with the project goals.
3. Establish clear communication channels: Set up regular communication channels to keep stakeholders informed about project progress, milestones, risks, and changes. This can include project status reports, meetings, email updates, or online collaboration platforms. Tailor the communication methods to suit the preferences of different stakeholders.
4. Define roles and responsibilities: Clearly define the roles and responsibilities of project sponsors and stakeholders. Establish who has decision-making authority, who needs to be consulted or informed, and who will provide resources or support. This helps avoid confusion and ensures accountability.
5. Build relationships: Develop strong relationships with project sponsors and stakeholders based on trust and transparency. Engage in active listening, address their concerns, and involve them in decision-making processes whenever possible. Regularly seek their feedback and make them feel valued and included in the project.
6. Manage expectations: Set realistic expectations with sponsors and stakeholders by providing accurate information about project scope, timeline, and limitations. Clearly communicate any potential risks, constraints, or changes that may impact the project. This helps prevent unrealistic expectations and ensures a shared understanding of project constraints.
7. Stakeholder engagement and involvement: Involve stakeholders at appropriate stages of the project. Conduct workshops, focus groups, or meetings to gather their input, validate requirements, and ensure their interests are considered. This enhances their ownership of the project and increases the likelihood of success.
8. Mitigate risks and conflicts: Identify potential conflicts or risks that may arise with stakeholders and sponsors. Proactively address these issues by seeking resolutions, finding compromises, or engaging in negotiation. Addressing concerns early on helps maintain positive relationships and minimizes the impact on the project.
9. Monitor and adapt: Continuously monitor stakeholder satisfaction and project sponsor engagement throughout the project lifecycle. Be open to feedback and adapt your management approach accordingly. Regularly reassess and update stakeholder and sponsor expectations to align them with changing project circumstances.
10. Celebrate achievements: Recognize and celebrate project milestones and achievements with project sponsors and stakeholders. Acknowledge their contributions and show appreciation for their support. This fosters positive relationships and motivates stakeholders to continue their

involvement and support for the project.

Remember that managing project sponsors and stakeholders is an ongoing process. By effectively communicating, engaging, and addressing their needs, you can build strong relationships and ensure their support for project success.

1.38. Why do developers sometime dislike project managers?

It is important to note that not all developers dislike project managers. The relationship between developers and project managers can vary depending on the individuals involved, the organizational culture, and the specific project circumstances. However, there are a few common reasons why some developers may have conflicts or frustrations with project managers:

1. Lack of technical understanding: Project managers are responsible for overseeing the project's progress, timeline, and resources. However, some project managers may not have a deep understanding of the technical aspects of software development. This can lead to miscommunication, unrealistic expectations, and difficulties in estimating project timelines or scope.
2. Unrealistic expectations and deadlines: Project managers often have to balance competing priorities and deadlines. They may push developers to complete tasks within tight timeframes without considering the complexities and challenges involved in the development process. This can lead to stress, compromised quality, and burnout among developers.
3. Micromanagement: Some project managers may engage in excessive micromanagement, closely monitoring every aspect of a developer's work and decision-making. This can hinder creativity, autonomy, and productivity, making developers feel undervalued and disempowered.
4. Ineffective communication and collaboration: Good communication and collaboration are crucial for successful project management. However, when project managers fail to provide clear requirements, feedback, or support, developers may struggle to deliver the desired results. Poor communication can lead to misunderstandings, rework, and wasted effort.
5. Scope creep and changing priorities: Project managers are responsible for managing project scope and ensuring that requirements are clearly defined. However, it is not uncommon for project requirements to change over time. When project managers fail to effectively manage scope changes or communicate them to developers, it can lead to confusion, frustration, and delays.
6. Lack of recognition and appreciation: Developers often invest significant time and effort in their work, and they appreciate recognition for their accomplishments. If project managers fail to acknowledge the contributions of developers or take credit for their work, it can create a sense of disengagement and demotivation.

It is worth noting that effective project managers who understand the technical aspects of software development, promote open communication, and respect the expertise of developers can foster positive relationships and contribute to successful project outcomes.

1.39. What is the future of project management?

The future of project management is likely to be shaped by several key trends:

1. Digital Transformation: Project management tools and techniques are becoming increasingly digitized, leveraging technologies like AI, machine learning, and automation to streamline processes, improve efficiency, and enhance decision-making.
2. Remote Work and Collaboration: The rise of remote work, accelerated by global events such as the COVID-19 pandemic, has led to a greater emphasis on virtual collaboration tools and strategies. Project managers will need to adapt to managing teams across different time zones and locations effectively.

3. Agile and Lean Methodologies: Agile and lean project management methodologies continue to gain popularity due to their flexibility, adaptability, and ability to deliver value incrementally. Expect to see further integration of these approaches into project management practices.
4. Focus on Sustainability: As environmental concerns become more prominent, project managers will need to consider sustainability factors in project planning and execution. This includes assessing the environmental impact of projects and incorporating sustainable practices into project management frameworks.
5. Data-Driven Decision Making: With the proliferation of data analytics tools, project managers will have access to more data than ever before. Utilizing data-driven insights can help optimize project performance, identify risks, and drive better decision-making throughout the project lifecycle.
6. Emphasis on Soft Skills: While technical skills remain important, there will be an increasing emphasis on soft skills such as communication, leadership, and emotional intelligence. Project managers need to effectively navigate complex interpersonal dynamics and foster collaboration among team members.
7. Integration of Project Management with Strategy: Project management is increasingly being viewed as a strategic function within organizations. Project managers will be expected to align projects with broader organizational goals and contribute to driving business value.

Overall, the future of project management will be characterized by innovation, adaptability, and a continued focus on delivering value in an increasingly dynamic and interconnected world.

1.40. How involved should the leadership be in projects?

The level of involvement that leadership should have in projects can vary depending on several factors, including the size and complexity of the project, the organizational structure, and the expertise of the team members involved. However, here are some general guidelines:

1. Setting Vision and Goals: Leadership should be heavily involved in setting the overall vision and goals for the project. This ensures alignment with the organization's objectives and provides clarity for the team.
2. Resource Allocation: Leaders should be involved in allocating resources (both human and financial) to projects based on their strategic importance and potential impact.
3. Monitoring Progress: Leadership should periodically monitor the progress of projects to ensure they are on track to achieve their objectives. This may involve regular check-ins, status reports, or milestone reviews.
4. Removing Obstacles: Leaders should be available to help remove obstacles or barriers that may impede the progress of the project. This could involve providing additional resources, resolving conflicts, or making strategic decisions.
5. Providing Support and Guidance: Leadership should provide support and guidance to project teams, offering expertise, advice, and mentorship when needed.
6. Decision Making: Leaders should be involved in key decision-making processes related to the project, especially those with strategic implications or significant resource allocation.
7. Celebrating Successes and Learning from Failures: Leadership should recognize and celebrate successes achieved through projects, while also encouraging a culture of learning from failures and using them as opportunities for improvement.

Overall, the level of involvement should strike a balance between providing direction and support while empowering teams to take ownership of their projects and drive them forward.

1.41. What are the primary goals of every project?

The primary goals of every project generally include:

1. Achieving Objectives: Projects are initiated to achieve specific objectives or outcomes. These objectives could be anything from creating a new product, implementing a new system, improving efficiency, or solving a problem.
2. Delivering Value: Projects are expected to deliver value to stakeholders, whether it is in the form of financial returns, improved processes, enhanced services, or any other measurable benefits.
3. Meeting Stakeholder Expectations: Projects need to meet the expectations of stakeholders, including clients, customers, sponsors, team members, and any other individuals or groups with an interest in the project's outcomes.
4. Managing Constraints: Projects operate within constraints such as time, budget, resources, and scope. A key goal is to manage these constraints effectively to deliver the project within the specified parameters.
5. Ensuring Quality: Quality is an essential goal of every project. Deliverables should meet predefined standards and specifications to satisfy the needs of stakeholders and ensure long-term success.
6. Managing Risks: Projects involve uncertainty, and managing risks is crucial to minimize the likelihood and impact of adverse events that could affect the project's success.
7. Maintaining Stakeholder Satisfaction: Keeping stakeholders informed, engaged, and satisfied throughout the project lifecycle is essential for its success. Communication and stakeholder management are critical aspects of achieving this goal.
8. Adhering to Schedule: Projects have timelines, and meeting deadlines is vital to ensure timely delivery and avoid disruptions to other initiatives or dependencies.
9. Optimizing Resources: Efficient utilization of resources, including human resources, materials, and budget, is essential to maximize project effectiveness and minimize waste.
10. Facilitating Learning and Improvement: Projects provide opportunities for learning and improvement, both at the individual and organizational levels. Evaluating project performance, identifying lessons learned, and implementing changes for future projects contribute to continuous improvement.

These goals may vary depending on the nature, size, and complexity of the project, as well as the specific needs and priorities of stakeholders. However, these are some of the fundamental objectives that guide project management practices across various industries and domains.

1.42. Why is not good project management enough?

While good project management is essential for the success of any endeavor, it is not always sufficient on its own due to several reasons:

1. Lack of Clear Objectives: Even with excellent project management, if the project's objectives are unclear or constantly changing, it can lead to confusion and inefficiencies.
2. Poor Communication: Effective communication is crucial for project success. If there are breakdowns in communication between team members, stakeholders, or project managers, even the best project management practices may not salvage the situation.
3. Insufficient Resources: Sometimes, projects fail due to a lack of adequate resources such as funding, skilled personnel, or time. Project management can help optimize the use of resources, but if they're insufficient from the start, success may be unattainable.
4. Unforeseen Risks: No matter how well a project is planned, unexpected events can occur that derail progress. Without robust risk management strategies in place, these unforeseen risks can escalate into major issues.
5. Poor Stakeholder Engagement: Projects often involve various stakeholders with different interests and expectations. If stakeholders are not adequately engaged or if their needs are not taken into account, it can lead to dissatisfaction and ultimately project failure.

6. Lack of Adaptability: Project management methodologies provide frameworks for planning and execution, but rigid adherence to these methodologies without flexibility can hinder a project's ability to adapt to changing circumstances or requirements.
7. Scope Creep: Projects can suffer from scope creep, where the project's scope gradually expands beyond its original boundaries. Without effective scope management, this can lead to resource depletion and delays.

In summary, while good project management is a crucial aspect of project success, it needs to be complemented by clear objectives, effective communication, sufficient resources, robust risk management, stakeholder engagement, adaptability, and scope management to ensure successful project outcomes.

1.43. How do you manage a project?

Managing a project involves several key steps and strategies to ensure its successful completion. Here is a general outline of how to manage a project effectively:

1. Define the Project Scope: Clearly outline the objectives, deliverables, and constraints of the project. This includes understanding the project's purpose, goals, and stakeholders' expectations.
2. Create a Project Plan: Develop a detailed plan that includes tasks, timelines, milestones, and resources required for each phase of the project. Use tools like Gantt charts, Kanban boards, or project management software to organize and track progress.
3. Allocate Resources: Identify and allocate the necessary resources (e.g., budget, personnel, equipment) to execute the project plan effectively. Ensure that resources are utilized efficiently and that roles and responsibilities are clearly defined.
4. Risk Management: Identify potential risks and develop strategies to mitigate them. Regularly assess and monitor risks throughout the project lifecycle to minimize any negative impacts on project objectives.
5. Communication: Establish clear lines of communication with stakeholders, team members, and any other relevant parties. Provide regular updates on project progress, milestones, and any changes to the plan. Encourage open communication to address any issues or concerns promptly.
6. Monitor Progress: Continuously monitor project progress against the established plan. Track key performance indicators (KPIs) and milestones to ensure that the project stays on schedule and within budget. Adjust the plan as needed to address any deviations or changes in project requirements.
7. Quality Assurance: Implement processes to ensure that deliverables meet quality standards and adhere to project requirements. Conduct regular quality checks and inspections throughout the project lifecycle to identify and address any issues or deficiencies promptly.
8. Manage Changes: Be prepared to adapt to changes in project scope, requirements, or constraints. Establish a change management process to evaluate, prioritize, and implement changes effectively while minimizing disruptions to the project.
9. Closure and Evaluation: Once the project is completed, conduct a thorough evaluation to assess its success against the original objectives and deliverables. Document lessons learned and best practices for future projects. Close out any remaining tasks, finalize project documentation, and ensure proper handover of deliverables to stakeholders.

By following these steps and applying effective project management principles, you can increase the likelihood of project success and achieve desired outcomes.

2. Project Scope and Requirements Management

Industry studies show that 30 to 40% of project costs are related to rework. Of that 70% is related to poor quality requirements. This means that 21 to 28% of your project costs are directly related to poor quality requirements.

Producing a good set of requirements is a team effort. It takes multiple players, including product manager, product owner, project managers, business analysts, UX experts, and QA professionals, to deliver what is needed to build and test solutions.

Requirements management remains a significant challenge for many organizations. Industry reports indicate that the primary contributors to issues with quality, cost, and schedule are a lack of understanding of customer needs, incomplete requirement specifications, and difficulties in managing changing requirements.

If our requirements are not right, it does not matter how well we do everything else, we can do a perfect job of creating the wrong software. To get the requirements right, we have to talk to the right people. This means we have to do a comprehensive job of identifying the stakeholders for our software. Some of the techniques to build a comprehensive set of software requirements include:

1. Interviews
2. Focus Groups
3. Facilitate Requirements Workshops
4. User Stories and Storyboards
5. Documentation Studies
6. Human Factors Studies

2.1. What is competitive advantage?

Competitive advantage is the ability of any organization or enterprise to dominate in the national and international markets. It refers to the unique attributes or capabilities that allow a company to outperform its competitors in the marketplace. These attributes could include superior products or services, innovative technology, efficient processes, strong brand reputation, access to unique resources, cost advantages, or highly skilled employees which are exceeding the requirements of the customers.

Having a competitive advantage enables a company to differentiate itself from competitors, attract customers, and generate higher profits. It is essentially what sets a company apart and gives it an edge in the industry. Competitive advantage can be temporary or sustainable depending on how difficult it is for competitors to replicate or surpass those attributes.

2.2. What is gap analysis?

Gap analysis is done to map the gap which exists between implied and specified customer requirements and existing process. It is a strategic planning tool used to assess the difference between the current state of affairs within an organization and where it desires to be in the future. This method involves comparing the actual performance of an organization (or a particular process or system within it) to its potential or desired performance. The "gap" refers to the difference or discrepancy between these two states.

Gap analysis typically involves several steps:

1. Identify objectives: Clearly define the goals and objectives that the organization wants to achieve.
2. Assess current state: Evaluate the current situation, including processes, resources, performance metrics, and any existing strategies.
3. Determine desired state: Define the ideal or desired state that the organization aims to reach.
4. Analyze the gap: Compare the current state with the desired state to identify any gaps or discrepancies.
5. Develop action plan: Once the gaps are identified, develop strategies and action plans to bridge these gaps and move closer to the desired state.
6. Implement and monitor: Execute the action plan and continually monitor progress to ensure that the gaps are being addressed effectively.

Gap analysis can be applied in various areas within an organization, including business processes, technology implementation, employee skills development, and market positioning. It helps organizations identify areas for improvement and develop targeted strategies to achieve their objectives.

2.3. What is the importance of requirements gathering?

Requirements gathering is crucial in any project for several reasons:

1. Understanding Client Needs: It helps in understanding what the client or stakeholders truly need from the project. This ensures that the final product meets their expectations and satisfies their requirements.
2. Scope Definition: Gathering requirements helps in defining the scope of the project. It delineates what is included and what is not, which is essential for managing expectations and avoiding scope creep.
3. Basis for Planning: Requirements serve as the basis for project planning. They guide the development team in creating project timelines, allocating resources, and estimating costs accurately.
4. Risk Management: Identifying requirements upfront allows for early identification and mitigation of risks. By understanding potential challenges and constraints, project teams can develop strategies to address them proactively.
5. Quality Assurance: Clear requirements facilitate effective testing and quality assurance. Test cases can be derived directly from requirements, ensuring that the final product meets the specified criteria.
6. Communication and Collaboration: Requirements gathering promotes communication and collaboration among stakeholders, project managers, and development teams. It ensures that everyone is aligned on project goals and objectives.
7. Basis for Design: Requirements serve as inputs for system design and architecture. They guide developers in designing solutions that meet the specified needs and functionalities.
8. Customer Satisfaction: Ultimately, gathering accurate requirements leads to higher customer satisfaction. When the final product meets or exceeds expectations, clients are more likely to be satisfied with the outcome.

In essence, requirements gathering sets the foundation for successful project delivery by ensuring clarity, alignment, and satisfaction among all stakeholders involved.

2.4. What should you know about requirements?

Understanding and caring about requirements is crucial for several reasons, all of which contribute to the overall success and efficiency of projects within an organization:

1. Mitigating Project Failures: Clear and well-defined requirements serve as the foundation upon which a project is built. By ensuring that all stakeholders have a common understanding of what needs to be delivered, the likelihood of project failure due to misunderstandings or misalignment decreases significantly.
2. Reducing Wasted Time and Money: When requirements are not properly defined or are constantly changing, it can lead to rework, delays, and increased costs. Investing time upfront to gather, analyze, and document requirements helps to identify potential issues early in the project lifecycle, ultimately saving both time and money by preventing costly rework later on.
3. Improving Relationships between Business and IT: Effective requirements management fosters collaboration and communication between business stakeholders and IT teams. By involving stakeholders from the outset and continuously engaging them throughout the project, organizations can ensure that the final deliverables meet the needs and expectations of the business.
4. Meeting Deadlines and Shortening Delivery Cycles: Clear requirements provide a roadmap for project execution, helping teams to stay focused and prioritize tasks effectively. By defining requirements upfront and establishing realistic timelines, organizations can better manage resources, mitigate risks, and deliver projects on time or even ahead of schedule.
5. Enhancing Quality and Customer Satisfaction: Well-defined requirements enable teams to build solutions that align closely with user needs and expectations. By delivering high-quality products that meet or exceed customer requirements, organizations can enhance customer satisfaction and loyalty, leading to increased competitiveness and business success.

Overall, prioritizing requirements management offers numerous benefits for organizations, including reducing project failures, minimizing wasted time and resources, improving stakeholder relationships, meeting deadlines, and enhancing product quality and customer satisfaction. By investing in effective requirements management practices, organizations can increase their chances of project success and achieve better outcomes in terms of both efficiency and effectiveness.

2.5. How do you test the requirements?

A requirement lacking testability is not truly a requirement. For instance, when faced with a requirement like "the product shall be user friendly," it is imperative to devise methods for testing it. While the originator may believe the requirement is valid, if it is not stated in a measurable way, it remains untestable. Effective requirements management involves testing to ensure they are well-defined, feasible, and not trivial, in addition to meeting any other quality standards you set. Always subject requirements to testing before incorporating them into the specification.

Furthermore, best practices dictate incorporating a fit criterion into your requirements. This criterion serves as a measurable standard, enabling testers to accurately gauge whether the solution aligns with the requirement.

Testing requirements involves ensuring that the software or system meets the specified criteria and functions correctly. Here is a general process for testing requirements:

1. Review Requirements: Ensure that the requirements are clear, complete, and testable. Ambiguous or contradictory requirements can lead to ineffective testing.
2. Create Test Cases: Based on the requirements, develop test cases that cover all aspects of the software functionality. Test cases should include inputs, expected outputs, and any other conditions necessary for testing.
3. Prioritize Test Cases: Not all test cases are equally important. Prioritize test cases based on

factors like criticality, risk, and frequency of use.

4. Execute Test Cases: Run the test cases against the software or system being developed. This can be done manually or using automated testing tools.
5. Record Results: Document the outcomes of each test case. Note any deviations from expected behavior, defects found, and other relevant information.
6. Traceability: Ensure that each requirement has associated test cases, and that the test cases cover all aspects of the requirements. This ensures that all requirements are adequately tested.
7. Regression Testing: As the software evolves, retest previously passed test cases to ensure that new changes have not introduced any regressions.
8. Validate Against User Needs: Ultimately, the software must meet the needs of its users. Validate that the tested requirements align with user expectations and needs.
9. Acceptance Testing: Once all requirements have been tested and validated, conduct acceptance testing with stakeholders to ensure that the software meets their expectations and requirements.
10. Iterative Process: Testing requirements is not a one-time activity. It is an iterative process that continues throughout the development lifecycle to ensure that the software meets the desired quality standards.

By following these steps, you can systematically test requirements and ensure that the software or system meets its intended functionality and quality standards.

2.6. What are the reasons for investing in requirements?

Investing in requirements is crucial for several reasons:

1. Clarity and Understanding: Clear requirements help all stakeholders understand what needs to be built or developed. This reduces misunderstandings and ensures everyone is on the same page regarding project objectives.
2. Reduced Costs: Investing time and effort in gathering and documenting requirements upfront can help identify potential issues early in the project lifecycle. Addressing these issues during the requirements phase is generally less costly than dealing with them later during development or after deployment.
3. Improved Quality: Well-defined requirements serve as a blueprint for the project. When developers have a clear understanding of what they need to build, they are more likely to produce a high-quality product that meets stakeholders' expectations.
4. Risk Mitigation: Requirements gathering helps identify potential risks and dependencies early in the project. This allows stakeholders to develop appropriate mitigation strategies and contingency plans, reducing the likelihood of project failure or delays.
5. Alignment with Business Goals: Requirements should always be aligned with the broader business goals and objectives. Investing in requirements ensures that the final product or solution will meet the needs of the business and deliver value to stakeholders.
6. Facilitates Communication: Clearly documented requirements serve as a common language for communication among project stakeholders, including business analysts, developers, testers, and end-users. This improves collaboration and reduces the likelihood of misunderstandings or misinterpretations.
7. Supports Change Management: Requirements provide a baseline against which changes can be assessed and managed. When changes are requested, they can be evaluated against the established requirements, and their impact on the project can be analyzed and communicated effectively.
8. Regulatory Compliance: In some industries, adherence to regulatory requirements is essential. Investing in requirements ensures that the final product or solution meets all relevant regulatory standards and compliance requirements.

Overall, investing in requirements is a critical step in the project lifecycle that can lead to improved project outcomes, reduced risks, and increased stakeholder satisfaction.

In summary, there are several compelling motives for investing in requirements:
1. Ensuring the development of the right product.
2. Expediting the delivery process.
3. Identifying the optimal product for sustained operational or sales triumph.
4. Leveraging requirements engineering to steer the project with informed decision-making.
5. Uncovering opportunities for product enhancement.
6. Recognizing the essential role of good design, exemplified by products like the iPad or iPhone.

2.7. What are some of the risks related to investing in requirements?

Most of the bugs in software are due to incomplete or inaccurate functional requirements. The software code, does not matter how well it is written, cannot do anything if there are ambiguities in requirements. About 60% of software errors are requirements errors. Investing in requirements, particularly in the context of software development or project management, can carry several risks:
1. Unclear Requirements: If the requirements are ambiguous or poorly defined, it can lead to misunderstandings and misinterpretations. This can result in building the wrong product or features, leading to wasted time and resources.
2. Scope Creep: Requirements may change or expand over time, leading to scope creep. This can result in project delays, increased costs, and difficulty in meeting deadlines.
3. Over-Engineering: Sometimes, there is a tendency to over-specify requirements, leading to over-engineering of the product. This can result in unnecessary complexity, increased development time, and higher costs.
4. Underestimation of Effort: Inaccurate estimation of the effort required to implement requirements can lead to underestimation of costs and timelines. This can result in projects going over budget and missing deadlines.
5. Lack of Stakeholder Involvement: If key stakeholders are not actively involved in the requirement gathering and validation process, there is a risk of building a product that does not meet their needs or expectations.
6. Technological Changes: Rapid advancements in technology can make requirements obsolete or outdated before the project is completed. This can result in the need for extensive rework or redevelopment.
7. Dependency on Third Parties: If the project relies on third-party components or services, there is a risk of delays or disruptions if these components or services are not available or fail to meet requirements.
8. Legal and Regulatory Compliance: Failure to consider legal and regulatory requirements can result in fines, lawsuits, or delays in product delivery.
9. Resource Constraints: Insufficient resources, such as skilled personnel or budget, can impact the ability to gather, validate, and implement requirements effectively.
10. Poor Communication: Inadequate communication among team members, stakeholders, and project managers can lead to misunderstandings, conflicts, and delays in requirement gathering and implementation.

Addressing these risks requires thorough analysis, effective communication, stakeholder involvement, continuous monitoring, and flexibility to adapt to changes throughout the project lifecycle.

2.8. What are the project groups' major concerns about stakeholders in discovering and specifying the requirements?

In the context of project management, project groups typically have several major concerns about stakeholders when it comes to discovering and specifying requirements:

1. Identifying Key Stakeholders: One major concern is ensuring that all relevant stakeholders are identified early in the process. Missing key stakeholders can lead to overlooking important requirements or perspectives.
2. Understanding Stakeholder Needs: Project groups need to understand the needs, expectations, and preferences of stakeholders. This involves effective communication and collaboration to ensure that requirements are accurately captured and prioritized.
3. Managing Conflicting Requirements: Stakeholders may have competing or conflicting requirements. Project groups must address these conflicts through negotiation, prioritization, and compromise to reach consensus and ensure project success.
4. Handling Changes in Requirements: Requirements may evolve throughout the project lifecycle due to changing stakeholder needs or external factors. Project groups need processes in place to manage and accommodate these changes while minimizing disruption to the project.
5. Ensuring Stakeholder Engagement: Engaging stakeholders throughout the requirements discovery and specification process is crucial for success. Project groups need strategies to keep stakeholders informed, involved, and invested in the project.
6. Addressing Stakeholder Resistance: Some stakeholders may be resistant to change or may have concerns about the project's impact. Project groups need to address these concerns proactively through communication, education, and addressing underlying issues.
7. Managing Expectations: Stakeholders may have unrealistic expectations about the project scope, timeline, or deliverables. Project groups must manage these expectations by providing clear and transparent communication about what is feasible and achievable within the project constraints.
8. Ensuring Alignment with Organizational Goals: Project requirements must align with the broader goals and objectives of the organization. Project groups need to ensure that stakeholder requirements contribute to the overall strategic direction and priorities of the organization.

By addressing these concerns effectively, project groups can improve the likelihood of successful requirements discovery and specification, ultimately leading to a more successful project outcome.

2.9. What is scope or feature creep? What are the causes of scope creep? How can you control scope creep?

Scope creep, also known as feature creep, refers to the gradual expansion of a project's goals, features, or requirements beyond its original intended scope. It typically involves the addition of new features, functionalities, or requirements that were not initially planned for, leading to increased complexity, time, and resources required to complete the project.

Causes of scope creep include:

1. Poorly Defined Requirements: Inadequate initial planning or unclear project requirements can lead to misunderstandings and ambiguity, making it easier for stakeholders to introduce new features later in the project.
2. Changing Stakeholder Expectations: As stakeholders become more involved in the project or gain new insights, they may request modifications or additions to the original scope based on their evolving needs or preferences.
3. Lack of Stakeholder Communication: Insufficient communication between project stakeholders, such as clients, users, and development teams, can result in misunderstandings and conflicting expectations, leading to scope creep.
4. Ambiguous Project Goals: When project goals are not clearly defined or are too broad, there is a higher likelihood of scope creep as stakeholders may interpret them differently and introduce new features or requirements to align with their interpretations.
5. Technological Advancements: Rapid advancements in technology may tempt stakeholders to

incorporate new technologies or features into the project, even if they were not part of the original plan, in order to stay competitive or meet evolving industry standards.

Controlling scope or feature creep requires proactive management strategies:

1. Clear Project Scope Definition: Establish clear and detailed project scope documents outlining the project's goals, objectives, deliverables, and constraints. This helps to set expectations and minimize misunderstandings among stakeholders.
2. Change Control Process: Implement a formal change control process that requires any proposed changes to be evaluated, documented, and approved by relevant stakeholders before implementation. This process helps to assess the impact of changes on the project's timeline, budget, and resources.
3. Regular Stakeholder Communication: Maintain open and transparent communication channels with project stakeholders to ensure that everyone is aligned with the project goals and objectives. Regular meetings and status updates can help identify and address potential scope creep issues early on.
4. Prioritization and Focus: Prioritize project requirements based on their importance and impact on the project's success. Avoid the temptation to incorporate every requested feature and focus on delivering the core functionalities that align with the project's objectives.
5. Monitor Progress Closely: Monitor project progress closely against the established scope and milestones to identify any deviations or potential scope creep. Early detection allows for timely intervention and corrective actions to mitigate the impact on the project.

By implementing these strategies, project managers can effectively control scope or feature creep and ensure the successful delivery of projects within the defined constraints of time, budget, and quality.

2.10. What are the top five frustrations of requirements and the tips to avoid them?

Managing requirements effectively is crucial for the success of any project, yet it often presents challenges that can lead to frustration. Here are five common frustrations of requirements management along with tips to avoid them:

1. Ambiguity:
    a. Frustration: Requirements are often stated in vague terms, leading to misunderstandings and misinterpretations.
    b. Tip: Invest time in clarifying requirements through discussions with stakeholders. Use techniques like user stories, use cases, and prototypes to provide clear and tangible examples of what is expected.
2. Scope Creep:
    a. Frustration: As the project progresses, new features and changes are continuously introduced, expanding the project scope beyond the initial agreement.
    b. Tip: Establish a robust change control process early on. Clearly define the scope and freeze requirements once they are agreed upon. Any changes should go through a formal approval process with consideration of their impact on time, cost, and resources.
3. Incomplete Requirements:
    a. Frustration: Some requirements are overlooked or omitted, leading to gaps in the project deliverables.
    b. Tip: Conduct thorough stakeholder analysis to identify all parties involved and gather comprehensive requirements. Utilize techniques such as brainstorming sessions, interviews, and workshops to capture requirements from different perspectives. Employ requirement traceability matrices to ensure all requirements are accounted for.
4. Inconsistency:
    a. Frustration: Requirements documents may contain conflicting or contradictory

information, causing confusion among project team members.
    b. Tip: Implement a structured approach to requirements documentation, such as using standardized templates and notation systems. Regularly review and validate requirements with stakeholders to identify and resolve inconsistencies early in the process.
5. Lack of Prioritization:
    a. Frustration: When all requirements are treated as equally important, it becomes challenging to focus on delivering high-value features within project constraints.
    b. Tip: Collaborate with stakeholders to prioritize requirements based on business value, urgency, and dependencies. Use techniques like MoSCoW (Must have, Should have, Could have, Won't have) prioritization to categorize requirements according to their criticality. Focus on delivering essential features first and iteratively incorporate additional requirements as time and resources allow.

By addressing these frustrations proactively and implementing best practices in requirements management, project teams can enhance communication, mitigate risks, and increase the likelihood of project success.

2.11. What is a project charter?

A project charter is a foundational document that outlines the key elements of a project. It serves as a formal authorization for the project to begin and provides a clear definition of the project's objectives, scope, participants, and overall direction. Here are the main components typically included in a project charter:

1. Project Title and Description: A concise title and a brief overview of what the project aims to achieve.
2. Objectives: Specific, measurable goals that the project is intended to accomplish. These should align with broader organizational objectives.
3. Scope: A detailed description of what the project will and will not include. This helps in setting boundaries and managing stakeholder expectations.
4. Deliverables: The tangible or intangible products or results that the project will produce.
5. Stakeholders: Identification of all parties involved or affected by the project, including their roles and responsibilities.
6. Milestones: Key points or significant stages in the project timeline that mark progress and facilitate monitoring.
7. Assumptions and Constraints: Any assumptions that are being made in planning the project, and constraints that might impact its execution, such as budget, time, or resources.
8. Budget: An overview of the financial resources allocated to the project.
9. Risks: Potential challenges or uncertainties that could affect the project's success, along with strategies for mitigating these risks.
10. Approval and Authorization: Signatures from key stakeholders or sponsors that formally authorize the project to proceed.

The project charter acts as a reference throughout the project's life cycle, ensuring that all team members and stakeholders have a common understanding of the project's purpose and structure. It also provides a basis for decision-making and a benchmark against which project progress and success can be measured.

2.12. How do you go about creating a project charter?

Creating a project charter is an essential first step in any project as it outlines the project's objectives, scope, stakeholders, and overall approach. Here is a step-by-step guide on how to create one:

1. Project Title and Overview: Begin by providing a clear and concise title for your project. Follow

it with a brief overview that describes the purpose of the project and its intended outcome.

2. Project Objectives: List the specific goals and objectives of the project. These should be measurable, achievable, relevant, and time-bound (SMART criteria).
3. Scope: Define the boundaries of the project. What is included and what is excluded from the project scope? This section helps prevent scope creep.
4. Stakeholders: Identify all stakeholders involved in the project. This includes sponsors, clients, end-users, team members, and any other individuals or groups affected by the project.
5. Project Deliverables: Outline the key deliverables that will be produced as part of the project. These are tangible outcomes that demonstrate the successful completion of the project.
6. Milestones and Timeline: Define the major milestones of the project and create a timeline indicating when each milestone is expected to be achieved. This helps track progress and ensure timely completion.
7. Constraints and Assumptions: Identify any constraints or limitations that may impact the project, such as budget, resources, or time constraints. Also, list any assumptions made about the project that could affect its outcome.
8. Risks and Mitigation Strategies: Identify potential risks that could arise during the project and outline strategies for mitigating or managing them. This helps minimize the impact of unexpected events on the project's success.
9. Resource Requirements: Specify the resources required to execute the project, including personnel, equipment, materials, and budgetary needs.
10. Project Governance: Define the project governance structure, including roles and responsibilities of team members, decision-making processes, and communication channels.
11. Approval Signatures: Once the project charter is complete, it should be reviewed and approved by key stakeholders, including the project sponsor and other relevant parties.
12. Document Revision History: Maintain a record of any changes made to the project charter over time, including the date of the change and the reason for it.

By following these steps, you can create a comprehensive project charter that provides a clear roadmap for the successful execution of your project.

2.13. What are some of the tips for writing a project charter?

Writing a project charter is crucial for ensuring clarity, alignment, and direction for a project. Here are some tips to help you craft an effective project charter:

1. Understand the Purpose: Clearly understand the purpose and objectives of the project. This will help you articulate them clearly in the charter.
2. Define Project Scope: Clearly define the scope of the project, including what is included and what is not included. This helps manage expectations and prevent scope creep.
3. Identify Stakeholders: Identify all stakeholders involved in the project and define their roles and responsibilities. This ensures clarity in communication and accountability.
4. Set SMART Goals: Ensure that the project goals are Specific, Measurable, Achievable, Relevant, and Time-bound. This helps in tracking progress and evaluating success.
5. Outline Deliverables: Clearly outline the deliverables or outcomes of the project. This helps in setting expectations and measuring success.
6. Establish Timeline: Define the timeline for the project, including major milestones and deadlines. This provides a clear roadmap for project execution.
7. Allocate Resources: Identify the resources required for the project, including human resources, budget, and materials. Ensure that resources are allocated effectively to support project success.
8. Risk Management: Identify potential risks and uncertainties associated with the project and develop strategies to mitigate them. This helps in minimizing disruptions and delays.
9. Communication Plan: Develop a communication plan outlining how information will be

communicated, to whom, and at what frequency. Effective communication is essential for project success.

10. Gain Approval: Ensure that the project charter is reviewed and approved by all relevant stakeholders before proceeding with the project. This helps in gaining buy-in and commitment.
11. Review and Update: Periodically review and update the project charter as needed to reflect any changes in project scope, goals, or stakeholders.

By following these tips, you can create a comprehensive and effective project charter that serves as a guiding document for the successful execution of your project.

2.14. What is a deliverable? What are different types of deliverables? What are internal and external deliverables?

A deliverable is any tangible or intangible output produced as a result of a project that is intended to be delivered to a customer (either internal or external). Deliverables can be documents, products, services, reports, or any other result of the project work that is completed and handed over to stakeholders. They are crucial for measuring the progress and success of a project.

Deliverables can be categorized based on various criteria such as their nature, purpose, or the phase of the project in which they are produced. Here are some common types of deliverables:

1. Tangible vs. Intangible Deliverables:
    a. Tangible Deliverables: Physical items that can be touched and seen, such as a product, a prototype, or a piece of equipment.
    b. Intangible Deliverables: Non-physical items such as software, a design, or a report.
2. Final vs. Interim Deliverables:
    a. Final Deliverables: The ultimate output that fulfills the project's objectives, delivered at the end of the project.
    b. Interim Deliverables: Outputs produced during the project lifecycle that contribute towards the final deliverable, such as drafts, models, or progress reports.
3. Process vs. Product Deliverables:
    a. Process Deliverables: Documents and plans that support the project management process, like project plans, schedules, and status reports.
    b. Product Deliverables: The actual output or end product that the project aims to deliver, like a completed software application or a constructed building.

Deliverables can also be classified based on their intended recipient:

1. Internal Deliverables:
    a. These are deliverables intended for internal stakeholders within the organization. They are typically used to manage and control the project, ensuring that everything is on track.
    b. Examples include project plans, internal progress reports, meeting minutes, and internal design documents.
    c. These deliverables are not typically shared with clients or external stakeholders.
2. External Deliverables:
    a. These are deliverables intended for external stakeholders, such as clients, customers, or regulatory bodies.
    b. Examples include final products, user manuals, customer reports, marketing materials, and compliance documents.
    c. These deliverables are the primary outputs that demonstrate the project's value to the client or external parties.

Importance of Deliverables

1. Deliverables are critical for the following reasons:
2. Tracking Progress: They serve as milestones to gauge the progress of the project.
3. Communication: They provide a means to communicate what has been accomplished to stakeholders.
4. Evaluation: They are used to evaluate the quality and success of the project.
5. Closure: They are necessary for project closure and acceptance by stakeholders.

In summary, deliverables are essential components of project management, providing clear outputs that can be measured, evaluated, and handed over to both internal and external stakeholders. Understanding the types and purposes of deliverables helps in planning, executing, and successfully completing a project.

2.15. What is a project justification? What are the different ways of describing the cost-benefit ratio for a project in order to justify it?

A project justification is a comprehensive explanation outlining the reasons why a project is necessary and beneficial. It provides the rationale for undertaking the project, detailing the problem it addresses, the objectives it aims to achieve, and the expected benefits. This justification is critical for securing approval and funding, as it convinces stakeholders of the project's value and alignment with organizational goals.

Ways to Describe the Cost-Benefit Ratio for Project Justification:

1. Cost-Benefit Analysis (CBA)
   a. Definition: This is a systematic approach for estimating the strengths and weaknesses of alternatives. It is used to determine options that provide the best approach to achieve benefits while preserving savings.
   b. Application: Calculate the total expected costs and benefits of the project. Express them in monetary terms to determine the net benefit (benefits minus costs).
   c. Example: If a project costs $1 million and generates $1.5 million in benefits, the net benefit is $500,000.
2. Return on Investment (ROI)
   a. Definition: ROI measures the gain or loss generated relative to the amount of money invested.
   b. Formula: ROI = ((Net Profit) / (Total Investment)) x 100
   c. Example: If a project costs $200,000 and generates $300,000 in returns, the ROI is 50%.
3. Payback Period
   a. Definition: The payback period is the time it takes for a project to generate enough benefits to recover its initial costs.
   b. Application: Calculate the duration required to recoup the investment.
   c. Example: If a project costs $100,000 and generates $25,000 annually, the payback period is 4 years.
4. Net Present Value (NPV)
   a. Definition: NPV calculates the present value of cash flows generated by the project, minus the initial investment. It accounts for the time value of money.
   b. Formula: $NPV=\sum(\text{Net Cash Flow}_t / (1+r)^t)$ - Initial Investment
   c. Example: A project with an initial investment of $50,000 and expected cash flows of $10,000 per year for 7 years, at a discount rate of 5%, might have an NPV of $12,000.
5. Internal Rate of Return (IRR)
   a. Definition: IRR is the discount rate that makes the NPV of all cash flows from a project equal to zero. It represents the project's potential rate of return.
   b. Application: A higher IRR indicates a more profitable project.
   c. Example: If a project's IRR is 12% and exceeds the company's required rate of return of

10%, the project is considered favorable.

6. Benefit-Cost Ratio (BCR)
    a. Definition: BCR compares the present value of benefits to the present value of costs. A BCR greater than 1 indicates that benefits exceed costs.
    b. Formula: BCR = (Present Value of Benefits) / (Present Value of Costs)
    c. Example: A BCR of 1.5 means that for every dollar spent, the project returns $1.50 in benefits.
7. Economic Value Added (EVA)
    a. Definition: EVA measures a project's financial performance based on residual wealth, calculated by deducting the cost of capital from the project's net operating profit.
    b. Formula: EVA = Net Operating Profit After Taxes (NOPAT) - (Capital * Cost of Capital)
    c. Example: If a project has a NOPAT of $200,000, capital of $1,000,000, and a cost of capital of 10%, the EVA is $100,000.

The break-even chart shown in Figure 2.15.1 is a basic justification method often employed in the early stages of project conceptualization. This rough technique is used to provide a preliminary comparison between alternatives. The chart plots the total expected cost of two alternatives over time, allowing for an easy visual comparison. The break-even point is where one alternative's total cost becomes less than the other's. Although it is possible to calculate the break-even point algebraically, a graphical approach is usually sufficient.

The chart is constructed on X and Y axes, where the Y axis represents total cost and the X axis represents time. The scales should be chosen so that the break-even point appears roughly in the middle of the chart.

New project alternatives typically incur a fixed cost, which is a one-time investment that does not recur throughout the project's life. This is known as the project's fixed cost. Additionally, there is a variable cost, which represents the ongoing expenses incurred as the project continues to be used over its useful life.

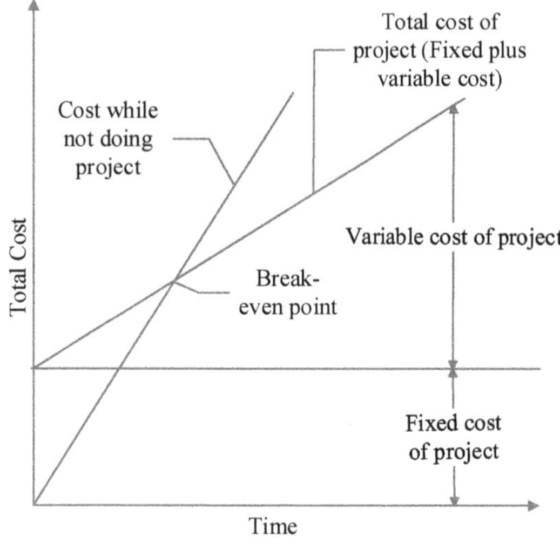

Figure 2.15.1 Break-Even Chart

When justifying a project, it is essential to clearly articulate the expected costs and benefits, using various financial metrics to demonstrate the project's value. These metrics help stakeholders understand the potential return on investment and make informed decisions about resource allocation. Each method provides a different perspective, contributing to a holistic view of the project's financial viability and strategic importance.

2.16. What is the requirements process of a project? What are the different ways to find out the deliverables of a project?

The requirements process of a project is a critical phase in project management that involves identifying, documenting, and managing the needs and expectations of stakeholders for a project. This process ensures that the project deliverables meet the desired outcomes and satisfy the stakeholders' requirements. The main steps in the requirements process typically include:

1. Stakeholder Identification and Engagement:
    a. Identify all stakeholders involved in the project.
    b. Engage stakeholders to understand their needs, expectations, and constraints.
2. Requirements Elicitation
    a. Interviews: Conducting one-on-one or group interviews with stakeholders to gather detailed information about their needs and expectations.
    b. Surveys/Questionnaires: Distributing surveys or questionnaires to a broader audience to collect quantitative and qualitative data.
    c. Workshops: Organizing facilitated sessions with stakeholders to discuss and prioritize requirements.
    d. Observation: Observing users in their work environment to understand the context and identify implicit requirements.
    e. Document Analysis: Reviewing existing documentation such as business plans, process descriptions, and previous project reports to extract relevant requirements.
    f. Focus Groups: Engaging a selected group of stakeholders to discuss and refine requirements collaboratively.
    g. Prototyping: Developing preliminary versions of the system or components to elicit feedback and clarify requirements.
3. Requirements Analysis
    a. Modeling: Creating visual models (e.g., use case diagrams, flowcharts, data models) to represent requirements and understand their relationships.
    b. Prioritization: Ranking requirements based on factors such as importance, urgency, feasibility, and stakeholder value.
    c. Validation: Ensuring that the requirements accurately reflect the stakeholders' needs and are feasible within the project's constraints.
4. Requirements Specification
    a. Requirements Document: Writing a comprehensive requirements specification document that clearly defines all functional and non-functional requirements.
    b. Use Cases/User Stories: Describing the interactions between users and the system to capture functional requirements in a user-centric manner.
5. Requirements Verification and Validation
    a. Review Sessions: Conducting reviews and walkthroughs of the requirements document with stakeholders to verify completeness and accuracy.
    b. Prototyping: Using prototypes to validate requirements and obtain stakeholder approval.
6. Requirements Management
    a. Change Control: Establishing a process for managing changes to requirements, including impact analysis and stakeholder approval.
    b. Traceability: Maintaining traceability matrices to track requirements throughout the project lifecycle and ensure they are addressed in the final deliverables.

Different Ways to Find Out the Deliverables of a Project

Identifying the deliverables of a project involves several techniques, including:

1. Stakeholder Analysis
    a. Stakeholder Interviews: Engaging with stakeholders to understand their needs, expectations, and desired outcomes.
    b. Stakeholder Meetings: Holding regular meetings with stakeholders to discuss and agree on the key deliverables.
2. Project Charter and Scope Statement
    a. Project Charter: Reviewing the project charter for high-level deliverables and objectives.
    b. Scope Statement: Developing a detailed scope statement that defines the boundaries of the project and lists the key deliverables.
3. Work Breakdown Structure (WBS)
    a. Decomposition: Breaking down the project into smaller, manageable components (tasks and sub-tasks) to identify all the deliverables.
    b. Hierarchy: Creating a hierarchical representation of all deliverables, starting from the main project deliverable down to individual work packages.
4. Requirements Documentation
    a. Requirements Specification: Reviewing the requirements documentation to extract specific deliverables that must be produced to meet the requirements.
    b. Use Cases/User Stories: Identifying deliverables from the use cases or user stories that describe the interactions between users and the system.
5. Prototyping
    a. Prototype Development: Developing prototypes to visualize and clarify the deliverables, and to obtain feedback from stakeholders.
6. Change Requests
    a. Change Control Process: Reviewing approved change requests to identify new or modified deliverables that result from changes to the project scope.
7. Project Management Tools
    a. Gantt Charts: Using Gantt charts to plan and track project activities and associated deliverables.
    b. Task Lists: Maintaining task lists that outline the work to be completed and the deliverables to be produced.

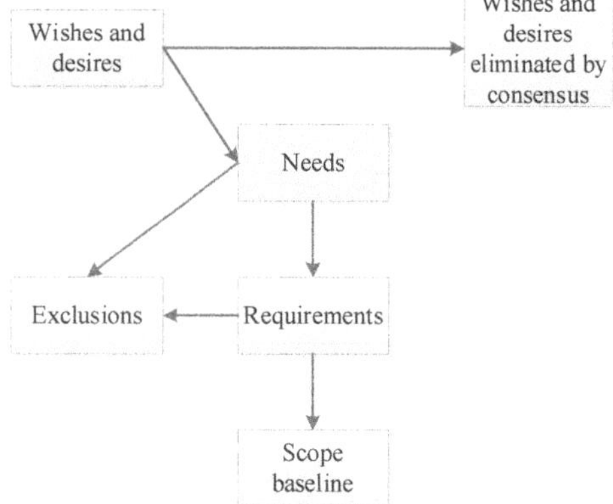

Figure 2.16.1 Requirements Process

There are several methods to create the required deliverables list. Figure 2.16.1 outlines a process that exemplifies the characteristics of an effective deliverables definition process.

The process begins by gathering the needs and desires of the stakeholders. While this step is straightforward, it can be time-consuming and result in a lengthy list. At this stage, we include anything that stakeholders want on the "wishes and desires" list. Many of these items will eventually be eliminated from the project. Allowing the creation of this list ensures that all stakeholders have an opportunity to voice their preferred requirements, fostering stakeholder engagement and satisfaction.

Next, we review the wishes and desires list. Items that can be unanimously agreed upon for elimination are removed. If there is any objection, the item remains on the list for further investigation. For smaller projects, all stakeholders can participate in this review. For larger projects, review committees composed of specific stakeholders can be organized to review related groups of items. The outcome of these meetings is the refined "needs" list.

The items on the needs list are then investigated. Some will require detailed justification, while others may need minimal investigation. Regardless of the investigation's depth, items excluded from the project are documented with reasons for their exclusion. At this stage, both included and excluded items are elaborated upon to prevent misunderstandings. The remaining items are identified as potential project deliverables, referred to as "requirements."

These requirements are not yet the final deliverables. Some may be eliminated for various reasons before establishing the scope baseline. Until the scope baseline is established, there is no need to process a change request through the change management process to add or delete requirements.

The requirements process is crucial for capturing and understanding what stakeholders need from the project. By systematically following the requirements process and utilizing various techniques to identify deliverables, project managers can ensure that all stakeholder needs are met and that the project stays on track to achieve its goals.

2.17. What is a scope statement? What should a project scope statement include?

A scope statement is an essential document in project management that defines the project's goals, deliverables, boundaries, and success criteria. It offers a clear and concise description of the tasks to be completed and establishes expectations for both the project team and stakeholders. This document outlines the outcomes the project will achieve and the conditions under which the work will be carried out. Before the project begins, all parties involved, including project owners and the project team, must agree on the terms outlined in the scope statement.

Here are the key components typically included in a scope statement:

1. Justification - You need to state how and why your project originated and the scope of the work expected. You also should add information such as the business requirements it deals with and how any related activities will affect the project.
2. Project Objectives: Defines the specific goals that the project aims to achieve. These objectives should be clear, measurable, and aligned with the overall strategic goals of the organization.
3. Deliverables: Lists the tangible and intangible outputs that the project will produce. This includes products, services, reports, and other outcomes that the project is expected to deliver.
4. Project Boundaries: Specifies what is included and what is excluded from the project scope. This helps to set clear limits on what the project will cover, preventing scope creep (the uncontrolled expansion of project scope).
5. Acceptance Criteria: Describes the conditions that must be met for the deliverables to be accepted by the project stakeholders. This includes quality standards, performance metrics, and other criteria for evaluating the project's outputs.
6. Constraints: Identifies any limitations or restrictions that the project must operate within. This

could include budget constraints, time constraints, resource availability, and other factors that could impact the project's execution.

7. Assumptions: Lists any assumptions that have been made during the planning of the project. These are conditions that are believed to be true but have not been verified, and they could impact the project's success if they turn out to be incorrect.
8. Stakeholders: Identifies the key stakeholders involved in the project, including their roles and responsibilities. This ensures that everyone knows who is responsible for what and who needs to be consulted or informed about project developments.

The scope statement serves as a reference point throughout the project lifecycle, helping to guide decision-making and manage changes to the project scope. It is often included as part of the project charter or project management plan and is typically developed during the project initiation phase. By clearly defining the scope, the scope statement helps to ensure that the project stays focused, within budget, and on schedule.

2.18. What is a work breakdown structure?

A Work Breakdown Structure (WBS) is a project management tool that breaks down a project into smaller, more manageable components. This hierarchical decomposition helps in organizing and defining the total scope of the project by dividing it into tasks, subtasks, and work packages. Each level of the WBS provides more detail, ensuring that all necessary work is captured and assigned.

Key Characteristics of a WBS:

1. Hierarchical Structure:
    a. The WBS is structured in a way that higher levels represent broader tasks, while lower levels represent more detailed tasks.
2. Deliverable-Oriented:
    a. It focuses on deliverables rather than processes, meaning each item in the WBS represents a tangible or measurable outcome.
3. Scope Definition:
    a. The WBS defines the full scope of the project by ensuring that all deliverables and related work are included.
4. Work Packages:
    a. At the lowest level, the WBS consists of work packages, which are the smallest units of work that can be assigned and managed.
5. Identification and Tracking:
    a. Each element in the WBS is typically assigned a unique identifier to help in tracking progress, resources, and costs.

Benefits of Using a WBS:

1. Improved Project Planning:
    a. By breaking down the project into smaller parts, it becomes easier to estimate costs, time, and resources.
2. Enhanced Communication:
    a. It provides a clear and detailed representation of the project, facilitating better communication among stakeholders.
3. Better Control and Monitoring:
    a. The detailed breakdown allows for better tracking of progress, making it easier to identify and address issues early.
4. Risk Management:
    a. By understanding all components of the project, potential risks can be identified and

managed more effectively.

Example of a WBS Structure:
Project Title
1.1 Major Deliverable 1
1.1.1 Sub-Deliverable 1.1
1.1.1.1 Work Package 1.1.1
1.1.1.2 Work Package 1.1.2
1.1.2 Sub-Deliverable 1.2
1.1.2.1 Work Package 1.2.1
1.2 Major Deliverable 2
1.2.1 Sub-Deliverable 2.1
1.2.1.1 Work Package 2.1.1

Steps to Create a WBS:

1. Identify the Project's Major Deliverables:
    a. Start by listing the main deliverables that need to be produced.
2. Decompose the Deliverables:
    a. Break down each deliverable into smaller components until manageable work packages are identified.
3. Define Work Packages:
    a. Ensure each work package is well-defined with clear descriptions, and allocate resources and time estimates.
4. Verify Completeness:
    a. Check that the WBS includes all the work required and no extraneous tasks.
5. Assign Unique Identifiers:
    a. Label each component for tracking purposes.

A very large project can be divided into multiple levels in the Work Breakdown Structure (WBS) until it reaches a manageable size. For a smaller project, this manageable element can be attained with fewer levels of breakdown. Thus, even the largest project can be reduced to a small, manageable subproject (see Figure 2.18.1).

The top level of any WBS represents the entire project. The levels between the top and the bottom consist of breakdown elements. The larger the project, the more intermediate levels of breakdown there are. Ultimately, the bottom level of the WBS represents the smallest detail that the project manager needs to oversee.

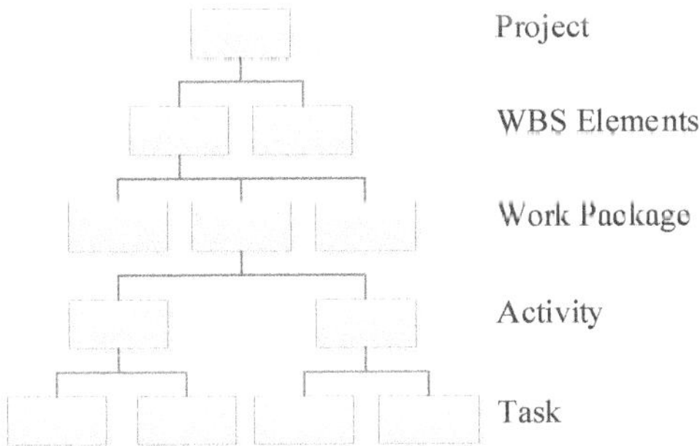

Figure 2.18.1 WBS Definitions

In summary, a Work Breakdown Structure is a fundamental project management tool that helps in planning, executing, and monitoring a project by breaking it down into manageable parts, ensuring nothing is overlooked, and facilitating effective communication and control.

2.19. How do I do a work breakdown structure?

A Work Breakdown Structure (WBS) is a key project management tool that helps in breaking down a project into smaller, more manageable components. Here is a step-by-step guide to creating a WBS:

Step-by-Step Guide to Creating a WBS

1. Understand the Scope of the Project
    a. Objective: Clearly define the project scope and objectives.
    b. Deliverables: Identify the final deliverables and outcomes expected from the project.
2. Identify Major Components (Phases)
    a. Phases: Break the project into major phases or high-level deliverables.
    b. Levels: Determine the levels of your WBS. Typically, Level 1 is the overall project, Level 2 consists of major deliverables or phases, and subsequent levels break down further into more detailed tasks.
3. Break Down the Phases into Work Packages
    a. Decomposition: Decompose each phase into smaller components until you reach a level of detail that can be easily managed and estimated.
    b. Work Packages: The smallest units in the WBS are called work packages. Each work package should be defined in terms of deliverables, effort, and cost.
4. Define Tasks and Activities
    a. Tasks: Break down work packages into tasks and activities necessary to complete them.
    b. Dependencies: Identify dependencies between tasks.
5. Review and Refine
    a. Consistency: Ensure that each level of the WBS provides a greater level of detail.
    b. Completeness: Verify that all necessary tasks are included and that there are no unnecessary tasks.
    c. Stakeholder Review: Have stakeholders review the WBS to ensure it meets their requirements and expectations.

Tips for Creating an Effective WBS

1. Use a Template: Starting with a WBS template can save time and ensure you do not miss key components.
2. Numbering System: Implement a consistent numbering system to uniquely identify each element in the WBS.
3. Clarity: Ensure that each element is clearly defined and understood by all stakeholders.
4. Team Involvement: Involve the project team in the creation of the WBS to ensure accuracy and completeness.
5. Consistency: Maintain a consistent level of detail across all branches of the WBS.
6. Inclusivity: Ensure all project work is included without overlap.
7. Visualization: Consider using software tools or graphical representations to visualize the WBS.

Example of a WBS Structure

1. Level 1: Project Name
    a. Level 2: Phase 1: Planning
        i. Level 3: Task 1.1: Define Scope
            1. Level 4: Activity 1.1.1: Meet with stakeholders
            2. Level 4: Activity 1.1.2: Document requirements
        ii. Level 3: Task 1.2: Develop Project Plan

            1. Level 4: Activity 1.2.1: Create timeline
            2. Level 4: Activity 1.2.2: Assign resources
    b. Level 2: Phase 2: Execution
        i. Level 3: Task 2.1: Implement Solution
            1. Level 4: Activity 2.1.1: Develop code
            2. Level 4: Activity 2.1.2: Conduct testing
    c. Level 2: Phase 3: Closure
        i. Level 3: Task 3.1: Final Report
            1. Level 4: Activity 3.1.1: Compile documentation
            2. Level 4: Activity 3.1.2: Obtain approvals

Tools for Creating a WBS

1. Software Tools: MS Project, Asana, Trello, or dedicated WBS software like WBS Chart Pro.
2. Visual Tools: Mind mapping software like MindMeister or XMind.
3. Templates: Various templates are available online that can be customized to fit your project's needs.

By following these steps and tips, you can create a clear, detailed, and structured WBS that will help guide your project to successful completion.

2.20. How do I test the work breakdown structure?

Testing a Work Breakdown Structure (WBS) involves ensuring that it is complete, accurate, and well-organized to serve as a foundation for project planning and execution. Here is a structured approach to testing your WBS:

1. Completeness Check
    a. Scope Alignment: Verify that the WBS includes all deliverables and work necessary to complete the project as defined in the project scope statement.
    b. Decomposition: Ensure that each deliverable is broken down into smaller, manageable components or work packages.
    c. Task Identification: Check that all tasks required to produce each deliverable are identified and included.
2. Hierarchy and Structure
    a. Level of Detail: Assess whether the WBS is detailed enough for project management needs but not so detailed that it becomes unwieldy.
    b. Consistent Decomposition: Ensure consistent levels of decomposition across all branches of the WBS.
    c. Parent-Child Relationship: Verify that each lower-level element (child) is necessary and sufficient to complete the higher-level element (parent).
3. Clarity and Understandability
    a. Naming Conventions: Ensure that each element is clearly and uniquely named.
    b. Descriptions: Check that each work package has a clear and concise description.
    c. Non-Overlapping Elements: Verify that there is no overlap between different elements of the WBS, avoiding redundancy.
4. Integration and Dependencies
    a. Interdependencies: Confirm that the WBS shows how different elements relate and depend on each other.
    b. Integration Points: Identify any integration points and ensure they are clearly defined within the WBS.
5. Validation with Stakeholders
    a. Stakeholder Review: Present the WBS to stakeholders for review and feedback to ensure

it meets their expectations and requirements.
    b. Expert Judgment: Consult with subject matter experts to validate the completeness and accuracy of the WBS.
6. Feasibility and Practicability
    a. Resource Availability: Ensure that the resources required to complete each work package are available or can be made available.
    b. Time and Cost Estimation: Validate that time and cost estimates derived from the WBS are realistic and achievable.
7. Compliance and Standards
    a. Standardization: Check if the WBS adheres to any organizational or industry standards.
    b. Compliance: Ensure that the WBS complies with any relevant regulatory or compliance requirements.
8. Updating and Maintenance
    a. Revision Process: Establish a process for updating the WBS as the project progresses and changes occur.
    b. Version Control: Implement version control to keep track of changes and ensure the team is working with the latest version of the WBS.

Testing Methods

1. Peer Review: Have team members and peers review the WBS for errors or omissions.
2. Scenario Analysis: Perform scenario analysis to test how well the WBS can handle changes and unforeseen events.
3. Walkthroughs: Conduct walkthroughs where team members explain their work packages to identify any gaps or misunderstandings.

By following these steps and utilizing these methods, you can thoroughly test and validate your Work Breakdown Structure, ensuring it serves as a solid foundation for your project management efforts.

2.21. What is task list?

A task list, also known as a to-do list, is a simple yet effective tool for organizing and managing tasks. It typically consists of a list of items, each representing a task that needs to be completed. Task lists can be handwritten, typed, or managed digitally through apps or software. Task list is a textual or column listing of the project plan. Usually includes the following minimal columns: Task Id, Task Name, Task Descriptions, Start Date, End Date, Duration, Priority Levels, Work Effort, and sometimes additional notes or subtasks.

Task lists are widely used in various contexts, including personal organization, project management, and professional tasks. They help individuals and teams stay focused, prioritize work, track progress, and ensure that important tasks are completed in a timely manner.

In essence, a task list is a compilation of all the work required to complete a project. It can be a personal list for individual tasks or a team list that captures the collective work needed to achieve project goals. Task lists are valuable for breaking down extensive project requirements into smaller, more manageable tasks, making big goals appear more achievable. By organizing and tracking tasks, you can work more efficiently and gain insights for better planning and execution. Whether you are managing your own workload or collaborating with a team, task lists help keep things organized and on track.

2.22. Why there is a need to manage diverse objectives and perspectives?

Managing diverse objectives and perspectives in projects is essential for several key reasons:

1. Enhanced Decision-Making:
    a. Broader Perspectives: Incorporating diverse viewpoints can lead to more comprehensive and well-rounded decision-making. Different team members bring unique experiences and insights, which can highlight potential risks and opportunities that might otherwise be overlooked.
    b. Creative Solutions: A diversity of ideas can foster creativity and innovation, leading to unique solutions that a more homogenous group might not conceive.
2. Stakeholder Satisfaction:
    a. Alignment with Stakeholder Needs: Different stakeholders often have varied interests and priorities. Managing these diverse objectives ensures that the project meets the expectations of all relevant parties, which is crucial for project acceptance and success.
    b. Improved Communication: Acknowledging and addressing different perspectives can enhance communication and trust among stakeholders, leading to smoother project execution.
3. Risk Management:
    a. Identifying Risks: Diverse teams are better at identifying and assessing a broader range of risks due to their varied experiences and viewpoints.
    b. Mitigating Conflicts: By understanding and managing different objectives early, potential conflicts can be mitigated before they escalate into major issues.
4. Resource Optimization:
    a. Effective Resource Utilization: Understanding the diverse objectives of a project helps in allocating resources more effectively, ensuring that the needs of various stakeholders are met without unnecessary expenditure.
    b. Balanced Workload: Diverse perspectives can lead to a more balanced distribution of tasks and responsibilities, leveraging the strengths of different team members.
5. Adaptability and Resilience:
    a. Dynamic Adaptation: Projects often face changing conditions and requirements. A team that embraces diverse objectives and perspectives is more adaptable and resilient to changes, as it can draw on a wide range of strategies and approaches.
    b. Flexibility in Approach: Diverse viewpoints encourage flexibility, allowing the project to pivot or adjust as needed to meet emerging challenges or opportunities.
6. Inclusion and Engagement:
    a. Team Morale: Recognizing and valuing diverse perspectives can improve team morale and engagement. When team members feel their input is valued, they are more likely to be motivated and committed to the project's success.
    b. Cultural Sensitivity: In global projects, cultural diversity must be managed to ensure that cultural sensitivities are respected, fostering a more inclusive and harmonious work environment.
7. Competitive Advantage:
    a. Innovation and Differentiation: Organizations that effectively manage diversity can often innovate more successfully and differentiate themselves in the market. Diverse teams can identify and exploit new market opportunities more effectively.
    b. Reputation and Compliance: Managing diverse objectives and perspectives can enhance an organization's reputation and ensure compliance with social and regulatory standards regarding diversity and inclusion.

In summary, managing diverse objectives and perspectives in projects is crucial for achieving comprehensive decision-making, stakeholder satisfaction, risk management, resource optimization, adaptability, inclusion, and competitive advantage. It ensures that projects are more likely to succeed and meet the varied needs of all stakeholders involved.

2.23. What is silo mentality, when and how does it happen, and how would you overcome it in your project team?

Silo Mentality refers to a mindset present in some organizations where different departments or teams do not share information, goals, tools, priorities, and processes with other departments. This isolationist behavior can create barriers to communication, reduce efficiency, and negatively impact overall organizational performance.

Silo mentality typically emerges under several circumstances:

1. Organizational Structure: A hierarchical structure with rigid departmental boundaries can lead to silos.
2. Lack of Communication: Poor inter-departmental communication or a lack of platforms for such communication encourages silos.
3. Competing Goals: Different departments focusing on their own goals rather than the organization's overall objectives.
4. Cultural Issues: A culture that does not promote teamwork or cross-functional collaboration.
5. Leadership Styles: Leaders who do not encourage collaboration or fail to set examples of cross-departmental teamwork.
6. Geographical Dispersion: Teams located in different physical locations might develop isolated working habits.
7. Resource Allocation: Limited resources might lead departments to prioritize their needs over collaborative efforts.

Overcoming silo mentality involves strategic initiatives and cultural changes. Here is how you can address it in your project team:

1. Promote Cross-Functional Collaboration:
    a. Regular Meetings: Hold regular inter-departmental meetings to discuss progress, challenges, and goals.
    b. Joint Projects: Create projects that require collaboration between different teams.
    c. Task Forces: Establish cross-functional task forces to address specific issues or projects.
2. Enhance Communication:
    a. Transparent Information Sharing: Use shared digital platforms (e.g., intranets, shared drives, collaboration tools like Teams, Slack, Trello, or Asana) to facilitate transparent and easy access to information.
    b. Open Channels: Create open communication channels and encourage team members to share information and updates freely.
3. Align Goals and Objectives:
    a. Unified Vision: Clearly articulate the organization's vision and ensure all teams understand how their work contributes to it.
    b. Shared Objectives: Set shared objectives and key results (OKRs) that align the goals of different teams with the overall organizational goals.
4. Leadership and Cultural Change:
    a. Model Behavior: Leaders should model collaborative behavior and actively encourage it among team members.
    b. Cultural Initiatives: Promote a culture of teamwork and collaboration through team-building activities and recognition programs.
    c. Training and Development: Provide training sessions on the importance of collaboration and how to work effectively in a team.
5. Integrated Performance Metrics:
    a. Collaborative Metrics: Develop performance metrics that reward collaborative behavior and inter-departmental success rather than just individual or departmental achievements.

6. Resource Sharing:
    a. Shared Resources: Encourage the sharing of resources, knowledge, and expertise between departments to break down barriers and build trust.
    b. Co-located Teams: Where possible, co-locate teams to facilitate better communication and collaboration.

To overcome silo mentality in your project team specifically, you can:

1. Conduct a Team Kickoff Meeting: Begin with a kickoff meeting involving all relevant departments to align on project goals, roles, and expectations.
2. Establish Clear Communication Protocols: Set up protocols for regular updates, shared documentation, and open forums for discussion.
3. Foster a Collaborative Culture: Encourage team-building exercises and regular inter-departmental workshops.
4. Utilize Technology: Leverage collaborative tools and software to ensure everyone has access to the same information and can contribute effectively.
5. Regular Feedback and Adjustment: Hold regular retrospectives to gather feedback on the collaboration process and make necessary adjustments.

By focusing on these strategies, you can mitigate the effects of silo mentality and foster a more collaborative and productive project team environment.

2.24. What are functional requirements or specifications?

Functional requirements or specifications refer to the detailed descriptions of the system's capabilities, features, and functionalities. These requirements outline what the system should do, defining its behavior and interactions with users, other systems, and the environment. Functional requirements are typically documented during the early stages of a project to guide development and testing processes. They serve as the basis for designing, implementing, and evaluating the system.

Functional requirements can include:

1. User interactions: Describing how users will interact with the system, such as through user interfaces, input methods, and navigation pathways.
2. Data processing: Defining how the system will handle and manipulate data, including data entry, storage, retrieval, processing, and output.
3. Business logic: Specifying the rules and algorithms governing the system's behavior, including calculations, validations, and decision-making processes.
4. Integration with other systems: Detailing how the system will communicate and exchange data with other systems, services, or components.
5. Security: Outlining the system's security requirements, such as authentication, authorization, encryption, and data protection measures.
6. Performance: Defining the system's performance requirements, including response times, throughput, scalability, and resource utilization.
7. Error handling: Describing how the system will detect, report, and handle errors, exceptions, and unexpected conditions.
8. Compliance: Ensuring that the system complies with relevant standards, regulations, and industry best practices.

Functional requirements are often documented using various techniques such as use cases, user stories, functional specifications documents, or requirement management tools. They provide a clear understanding of what the system is expected to deliver and serve as a basis for stakeholders to evaluate the system's success.

2.25. How do you go about obtaining requirements from your customer?

Business requirements analysis is a high-level assessment for the entire project that addresses the what, where, when, why, who, and how for the project. Obtaining requirements from customers is a crucial step in any project, ensuring that the final product meets their needs and expectations. Here is a general process for gathering requirements:

1. Identify Stakeholders: Determine who the key stakeholders are for the project. These could include end-users, decision-makers, subject matter experts (SME), etc.
2. Engage Stakeholders: Reach out to the identified stakeholders and engage them in discussions about their needs, preferences, and expectations regarding the project.
3. Conduct Interviews: Schedule one-on-one interviews with stakeholders to delve deeper into their requirements. Ask open-ended questions to encourage them to articulate their needs and concerns.
4. Hold Workshops or Focus Groups: Bring together groups of stakeholders for workshops or focus groups where they can discuss requirements collectively. This can help identify common themes and priorities.
5. Use Surveys or Questionnaires: Distribute surveys or questionnaires to a broader audience if applicable. This can be useful for gathering input from a large number of stakeholders or users.
6. Document Requirements: Record all gathered requirements systematically. This could be in the form of user stories, use cases, feature lists, or any other format that suits the project.
7. Validate Requirements: Once requirements are documented, validate them with stakeholders to ensure accuracy and completeness. This may involve reviewing the documentation with stakeholders or conducting follow-up interviews.
8. Prioritize Requirements: Work with stakeholders to prioritize requirements based on importance, urgency, feasibility, etc. This helps in managing scope and resources effectively.
9. Iterate: Requirements gathering is often an iterative process. Be prepared to revisit and refine requirements as the project progresses and new information becomes available.
10. Communicate: Maintain open communication with stakeholders throughout the project to keep them informed of any changes to requirements and to ensure alignment between their needs and the project's deliverables.

By following these steps, you can effectively gather requirements from customers and lay a solid foundation for successful project delivery.

2.26. What structure you will follow to obtain requirements from stakeholders, key managers, and end users?

Obtaining requirements from stakeholders, key managers, and end users is a critical part of the project management and software development process. A well-structured approach ensures that all perspectives are considered, resulting in a comprehensive set of requirements. Here is a structured approach to obtain requirements:

1. Preparation
    a. Define Objectives
        i. Objective: Clearly define the purpose of the requirements gathering process.
        ii. Scope: Determine the scope of the requirements to be gathered, including what is in and out of scope.
    b. Identify Stakeholders
        i. Stakeholder Analysis: Identify all key stakeholders, including end users, key managers, and other relevant parties.
        ii. Stakeholder Map: Create a stakeholder map to understand their influence and interest levels.
2. Information Gathering Techniques

a. Interviews
    i. Select Participants: Choose a representative sample of stakeholders and end users.
    ii. Prepare Questions: Develop a list of open-ended questions tailored to each stakeholder group.
    iii. Conduct Interviews: Conduct one-on-one or group interviews to gather detailed information.
b. Surveys and Questionnaires
    i. Design Surveys: Create structured surveys with both open-ended and closed-ended questions.
    ii. Distribute Surveys: Distribute surveys to a broad audience to gather quantitative data.
    iii. Analyze Results: Analyze survey results to identify common themes and priorities.
c. Workshops and Focus Groups
    i. Plan Workshops: Organize workshops with stakeholders and end users to facilitate interactive discussions.
    ii. Conduct Workshops: Use techniques such as brainstorming, mind mapping, and affinity diagrams.
    iii. Document Outcomes: Record the outcomes and insights from workshops.
d. Observation
    i. Observe End Users: Observe end users in their natural environment to understand their workflows and challenges.
    ii. Document Observations: Take detailed notes and, if possible, record sessions to capture real-time data.
e. Document Analysis
    i. Review Existing Documentation: Analyze existing documentation such as business plans, system documentation, and user manuals.
    ii. Extract Requirements: Identify relevant information and extract potential requirements.

3. Requirement Analysis
    a. Categorize Requirements
        i. Functional Requirements: Define what the system should do (features, functionalities).
        ii. Non-Functional Requirements: Define system attributes such as performance, security, usability, etc.
        iii. Business Requirements: Define high-level business needs and objectives.
    b. Prioritize Requirements
        i. MoSCoW Method: Classify requirements into Must-have, Should-have, Could-have, and Won't-have.
        ii. Stakeholder Prioritization: Involve stakeholders in prioritizing requirements based on business value and feasibility.
    c. Validate Requirements
        i. Review Sessions: Conduct review sessions with stakeholders to validate and verify the gathered requirements.
        ii. Feedback Loop: Incorporate feedback and make necessary adjustments.
4. Documentation
    a. Create Requirement Documents
        i. Requirement Specification: Document detailed requirements in a clear, concise, and structured manner.
        ii. User Stories/Use Cases: Create user stories or use cases to describe interactions

from the user's perspective.

   b. Review and Approval
      i. Stakeholder Review: Share the documented requirements with stakeholders for review.
      ii. Approval Process: Obtain formal approval and sign-off from key stakeholders.

5. Management and Tracking
   a. Requirement Traceability Matrix (RTM)
      i. Develop RTM: Create a traceability matrix to map requirements to design, development, and testing phases.
      ii. Track Changes: Establish a process for managing changes to requirements.
   b. Ongoing Communication
      i. Regular Updates: Provide regular updates to stakeholders on the status of requirements.
      ii. Feedback Mechanism: Maintain an open channel for continuous feedback and clarification.

Following this structured approach ensures that all stakeholder perspectives are considered, and the requirements gathered are comprehensive, prioritized, and validated. This helps in reducing misunderstandings, managing expectations, and increasing the chances of project success.

2.27. How do you validate the requirements you got from customer? How do you make certain you understand what they want?

Validating requirements from customers is a crucial step in ensuring that a project meets their expectations and needs. Here is a general process for validating requirements:

1. Understand the Requirements: First, thoroughly understand the requirements provided by the customer. Break them down into smaller, more manageable components if necessary. Ensure clarity and completeness by asking questions to clarify any ambiguities.
2. Document the Requirements: Document the requirements in a clear and structured manner. Use tools like requirement documents, user stories, or use cases to capture and organize the information.
3. Review with Stakeholders: Review the requirements with relevant stakeholders, including the customer, project managers, developers, and end-users if possible. This review ensures that everyone is on the same page and that the requirements are well understood.
4. Prototype or Mockups: Create prototypes, wireframes, or mockups based on the requirements to provide a visual representation of the proposed solution. This allows stakeholders to better understand how the system will look and function.
5. Feedback Collection: Gather feedback from stakeholders on the documented requirements and prototypes. Encourage open communication and address any concerns or discrepancies raised during this stage.
6. Validation Testing: Develop test cases based on the requirements to validate them against the expected outcomes. This may involve functional testing, usability testing, or other forms of testing depending on the nature of the project.
7. Iterative Process: Requirements validation is often an iterative process. As feedback is received and testing is conducted, it may be necessary to revise and refine the requirements accordingly.
8. Sign-off: Once the requirements have been validated and approved by the stakeholders, obtain formal sign-off to confirm their acceptance. This sign-off indicates that the requirements meet the customer's expectations and can serve as a baseline for further development.
9. Continuous Communication: Maintain open communication with the customer throughout the project to ensure that any changes or updates to the requirements are properly addressed and incorporated.

By following these steps, you can effectively validate the requirements provided by the customer and ensure that the resulting solution meets their needs and expectations.

2.28. Once you have the requirements, what do you do with them?

Once you have the requirements for a project, there are several steps you typically take to ensure they are effectively utilized:

1. Review and Analyze: Carefully go through the requirements to understand the scope of the project, the objectives, and any constraints or dependencies.
2. Clarify Ambiguities: If any requirements are unclear or ambiguous, seek clarification from stakeholders or the client to ensure a clear understanding.
3. Prioritize: Identify and prioritize requirements based on their importance to the project goals, feasibility, and potential impact on the final product.
4. Document: Document the requirements in a clear and organized manner, using tools such as requirement documents, user stories, or use cases. This documentation serves as a reference for all stakeholders throughout the project lifecycle.
5. Communicate: Ensure that all members of the project team, as well as stakeholders, have a shared understanding of the requirements. Regular communication helps prevent misunderstandings and ensures everyone is aligned on the project objectives.
6. Validate: Validate the requirements with stakeholders to confirm that they accurately reflect their needs and expectations. This may involve conducting meetings, reviews, or demonstrations to gather feedback.
7. Manage Changes: Be prepared to manage changes to the requirements throughout the project lifecycle. Changes may arise due to evolving business needs, technology advancements, or other factors. It is important to assess the impact of changes and communicate them effectively to all stakeholders.
8. Track Progress: Use the requirements as a basis for tracking the progress of the project. Regularly compare the project deliverables against the requirements to ensure alignment and identify any deviations that need to be addressed.

By following these steps, you can ensure that the requirements are effectively used to guide the project to successful completion while meeting the needs of stakeholders.

2.29. How do you request a project scope change?

Requesting a project scope change typically involves a structured approach to ensure clarity and alignment with stakeholders. Here is a step-by-step guide:

1. Document the Change: Clearly articulate the proposed change in detail. Include the reasons for the change, the expected outcomes, and any potential impacts on the project timeline, budget, and resources.
2. Identify Stakeholders: Determine who needs to be involved in the decision-making process. This may include project sponsors, clients, team members, and any other relevant stakeholders.
3. Prepare a Change Request Form: Use a standardized template or form to document the change request. Include fields for the description of the change, rationale, impact analysis, and proposed mitigation strategies.
4. Assess Impact: Evaluate how the proposed change will affect the project scope, timeline, budget, resources, and deliverables. Consider both the positive and negative impacts of the change.
5. Risk Analysis: Identify any potential risks associated with the change and develop strategies to mitigate them. Consider how the change may affect project dependencies, quality, and stakeholder expectations.

6. Cost-Benefit Analysis: Assess the costs and benefits of implementing the change. Determine whether the benefits outweigh the costs and whether the change aligns with the project's objectives and priorities.
7. Communicate with Stakeholders: Present the change request to relevant stakeholders and seek their input and approval. Clearly communicate the reasons for the change, the expected outcomes, and any potential implications.
8. Gain Approval: Obtain formal approval from the appropriate stakeholders before proceeding with the change. This may involve obtaining signatures on the change request form or holding a formal review meeting.
9. Update Project Documentation: Once the change request is approved, update the project documentation, including the project plan, requirements document, and any other relevant documents.
10. Implement the Change: Execute the necessary changes to the project scope, schedule, budget, and resources in accordance with the approved change request.
11. Monitor and Control: Continuously monitor the implementation of the change and its impact on the project. Take corrective action as needed to ensure that the project remains on track.

By following these steps, you can effectively request and manage changes to the project scope while ensuring transparency, accountability, and alignment with stakeholder expectations.

2.30. How do you communicate project scope changes?

Communicating project scope changes effectively is crucial for maintaining transparency and managing stakeholders' expectations. Here is a step-by-step guide:

1. Document the Changes: Clearly outline the scope changes in a formal document. This document should include details such as the reason for the change, the impact on the project timeline, budget, and resources, as well as any new deliverables or requirements.
2. Identify Stakeholders: Determine who needs to be informed about the scope changes. This typically includes project sponsors, clients, team members, and any other relevant stakeholders.
3. Schedule a Meeting or Communication: Depending on the size and complexity of the project, schedule a meeting or send out a formal communication to stakeholders. Make sure to provide ample notice so that stakeholders can prepare for the discussion.
4. Present the Changes: Clearly communicate the scope changes, highlighting the reasons behind them and how they will affect the project. Use visuals such as charts or diagrams if necessary to help stakeholders understand the impact.
5. Address Concerns: Be prepared to address any concerns or questions that stakeholders may have about the scope changes. This may involve providing additional clarification or reassurance about the project's direction.
6. Update Project Documentation: After the scope changes have been communicated and approved, update all relevant project documentation, including the project plan, requirements documents, and any other related materials.
7. Monitor and Adjust: Keep a close eye on how the scope changes impact the project and be prepared to make further adjustments if necessary. Regularly communicate updates to stakeholders to ensure everyone remains informed throughout the project lifecycle.

By following these steps, you can effectively communicate project scope changes and ensure that all stakeholders are on the same page.

2.31. How do you go about developing a feasibility study for a project?

Developing a feasibility study for a project involves several key steps to assess whether the project is viable and worth pursuing. Here is a general outline of the process:

1. Define the Project Scope and Objectives: Clearly define what the project aims to achieve, its intended outcomes, and the scope of work involved.
2. Conduct Market Research: Gather data on the market demand, trends, competitors, and potential customers. Analyze the market to understand if there is a need for the proposed product or service.
3. Evaluate Technical Feasibility: Assess whether the project is technically feasible. This involves examining the technology required, availability of resources, and any potential technical challenges.
4. Assess Financial Feasibility: Calculate the costs associated with the project, including initial investment, operating expenses, and potential revenue streams. Conduct a cost-benefit analysis to determine if the project is financially viable.
5. Evaluate Legal and Regulatory Considerations: Identify any legal or regulatory requirements that may impact the project. Ensure compliance with laws and regulations related to the industry, environment, safety, etc.
6. Consider Resource Availability: Evaluate the availability of resources such as manpower, materials, equipment, and facilities needed to execute the project.
7. Risk Assessment: Identify potential risks and uncertainties associated with the project, such as market risks, technical risks, financial risks, and operational risks. Develop strategies to mitigate these risks.
8. Environmental Impact Assessment: Evaluate the potential environmental impact of the project and identify measures to minimize negative effects on the environment.
9. Stakeholder Analysis: Identify key stakeholders involved in or affected by the project and assess their interests, concerns, and potential impact on the project's success.
10. Document Findings and Recommendations: Compile all the information gathered during the feasibility study into a comprehensive report. Present the findings, conclusions, and recommendations to stakeholders for review and decision-making.
11. Decision Making: Based on the findings of the feasibility study, stakeholders can make an informed decision on whether to proceed with the project, modify it, or abandon it altogether.
12. Update the Feasibility Study: As the project progresses, periodically review and update the feasibility study to incorporate any changes in circumstances, assumptions, or project requirements.

By following these steps, you can develop a thorough feasibility study that provides valuable insights into the viability of the project and helps stakeholders make informed decisions.

3. Project Estimation

Project estimation is the process of predicting the time, resources, and costs required to complete a project. This involves evaluating the scope of the project, breaking down tasks, and using various methodologies such as expert judgment, historical data analysis, and algorithmic models to forecast the necessary effort and expenses. Accurate estimation is crucial for planning, budgeting, and managing stakeholder expectations, ensuring that the project can be delivered on time and within budget while meeting its objectives. It is an iterative process, often refined as more information becomes available and as the project progresses.

3.1. What is a project estimate? What are the major things that we estimate in a project? What are the various approaches or estimating methods used to estimate for a project? What are the various pitfalls in producing a good estimate for a project?

A project estimate is a calculated approximation of the resources, time, and costs required to complete a project. It serves as a foundation for budgeting, scheduling, and resource planning. Accurate project estimates are crucial for setting realistic expectations, managing project risks, and ensuring successful project completion.

Major Things We Estimate in a Project

1. Time (Schedule):
    a. Duration of tasks and activities
    b. Start and finish dates for project milestones
    c. Overall project timeline
2. Cost:
    a. Direct costs (e.g., labor, materials, equipment)
    b. Indirect costs (e.g., overhead, administration)
    c. Contingencies for unforeseen expenses
3. Resources:
    a. Human resources (e.g., number of personnel, skill levels)
    b. Physical resources (e.g., equipment, facilities)
    c. Financial resources
4. Scope:
    a. Work breakdown structure (WBS)
    b. Specific deliverables and their requirements

Approaches or Estimating Methods

1. Top-Down Estimating:
    a. Estimates are made at a high level and then broken down into smaller components.
    b. Suitable for early project phases or when detailed information is lacking.
2. Bottom-Up Estimating:
    a. Estimates are made for individual tasks or components and then aggregated.
    b. Provides higher accuracy and detail, ideal for later project stages.
3. Analogous Estimating:
    a. Uses historical data from similar projects to estimate current project parameters.
    b. Relatively quick and less costly but relies on the similarity and accuracy of past projects.
4. Parametric Estimating:
    a. Uses statistical relationships between historical data and other variables.
    b. Involves mathematical models (e.g., cost per unit, time per unit).
5. Three-Point Estimating:
    a. Incorporates three estimates: optimistic, pessimistic, and most likely.
    b. Uses formulas to calculate the expected estimate, accounting for uncertainty and risk.
6. Expert Judgment:

    a. Relies on the experience and knowledge of experts to provide estimates.
    b. Often used in combination with other methods for validation.
7. Delphi Technique:
    a. Gathers estimates from a panel of experts through multiple rounds of anonymous feedback.
    b. Aims to achieve a consensus estimate.
8. Monte Carlo Simulation:
    a. Uses probability distributions and random sampling to model potential outcomes.
    b. Provides a range of possible scenarios and their likelihoods.

Pitfalls in Producing a Good Estimate

1. Inaccurate or Incomplete Information:
    a. Lack of detailed project requirements or scope can lead to incorrect estimates.
2. Over-Optimism:
    a. Underestimating time, cost, or complexity due to an overly positive outlook.
3. Underestimating Complexity:
    a. Failing to account for the complexity and interdependencies of tasks.
4. Changes in Scope (Scope Creep):
    a. Frequent changes to project scope can invalidate initial estimates.
5. Ignoring Risks and Contingencies:
    a. Not accounting for potential risks and uncertainties that can impact the project.
6. Poor Communication:
    a. Misunderstandings or lack of communication among stakeholders and team members.
7. Historical Data Misuse:
    a. Relying on outdated or irrelevant historical data that does not match current project conditions.
8. Bias:
    a. Personal biases of the estimators can skew the estimates.
9. Inadequate Tools and Techniques:
    a. Using inappropriate or outdated estimating tools and techniques.
10. Time Pressure:
    a. Rushing the estimating process due to tight deadlines can compromise accuracy.

By understanding and addressing these pitfalls, project managers can improve the accuracy and reliability of their project estimates, leading to more successful project outcomes.

3.2. Why do project estimate at all for a project?

Project estimation serves several important purposes:

1. Resource Planning: Estimating helps in planning the allocation of resources such as time, money, manpower, and materials required for the project. This ensures that resources are utilized optimally and that there are no shortages or overages during project execution.
2. Budgeting: Accurate estimation is crucial for creating a budget for the project. It allows stakeholders to understand the financial requirements of the project and allocate funds accordingly.
3. Risk Management: Estimation helps in identifying potential risks and uncertainties associated with the project. By considering different scenarios and estimating their impact, project managers can develop risk mitigation strategies to minimize the adverse effects on the project's progress.
4. Setting Expectations: Estimation helps in setting realistic expectations with stakeholders regarding project timelines, deliverables, and outcomes. It enables project managers to communicate effectively with clients, team members, and other stakeholders about what can be

achieved within the given constraints.
5. Decision Making: Estimation provides valuable information for decision-making throughout the project lifecycle. It helps in prioritizing tasks, selecting appropriate strategies, and making adjustments to the project plan as necessary.
6. Performance Measurement: Estimation provides a baseline against which actual performance can be measured. By comparing estimated versus actual costs, timelines, and deliverables, project managers can assess project performance and identify areas for improvement.

Overall, project estimation is essential for effective project planning, management, and control, ultimately contributing to the successful completion of the project within constraints.

3.3. What terms are used in estimating?

Estimating in the context of project management, construction, software development, or any field that involves planning and budgeting, involves several key terms and concepts. Here is a detailed overview of the most commonly used terms:

1. Effort refers to the amount of work required to complete a task or project. It is usually measured in person-hours, person-days, person-weeks, or person-months. Effort focuses on the total time individual team members spend working on the task, regardless of the calendar duration over which this work is spread. For example, if a task requires 80 hours of effort, that means it will take one person 80 hours to complete the task, or two people 40 hours each, and so on.
2. Duration is the total time span from the start to the completion of a task or project. It includes all the calendar time that passes, including non-working time such as weekends and holidays. Duration is measured in calendar units like days, weeks, or months. For instance, if a task starts on January 1st and ends on January 10th, its duration is 10 calendar days.
3. Level of Effort (LOE) Work refers to tasks that are typically supportive in nature and do not produce direct deliverables but are necessary for the project's progression. These tasks usually have a fixed, ongoing nature, such as project management, maintenance, or administrative tasks. LOE is often measured by the consistent amount of effort per time period, like hours per week. It is used for activities that are not easily quantified by specific outputs but are necessary for the project.
4. Work Time is the actual productive time spent working on a task, excluding breaks, downtime, or any non-productive periods. It is the portion of the effort that directly contributes to completing the task. For example, in an 8-hour workday, if 6 hours are spent directly on task-related activities and 2 hours are taken up by meetings and breaks, the work time is 6 hours.
5. Elapsed Time is similar to duration but is used specifically to highlight the total time taken to complete a task from start to finish, considering all real-world interruptions. It includes all periods of inactivity such as waiting times, delays, or any non-working periods. Elapsed time helps in understanding the actual time frame needed for project completion, including all delays. For instance, if a task starts on January 1st and the actual work takes 5 days but due to waiting periods the task completes on January 15th, the elapsed time is 15 days.
6. Availability refers to the amount of time a resource (such as a team member) is available to work on a project. It is often expressed as a percentage of full-time availability. For example, if a team member is working on multiple projects and is available to dedicate 50% of their time to a specific project, their availability is 50%. Availability takes into account holidays, part-time schedules, and other commitments that might limit the time a resource can dedicate to a project.
7. Estimate. An approximation or educated guess of the resources (time, cost, materials, etc.) required to complete a task or project.
8. Baseline. A fixed reference point or standard against which actual performance can be compared. It typically includes the approved project scope, schedule, and cost.
9. Bid. A proposal submitted by a contractor or service provider to complete a project for a specified

cost. It includes a detailed cost estimate and may also include time estimates and other relevant details.

10. Budget. The total amount of money allocated for the project. It includes all estimated costs and provides a financial framework for the project.
11. Contingency. A provision within the estimate to cover unexpected costs or risks that may arise during the project. It is typically expressed as a percentage of the total estimated cost.
12. Direct Costs. Costs that can be directly attributed to a specific task or component of a project. Examples include labor, materials, and equipment specifically used for the project.
13. Indirect Costs. Costs that are not directly attributable to a specific task but are necessary for the project. Examples include overhead costs, utilities, and administrative expenses.
14. Labor Costs. The cost of human resources needed to complete the project. This includes wages, benefits, and other related expenses.
15. Material Costs. The cost of raw materials or components required to complete the project. This includes purchasing, shipping, and handling costs.
16. Overhead. The ongoing business expenses not directly tied to a specific project, such as rent, utilities, and administrative salaries.
17. Unit Cost. The cost associated with a single unit of measure, which can be useful in estimating large quantities of items or repetitive tasks.
18. Scope. The defined objectives and deliverables of a project. It details what is included and what is excluded from the project.
19. Scope Creep. The gradual expansion of the project scope without corresponding adjustments to time, cost, and resources, often leading to project overruns.
20. Schedule. The timeline for project tasks and activities, detailing when each task will be started and completed.
21. Work Breakdown Structure (WBS). A hierarchical decomposition of the total scope of work to be carried out by the project team. It breaks down the project into smaller, more manageable components.
22. Quantity Takeoff. A detailed measurement of materials and labor needed to complete a project, typically derived from blueprints and specifications.
23. Phased Estimating. An approach where the estimate is progressively refined as the project scope and details become clearer over time. It involves creating preliminary estimates early and updating them as more information becomes available.
24. Accuracy. The degree to which the estimated values are close to the actual values. Higher accuracy implies less deviation from the real costs and time.
25. Risk Analysis. The process of identifying and assessing potential risks that could impact the project's cost, schedule, or quality. It includes evaluating the likelihood and potential impact of each risk.
26. Monte Carlo Simulation. A statistical technique used in estimating to model the probability of different outcomes in a process that cannot easily be predicted due to the intervention of random variables.
27. Parametric Estimating. An estimating technique that uses statistical relationships between historical data and other variables (such as square footage in construction projects) to calculate an estimate.
28. Analogous Estimating. An estimating technique that uses the actual cost or duration of a previous, similar project as the basis for estimating the cost or duration of the current project.
29. Bottom-Up Estimating. An estimating technique that involves estimating the cost of individual work packages or activities with the greatest level of detail, and then summing them to get a total project estimate.
30. Top-Down Estimating. An estimating technique that uses the overall scope of the project to estimate the cost and duration, often based on experience or high-level information.

Understanding these terms is crucial for accurate project planning and estimation, ensuring that project managers can allocate resources effectively and anticipate potential delays or constraints in project timelines.

3.4. What are the key steps in project estimation?

Project estimation is the process of predicting the time, cost, resources, and effort required to complete a project. It involves several key steps:

1. Defining Scope: Clearly outline what the project entails, including objectives, deliverables, and boundaries.
2. Identifying Activities: Break down the project into smaller, manageable tasks or activities.
3. Estimating Effort: Determine the amount of work needed for each activity. This can involve various methods such as expert judgment, analogous estimating, parametric estimating, and bottom-up estimating.
4. Estimating Duration: Calculate how long each activity will take based on the estimated effort and the availability of resources.
5. Estimating Costs: Predict the financial resources required by considering labor, materials, equipment, and other expenses.
6. Risk Assessment: Identify potential risks and uncertainties that could impact the project, and include contingencies in the estimates to account for these risks.
7. Consolidation and Review: Aggregate all estimates to form a comprehensive project plan and review it for accuracy, feasibility, and alignment with project goals.

Effective project estimation is crucial for setting realistic expectations, planning resources, and ensuring the project stays on track and within budget.

3.5. What factors are we concerned with when doing estimation for projects?

Estimating for projects involves a comprehensive analysis of various factors to ensure accuracy and feasibility. The key factors to consider include:

1. Scope of Work:
    a. Project Requirements: Detailed understanding of what needs to be done, including deliverables and objectives.
    b. Specifications: Detailed description of the materials, standards, and techniques to be used.
2. Time:
    a. Project Schedule: Timeline for project completion, including start and end dates.
    b. Milestones: Significant phases or checkpoints in the project.
    c. Deadlines: Specific dates by which parts of the project need to be completed.
3. Resources:
    a. Human Resources: Availability and skill level of the project team.
    b. Material Resources: Availability and cost of materials required.
    c. Equipment: Availability, cost, and condition of equipment needed.
4. Costs:
    a. Labor Costs: Wages and benefits for project team members.
    b. Material Costs: Price of materials and supplies.
    c. Overhead Costs: Indirect costs such as utilities, rent, and administration.
    d. Contingency Costs: Budget reserved for unexpected expenses.
5. Risk Factors:
    a. Identified Risks: Potential issues that could impact the project (technical, financial,

environmental).
    b. Risk Mitigation Plans: Strategies to reduce or manage risks.
6. Quality:
    a. Quality Standards: Standards and benchmarks that the project must meet.
    b. Quality Assurance: Processes to ensure the project meets the required standards.
7. Dependencies and Constraints:
    a. Internal Dependencies: Tasks within the project that depend on the completion of other tasks.
    b. External Dependencies: Factors outside the project that might impact its progress.
    c. Constraints: Limitations related to time, budget, resources, or scope.
8. Historical Data:
    a. Previous Projects: Data and outcomes from similar past projects to guide estimations.
    b. Lessons Learned: Insights and improvements identified from past projects.
9. Stakeholder Requirements:
    a. Stakeholder Expectations: Needs and expectations of those with an interest in the project.
    b. Communication Plan: How information will be disseminated to stakeholders.
10. Market Conditions:
    a. Economic Factors: Current market conditions affecting costs and availability of resources.
    b. Regulatory Environment: Compliance with relevant laws and regulations.
11. Technology:
    a. Tools and Software: Availability and capability of technology to support project activities.
    b. Technological Trends: Emerging technologies that could impact project execution.

By thoroughly analyzing these factors, project managers can develop more accurate and reliable estimates, ultimately leading to better project planning and execution.

3.6. How does productivity and utilization factors play a role when doing estimating for projects?

Productivity and utilization factors are critical elements in project estimating, especially in industries such as construction, manufacturing, software development, and other fields where resource allocation and time management are crucial for project success. Here is how they play a role:

Productivity Factors

1. Defining Productivity:
    a. Productivity refers to the rate at which work is completed. It is typically measured as output per unit of time, such as units produced per hour or lines of code written per day.
2. Impact on Estimates:
    a. Time Estimates: Accurate productivity measurements help in estimating the time required to complete specific tasks or the entire project. For example, knowing that a team can lay 100 bricks per hour allows you to estimate the time needed for a wall of a given size.
    b. Resource Allocation: Understanding productivity helps in determining how many resources (e.g., workers, machines) are needed to meet project deadlines.
    c. Cost Estimates: Productivity directly influences labor costs. Higher productivity can lower labor costs per unit of output, while lower productivity can increase costs.
3. Factors Influencing Productivity:
    a. Skill Levels: The expertise and experience of the workforce.
    b. Tools and Technology: The efficiency of tools and technology used.
    c. Working Conditions: The environment and conditions under which the work is

performed.

    d. Processes and Methods: The efficiency of the methods and processes in place.

Utilization Factors

1. Defining Utilization:
    a. Utilization refers to the extent to which available resources are used in productive activities. It is typically expressed as a percentage of total available time that resources (e.g., employees, equipment) are actively working on project tasks.
2. Impact on Estimates:
    a. Capacity Planning: Utilization rates help in understanding how much of the available capacity (workforce, equipment) can be realistically expected to contribute to project tasks. For example, if employees are only utilized 70% of the time due to meetings, training, and breaks, this needs to be factored into estimates.
    b. Schedule Accuracy: Higher utilization means more work is being done in a given time, which can shorten project timelines. Conversely, lower utilization extends project duration.
    c. Resource Requirements: Utilization rates help in determining the number of resources required to meet project demands. Lower utilization might necessitate hiring more staff or acquiring more equipment.
3. Factors Influencing Utilization:
    a. Non-Productive Time: Time spent on activities not directly contributing to project goals, such as administrative tasks, training, or maintenance.
    b. Availability: The actual time resources are available to work, which can be affected by holidays, sick leave, or shift patterns.
    c. Work Distribution: How well tasks are distributed among available resources to maximize productivity.

Integrating Productivity and Utilization into Project Estimates

1. Data Collection:
    a. Collect historical data on productivity rates and utilization percentages from past projects. This provides a benchmark for future estimates.
2. Estimation Models:
    a. Use estimation models that incorporate both productivity and utilization factors. For example, software estimation models like COCOMO (Constructive Cost Model) consider productivity variations among different teams.
3. Continuous Monitoring:
    a. Monitor productivity and utilization throughout the project to adjust estimates and resource allocations as necessary. This helps in maintaining realistic timelines and budgets.
4. Scenario Analysis:
    a. Perform scenario analysis to understand how changes in productivity and utilization can impact the project. This can involve best-case, worst-case, and most likely scenarios to prepare for potential variances.
5. Communication and Training:
    a. Ensure clear communication of productivity expectations and provide training to improve both productivity and utilization. Well-informed and well-trained teams are more likely to meet estimated targets.

In summary, productivity and utilization factors are fundamental to creating accurate project estimates. They influence how resources are allocated, the time required to complete tasks, and the overall cost of the project. Properly accounting for these factors helps in developing realistic and achievable project plans, reducing the risk of overruns in both time and budget.

3.7. What is life cycle cost?

Life cycle cost (LCC) refers to the total cost of owning, operating, maintaining, and eventually disposing of an asset over its entire lifespan. This comprehensive approach considers all phases of an asset's life, from acquisition to decommissioning, providing a holistic view of the financial implications involved. The goal of life cycle cost analysis (LCCA) is to help decision-makers evaluate the long-term economic performance of different investment options and choose the one that offers the best value over time.

Key Components of Life Cycle Cost

1. Acquisition Costs:
    a. Purchase Price: The initial cost to acquire the asset.
    b. Financing Costs: Interest and other costs associated with borrowing funds to purchase the asset.
    c. Installation Costs: Expenses for setting up or installing the asset.
2. Operation Costs:
    a. Energy and Utility Costs: Expenses for energy consumption and utilities required to operate the asset.
    b. Labor Costs: Costs for personnel required to operate the asset.
3. Maintenance Costs:
    a. Routine Maintenance: Regular upkeep to keep the asset in working condition.
    b. Repairs: Costs associated with fixing any issues that arise during the asset's use.
    c. Upgrades and Replacements: Expenses for parts or systems that need to be replaced or upgraded over time.
4. Downtime Costs:
    a. Loss of Productivity: Financial losses due to the asset being out of service for maintenance or repairs.
    b. Emergency Repairs: Additional costs incurred from unexpected breakdowns.
5. End-of-Life Costs:
    a. Decommissioning Costs: Expenses for safely removing the asset from service.
    b. Disposal Costs: Costs for disposing of the asset, which may include recycling or hazardous material handling.
    c. Salvage Value: Any residual value or income from selling parts or materials from the decommissioned asset.

Benefits of Life Cycle Cost Analysis

1. Informed Decision-Making: By understanding the total cost of ownership, organizations can make better investment decisions.
2. Cost Efficiency: Identifying and planning for all potential costs helps in managing and reducing unnecessary expenses.
3. Budget Planning: Provides a clearer picture of long-term financial commitments, aiding in more accurate budgeting.
4. Sustainability: Encourages the selection of options that may have higher initial costs but lower long-term environmental and operational costs.
5. Risk Management: Understanding the total cost helps in anticipating future financial requirements and mitigating risks related to cost overruns or unexpected expenditures.

Applications of Life Cycle Cost Analysis: Life cycle cost analysis is widely used in various fields, including:

1. Construction and Infrastructure: Evaluating the total cost of building projects, including future

maintenance and operation expenses.
2. Manufacturing and Industrial Equipment: Assessing the cost-effectiveness of machinery and production systems.
3. Energy and Utilities: Comparing different energy systems or technologies based on their total cost of ownership.
4. Transportation: Analyzing the costs associated with vehicles, including fuel, maintenance, and depreciation.

Example: For a new building project, a life cycle cost analysis might include:
1. Initial Costs: Construction, land acquisition, architectural design.
2. Operational Costs: Utility bills, staffing, security, insurance.
3. Maintenance Costs: Regular cleaning, HVAC system maintenance, landscaping.
4. End-of-Life Costs: Demolition, site cleanup, potential resale, or salvage value.

In summary, life cycle cost is a critical financial analysis tool that provides a comprehensive view of all costs associated with an asset over its lifespan, helping organizations make more economically sound decisions. By evaluating all these aspects, project managers can make more strategic decisions that balance upfront expenses with long-term savings and benefits, leading to more sustainable and cost-effective projects.

3.8. What is life cycle cost as relates to software development projects?

Life cycle cost (LCC) in the context of software development projects refers to the total cost associated with the entire lifespan of a software system, from its initial conception to its eventual retirement. This encompasses all costs incurred during the various phases of the software development life cycle (SDLC), including planning, development, deployment, maintenance, and decommissioning. Here is a breakdown of what life cycle cost entails in software development:
1. Planning and Requirements Analysis:
    a. Costs related to feasibility studies, requirement gathering, and analysis.
    b. Expenses for stakeholder meetings, market research, and initial project planning.
2. Design:
    a. Costs for system and software design, including architectural design and user interface design.
    b. Expenses related to prototyping and design validation.
3. Development:
    a. Costs of coding, unit testing, integration, and configuration.
    b. Expenses for development tools, environments, and third-party libraries or components.
    c. Personnel costs, including salaries of developers, testers, and project managers.
4. Testing:
    a. Costs for various testing activities such as system testing, integration testing, user acceptance testing (UAT), and performance testing.
    b. Expenses for testing tools, environments, and test data preparation.
5. Deployment:
    a. Costs associated with deploying the software to production environments.
    b. Expenses for hardware, cloud services, and other infrastructure needed to host the software.
6. Operation and Maintenance:
    a. Ongoing costs for software updates, bug fixes, and enhancements.
    b. Expenses for operational support, including help desk services and user training.
    c. Costs related to software upgrades, scalability improvements, and performance tuning.
7. End-of-Life (Decommissioning):

   a. Costs for retiring the software, including data migration to new systems, archival of data, and decommissioning of related hardware and infrastructure.
   b. Expenses related to any contractual obligations or compliance requirements for data retention and disposal.

Key Considerations in Life Cycle Cost Analysis:

1. Direct vs. Indirect Costs:
   a. Direct costs are directly attributable to the project, such as salaries and software licenses.
   b. Indirect costs may include overheads, such as office space, utilities, and administrative support.
2. Cost Estimation Accuracy:
   a. Accurate estimation of life cycle costs is crucial for budgeting and financial planning.
   b. Techniques like cost-benefit analysis, return on investment (ROI), and total cost of ownership (TCO) are often used.
3. Risk Management:
   a. Identifying and managing risks that could affect costs, such as changes in technology, scope creep, or regulatory changes.
4. Sustainability and Scalability:
   a. Ensuring that the software can be maintained and scaled efficiently over its life cycle.
   b. Considering long-term operational costs and potential savings from efficient design and architecture.

Life cycle cost analysis helps organizations make informed decisions about software investments by providing a comprehensive view of all costs associated with a software system over its entire life span. It enables better financial planning, resource allocation, and helps in evaluating the total economic impact of the software project.

3.9. What is statistical cost estimating?

Statistical cost estimating is a method used to predict the cost of a project or product based on historical data and statistical analysis. This technique employs mathematical models to analyze past cost data and establish relationships between various cost drivers and the final cost. It is particularly useful when there is a substantial amount of historical data available, and it allows for more accurate and reliable cost predictions.

Key Steps in Statistical Cost Estimating:

1. Data Collection: Gather historical cost data and relevant variables (cost drivers) that influence the cost.
2. Data Analysis: Use statistical techniques to analyze the data and identify trends, correlations, and patterns.
3. Model Development: Develop a mathematical model (e.g., regression analysis) that relates the cost drivers to the total cost.
4. Validation: Test the model using a separate dataset to ensure its accuracy and reliability.
5. Cost Estimation: Apply the model to predict future costs based on new data or scenarios.

Let us consider an example in the construction industry where a company wants to estimate the cost of building new residential houses.

Step-by-Step Illustration:

1. Data Collection:
   a. The company collects data from 50 previously completed residential projects.

   b. The data includes the total cost of each project, the size of the house (in square feet), the number of floors, the type of materials used, the labor hours, and the location of the project.
2. Data Analysis:
   a. The company uses statistical software to analyze the data.
   b. They identify that the size of the house (square footage) and the number of floors are strongly correlated with the total cost.
3. Model Development:
   a. Using regression analysis, they develop a model that predicts the total cost based on the size of the house and the number of floors.
   b. The regression equation might look like this: Total Cost = a + b × Size + c × Number of Floors
   c. Where a, b, and c are coefficients determined by the regression analysis.
4. Validation:
   a. They validate the model by comparing the predicted costs with actual costs from another set of completed projects not used in the model development.
   b. If the model's predictions are close to the actual costs, it is considered valid.
5. Cost Estimation:
   a. Now, the company can use this model to estimate the cost of future projects.
   b. For example, if a new project involves building a 2,500 square foot house with 2 floors, the model can estimate the cost by plugging these values into the regression equation.

Application:
Suppose the regression analysis resulted in the following equation:
Total Cost = 50,000 + 100 × Size + 30,000 × Number of Floors
For a 2,500 square foot house with 2 floors:
Total Cost = 50,000 + 100 × 2,500 + 30,000 × 2
Total Cost = 50,000 + 250,000 + 60,000
Total Cost = 360,000
Therefore, the estimated cost to build this house would be $360,000.

Advantages of Statistical Cost Estimating:
1. Accuracy: Provides more accurate estimates by leveraging historical data and statistical relationships.
2. Objectivity: Reduces the reliance on subjective judgment.
3. Scalability: Can be applied to various types of projects as long as relevant historical data is available.

Limitations:
1. Data Dependency: Requires a substantial amount of accurate historical data.
2. Complexity: Developing and validating statistical models can be complex and requires expertise.
3. Assumption of Continuity: Assumes that future projects will follow similar patterns to past projects, which may not always be the case.

In summary, statistical cost estimating is a powerful technique that uses historical data and statistical methods to forecast future costs, providing a more scientific approach to cost estimation in various industries.

3.10. What is Program Evaluation and Review Technique? Provide practical examples.

The Program Evaluation and Review Technique (PERT) is a project management tool used to analyze and represent the tasks involved in completing a given project. It was originally developed by the United States Navy in the 1950s to manage the Polaris submarine missile program. PERT aims to streamline the scheduling and coordination of tasks within a project by estimating the time and resources required for each task and identifying the critical path - the sequence of tasks that determines the project's overall duration.

Practical applications of PERT can be found in various industries and fields, including:

1. Construction Projects: PERT can help construction companies manage the complex network of tasks involved in building structures. For example, when constructing a new office building, PERT can be used to schedule tasks such as site preparation, foundation laying, framing, electrical wiring, plumbing installation, and finishing work. By identifying the critical path, project managers can focus resources on tasks that have the greatest impact on the project timeline.
2. Product Development: PERT is valuable in managing the development of new products, especially those with multiple components and dependencies. For instance, a company developing a new smartphone might use PERT to schedule tasks such as design, prototyping, testing, manufacturing, and marketing. By using PERT, project managers can allocate resources effectively and ensure that the product is launched on time.
3. Event Planning: Event planners can use PERT to organize and coordinate all the tasks involved in hosting an event, such as conferences, weddings, or concerts. Tasks might include booking venues, arranging catering, coordinating entertainment, managing invitations, and overseeing setup and teardown. PERT can help ensure that each task is completed on schedule to guarantee a successful event.
4. Research Projects: PERT can be applied in academic and scientific research to manage the various stages of a research project, from literature review to data collection and analysis to manuscript writing. By breaking down the research process into tasks and estimating the time required for each task, researchers can effectively plan and execute their projects, meeting deadlines and milestones along the way.
5. Software Development: In software development, PERT can assist in managing the development lifecycle, including requirements gathering, design, coding, testing, and deployment. By using PERT to schedule tasks and identify dependencies, software development teams can deliver high-quality products on time and within budget.

The PERT is applied to estimating cost

Expected value of cost = (Optimistic + (4 x Most Likely) + Pessimistic) / 6
Standard deviation = (Pessimistic - Optimistic) / 6

In cost estimating, we typically aim for an estimated range of values with a 95 percent probability that the actual cost will fall within this range. This range includes the expected cost plus or minus two standard deviations.

In the Program Evaluation and Review Technique (PERT), we seek to determine the probability of a project being completed within a specific time frame. This time frame is defined by the expected completion date plus or minus two standard deviations, calculated using the given equations. Although these dates are approximations based on a normal distribution, a skewed probability distribution, such as the beta distribution (see Figure 3.10.1), would be more accurate. Nonetheless, the approximations are sufficiently accurate for scheduling estimates. These assumptions are also valid for cost estimating.

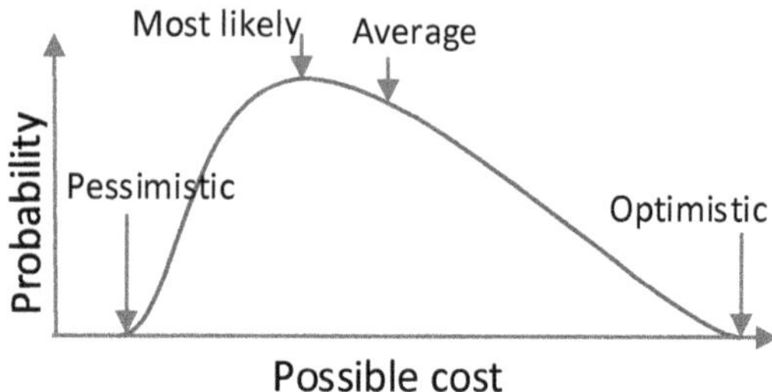

Figure 3.10.1 Skewed Probability Distribution

In essence, PERT provides a structured approach to project management, enabling organizations to effectively plan, execute, and monitor projects of varying complexity across different industries.

3.11. What is the difference between estimated cost and price of completing a project?

The terms "estimated cost" and "price" of completing a project refer to different financial aspects in project management and have distinct meanings:

1. Estimated Cost:
    a. Definition: The estimated cost is the anticipated expense incurred to complete a project. It encompasses all resources needed, including materials, labor, equipment, and overheads.
    b. Components: This includes direct costs (e.g., salaries, raw materials) and indirect costs (e.g., administrative expenses, utilities).
    c. Purpose: It serves as a financial forecast to guide budgeting, funding, and resource allocation. It is primarily used internally by the project team and stakeholders to plan and control project finances.
    d. Calculation Basis: The estimated cost is based on historical data, expert judgment, cost estimation techniques, and analysis of project scope and requirements.
2. Price:
    a. Definition: The price is the amount charged to the client or customer for delivering the completed project. It is what the project owner expects to receive as revenue.
    b. Components: The price includes the estimated cost plus a profit margin and may also factor in market conditions, client's ability to pay, and competitive considerations.
    c. Purpose: The price is a contractual figure used in agreements between the project provider and the client. It represents the financial terms under which the project will be delivered.
    d. Calculation Basis: The price is determined based on the estimated cost, desired profit margin, competitive pricing strategies, and negotiation outcomes.

Key Differences:

1. Objective:
    a. Estimated Cost: Focuses on the internal financial needs to complete the project.
    b. Price: Focuses on the external financial agreement with the client.
2. Usage:
    a. Estimated Cost: Used for budgeting, planning, and internal cost control.
    b. Price: Used for invoicing, revenue generation, and contractual obligations.
3. Inclusion of Profit:
    a. Estimated Cost: Does not include profit margin; it is purely the expected expense.
    b. Price: Includes profit margin and possibly other factors like risk premiums.
4. Determination Process:
    a. Estimated Cost: Based on detailed cost estimation methodologies and internal analysis.

b. Price: Based on the estimated cost, market factors, and strategic pricing decisions.

Understanding these differences is crucial for effective project financial management, ensuring both accurate budgeting and competitive, profitable pricing.

3.12. What is the law of diminishing returns? How this concept relates to project management?

The law of diminishing returns, also known as the principle of diminishing marginal returns, is an economic concept that describes how, after a certain point, adding more of one factor of production while holding others constant will result in smaller incremental increases in output. Essentially, as more of a variable input (e.g., labor, capital) is added to a fixed input (e.g., land, machinery), the additional output produced by each additional unit of the variable input will eventually decrease.

Key Points of the Law of Diminishing Returns:

1. Initial Increase: Initially, adding more of the variable input increases total output at an increasing rate due to improved efficiencies and optimal utilization of fixed resources.
2. Diminishing Returns: After reaching a certain level of input, the rate of increase in total output begins to slow down. Each additional unit of input contributes less to the total output.
3. Negative Returns: If the variable input continues to increase beyond the point of diminishing returns, it can lead to an overall decrease in total output due to overcrowding, overuse, or inefficiencies.

Example: Consider a factory that produces widgets. Initially, as more workers are hired, production increases rapidly because workers can specialize and collaborate. However, after reaching an optimal level of staffing, adding more workers leads to smaller increases in production because there is a finite number of machines and space. Beyond a certain point, additional workers may even hinder production by getting in each other's way.

Graphical Representation: On a graph, the total product curve first increases at an increasing rate, then at a decreasing rate, and may eventually decline.

Key Takeaway: The law of diminishing returns highlights the importance of balancing the inputs in a production process. It underscores that continuously increasing one input while keeping others constant will yield progressively smaller improvements in output, eventually leading to inefficiency.

In project management, the law of diminishing returns can be observed in various scenarios where increasing resources do not proportionally increase productivity or project outcomes. Here are some specific ways this concept relates to project management:

1. Resource Allocation: Adding more team members to a project does not always result in faster completion times. After a certain point, more team members can lead to communication overhead, coordination issues, and reduced efficiency.
2. Task Overload: Overloading team members with additional tasks can reduce their productivity and the quality of their work. There is a limit to how much work an individual can handle efficiently before their performance starts to decline.
3. Project Scheduling: Extending work hours (overtime) to meet deadlines might initially increase output, but prolonged overtime can lead to fatigue, burnout, and errors, reducing overall productivity and potentially increasing project delays.
4. Technology and Tools: Investing in new tools and technologies can improve project performance up to a point. However, if the team is overwhelmed with too many tools or if the tools are not adequately integrated, the expected benefits may not materialize, and efficiency could decrease.

Examples in Project Management:

1. Team Expansion: Imagine a software development project where the team size is increased from 5 to 15 developers. Initially, the project may benefit from the additional manpower, but beyond a certain number, the coordination efforts, communication breakdowns, and merging of code can lead to diminishing returns in productivity.
2. Overtime and Productivity: A project manager might push for longer work hours to meet a tight deadline. Initially, this may result in higher output, but as team members become exhausted, their productivity will drop, leading to mistakes and potentially longer timelines to correct these errors.
3. Tool Integration: Implementing a new project management software might streamline processes initially. However, adding too many complex tools can create confusion, require extensive training, and lead to reduced overall efficiency if not managed properly.

Understanding the law of diminishing returns helps project managers make informed decisions about resource allocation, team size, work schedules, and tool adoption. It emphasizes the importance of finding an optimal balance and recognizing the point at which additional inputs may no longer produce proportional benefits. This awareness can lead to more effective project planning, execution, and successful project outcomes.

3.13. What is a cost improvement curve?

A cost improvement curve, also known as a learning curve, is a graphical representation that shows how the cost per unit decreases as the cumulative production of units increases. This concept is based on the observation that as workers gain more experience in producing a product, they become more efficient, leading to lower production costs. In the context of projects, this curve illustrates how project costs decrease over time as the team becomes more familiar with the processes, tools, and tasks involved.

Key Principles of Cost Improvement Curves

1. Experience Leads to Efficiency: As the team completes more units or tasks, they find faster and more efficient ways to do the work.
2. Predictable Cost Reductions: The rate of cost reduction can often be predicted based on past performance.
3. Cumulative Production: The total output to date is crucial; the more units produced, the greater the experience and thus the lower the costs.

Examples of Cost Improvement Curves in Projects

1. Example 1: Manufacturing. In a car manufacturing plant, the cost per car might decrease as more cars are produced. Initially, workers spend more time and resources figuring out the best assembly methods. Over time, they identify shortcuts and optimize their processes, leading to lower costs per car. For example:
    a. First 100 cars: $25,000 per car
    b. Next 200 cars: $22,000 per car
    c. Next 500 cars: $20,000 per car
2. Example 2: Software Development. In a software development project, the initial phase may involve higher costs due to the team's unfamiliarity with the project's specific requirements, tools, and technologies. As the project progresses, the team gains expertise, resulting in faster development times and reduced costs. For instance:
    a. First release: High cost due to initial setup, debugging, and learning new frameworks.
    b. Subsequent releases: Lower costs as the team becomes proficient and refines their processes.
3. Example 3: Construction. In a construction project, the cost of building similar types of houses

might decrease as more houses are built. Workers become more skilled, equipment usage is optimized, and processes are streamlined. For example:

a. First 10 houses: $150,000 per house
b. Next 20 houses: $140,000 per house
c. Next 50 houses: $130,000 per house

Benefits of Understanding Cost Improvement Curves

1. Forecasting and Budgeting: Helps in predicting future costs and setting more accurate budgets.
2. Resource Allocation: Assists in planning the allocation of resources more effectively as efficiencies improve.
3. Competitive Pricing: Enables businesses to offer competitive prices as production becomes cheaper over time.

Application in Project Management: Project managers can use cost improvement curves to:

1. Set Realistic Cost Targets: By understanding how costs are likely to decrease over time.
2. Monitor Efficiency Gains: Track the team's progress and identify areas where further improvements can be made.
3. Plan Training Programs: Invest in training early in the project to accelerate the learning process and achieve cost reductions faster.

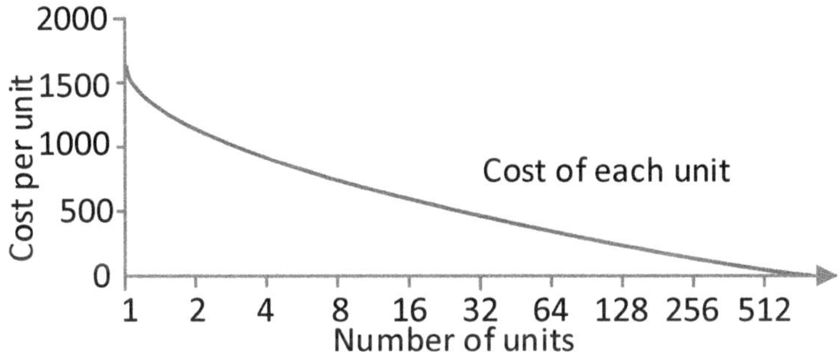

Figure 3.13.1 Cost Improvement Curve

Improvement curves (see Figure 3.13.1) resemble learning curves in that they apply a fixed percentage reduction in price with each doubling of product delivery. However, unlike learning curves, improvement curves are not derived from the concept of learning. Instead, they are based on the principle that similar project deliverables are more expensive at the beginning of a project than at later stages. Improvement curves consistently acknowledge that cost reductions occur over time, with the most significant improvements happening earlier in the project.

In summary, a cost improvement curve is a valuable tool for understanding how costs decrease with increased production or experience. It highlights the importance of learning and efficiency gains in reducing project costs over time.

3.14. What approach you follow for software estimation? Why use more than one estimating processes?

We can follow one or more of the following estimation approaches: COCOMO (Constructive Cost Model), LOC (Lines Of Code), WBS (Work Breakdown Structure), and FPA (Function Point Analysis).

The WBS-based estimating method is a detailed, micro-level method that can be used for all projects.

FPA is a generic, macro-level method that is used for any project that includes software development. Both of these methods are used to estimate size, schedule, work effort, and cost. Each method is used throughout the project, but at different times, depending on how much information is available; each method cross-checks the other.

In software estimation, we typically follow a combination of several approaches to get a more comprehensive understanding of the effort, time, and resources required for a project:

1. Expert Judgment: Consulting with individuals or teams who have experience in similar projects can provide valuable insights into potential challenges, risks, and required resources. This approach relies on the expertise and experience of individuals to make informed estimates.
2. Analogous Estimation: This involves comparing the current project with similar past projects and using their metrics (such as size, complexity, and duration) as a basis for estimating the current project's parameters. This method is useful when historical data is available and applicable to the current project.
3. Parametric Estimation: Parametric estimation involves using mathematical models based on historical data to estimate project parameters. These models typically consider factors like project size, team productivity, and technology used. Parametric models can provide more systematic and data-driven estimates.
4. Bottom-Up Estimation: This approach involves breaking down the project into smaller, more manageable tasks and estimating the effort required for each task individually. These estimates are then aggregated to provide an overall estimate for the project. Bottom-up estimation is particularly useful for complex projects with many interdependent tasks.
5. Top-Down Estimation: In contrast to bottom-up estimation, top-down estimation starts with an overall estimate for the project and then breaks it down into smaller components. This approach is useful for quickly generating high-level estimates but may require refinement as more details about the project become available.
6. Three-Point Estimation: This technique involves estimating three scenarios for each task or project: optimistic, pessimistic, and most likely. These estimates are then combined to calculate a weighted average, which provides a more realistic estimate while also accounting for uncertainty.

Using more than one estimating process is beneficial for several reasons:

1. Redundancy: Different estimation methods may produce different results due to their inherent assumptions and biases. Using multiple methods allows for cross-validation and helps identify outliers or inconsistencies.
2. Risk Mitigation: Relying on a single estimation method can be risky, as it may overlook certain factors or uncertainties. By using multiple methods, you can better account for various risks and uncertainties inherent in software projects.
3. Accuracy Improvement: Each estimation method has its strengths and weaknesses. By combining multiple methods, you can leverage the strengths of each approach while mitigating their weaknesses, leading to more accurate overall estimates.
4. Stakeholder Confidence: Using multiple estimation methods demonstrates a thorough and systematic approach to estimation, which can instill confidence in stakeholders regarding the reliability of the estimates.

In summary, employing multiple software estimation processes provides a more comprehensive and robust estimation framework, leading to more accurate and reliable project estimates.

4. Project Planning

Unless commitment is made, there are only promises and hopes; but no plans. - Peter F. Drucker

It is no secret that we are living in somewhat turbulent times. There is the very real threat of climate change, energy prices have skyrocketed, the arrival of AI threatens to take all of our jobs... you'd be forgiven for thinking you cannot plan for the future with the world in such a constant state of flux.

But long-term planning is essential to the future of your organization. Plans provide clarity, they inform strategy, they help provide a roadmap for where you want to get to. Above all, they enable you to focus on the things you and your people can control - and help to alleviate anxiety over the things you cannot.

Planning is the major component of project management success. A successful project manager relies on an effective project management plan that provides a baseline for monitoring progress, identifying variances, and taking action to mitigate the impact of problems.

4.1. What is the point of planning in organizations?

The point of planning in organizations is to set a direction, establish objectives, and determine the best course of action to achieve those objectives. Planning is a fundamental management function that helps organizations navigate uncertainty and complexity by anticipating future events and developing strategies to respond effectively.

Here are some key reasons why planning is important in organizations:

1. Goal Setting: Planning enables organizations to define their goals and objectives clearly. It provides a roadmap for the organization to know where it wants to go and what it wants to achieve.
2. Decision Making: Planning helps in making informed decisions. It involves gathering information, analyzing options, and evaluating potential outcomes. This enables organizations to select the most appropriate course of action based on available resources and constraints.
3. Resource Allocation: Effective planning ensures that resources such as financial, human, and material are allocated efficiently. It helps in identifying resource requirements, determining priorities, and optimizing resource utilization to achieve desired outcomes.
4. Coordination: Planning promotes coordination and collaboration among different departments and individuals within an organization. It establishes a common understanding of goals and ensures that everyone is working towards a unified purpose.
5. Risk Management: Through planning, organizations can identify potential risks and develop strategies to mitigate them. It allows proactive measures to be taken to minimize the impact of uncertainties, thereby increasing the likelihood of success.
6. Performance Measurement: Planning provides a basis for evaluating performance. By setting clear objectives and targets, organizations can monitor progress and measure achievements. This helps in identifying areas of improvement and taking corrective actions when necessary.
7. Adaptability: Planning enables organizations to adapt to changing circumstances and seize

opportunities. It allows for flexibility and agility in responding to internal and external changes, facilitating the organization's ability to stay relevant and competitive.

Overall, planning helps organizations align their actions with their strategic objectives, improve decision-making processes, optimize resource allocation, and enhance overall performance. It provides a structured approach to achieve desired outcomes and contributes to the long-term success and sustainability of the organization.

4.2. Why is the project plan so important?

The project plan is vital for several reasons:

1. Roadmap: It serves as a roadmap, outlining the sequence of tasks and activities needed to achieve project objectives. This clarity helps keep everyone on the same page regarding what needs to be done and when.
2. Resource Allocation: The plan details resource requirements, including human resources, time, budget, and materials. This allows for efficient allocation of resources, preventing overallocation or shortages that could delay the project.
3. Risk Management: By identifying potential risks and including contingencies in the plan, it helps mitigate risks and uncertainties that could otherwise derail the project.
4. Communication Tool: The plan acts as a communication tool, providing stakeholders with a clear understanding of project goals, timelines, milestones, and dependencies. It facilitates effective communication among team members, clients, sponsors, and other stakeholders.
5. Baseline for Monitoring and Control: It establishes a baseline against which actual progress can be compared. This enables project managers to monitor progress, identify deviations from the plan, and take corrective actions as needed to keep the project on track.
6. Decision Making: The plan provides a basis for decision-making throughout the project lifecycle. It helps prioritize tasks, allocate resources, and make informed decisions when faced with changes, challenges, or unexpected events.

In summary, the project plan is essential for guiding project execution, managing resources effectively, mitigating risks, facilitating communication, monitoring progress, and making informed decisions to ensure project success.

4.3. What should be in a project plan?

A comprehensive project plan typically includes several key components to ensure clarity, organization, and effective management throughout the project lifecycle. Here are the main areas you should cover in your project plan:

1. Project Overview:
    a. Brief description of the project's purpose, objectives, and scope.
    b. Identification of stakeholders and their roles.
2. Scope Management:
    a. Detailed description of what is included and excluded from the project.
    b. Scope statement outlining project deliverables, assumptions, and constraints.
3. Schedule Management:
    a. Project timeline with key milestones, tasks, and dependencies.
    b. Gantt chart or timeline visualization to illustrate the schedule.
4. Resource Management:
    a. Allocation of human, financial, and material resources.
    b. Roles and responsibilities of team members.
    c. Resource availability and utilization plan.

5. Risk Management:
    a. Identification of potential risks and uncertainties that may impact the project.
    b. Risk assessment, prioritization, and mitigation strategies.
    c. Contingency plans for addressing unforeseen events.
6. Communication Plan:
    a. Channels of communication among team members, stakeholders, and project manager.
    b. Frequency and format of status updates, meetings, and reports.
    c. Protocols for resolving conflicts and escalating issues.
7. Quality Management:
    a. Standards and metrics for measuring project quality.
    b. Quality assurance processes to ensure deliverables meet requirements.
    c. Testing and validation procedures.
8. Budget and Cost Management:
    a. Estimated budget for the project, including costs for resources, materials, and overhead.
    b. Budget allocation and tracking mechanisms.
    c. Strategies for cost control and management of budget variances.
9. Change Management:
    a. Procedures for handling change requests and scope modifications.
    b. Impact analysis of proposed changes on schedule, budget, and resources.
    c. Change control board or process for approving changes.
10. Closure Plan:
    a. Criteria for project completion and acceptance.
    b. Handover procedures for transitioning deliverables to stakeholders.
    c. Post-project review and lessons learned documentation.
11. Dependencies and Constraints:
    a. Identification of external dependencies, such as regulatory requirements or dependencies on other projects.
    b. Constraints that may limit project execution, such as budgetary restrictions or resource availability.
12. Monitoring and Reporting:
    a. Methods for tracking project progress, including key performance indicators (KPIs) and metrics.
    b. Reporting mechanisms for communicating project status, issues, and risks to stakeholders.
    c. Regular review and update intervals for the project plan.

By covering these main areas in your project plan, you will create a comprehensive roadmap that guides the project from initiation to completion while minimizing risks and maximizing success.

4.4. Why would you build a project plan?

A project plan serves as a guiding map for effectively implementing a system and ensuring its success. It communicates expectations and deadlines to all involved parties, aiding the project manager in keeping upper management, business users, and support groups informed about project progress and resource allocation. With built-in dependencies, it facilitates quick assessment of any delays. By comparing actual progress to the plan, valuable insights are gained for future project planning, highlighting areas of over- or under-estimation.

Project plans serve as crucial milestones in project assignments, directing efforts towards achieving business objectives. They are not only essential for new development but also for support and maintenance activities. However, many managers tailor plans without integrating actual progress, often neglecting the plan altogether.

Building a project plan is crucial for several reasons:

1. Clarity of Objectives: A project plan outlines the objectives, scope, and deliverables of the project. It helps everyone involved understand what needs to be achieved and how it will be accomplished.
2. Resource Management: A project plan identifies the resources required for the project, such as manpower, materials, and budget. It helps in effectively allocating these resources to ensure smooth project execution.
3. Time Management: By breaking down the project into smaller tasks and assigning timeframes to each task, a project plan helps in managing time effectively. It ensures that the project stays on track and deadlines are met.
4. Risk Management: A project plan identifies potential risks and uncertainties associated with the project and outlines strategies to mitigate them. It helps in proactively addressing risks and minimizing their impact on the project.
5. Communication: A project plan serves as a communication tool among stakeholders. It provides a structured framework for discussing project progress, milestones, and any issues or changes that arise during the project lifecycle.
6. Accountability: With a project plan in place, responsibilities are clearly defined, and team members know what is expected of them. This fosters accountability and ensures that everyone is working towards the common goal.
7. Quality Control: A project plan includes checkpoints and quality assurance measures to ensure that the project meets the desired quality standards. It helps in identifying deviations from the plan and taking corrective actions as necessary.

Overall, building a project plan is essential for organizing, coordinating, and executing a project effectively, ensuring its success within the constraints of time, budget, and resources.

4.5. How would you go about planning a project?

Scheduling is a nuanced skill, drawing from a blend of business objectives, company standards (if applicable), and past experiences. It commences with a clear definition of scope and objectives, alongside the documentation of assumptions, risks, and constraints. Inaccurate estimations often result from a lack of understanding about the business and the intricacies within the project scope.

Next, the project can be broken down into manageable tasks, including phases, activities within each phase, and tasks within each activity. Key milestones and deliverables should be identified and documented.

The project plan evolves continuously, requiring refinement in stages as information unfolds. Any schedule modifications must be meticulously recorded for the project manager, team members, support groups, upper management, and business users to ensure transparency and alignment.

Planning a project involves several key steps to ensure its success. Here is a general framework:

1. Define Objectives and Scope: Clearly outline the goals and deliverables of the project. Understand what needs to be achieved and what falls within the project's boundaries.
2. Identify Stakeholders: Determine who will be affected by the project and involve relevant stakeholders from the beginning. This could include team members, clients, end-users, and any other parties with an interest in the project.
3. Create a Project Plan: Develop a detailed plan that outlines tasks, timelines, resources, and dependencies. Break down the project into smaller, manageable components and assign

responsibilities to team members.
4. Allocate Resources: Determine the resources required for each task, including personnel, budget, equipment, and materials. Ensure that resources are available when needed to prevent delays.
5. Risk Management: Identify potential risks and develop strategies to mitigate them. This could involve creating contingency plans, allocating additional resources, or adjusting the project timeline.
6. Communication Plan: Establish clear communication channels and protocols for sharing updates, progress reports, and addressing issues. Regular communication is essential for keeping stakeholders informed and aligned.
7. Monitor Progress: Track the progress of the project against the plan to ensure that it stays on schedule and within budget. Use key performance indicators (KPIs) to measure progress and identify any deviations from the plan.
8. Adjustments and Iterations: Be prepared to adapt the project plan as needed based on changing circumstances or new information. Flexibility is key to overcoming obstacles and achieving success.
9. Quality Assurance: Implement processes to ensure that deliverables meet the required quality standards. This could involve regular testing, reviews, and feedback loops to identify and address any issues early on.
10. Closure and Evaluation: Once the project is complete, conduct a thorough evaluation to assess its success against the initial objectives. Identify lessons learned and areas for improvement to inform future projects.

By following these steps and maintaining a proactive approach, you can effectively plan and execute projects to achieve their desired outcomes.

4.6. How would you go about building a project plan?

Building a project plan involves several key steps to ensure its effectiveness. Here is a structured approach you can follow:

1. Define Project Objectives: Clearly articulate the purpose and goals of the project. What do you aim to achieve? What are the expected outcomes?
2. Identify Stakeholders: Identify all individuals and groups who will be impacted by or have an interest in the project. This includes both internal and external stakeholders.
3. Scope Definition: Clearly outline the boundaries of the project. What is included and what is not? Define the deliverables and constraints.
4. Create Work Breakdown Structure (WBS): Break down the project into smaller, manageable components or tasks. This hierarchical decomposition helps in organizing and understanding the work involved. Type in the identified tasks under the appropriate activity and phase or other summary level descriptions. Associate the appropriate deliverables and milestones to the specific task.
5. Sequence Activities: Determine the order in which tasks need to be performed. Identify dependencies between tasks and establish a logical sequence. Link all tasks requiring dependency associations.
6. Estimate Resources: Estimate the resources (human, financial, equipment, etc.) required for each task. This helps in resource allocation and budgeting. Add resource roles or resource names to each task.
7. Develop Schedule: Use the information from the WBS and activity sequencing to create a project schedule. Assign start and end dates to each task and establish milestones.
8. Allocate Resources: Assign resources to tasks based on availability, skills, and dependencies. Ensure that resources are adequately allocated to meet project requirements.
9. Risk Assessment and Management: Identify potential risks that could impact the project's

success. Develop strategies to mitigate or respond to these risks.

10. Communication Plan: Define how information will be communicated within the project team and to stakeholders. Establish channels, frequency, and methods of communication.
11. Quality Management Plan: Outline how quality will be ensured throughout the project lifecycle. Define quality standards, processes, and metrics.
12. Procurement Plan (if applicable): If the project involves procurement of goods or services, outline the procurement process, including vendor selection, contracts, and delivery schedules.
13. Create Baselines: Once the plan is developed, establish baselines for scope, schedule, and budget. These baselines serve as benchmarks for monitoring and controlling the project.
14. Monitor and Control: Continuously monitor project progress against the plan. Compare actual performance to the baseline and take corrective actions as necessary to keep the project on track.
15. Closure: Once the project objectives are met, close out the project formally. Document lessons learned, conduct post-project reviews, and celebrate successes.

By following these steps, you can create a comprehensive project plan that serves as a roadmap for successful project execution.

4.7. What is the distinction between planning and scheduling?

Planning and scheduling are both crucial aspects of project management, but they serve distinct purposes:

1. Planning:
    a. Definition: Planning involves determining what needs to be done, how it will be done, and who will do it. It is about setting objectives, identifying tasks, estimating resources, and establishing timelines.
    b. Focus: Planning focuses on the big picture, overarching goals, and the sequence of activities required to achieve those goals.
    c. Output: The output of planning is typically a comprehensive project plan that outlines the scope, objectives, resources, timelines, risks, and strategies for execution. This plan serves as a roadmap for the project.
2. Scheduling:
    a. Definition: Scheduling is the process of determining when each task or activity identified during planning will be performed. It involves creating a timetable or calendar that allocates resources and sets deadlines for completing specific tasks.
    b. Focus: Scheduling focuses on the detailed timing of activities, considering dependencies between tasks, resource availability, and constraints such as deadlines and milestones.
    c. Output: The output of scheduling is typically a project schedule, which specifies start and end dates for each task, along with dependencies and resource allocations. This schedule provides a detailed timeline for project execution.

In summary, planning establishes the overall framework and strategy for a project, while scheduling translates that strategy into a detailed timetable for execution. Planning answers the questions of what, why, and how, while scheduling answers the question of when. Both planning and scheduling are essential for successful project management, and they often overlap and inform each other throughout the project lifecycle.

4.8. How do you determine staffing requirements?

Determining staffing requirements for a project involves several key steps:

1. Define Project Scope: Understand the project's objectives, deliverables, timeline, and complexity. This provides a foundation for estimating the necessary resources.
2. Identify Tasks and Activities: Break down the project into smaller tasks and activities. This helps

in assessing the specific skills and expertise needed for each component.

3. Estimate Work Effort: Estimate the amount of work required for each task or activity. This includes considering factors like duration, complexity, and dependencies.
4. Assess Skill Sets: Identify the skills and expertise required to complete each task effectively. Consider technical skills, domain knowledge, experience, and any specialized qualifications needed.
5. Consider Resource Availability: Evaluate the availability of existing team members and their capacity to take on additional work. Determine if any skills gaps exist that need to be filled through hiring or outsourcing.
6. Account for Risks and Contingencies: Anticipate potential risks and uncertainties that could impact staffing needs, such as unexpected delays, changes in scope, or resource constraints.
7. Use Historical Data: Refer to past projects with similar characteristics to inform staffing decisions. Analyze past resource allocations, productivity rates, and any lessons learned.
8. Consult Stakeholders: Involve relevant stakeholders, including project sponsors, managers, and team members, in the staffing planning process. Gather their input and insights to ensure alignment with project objectives and expectations.
9. Optimize Resource Allocation: Balance workload distribution across team members to avoid overloading or underutilizing resources. Consider factors like individual strengths, availability, and development opportunities.
10. Review and Adjust: Continuously monitor staffing levels throughout the project lifecycle. Regularly review progress, adjust resource allocations as needed, and be prepared to make changes in response to evolving requirements or unforeseen challenges.

4.9. Which planning method have you found yields the most accurate results?

The accuracy of planning methods can vary depending on the context and the specific requirements of a project. However, some commonly used planning methods that have been found to yield relatively accurate results include:

1. Work breakdown structure
2. Critical Path Method (CPM): CPM is a widely used technique for planning and managing complex projects. It identifies the critical path, which is the sequence of tasks that determine the total duration of the project. By focusing on the critical path, project managers can prioritize tasks and allocate resources effectively.
3. Program Evaluation and Review Technique (PERT): PERT is another project management tool used to analyze and represent the tasks involved in completing a project. It involves estimating the time required to complete each task, considering optimistic, pessimistic, and most likely scenarios, to calculate the expected duration of the project.
4. Agile Methodology: Agile methodologies, such as Scrum or Kanban, are often preferred for projects where requirements are likely to change or evolve over time. Agile emphasizes iterative development, frequent collaboration with stakeholders, and adaptability to change, which can lead to more accurate planning and better alignment with evolving project needs.
5. Earned Value Management (EVM): EVM integrates cost, schedule, and scope to provide an overall view of project performance. It compares the planned value (budgeted cost of work scheduled) with the earned value (budgeted cost of work performed) to assess project progress and forecast future performance.
6. Monte Carlo Simulation: Monte Carlo simulation involves running multiple simulations with random inputs to forecast the likely outcomes of a project. It helps in understanding the range of possible outcomes and the probabilities associated with them, which can improve the accuracy of project planning and risk management.
7. Rolling wave scheduling is a project management technique where the project plan is developed in waves, with details planned for the near term and broader outlines for the future. It is

particularly useful in situations where detailed information or requirements are not available for the entire project duration. Here is how it typically works:

a. Initial Planning: Detailed planning is done for the near term, usually for the next few weeks or months, where requirements and resources are well understood.
b. Future Phases: Future phases of the project are planned at a higher level, with less detail. This allows for flexibility and adaptation as more information becomes available over time.
c. Regular Updates: The project plan is continuously updated as new information emerges or as the project progresses. Detailed planning for future phases is done as the project moves forward.

Rolling wave scheduling can be used in various industries and project types, but it is particularly beneficial in industries where requirements may change frequently, such as software development, construction, and research and development projects. It allows teams to adapt to changes and uncertainties more effectively while still maintaining a structured approach to project management.

Ultimately, the choice of planning method depends on factors such as project complexity, team expertise, available resources, and organizational culture. Combining multiple methods or tailoring them to suit specific project requirements may also enhance accuracy.

4.10. How and why would you build dependencies into the project plan?

Implementing dependencies into the project plan offers valuable insights, including identifying the critical path and assessing the impact of delays on the entire project. Depending on the software utilized, dependencies can establish both predecessor and successor links by associating task IDs.

Dependencies highlight the necessity for task coordination. For instance, one task may need to commence and potentially conclude before another can begin; for example, completing the logical data model before initiating the physical data model. However, not all programming tasks must be finished before testing can commence, especially if incomplete programming does not affect specific tests.

Building dependencies into a project plan is crucial for ensuring that tasks are completed in the right order and that resources are allocated efficiently. Here is how and why you would do it:

1. Identifying Dependencies: Before you can build dependencies into the project plan, you need to identify them. Dependencies are the relationships between tasks or activities where the completion of one task is reliant on the completion of another.
2. Types of Dependencies: There are four main types of dependencies:
    a. Finish-to-Start (FS): The most common type, where the successor task cannot start until the predecessor task is finished.
    b. Start-to-Start (SS): The successor task can start when the predecessor task starts.
    c. Finish-to-Finish (FF): The successor task can finish only when the predecessor task finishes.
    d. Start-to-Finish (SF): The successor task can finish only when the predecessor task starts.
3. Mapping Dependencies: Once identified, dependencies should be mapped out visually, either through a Gantt chart or a network diagram. This helps in understanding the sequence of tasks and their interdependencies.
4. Reasons for Building Dependencies:
    a. Sequence Management: Dependencies ensure that tasks are completed in the correct order, preventing chaos, and ensuring smooth progress.
    b. Resource Allocation: Dependencies help in allocating resources effectively since you know which tasks need to be completed before others can start.

c. Risk Management: By understanding dependencies, you can identify potential bottlenecks or areas where delays might occur, allowing you to mitigate risks proactively.
d. Communication: Dependencies provide a clear roadmap for team members, stakeholders, and other parties involved in the project. Everyone knows what needs to be done and when.

5. Building Dependencies into the Project Plan: This involves integrating the dependencies into the project schedule or plan, ensuring that they are clearly documented and understood by all stakeholders. This might involve adjusting task durations, setting milestones, or establishing constraints within project management software.
6. Monitoring Dependencies: Once the project is underway, it is essential to monitor dependencies closely. Any changes to task durations or dependencies should be updated promptly in the project plan to avoid delays or resource conflicts.

By building dependencies into the project plan, you create a structured framework that enhances efficiency, reduces risks, and improves communication, ultimately increasing the likelihood of project success.

4.11. How would you incorporate a person's work pace into the plan?

Incorporating a person's work pace into a project plan is crucial for optimizing productivity and ensuring realistic timelines. Depending upon the specific tool the organization is using, a resource can be adjusted to be less than a full resource/unit or you can adjust each task the individual is working on to a lower percentage of time. Here are some steps to accomplish this:

1. Understand Individual Work Pace: Start by understanding each team member's typical work pace. This can vary based on factors such as experience, skill level, work habits, and personal preferences.
2. Communication and Collaboration: Encourage open communication within the team. Discuss work pace preferences and any constraints team members might have. Understanding each other's working styles can help in accommodating different speeds.
3. Task Allocation: When assigning tasks, consider the individual work pace of team members. Match tasks to individuals who can complete them efficiently based on their pace and expertise.
4. Time Estimates: Incorporate individual work pace into time estimates for tasks. Adjust timeframes accordingly, accounting for faster or slower workers. This ensures that deadlines are realistic and achievable.
5. Flexibility: Build flexibility into the project plan to accommodate variations in work pace. Allow for buffer time in case tasks take longer than anticipated. This can prevent bottlenecks and reduce the risk of delays.
6. Regular Check-ins: Conduct regular check-ins with team members to monitor progress and address any issues related to work pace. Provide support and resources as needed to help team members meet deadlines.
7. Adjustments: Be prepared to make adjustments to the project plan as necessary. If it becomes apparent that a team member's work pace is significantly different from what was initially anticipated, reevaluate task assignments and deadlines accordingly.
8. Feedback and Iteration: Encourage feedback from team members on the project plan and their individual workloads. Use this feedback to refine the plan and make improvements for future projects.

By incorporating a person's work pace into the project plan, you can create a more realistic and achievable roadmap, leading to increased productivity and project success.

4.12. How would you incorporate training, holidays, and individuals' education

schedules?

Integrating training, holidays, and individual education schedules into a project plan demands careful coordination and scheduling to avoid disrupting project timelines. Each product has a corporate or global calendar that highlights common days off, and an individual resource calendar that tracks specific time off for each person. If education or training is essential for the project, it should be included as a task within the project plan. Here is a step-by-step approach:

1. Identify Training Needs: Determine the training requirements for team members based on the project scope, technology, or skill gaps. This could include technical training, soft skills development, or specific certifications.
2. Schedule Training Sessions: Coordinate with relevant training providers or internal trainers to schedule sessions. Consider both in-person and virtual training options based on team availability and preferences.
3. Allocate Time for Training: Block out specific time slots in the project schedule for training sessions. Ensure that these time slots do not overlap with critical project milestones or deadlines.
4. Account for Holidays: Identify public holidays and team-specific holidays (if applicable) during the project duration. Adjust the project timeline accordingly to account for potential decreases in productivity during holiday periods.
5. Plan Around Individual Education Schedules: Gather information about individual team members' education schedules, such as classes or exams. Coordinate with team members to understand their availability and any potential conflicts with project timelines.
6. Flexible Resource Allocation: Incorporate flexibility into resource allocation to accommodate individual schedules. Assign tasks and responsibilities with an understanding of each team member's availability due to training or education commitments.
7. Communication and Collaboration: Maintain open communication channels with team members to ensure that training and education schedules are effectively integrated into the project plan. Encourage team members to proactively communicate any scheduling conflicts or concerns.
8. Regular Review and Adjustment: Regularly review the project plan to assess progress and make any necessary adjustments to accommodate changes in training schedules, holidays, or individual commitments.
9. Documentation and Tracking: Document all training sessions, holidays, and individual education schedules in the project plan or a centralized calendar. Use project management tools or software to track progress and ensure that everyone stays informed.
10. Contingency Planning: Develop contingency plans to address unexpected disruptions caused by training schedules, holidays, or individual commitments. Identify backup resources or adjust timelines as needed to mitigate risks to the project schedule.

By incorporating these steps into the project planning process, you can effectively manage training, holidays, and individual education schedules while ensuring that project timelines are met and resources are utilized efficiently.

4.13. How do you spread a task that occurs throughout the project requiring little time and effort, such as status meetings?

Spreading out tasks that occur throughout a project, such as status meetings, can help manage time and effort effectively. Duration would be set for the entire length of the project. Work effort would be listed as a small percentage of days. Everyone assigned to the task would have an extremely low percentage of time dedicated to the task. Here are some strategies to consider:

1. Regular Schedule: Set a regular schedule for these tasks, such as holding status meetings every Monday morning or every other day. This consistency helps team members anticipate and prepare for these activities.

2. Shorter Duration: Keep these tasks brief and focused. For example, limit status meetings to 15-30 minutes to ensure they do not consume too much time. This also helps maintain everyone's attention and engagement.
3. Delegate Responsibility: Rotate the responsibility for leading these tasks among team members. This not only lightens the load on any single individual but also provides opportunities for skill development and engagement.
4. Automation: Where possible, automate routine aspects of these tasks. For example, use project management software to automatically send out meeting reminders or generate status reports, reducing the manual effort required.
5. Combine Tasks: Look for opportunities to combine similar tasks to minimize interruptions and streamline workflow. For instance, if team members are already meeting to discuss project updates, consider addressing other related topics during the same meeting to avoid scheduling multiple sessions.
6. Optimize Communication Channels: Utilize efficient communication channels, such as email updates or dedicated project management platforms, to convey information that does not necessarily require synchronous meetings. Reserve in-person or virtual meetings for discussions that truly benefit from real-time interaction.
7. Continuous Improvement: Regularly review the effectiveness of these tasks and seek feedback from team members on how they can be optimized further. Continuous improvement ensures that time and effort are utilized efficiently throughout the project lifecycle.

By implementing these strategies, you can effectively spread out tasks like status meetings throughout the project, minimizing the time and effort required while still ensuring effective communication and coordination among team members.

4.14. What value does metrics add to the project?

Effective utilization of metrics can significantly enhance project development processes. They offer a consistent means of gauging complexity and effort, thereby aiding in the creation of comprehensive project plans. Moreover, metric results serve as invaluable historical data, enabling teams to discern development trends' impacts. Consequently, software metrics play a pivotal role in facilitating the creation of superior software solutions. Nevertheless, it is advisable to have a three-year historical perspective.

Mismanagement or misuse of metrics can yield adverse consequences. It is imperative to incorporate them judiciously into project planning and gather statistical data throughout various project stages. Such data provides invaluable insights for planning future projects or phases. Inappropriate utilization of metrics, such as evaluating individual performance, can be counterproductive.

Metrics add significant value to a project in several ways:

1. Objective Evaluation: Metrics provide an objective way to evaluate the progress and success of a project. Instead of relying solely on subjective assessments, metrics offer quantifiable data that can be used to gauge performance.
2. Performance Monitoring: Metrics allow project managers and stakeholders to monitor performance in real-time or over specific intervals. This monitoring helps identify issues early on, enabling timely adjustments and interventions to keep the project on track.
3. Identifying Trends: By analyzing trends in metrics over time, patterns and tendencies within the project can be identified. This allows for proactive measures to address emerging issues or capitalize on positive developments.
4. Data-Driven Decision Making: Metrics provide the data necessary for informed decision-making. Whether it is allocating resources, adjusting timelines, or changing strategies, having reliable

metrics ensures decisions are based on concrete evidence rather than guesswork.

5. Communication and Transparency: Metrics serve as a common language for project teams and stakeholders. They facilitate communication by providing a clear picture of project status and progress. Transparency is enhanced when everyone has access to the same set of metrics, fostering trust and collaboration.
6. Continuous Improvement: Metrics help drive continuous improvement by highlighting areas for optimization and efficiency gains. By identifying bottlenecks, inefficiencies, or areas of underperformance, teams can focus their efforts on making targeted improvements.
7. Alignment with Goals: Metrics ensure that the project remains aligned with its goals and objectives. By regularly assessing progress against predefined metrics, teams can ensure that their efforts are contributing to the desired outcomes.

In summary, metrics play a crucial role in enhancing project management by providing objective evaluation, enabling performance monitoring, identifying trends, facilitating data-driven decision-making, promoting communication and transparency, driving continuous improvement, and ensuring alignment with project goals.

4.15. How would you incorporate the use of a new technology into a project plan?

Incorporating a new technology into a project plan involves careful consideration and integration at various stages of the project lifecycle. Add tasks for training as well as expanding the work effort and lowering each individual's unit of work. Add extra prototypes and checkpoints (milestones) in evaluating the impact of the new technology on the development effort. Here is a step-by-step approach:

1. Identify Needs and Goals: Begin by identifying the specific needs and goals of the project. Understand the challenges you are facing and the objectives you aim to achieve. Determine how the new technology can address these needs and contribute to the success of the project.
2. Technology Assessment: Conduct a thorough assessment of the new technology. Evaluate its features, functionalities, compatibility with existing systems, scalability, security considerations, and potential impact on the project timeline and budget. Consider consulting with experts or conducting pilot tests to gather more insights.
3. Integration Strategy: Develop a clear integration strategy for incorporating the new technology into the project plan. Define how the technology will be implemented, including any modifications to existing processes, infrastructure requirements, and dependencies on other project components.
4. Resource Planning: Determine the resources required for implementing the new technology, including personnel, hardware, software, and training. Allocate sufficient time and budget for procurement, installation, configuration, and testing of the technology.
5. Risk Management: Identify potential risks associated with the adoption of the new technology and develop mitigation strategies. This may include risks related to technical issues, data security, vendor reliability, and changes in project scope. Implement measures to minimize these risks and ensure project continuity.
6. Stakeholder Engagement: Engage relevant stakeholders throughout the process of incorporating the new technology into the project plan. Communicate the benefits, risks, and implications of the technology adoption, and solicit feedback to ensure alignment with project objectives and stakeholder expectations.
7. Training and Change Management: Provide comprehensive training and support to project team members who will be using the new technology. Ensure they have the necessary skills and knowledge to effectively leverage the technology to achieve project goals. Implement change management strategies to address any resistance or concerns among team members.
8. Monitoring and Evaluation: Establish key performance indicators (KPIs) to monitor the performance and impact of the new technology on the project. Continuously evaluate its

effectiveness, efficiency, and alignment with project objectives. Use feedback from stakeholders and project metrics to make adjustments and improvements as needed.
9. Documentation and Knowledge Sharing: Document the implementation process, lessons learned, best practices, and troubleshooting guidelines related to the new technology. Foster knowledge sharing among project team members to facilitate ongoing support and collaboration.
10. Continuous Improvement: Foster a culture of continuous improvement by actively seeking opportunities to optimize the use of the new technology throughout the project lifecycle. Stay informed about updates, upgrades, and emerging trends in technology that may further enhance project outcomes.

By following these steps, you can effectively incorporate the use of a new technology into your project plan, enabling you to leverage its benefits and achieve successful project outcomes.

4.16. How are actuals supplied to a project plan and what is the value of comparing the original estimates to actuals?

Actuals are supplied to a project plan by recording the real-time progress, costs, and resources utilized during the execution phase of the project. This data is typically collected through various means such as timesheets, expense reports, task completion reports, and other tracking mechanisms.

Comparing the original estimates to actuals provides several valuable insights:

1. Performance Evaluation: It allows project managers to evaluate the performance of the project against the initial estimates. By comparing planned vs. actual timelines, costs, and resource allocations, they can identify areas where the project is ahead or behind schedule, over or under budget, and whether resources are being utilized efficiently.
2. Variance Analysis: Analyzing the differences between estimated and actual values helps in identifying deviations or variances. This analysis enables project managers to understand the reasons behind these discrepancies, whether they are due to inaccurate estimation, unforeseen circumstances, resource constraints, or other factors.
3. Decision Making: The comparison of estimates to actuals aids in making informed decisions regarding project adjustments. It allows project managers to reallocate resources, revise timelines, adjust budgets, or implement corrective actions to keep the project on track and within the desired parameters.
4. Improvement Opportunities: By understanding where the estimates were inaccurate and why, project teams can learn from their experiences and improve their estimation processes for future projects. This continuous improvement cycle helps in enhancing project management practices and increasing the accuracy of future estimates.

Overall, comparing actuals to original estimates is essential for maintaining project control, optimizing performance, and achieving project success. It enables project managers to proactively manage risks, mitigate issues, and deliver projects within the defined scope, schedule, and budget

4.17. Describe what development project life cycle phases, activities, and deliverables you would include in a project plan for a software application product.

Creating a project plan for a software application involves several key phases, activities, and deliverables to ensure a successful development process. Here is a breakdown:

1. Initiation Phase:
    a. Activities: Identify the project scope, objectives, stakeholders, and initial requirements.
    b. Deliverables: Project charter, preliminary requirements document, stakeholder analysis.
2. Planning Phase:

    a. Activities: Define project scope in detail, create a work breakdown structure (WBS), identify resources, estimate costs and timelines, and define risk management strategies.
    b. Deliverables: Project plan, WBS, resource plan, cost estimation, risk management plan, communication plan.
3. Analysis Phase:
    a. Activities: Gather and analyze detailed requirements from stakeholders, create use cases, develop prototypes if necessary.
    b. Deliverables: Detailed requirements document, use cases, user stories, prototype (if applicable).
4. Design Phase:
    a. Activities: Design system architecture, database schema, user interface, and detailed technical specifications.
    b. Deliverables: System architecture diagram, database schema, UI wireframes/mockups, technical design document.
5. Development Phase:
    a. Activities: Write code, perform unit testing, integrate components, and ensure adherence to design specifications.
    b. Deliverables: Working software modules, code documentation, unit test reports.
6. Testing Phase:
    a. Activities: Conduct various testing types such as unit testing, integration testing, system testing, and user acceptance testing (UAT).
    b. Deliverables: Test cases, test results, defect reports, UAT sign-off.
7. Deployment Phase:
    a. Activities: Prepare for deployment, configure production environment, perform deployment, and provide user training if necessary.
    b. Deliverables: Deployment plan, production-ready software, user manuals or documentation.
8. Operations and Maintenance Phase:
    a. Activities: Provide ongoing support, perform maintenance tasks, address user feedback, and implement updates or patches.
    b. Deliverables: Support documentation, bug fixes, software updates.

Throughout the project, it is crucial to have regular reviews, status updates, and communication channels established to ensure alignment with stakeholders and mitigate risks. Additionally, a change management process should be in place to handle any modifications to requirements or scope.

4.18. What are the most important considerations in planning a major capital project?

Planning a major capital project involves numerous considerations, and their importance can vary depending on the specific project and context. However, in general, the following considerations are often ranked in decreasing order of importance:

1. Financial Viability and Budgeting: Ensuring the project is financially feasible and fits within the allocated budget is paramount. This includes accurately estimating costs, securing funding, and forecasting potential financial risks and contingencies.
2. Risk Management: Identifying and mitigating risks that could derail the project is crucial. This involves assessing various types of risks such as financial, technical, regulatory, environmental, and operational risks, and developing strategies to minimize their impact.
3. Stakeholder Engagement and Communication: Engaging with stakeholders, including government entities, communities, investors, employees, and suppliers, is essential for garnering support, managing expectations, and addressing concerns throughout the project lifecycle.

4. Project Scope and Objectives: Clearly defining the project scope, objectives, and deliverables helps ensure alignment with organizational goals and prevents scope creep. This involves outlining specific tasks, timelines, milestones, and performance metrics.
5. Resource Management: Efficiently managing resources such as manpower, materials, equipment, and technology is critical for achieving project success within schedule and budget constraints. This includes optimizing resource allocation, procurement, and utilization.
6. Regulatory Compliance and Permitting: Adhering to relevant laws, regulations, codes, and permitting requirements is essential for avoiding legal issues, fines, and delays. This involves obtaining necessary permits, approvals, and licenses from regulatory authorities.
7. Quality Assurance and Control: Implementing robust quality assurance and control processes ensures that the project meets specified standards, specifications, and customer requirements. This includes conducting inspections, testing, and audits at various stages of the project.
8. Procurement and Contract Management: Selecting the right vendors, subcontractors, and suppliers through a transparent and competitive procurement process is vital. Effective contract management also involves negotiating terms, monitoring performance, and resolving disputes.
9. Scheduling and Time Management: Developing a realistic project schedule, timeline, and critical path analysis is essential for managing deadlines, dependencies, and resource allocation efficiently. This includes identifying potential scheduling conflicts and implementing strategies to mitigate them.
10. Environmental and Sustainability Considerations: Incorporating environmentally sustainable practices and minimizing the project's ecological footprint are increasingly important considerations. This involves assessing environmental impacts, implementing mitigation measures, and promoting sustainable practices.
11. Health and Safety: Ensuring the health and safety of workers, contractors, and the public is paramount. This includes implementing robust safety protocols, providing training, conducting risk assessments, and maintaining a safe work environment.
12. Change Management: Anticipating and managing changes to project scope, requirements, or objectives is essential for adapting to evolving circumstances and minimizing disruptions. This involves establishing change control processes and communicating effectively with stakeholders.

While these considerations are typically ranked in decreasing order of importance, the relative significance of each may vary depending on the nature, scale, and complexity of the capital project. Additionally, effective project management involves integrating these considerations holistically to optimize project outcomes.

4.19. How do you use data to make project decisions?

Using data to make project decisions involves a systematic and analytical approach. Here are the general steps you can follow:

1. Define project objectives: Clearly define the goals and objectives of your project. What outcomes do you want to achieve? This clarity will guide your data collection and analysis efforts.
2. Identify relevant data: Determine the types of data that are relevant to your project objectives. This may include internal data (e.g., project metrics, customer feedback, sales data) and external data (e.g., market research, industry benchmarks, competitor analysis).
3. Collect and organize data: Gather the necessary data from various sources. This may involve conducting surveys, interviews, or experiments, or accessing existing data repositories. Ensure that the data is accurate, reliable, and representative of the project's scope.
4. Clean and preprocess data: Data often requires cleaning and preprocessing to remove errors, duplicates, or outliers, and to transform it into a consistent format. This step is crucial for ensuring the quality and integrity of the data.
5. Analyze data: Apply appropriate analytical techniques to extract insights from the data. This can

involve descriptive statistics, data visualization, regression analysis, machine learning algorithms, or other statistical methods, depending on the nature of your project and the questions you want to answer.

6. Interpret the results: Examine the findings from your data analysis and interpret them in the context of your project objectives. Identify patterns, trends, correlations, or causal relationships that can inform your decision-making process.
7. Make informed decisions: Use the insights gained from data analysis to inform your project decisions. Consider the implications of the data in relation to your objectives, risks, constraints, and other relevant factors. Data should not be the sole basis for decision-making, but it should be a valuable input in conjunction with domain expertise and other qualitative considerations.
8. Monitor and iterate: Continuously monitor the outcomes of your decisions and assess their impact on the project. Track relevant metrics and compare them against your initial objectives. If necessary, iterate and refine your decisions based on new data or changing circumstances.

Remember that data is a tool for decision-making, and it should be used in conjunction with other sources of information and expertise. Contextual understanding, critical thinking, and domain knowledge play crucial roles in effectively using data to make project decisions.

4.20. What is the purpose of the project plan memorandum?

A project plan memorandum serves several purposes:

1. Communication: It provides a formal document that communicates the details of a project plan to stakeholders, team members, and other relevant parties. It ensures that everyone involved in the project understands the objectives, scope, timelines, responsibilities, and resources required.
2. Documentation: It serves as a record of the project plan. Having a written document helps in tracking progress, making revisions, and referring back to initial agreements or decisions throughout the project lifecycle.
3. Alignment: It helps in aligning the project team and stakeholders towards common goals and objectives. By clearly outlining the project plan, it reduces misunderstandings and ensures that everyone is working towards the same vision.
4. Risk Management: It allows for the identification and mitigation of risks associated with the project. By documenting potential risks and outlining strategies to address them, the project plan memorandum helps in minimizing the impact of unforeseen events on project outcomes.
5. Resource Allocation: It facilitates the allocation of resources such as budget, personnel, and equipment. By outlining resource requirements and timelines, it helps in ensuring that resources are utilized effectively and efficiently throughout the project.

Overall, the project plan memorandum serves as a roadmap for the successful execution of a project by providing clarity, direction, and accountability to all involved parties.

4.21. How do you write the project plan memorandum for the executive team and what does it look like?

Writing a project plan memorandum for the executive team involves several key steps to ensure clarity, conciseness, and relevance. Here is a general outline of what it should include and how it might be structured:

1. Header:
    a. Start with the name and logo of your company or organization.
    b. Include the title "Project Plan Memorandum" prominently.
    c. Add the date of the memorandum and any reference numbers if applicable.
2. Introduction:

a. Briefly introduce the purpose of the memorandum, which is to outline the project plan for a specific initiative.
b. Provide a concise overview of the project, its objectives, and its significance to the organization.

3. Project Overview:
    a. Provide a detailed description of the project, including its scope, goals, and expected outcomes.
    b. Explain why the project is necessary and how it aligns with the organization's strategic objectives.
4. Project Deliverables:
    a. List the specific deliverables or outcomes that the project aims to achieve.
    b. Clearly define each deliverable and explain how it contributes to the overall success of the project.
5. Timeline and Milestones:
    a. Present a timeline that outlines the key phases of the project from start to finish.
    b. Identify important milestones or checkpoints along the way.
    c. Include estimated timeframes for each phase and milestone.
6. Resource Requirements:
    a. Detail the resources needed to execute the project, including personnel, equipment, and budgetary allocations.
    b. Specify any external dependencies or constraints that may impact resource availability.
7. Risk Management:
    a. Identify potential risks and challenges that could affect the project's progress or success.
    b. Provide strategies for mitigating these risks and contingency plans for handling unforeseen issues.
8. Communication Plan:
    a. Outline how project updates and communications will be shared with stakeholders, including the executive team.
    b. Specify the frequency and format of communication, as well as the channels to be used.
9. Conclusion:
    a. Summarize the key points of the project plan memorandum.
    b. Reiterate the importance of the project and the anticipated benefits to the organization.
10. Approval Section:
    a. Provide space for the executive team members to sign off on the project plan, indicating their approval and support
11. Attachments (if applicable):
    a. Include any supplementary documents or supporting materials that provide further details on the project plan.
12. Footer:
    a. End with the contact information of the project manager or other relevant personnel for inquiries or further discussion.

The appearance of the memorandum should be professional and easy to read, with clear headings and formatting to help guide the reader through the document. Using bullet points, tables, and graphs can also enhance clarity and comprehension.

4.22. How do develop communications plan for a project and what does it look like?

Developing a communication plan for a project involves several key steps to ensure that all stakeholders are informed effectively and timely throughout the project lifecycle. Here is a general outline of how to develop a communication plan and what it typically includes:

1. Identify Stakeholders: Determine who the key stakeholders are for your project. These could include project team members, sponsors, clients, end-users, vendors, and any other individuals or groups impacted by the project.
2. Understand Communication Needs: Understand the communication needs and preferences of each stakeholder group. Some stakeholders may require frequent updates, while others may only need to be informed of major milestones.
3. Define Objectives: Clearly define the objectives of your communication plan. What do you aim to achieve through your communication efforts? This could include keeping stakeholders informed, managing expectations, resolving conflicts, etc.
4. Choose Communication Channels: Select the most appropriate communication channels for each stakeholder group. This could include emails, meetings, status reports, project management tools, newsletters, social media, etc.
5. Create a Communication Matrix: Develop a communication matrix that outlines who needs to receive what information, when, and through which channels. This matrix helps ensure that all necessary communications are planned and executed.
6. Establish Frequency and Timing: Determine how often communication should occur and when it should take place. For example, you may schedule weekly status meetings with the project team and monthly progress reports for stakeholders.
7. Craft Key Messages: Develop key messages that you want to convey to each stakeholder group. These messages should be clear, concise, and tailored to the audience's needs and interests.
8. Assign Responsibilities: Assign responsibilities for communication tasks to specific individuals or teams. Make sure everyone understands their role in the communication plan and is accountable for their contributions.
9. Plan for Feedback: Build mechanisms for collecting feedback from stakeholders and incorporate it into your communication plan. This could include surveys, feedback sessions, or regular check-ins.
10. Monitor and Adjust: Continuously monitor the effectiveness of your communication plan and be prepared to adjust it as needed. If certain channels or messages are not resonating with stakeholders, be flexible and try alternative approaches.

A typical communication plan document might include sections such as:

1. Introduction: Overview of the project and the purpose of the communication plan.
2. Stakeholder Analysis: Identification of key stakeholders and their communication needs.
3. Communication Objectives: Clear statement of what the communication plan aims to achieve.
4. Communication Channels: Description of the communication channels selected for each stakeholder group.
5. Communication Matrix: Detailed table outlining who needs to receive what information, when, and through which channels.
6. Key Messages: List of key messages to be communicated to each stakeholder group.
7. Responsibilities: Assignment of communication responsibilities to specific individuals or teams.
8. Feedback Mechanisms: Explanation of how feedback will be collected and utilized.
9. Monitoring and Evaluation: Plan for monitoring the effectiveness of the communication plan and making adjustments as necessary.

Remember, the communication plan should be a dynamic document that evolves as the project progresses and as stakeholder needs change.

4.23. How do you develop an operations integration plan?

Developing an operations integration plan involves several key steps to ensure a smooth transition and alignment of processes, systems, and teams. Here is a structured approach to creating such a plan:

1. Understand Business Objectives: Begin by clearly defining the objectives of the integration. What are the strategic goals driving this integration? Understanding this will guide the entire process.
2. Assessment of Current Operations: Conduct a thorough assessment of the existing operations of both entities involved in the integration. This includes processes, systems, workflows, organizational structures, and culture.
3. Identify Integration Points: Determine the areas where integration is necessary. This could involve supply chain, IT systems, customer service, human resources, etc.
4. Develop a Project Plan: Create a detailed project plan outlining tasks, timelines, responsibilities, and dependencies. Break down the integration process into manageable phases or milestones.
5. Communication Plan: Develop a comprehensive communication plan to keep all stakeholders informed throughout the integration process. This includes employees, customers, suppliers, and other relevant parties.
6. Risk Management: Identify potential risks and challenges associated with the integration and develop mitigation strategies. This could include IT system compatibility issues, cultural clashes, or resistance from employees.
7. Alignment of Processes and Systems: Ensure that processes and systems are aligned between the two entities. This may involve standardizing processes, integrating IT systems, or developing new workflows.
8. Change Management: Implement a change management strategy to help employees adapt to the changes brought about by the integration. Provide training and support to ensure a smooth transition.
9. Performance Measurement: Define key performance indicators (KPIs) to measure the success of the integration. Regularly monitor and evaluate performance against these metrics to identify areas for improvement.
10. Continuous Improvement: Integration is an ongoing process. Encourage a culture of continuous improvement to refine operations and maximize the benefits of the integration over time.
11. Legal and Regulatory Compliance: Ensure that the integration plan complies with relevant legal and regulatory requirements. This may involve obtaining approvals from regulatory bodies or addressing any legal issues that arise.
12. Post-Integration Review: After the integration is complete, conduct a thorough review to assess the overall success of the integration process. Identify lessons learned and areas for improvement to inform future integration efforts.

By following these steps, you can develop a comprehensive operations integration plan that aligns processes, systems, and teams effectively, ultimately driving the success of the integration.

4.24. How do you respond to a question: "Tell me about a time... You had to proceed on a project with little information, etc."

When asked about a time you had to proceed on a project with little information, it is crucial to frame your response effectively. Here is a structured approach:

1. Context: Briefly describe the project you were working on and the circumstances that led to the lack of information. Highlight the importance of the project and the challenges posed by the limited information.
2. Actions: Explain the steps you took to move forward despite the lack of information. This could include:
    a. Research: Detail how you gathered whatever information was available through research, data analysis, or consultations with relevant stakeholders.
    b. Assumptions: Discuss any assumptions you made based on the available information and how you validated or adjusted them as the project progressed.
    c. Decision-making: Describe how you made decisions under uncertainty, considering

potential risks and trade-offs.

   d. Communication: Emphasize the importance of clear and frequent communication with team members or stakeholders to manage expectations and gather insights.

3. Challenges: Acknowledge any difficulties or setbacks you encountered due to the lack of information. Highlight how you navigated these challenges and adapted your approach to mitigate risks.
4. Results: Summarize the outcomes of your actions. Highlight any successes achieved despite the initial limitations, such as meeting project deadlines, delivering quality results, or learning valuable lessons for future projects.
5. Reflection: Conclude by reflecting on what you learned from the experience. Discuss how you would approach similar situations differently in the future and any strategies you developed for handling uncertainty effectively.

By following this structure, you can provide a comprehensive and insightful response that demonstrates your ability to thrive in ambiguous situations and drive projects forward despite limited information.

4.25. How do you respond to a question: "Tell me about a time... You disagreed with the project design but had to deliver ..."

When faced with a situation like that, I believe it is crucial to balance professional disagreement with commitment to project success. I encountered a similar scenario during [describe relevant project or job experience]. While I had reservations about certain aspects of the project design, I recognized the importance of meeting deadlines and delivering results.

So, I approached the situation by first thoroughly understanding the rationale behind the project design. I engaged in constructive dialogue with team members and stakeholders to express my concerns and suggest alternative approaches. This allowed us to consider different perspectives and refine the design collaboratively.

Ultimately, I committed myself fully to executing the project according to the agreed-upon design, even if it was not my initial preference. Through effective communication and teamwork, we were able to deliver a successful outcome that met the project goals and satisfied all stakeholders.

4.26. How do you ensure that projects are delivered on time and with high quality?

Ensuring projects are delivered on time and with high quality requires a combination of effective planning, clear communication, diligent execution, and continuous monitoring. Here is a structured approach:

1. Detailed Planning: Start by outlining clear objectives, defining scope, identifying tasks, setting deadlines, and allocating resources. Develop a project plan that breaks down the work into manageable tasks with realistic timelines.
2. Resource Allocation: Ensure that you have the right people with the necessary skills assigned to each task. Optimize resource allocation to avoid bottlenecks and ensure smooth progress.
3. Clear Communication: Maintain open communication channels among team members, stakeholders, and clients. Regularly update everyone on project progress, milestones achieved, and any issues or risks that arise. This fosters transparency and keeps everyone aligned.
4. Risk Management: Identify potential risks and develop mitigation strategies. Proactively address issues as they arise to prevent them from escalating and impacting project timelines or quality.
5. Quality Assurance: Implement quality control measures throughout the project lifecycle. Define quality standards and conduct regular reviews to ensure that deliverables meet these standards. Encourage feedback and iteration to continuously improve quality.

6. Monitoring and Control: Track progress against the project plan using key performance indicators (KPIs) such as schedule variance, cost variance, and quality metrics. Adjust plans as needed based on insights gained from monitoring to keep the project on track.
7. Adaptability and Flexibility: Be prepared to adapt to changing circumstances, priorities, or requirements. Agile methodologies, such as Scrum or Kanban, can be particularly useful for managing evolving projects.
8. Continuous Improvement: Conduct post-project reviews to identify lessons learned and areas for improvement. Use this feedback to refine processes and practices for future projects, fostering a culture of continuous improvement.

By following these steps and staying vigilant throughout the project lifecycle, you can increase the likelihood of delivering projects on time and with high quality.

5. Project Cost Management

Effectively managing costs within your project ranks among the most formidable challenges in project management. Finances permeate every aspect of a project, from its inception to its execution. Despite meticulous planning, projects often exceed their initial budgetary constraints, with change orders and unforeseen expenses driving up costs. The reality is that for every project that stays within budget, there are approximately fifty that surpass their financial projections. This phenomenon stems from various factors such as ambiguous requirements, inaccurate estimations, and the introduction of change orders.

As project managers, we excel in procuring resources, delegating tasks, monitoring progress, and delivering results. However, the omnipresence of costs adds layers of complexity and difficulty to our role. Ensuring precise cost estimation at the project's outset, allocating budgets across different phases, and implementing robust cost-control measures throughout the project lifecycle become imperative.

The ability to navigate financial decisions adeptly is paramount for effective project management. Those project managers who possess a profound comprehension of economic analysis and are adept at managing the financial dynamics of projects, both large and small, emerge as invaluable assets to their organizations.

5.1. How do you go about cost estimation through the life cycle of a project?

Cost estimation is a crucial aspect of project management that involves predicting the expenses associated with executing a project. It is typically performed iteratively throughout the project life cycle to ensure accurate budgeting and resource allocation. Here is a breakdown of the various cost estimation stages and how they relate to different phases of a project:

1. Initiation Phase:

   a. Preliminary Cost Estimation: During project initiation, high-level cost estimates are made based on limited information and assumptions. These estimates help stakeholders decide whether to proceed with the project.
   b. Feasibility Study: Cost estimation is used to assess the feasibility of the project by comparing estimated costs with expected benefits.
2. Planning Phase:
   a. Detailed Cost Estimation: As project requirements become clearer, detailed cost estimation is performed for each activity or work package. Various techniques such as bottom-up estimation, parametric estimation, and analogous estimation are employed.
   b. Budget Development: The detailed cost estimates are aggregated to develop a comprehensive project budget, including contingency reserves to account for uncertainties.
   c. Risk Analysis: Cost estimation is used to identify and quantify risks that could impact project costs. Contingency reserves are allocated based on the level of risk exposure.
3. Execution Phase:
   a. Cost Tracking: Actual costs are monitored and compared to the budget throughout the execution phase. Cost tracking ensures that expenses are within the approved budget and helps identify deviations that require corrective action.
   b. Resource Management: Cost estimation informs resource allocation decisions, ensuring that resources are utilized efficiently to minimize costs while meeting project objectives.
4. Monitoring and Controlling Phase:
   a. Variance Analysis: Cost variances are analyzed to understand the reasons behind deviations from the budget. This analysis helps identify areas where corrective actions are needed to bring costs back on track.
   b. Change Management: Cost estimation is used to assess the financial impact of project changes, such as scope modifications or schedule delays. Changes are evaluated against the baseline budget, and adjustments are made as necessary.
5. Closure Phase:
   a. Final Cost Analysis: At project closure, a final analysis is performed to compare actual costs against the initial estimates and budget. Any remaining funds are accounted for, and lessons learned are documented for future projects.
   b. Post-Project Review: Cost estimation performance is evaluated as part of the overall project review process, highlighting areas of improvement for future cost estimation efforts.

Throughout the life cycle, it is essential to engage relevant stakeholders, maintain transparency in cost estimation and management processes, and adapt strategies based on evolving project dynamics. Additionally, leveraging project management tools and software can streamline the estimation process and facilitate effective cost tracking and control.

5.2. What is the cost baseline?

The cost baseline in project management is a key component of the project's overall financial planning and control. It represents an approved version of the project budget that includes all planned expenses for completing the project. The cost baseline is used as a benchmark to measure and monitor the project's financial performance throughout its lifecycle.

Key Aspects of the Cost Baseline:

1. Development:
   a. Estimation: It is developed based on detailed cost estimates derived from the project's work breakdown structure (WBS). These estimates include direct and indirect costs,

contingency reserves, and sometimes management reserves.

   b. Approval: Once estimated, the cost baseline must be approved by relevant stakeholders, which may include project sponsors, project managers, and financial controllers.
2. Components:
   a. Planned Costs: It incorporates all anticipated costs, including labor, materials, equipment, and overheads.
   b. Time-phased Budget: The costs are usually spread over the project's timeline, aligning with the project's schedule to track expenses over specific periods (e.g., monthly, or quarterly).
3. Monitoring and Control:
   a. Performance Measurement: The cost baseline serves as a reference point for evaluating actual financial performance against planned costs. This comparison helps in identifying variances and taking corrective actions.
   b. Earned Value Management (EVM): Often, EVM is used in conjunction with the cost baseline to provide a comprehensive view of cost performance and project health by comparing planned value (PV), earned value (EV), and actual cost (AC).
4. Adjustments and Revisions:
   a. Change Control: Any changes to the project scope, schedule, or resources that impact the budget require formal change control processes. Adjustments to the cost baseline are made through approved changes only, ensuring all stakeholders are aware of modifications and their implications.

Importance of the Cost Baseline:

1. Financial Control: It provides a structured approach to managing the project's financial resources, ensuring expenditures align with planned budgets.
2. Performance Measurement: By establishing a baseline, project managers can measure actual progress against planned progress, facilitating proactive management and decision-making.
3. Stakeholder Communication: It offers a clear and agreed-upon financial plan that stakeholders can reference, enhancing transparency and accountability.

In summary, the cost baseline is a fundamental element in project management, forming the financial foundation upon which the project's cost performance is measured and managed. It helps in ensuring that the project stays within budget, meets financial goals, and delivers value to stakeholders.

5.3. How do you plan for and create a cost baseline in a project?

Creating a cost baseline for a project involves several key steps that ensure the project's financial planning is accurate, comprehensive, and aligned with the overall project objectives. Here is a detailed guide on how to plan for and create a cost baseline:

1. Define the Scope of the Project
   a. Scope Statement: Clearly define the project scope to understand what is included and what is not.
   b. Work Breakdown Structure (WBS): Break down the project into smaller, manageable components or deliverables.
2. Identify Resources
   a. Resource Planning: Determine the types and quantities of resources (human, material, equipment) required for each task.
   b. Resource Allocation: Allocate resources to each task based on availability and project requirements.
3. Estimate Costs
   a. Cost Estimating Techniques:

        i. Analogous Estimating: Use historical data from similar projects.
        ii. Parametric Estimating: Use statistical relationships between historical data and other variables.
        iii. Bottom-Up Estimating: Estimate costs for individual tasks and roll them up to the project level.
        iv. Three-Point Estimating: Use optimistic, pessimistic, and most likely estimates to calculate an average.
    b. Direct and Indirect Costs: Include both direct costs (labor, materials) and indirect costs (overhead, administrative expenses).
4. Develop the Budget
    a. Cost Aggregation: Aggregate estimated costs for individual tasks to develop a total project cost.
    b. Contingency Reserves: Add contingency reserves for identified risks.
    c. Management Reserves: Set aside management reserves for unforeseen changes.
5. Create the Cost Baseline
    a. Time-Phased Budget: Spread the budget over the project timeline based on when costs are expected to be incurred.
    b. Approval Process: Obtain approval from stakeholders and sponsors to finalize the cost baseline.
6. Implement the Cost Baseline
    a. Cost Baseline Integration: Integrate the approved cost baseline into the project management plan.
    b. Monitoring and Control: Regularly compare actual expenditures against the cost baseline to identify variances.
7. Monitor and Control Costs
    a. Earned Value Management (EVM): Use EVM techniques to measure project performance and progress.
        i. Planned Value (PV): The authorized budget assigned to scheduled work.
        ii. Earned Value (EV): The value of work actually performed.
        iii. Actual Cost (AC): The actual costs incurred for work performed.
    b. Variance Analysis: Analyze cost variances to understand deviations from the cost baseline.
        i. Cost Variance (CV): EV - AC
        ii. Schedule Variance (SV): EV - PV
        iii. Cost Performance Index (CPI): EV / AC
        iv. Schedule Performance Index (SPI): EV / PV
8. Update and Re-baseline (if necessary)
    a. Change Control Process: Use a formal change control process to manage changes to the cost baseline.
    b. Re-baseline: If significant changes occur, update the cost baseline to reflect new estimates and budgets.

Tools and Techniques

1. Project Management Software: Use software like Microsoft Project, Primavera, or similar tools for cost estimation, budgeting, and tracking.
2. Spreadsheets: Utilize spreadsheets for detailed cost analysis and aggregation.
3. Expert Judgment: Leverage expertise from experienced team members or consultants for accurate cost estimation and risk assessment.

By following these steps, you can create a well-defined cost baseline that serves as a benchmark for project financial performance, helping to ensure the project is completed within the approved budget.

Regular monitoring and control are crucial to manage any deviations and make necessary adjustments to keep the project on track financially.

5.4. Why should we be concerned with cost budgeting or setting the cost baseline for a project?

Cost budgeting and setting the cost baseline for a project are crucial for several reasons, all of which contribute to the overall success and efficiency of the project. Here are the key reasons why these processes are important:

1. Financial Control and Oversight:
    a. Predictability: Establishing a cost baseline provides a reference point against which actual project performance can be measured. This helps in predicting future expenditures and identifying potential overruns early.
    b. Monitoring and Controlling Costs: By setting a budget, project managers can regularly compare actual costs against the budgeted costs to ensure that the project is on track financially. This enables timely corrective actions if the project starts to deviate from the plan.
2. Resource Allocation:
    a. Efficient Use of Resources: Budgeting helps in allocating financial resources efficiently across various project activities. This ensures that critical tasks receive adequate funding while avoiding overallocation or underutilization of funds.
3. Stakeholder Communication and Confidence:
    a. Transparency: A well-defined cost baseline enhances transparency with stakeholders, providing a clear picture of how funds will be spent and what the financial expectations are. This builds trust and confidence among stakeholders, including investors, sponsors, and team members.
    b. Decision-Making: It aids in making informed decisions by providing a clear financial framework within which the project operates. Stakeholders can make better choices regarding scope changes, additional investments, or contingency plans based on the established budget.
4. Risk Management:
    a. Identifying Financial Risks: Budgeting helps identify potential financial risks early in the project. Understanding these risks allows for the development of mitigation strategies and contingency plans to manage cost-related uncertainties.
    b. Contingency Planning: A robust cost baseline includes contingencies for unexpected expenses, ensuring that the project can handle unforeseen financial challenges without derailing.
5. Performance Measurement:
    a. Benchmarking: The cost baseline serves as a benchmark for measuring project performance. Key performance indicators (KPIs) related to cost, such as Cost Performance Index (CPI) and Earned Value Management (EVM), rely on the cost baseline to assess the efficiency and progress of the project.
    b. Evaluation: Post-project evaluation of financial performance against the budget helps in understanding what worked well and what did not, providing valuable lessons for future projects.
6. Legal and Compliance Requirements:
    a. Contractual Obligations: Many projects involve contractual agreements that specify budget constraints and financial obligations. Adhering to a cost baseline ensures compliance with these contractual terms, reducing the risk of legal disputes.
    b. Regulatory Compliance: Certain industries have regulatory requirements related to financial reporting and accountability. Proper cost budgeting ensures adherence to these

regulations.

In summary, cost budgeting and setting a cost baseline are fundamental to project management as they provide a structured approach to managing financial resources, ensure transparency and accountability, support informed decision-making, facilitate risk management, and enable effective performance measurement. All these factors contribute to the successful delivery of the project within the allocated budget.

5.5. What are the key elements to include in your cost management plan, what kind of information should be in each section, and how to do it?

Creating a comprehensive cost management plan is crucial for ensuring that a project stays within budget and achieves its financial goals. Here are the key elements to include in your cost management plan, along with the kind of information that should be in each section:

1. Introduction and Overview:
    a. Brief overview of the project.
    b. Objectives of the cost management plan.
    c. Scope of the plan.
2. Roles and Responsibilities:
    a. Define who will be responsible for cost management.
    b. Roles of project manager, finance team, procurement team, etc.
    c. Communication channels for cost-related issues.
3. Cost Estimation:
    a. Methods and techniques used for estimating costs.
    b. Detailed breakdown of cost categories (labor, materials, equipment, etc.).
    c. Assumptions made during the estimation process.
4. Budget Allocation:
    a. Total project budget.
    b. Budget allocation for different phases or tasks.
    c. Contingency reserves and how they will be managed.
5. Cost Control Procedures:
    a. Processes for tracking and monitoring costs.
    b. Tools and software to be used for cost control.
    c. Frequency of cost reporting (weekly, monthly, etc.).
    d. Thresholds for cost variances and escalation procedures.
6. Change Management:
    a. Procedures for managing changes that affect project costs.
    b. Approval process for change requests.
    c. Impact assessment of proposed changes on the budget.
7. Risk Management:
    a. Identification of potential cost-related risks.
    b. Mitigation strategies for managing cost risks.
    c. Contingency plans for unforeseen cost overruns.
8. Reporting and Documentation:
    a. Formats for cost reports.
    b. Documentation requirements for cost-related decisions.
    c. Archiving procedures for historical cost data.
9. Cost Baseline and Performance Measurement:
    a. Establishing a baseline for comparing actual costs against planned costs.
    b. Key performance indicators (KPIs) for measuring cost performance.
    c. Earned Value Management (EVM) metrics if applicable.

10. Quality Assurance:
    a. Ensuring that cost management processes align with quality standards.
    b. Reviews and audits to validate cost data accuracy.
    c. Continuous improvement initiatives for cost management practices.

When developing each section, it is essential to involve key stakeholders and subject matter experts to ensure accuracy and relevance. Additionally, the plan should be flexible enough to accommodate changes throughout the project lifecycle while maintaining a focus on controlling costs effectively. Regular reviews and updates to the cost management plan are also necessary to adapt to evolving project requirements and circumstances.

5.6. What is the most difficult aspect of controlling project costs?

Controlling project costs involves several challenges, and their importance can vary depending on the project's nature and scope. However, here are some of the most difficult aspects in decreasing order of importance:

1. Scope Management: Ensuring that the project stays within its defined scope is crucial for cost control. Scope creep, where additional features or requirements are added without proper evaluation, can lead to cost overruns.
2. Resource Allocation and Costs: Efficiently allocating resources such as labor, materials, and equipment is essential for controlling costs. Mismanagement or underestimation of resource needs can result in budgetary issues.
3. Risk Management: Identifying and mitigating risks that could impact project costs is challenging but necessary. Failure to anticipate and address potential risks can lead to unexpected expenses.
4. Vendor Management: Dealing with external vendors or suppliers adds complexity to cost control. Negotiating contracts, monitoring vendor performance, and ensuring adherence to budgetary constraints are critical tasks.
5. Time Management: Delays in project timelines can have significant cost implications. Efficiently managing schedules and minimizing disruptions are essential for cost control.
6. Quality Management: Balancing quality requirements with cost constraints is often challenging. Cutting corners to save money can lead to rework or customer dissatisfaction, ultimately impacting project costs.
7. Communication: Effective communication among project stakeholders is vital for cost control. Misunderstandings or lack of communication can lead to budgetary discrepancies and hinder the ability to address cost related issues promptly.
8. Change Management: Handling changes to project requirements or objectives can disrupt cost estimates and budgets. Implementing effective change management processes is essential for minimizing cost impacts.
9. Monitoring and Control: Continuously monitoring project performance against cost baselines and implementing corrective actions as needed is critical. Without robust monitoring and control mechanisms, cost overruns may go unnoticed until it is too late to address them effectively.

Addressing these challenges requires a combination of thorough planning, diligent execution, and proactive risk management throughout the project lifecycle.

5.7. What steps companies can take to optimize the efficiency of its business processes?

Optimizing efficiency in business processes involves a variety of strategies. Here are some steps companies can take, listed in decreasing order of importance:

1. Process Analysis and Documentation: Begin by thoroughly analyzing existing processes to

identify inefficiencies, redundancies, and bottlenecks. Document each step involved in the process to gain a clear understanding of how it operates.
2. Automation and Technology Integration: Implement automation tools and integrate appropriate technologies to streamline repetitive tasks and reduce manual errors. This could include using workflow automation software, AI-driven systems, or robotic process automation (RPA).
3. Standardization: Standardize processes wherever possible to establish consistency and efficiency across departments and teams. This involves defining best practices, creating templates, and enforcing standardized procedures.
4. Training and Skill Development: Invest in training programs to ensure employees have the necessary skills and knowledge to perform their tasks efficiently. Continuous learning opportunities can help employees adapt to new technologies and optimize their workflow.
5. Performance Monitoring and KPIs: Establish key performance indicators (KPIs) to track the effectiveness of business processes. Regularly monitor performance metrics and use data-driven insights to identify areas for improvement and measure success.
6. Cross-Functional Collaboration: Foster collaboration between different departments and teams to streamline communication and coordination. Encourage cross-functional teams to work together towards common goals and share insights for process improvement.
7. Customer-Centric Approach: Prioritize customer needs and satisfaction when designing and optimizing business processes. By aligning processes with customer expectations, companies can improve customer experience and loyalty while driving efficiency.
8. Continuous Improvement Culture: Cultivate a culture of continuous improvement where employees are encouraged to identify and propose enhancements to existing processes. Implement feedback mechanisms and regularly review processes to incorporate improvements.
9. Outsourcing and Offshoring: Evaluate opportunities for outsourcing non-core or resource-intensive tasks to external vendors or offshoring to locations with lower labor costs. This can free up internal resources and improve overall efficiency.
10. Risk Management and Compliance: Ensure that business processes are designed to comply with relevant regulations and mitigate potential risks. Incorporate risk management practices into process design and regularly assess compliance to avoid costly errors or penalties.

Prioritizing these steps can vary depending on the nature of the business and its specific challenges. However, focusing on process analysis, automation, standardization, and continuous improvement tends to yield significant efficiency gains across industries.

5.8. What are some of the tips on managing and reducing project costs?

Managing project costs presents one of the most formidable challenges in project management. While we excel at securing resources, delegating tasks, monitoring progress, and finalizing projects, the omnipresence of costs adds layers of complexity and difficulty to our role. Precise cost estimation at project inception, allocation of budgets across different project components, and the ability to wield cost-control tools throughout the project lifecycle are all essential facets of our responsibility.

Managing and reducing project costs is crucial for ensuring the success and profitability of a project. Here are some tips to help you achieve this:

1. Create a Detailed Budget: Develop a comprehensive budget that includes all project expenses, from labor and materials to overhead costs and contingencies. Ensure that it is realistic and accounts for potential fluctuations.
2. Identify Cost Drivers: Analyze the factors that contribute most significantly to project costs. By understanding the key cost drivers, you can focus your efforts on managing those areas more effectively.
3. Prioritize Requirements: Work with stakeholders to prioritize project requirements based on their

importance and impact on the overall project goals. Focus resources on high-priority items and consider deferring or eliminating low-priority features. Match costs and benefits and link them to objectives and deliverables.

4. Use Cost Estimation Techniques: Employ various cost estimation techniques such as bottom-up estimating, analogous estimating, and parametric estimating to forecast project costs accurately. Regularly revisit and update cost estimates as the project progresses.
5. Optimize Resource Allocation: Efficiently allocate resources such as labor, equipment, and materials to minimize waste and maximize productivity. Consider outsourcing certain tasks or using flexible staffing arrangements to better match resource availability with project demands.
6. Monitor and Control Expenses: Implement robust monitoring and control mechanisms to track project expenses against the budget in real-time. Identify cost variances early and take corrective actions promptly to prevent budget overruns.
7. Negotiate Contracts: Negotiate favorable terms with suppliers, contractors, and vendors to secure competitive pricing and favorable payment terms. Explore opportunities for volume discounts or long-term agreements to reduce costs further. Consider lower cost alternatives.
8. Manage Scope Creep: Define project scope clearly and manage scope creep effectively by addressing changes promptly through formal change control processes. Avoid unnecessary scope changes that can drive up costs and extend the project timeline. Reduce scope where little added value is evident. Enforce tight discipline and adherence to agreed change and risk management approach.
9. Improve Efficiency: Streamline processes and workflows to improve efficiency and productivity across the project lifecycle. Eliminate unnecessary bureaucracy and optimize workflows to minimize delays and reduce costs.
10. Continuous Improvement: Encourage a culture of continuous improvement within the project team by soliciting feedback, analyzing performance metrics, and implementing lessons learned from past projects. Identify opportunities to refine processes and reduce costs for future projects.
11. Automation: Use project and resource management software that provides resource availability and task completion alerts/triggers; escalation filters and root cause analysis (RCA); and exception reporting on tasks not started, not progressing, and/or escalated

By implementing these tips effectively, you can better manage and reduce project costs while delivering value to stakeholders and achieving project objectives.

5.9. Why do we need to have two separate reserves like the contingency reserve and the management reserve set up to budget for risks?

Having two separate reserves - contingency reserves and management reserves - helps organizations effectively manage and budget for risks in projects. Each reserve serves a distinct purpose and addresses different types of uncertainties, providing a more structured and comprehensive risk management approach. Here is a detailed explanation of why both reserves are necessary:

1. Purpose and Scope of Each Reserve
   a. Contingency Reserve:
      i. Purpose: To cover identified risks.
      ii. Scope: These are risks that have been recognized, analyzed, and quantified. The contingency reserve is calculated based on risk assessment processes, including quantitative risk analysis.
      iii. Example: If a project involves construction, the contingency reserve might cover potential delays due to weather conditions, which have been identified as a probable risk.
   b. Management Reserve:

    i. Purpose: To cover unidentified or unforeseen risks.
    ii. Scope: These are risks that are unknown or unpredictable at the time of planning. The management reserve is not tied to specific risks but is a buffer for unexpected events or changes that cannot be anticipated.
    iii. Example: If a new regulation is suddenly introduced that affects the project, the management reserve can be used to address the additional costs or delays that were not previously anticipated.

2. Risk Management Process
    a. Contingency Reserve:
        i. Involves detailed risk identification and analysis.
        ii. Uses tools like risk registers, probability-impact matrices, and scenario analysis.
        iii. Quantifies risks based on likelihood and impact, allowing for a calculated reserve.
    b. Management Reserve:
        i. Acknowledges the presence of unknown unknowns.
        ii. Is usually determined as a percentage of the overall project budget.
        iii. Provides flexibility to deal with surprises that standard risk management processes cannot foresee.
3. Governance and Control
    a. Contingency Reserve:
        i. Typically managed by the project manager.
        ii. Its use is planned and controlled based on the occurrence of identified risks.
        iii. There is often a clear process for accessing and utilizing these funds, ensuring they are used for their intended purpose.
    b. Management Reserve:
        i. Controlled at a higher organizational level, often by senior management or project sponsors.
        ii. Its use requires approval from higher authority, ensuring that it is not depleted on minor issues and is available for significant unforeseen events.
        iii. Helps maintain strategic control and oversight over large, unexpected deviations from the plan.
4. Psychological and Practical Benefits
    a. Focused Risk Management: By separating the two reserves, teams can focus their risk management efforts more effectively. The contingency reserve allows for detailed planning and proactive management of known risks, while the management reserve provides a safety net for the unknown, reducing anxiety about unforeseen events.
    b. Budget Accuracy and Stability: Projects can be budgeted more accurately by segregating known risks and unknown risks. This segregation ensures that the project is neither over-budgeted with excessive reserves nor under-budgeted by failing to account for potential uncertainties.
    c. Enhanced Decision-Making: Clear distinction between the reserves supports better decision-making. Project managers can decide on the use of the contingency reserve based on specific risk triggers, while senior management can make strategic decisions regarding the use of the management reserve for significant unforeseen changes.

In summary, having both contingency reserves and management reserves allows for a more nuanced and effective approach to risk management. Contingency reserves address identified risks with planned responses, while management reserves provide a buffer for unforeseen risks, ensuring that projects have the flexibility and resources needed to handle uncertainties comprehensively. This dual-reserve system enhances the robustness of project planning, governance, and execution.

5.10. What is the time value of money?

The time value of money (TVM) is a financial concept that recognizes the greater benefit of receiving money now rather than an identical sum later. This principle is based on the potential earning capacity of money, which can be invested to earn interest or returns over time. Essentially, a dollar today is worth more than a dollar in the future due to its potential to generate earnings.

Key Components of Time Value of Money

1. Present Value (PV): The current worth of a future sum of money or stream of cash flows, given a specified rate of return. It discounts future amounts back to the present time.
2. Future Value (FV): The value of a current sum of money at a specified date in the future, based on an assumed rate of growth or interest.
3. Interest Rate (r): The rate at which money grows over time. This can be seen as the opportunity cost of having money now rather than later.
4. Time Period (t): The duration over which the money is invested or the loan is taken.
5. Discount Rate: The interest rate used to discount future cash flows to their present values. It reflects the opportunity cost and risk associated with the money.

Formulas Involving Time Value of Money

1. Future Value of a Single Sum: $FV = PV \times (1 + r)^t$ where PV is the present value, r is the interest rate, and t is the number of periods.
2. Present Value of a Single Sum: $PV = FV / (1 + r)^t$ where FV is the future value, r is the interest rate, and t is the number of periods.
3. Future Value of an Annuity: $FV_{annuity} = P \times ((1 + r)^t - 1) / r$ where P is the periodic payment, r is the interest rate per period, and t is the number of periods.
4. Present Value of an Annuity: $PV_{annuity} = P \times ((1 - (1 + r)^{-t}) / r$ where P is the periodic payment, r is the interest rate per period, and t is the number of periods.

Importance of Time Value of Money

1. Investment Decisions: TVM helps investors compare the value of investments that offer returns at different times.
2. Loan Amortization: It is crucial in determining the payments for mortgages and other loans, as well as understanding how interest accrues.
3. Valuation: TVM is used to value financial assets like bonds, stocks, and annuities.
4. Retirement Planning: It helps in estimating how much to save and invest to achieve financial goals for retirement.
5. Corporate Finance: Companies use TVM in capital budgeting to assess the profitability of projects.

Understanding TVM is fundamental in finance and economics because it underpins many key concepts such as interest rates, present and future value calculations, and the valuation of cash flows.

5.11. What is depreciation as relates to projects? How is it used as an accounting method? What are the different methods of depreciation?

Depreciation in the context of projects refers to the allocation of the cost of a tangible asset over its useful life. In project management and accounting, it is important to account for the wear and tear, obsolescence, or decrease in value of assets over time. Depreciation helps spread out the cost of acquiring an asset over its useful life, matching the expense to the periods in which it contributes to revenue generation.

Depreciation is used as an accounting method to accurately reflect the decrease in value of an asset over time. It allows businesses to allocate the cost of an asset as an expense in each accounting period, rather than recognizing the entire cost in the period the asset was acquired. This is essential for matching expenses with the revenue generated by the asset.

There are several methods of depreciation, each with its own set of rules and implications. Some common methods include:

1. Straight-line depreciation: This method evenly allocates the cost of the asset over its useful life. The formula for straight-line depreciation is: (Cost of asset - Salvage value) / Useful life.
2. Declining balance depreciation: Also known as accelerated depreciation, this method allocates more depreciation expense in the earlier years of the asset's life and less in later years. Commonly used rates for this method are double the straight-line rate or a percentage set by the business.
3. Units of production depreciation: This method allocates depreciation based on the actual usage or production of the asset. The formula involves dividing the depreciable cost of the asset by the total estimated units of production expected from the asset over its useful life.
4. Sum-of-the-years'-digits depreciation: This method accelerates depreciation, allocating more depreciation expense in the earlier years and less in later years. It involves using a fraction based on the sum of the years of the asset's useful life.
5. MACRS (Modified Accelerated Cost Recovery System): This method is commonly used for tax purposes in the United States. It assigns assets to specific classes and uses predetermined recovery periods and percentages to calculate depreciation.

The choice of depreciation method depends on various factors such as the nature of the asset, its expected pattern of use, regulatory requirements, and the company's financial objectives. Each method has its own impact on financial statements and tax liabilities.

5.12. What is the fundamental accounting equation?

The fundamental accounting equation is:
Assets = Liabilities + Equity

This equation forms the basis of the double-entry accounting system, which ensures that the balance sheet of a company always balances. Here is a brief explanation of each component:

1. Assets: Resources owned by the company that have economic value and can provide future benefits. Examples include cash, inventory, property, and equipment.
2. Liabilities: Obligations or debts that the company owes to external parties. Examples include loans, accounts payable, and mortgages.
3. Equity: The residual interest in the assets of the company after deducting liabilities. It represents the ownership interest of the shareholders. Examples include common stock, retained earnings, and additional paid-in capital.

The fundamental accounting equation shows that a company's resources (assets) are funded either by borrowing money (liabilities) or by using the owners' funds (equity). This relationship ensures that the balance sheet remains balanced, reflecting the true financial position of the company.

6. Project Time Management

Effective time management skills significantly impact productivity, work quality, and stress levels.

Project Time Management encompasses the procedures for scheduling project components and resources required to achieve final deliverables. This entails establishing the sequence of tasks, identifying the critical path, and defining milestones to ensure project progress within set constraints.

Prioritizing tasks based on importance is essential. Embracing strategies like "Full Warrior Mode" or "Ruthlessness" may seem more fitting for battle tactics than time management, but if daily chaos leads to frequent stress, it might be time to combat distractions, interruptions, and clutter to reclaim control of your time at work and home.

Do you:

1. Find yourself overloaded with work?
2. Feel so stretched to the limit you cannot set priorities?
3. Exhaust yourself daily without accomplishing your goals?

If you are doing more and enjoying it less, it is time to make real choices about how and when to spend your time. Take control, prioritize, and get out from under. The following questions and answers allow you to find a balance, achieve your goals and be more effective and productive.

6.1. What are dependencies?

Dependencies typically refer to the relationships or connections between different elements within a system or project. In various contexts, dependencies can take on different meanings:

1. Software Development: In software development, dependencies often refer to external libraries, modules, or packages that a piece of software relies on to function properly. For instance, if you are developing a web application using a framework like Django, Django itself becomes a dependency of your project.
2. Project Management: Dependencies in project management refer to tasks or activities that are reliant on other tasks or activities to be completed before they can start or finish. Dependencies are the links between tasks indicating which tasks have an impact on the start of other tasks. For instance, you cannot code until you have identified and understood the requirements. Identifying and managing dependencies is crucial for ensuring that projects are completed on time and within budget.
3. Data Dependencies: In data analysis or data processing, dependencies refer to the relationships between different datasets or variables. For example, in a machine learning model, certain features might be dependent on other features for accurate predictions.
4. Infrastructure: Dependencies can also refer to the relationships between different components of an infrastructure. For instance, in a network, certain devices may depend on others for connectivity or functionality.
5. Business: In a business context, dependencies can refer to the reliance of one department or team on another for resources, information, or support to accomplish tasks or goals.

In all these contexts, understanding dependencies is important for managing complexity, ensuring reliability, and facilitating effective coordination and collaboration.

6.2. What is a lag?

In various contexts, a "lag" refers to a delay or a period of time between two events or actions. Lag is elapsed time between the end of one task and the start of the dependent one. This facility allows overlaps or long stretches of time between the end of one task and the start of the other. Here are a few common uses:

1. Project Management: In project management, a lag refers to a delay or waiting period between the completion of one task and the start of another. Lags are often used to represent dependencies between tasks, indicating that the start of one task must wait for a certain amount of time after the completion of another task. For example, if Task A must be completed before Task B can start, but there is a two-day lag between the two tasks, Task B cannot start until two days after Task A is finished. Lags can be used strategically to account for factors such as resource availability, waiting for materials or information, or to align with external dependencies. They are an important aspect of project scheduling and critical path analysis.
2. Economics and Finance: In economics and finance, a lag often refers to the time delay between a cause and its effect. For example, in monetary policy, there may be a lag between when a central bank adjusts interest rates and when those changes affect the economy.
3. Statistics and Time Series Analysis: In statistics and time series analysis, a lag is a fixed amount of time by which a series of data points is shifted. This is often done to identify patterns or correlations between variables.
4. Technology and Computing: In computing, particularly in networking, a lag can refer to a delay in data transmission. It could also refer to a delay in response time, such as lag in video games, where there is a delay between the player's input and the game's reaction.
5. Environmental Science: In environmental science, lag can refer to the delay between a change in an environmental factor (like carbon emissions) and the resulting effects on the environment (like climate change).

In essence, a lag denotes a temporal delay or gap between cause and effect, action and consequence, or input and output in various fields.

6.3. What is a milestone?

In project management, a milestone is a specific point or event in a project timeline that marks a significant achievement or stage of progress. Milestones are typically used to track and monitor the project's progress, ensuring that the project stays on schedule and meets its objectives.

Key characteristics of milestones include:

1. No Duration: Unlike tasks, milestones do not have a duration. They represent a moment in time, such as the completion of a key deliverable or the approval of a phase.
2. Checkpoint: Milestones serve as checkpoints that indicate whether the project is on track. They are often associated with decision points, such as whether to proceed to the next phase of the project.
3. Key Deliverables: Milestones are usually tied to the completion of important deliverables or the achievement of significant project outcomes, like the completion of a project phase, finalization of a design, or the signing of a contract.
4. Stakeholder Communication: Milestones are often used to communicate progress to stakeholders, as they highlight the completion of critical stages in the project.

For example, in a software development project, milestones might include the completion of the requirements analysis, the end of the coding phase, the start of testing, and the final product release.

6.4. What do you mean by resource constraint?

A resource constraint refers to a limitation or restriction on the availability of resources necessary for completing a particular task, project, or goal. These constraints can include limitations on finances, time, materials, personnel, or any other essential resources. Essentially, it is a condition where the demand for resources exceeds their availability.

In project management, a resource constraint refers to limitations or restrictions on the availability of resources necessary for completing a project. A plan and schedule developed with consideration of the resources available, the level of skills of each resource, and the resource work schedule. These resources can include finances, personnel, equipment, materials, and time.

Resource constraints can arise due to various factors such as budget limitations, limited availability of skilled staff, shortage of necessary equipment or materials, or time constraints imposed by project deadlines.

Project managers must carefully plan and manage resources to ensure that the project stays within the allocated budget, meets its deadlines, and achieves its objectives despite these constraints. This often involves prioritizing tasks, allocating resources efficiently, and sometimes making trade-offs or adjustments to the project plan to accommodate resource limitations.

Here are some examples across various contexts:

1. Financial Constraints: A startup company might have limited funding, restricting its ability to hire employees, purchase equipment, or invest in marketing.
2. Time Constraints: A student may have a deadline for submitting a project, limiting the time available for research, writing, and editing.
3. Material Constraints: A construction project might face limitations in the availability of raw materials like cement, steel, or lumber, impacting the progress and quality of the construction.
4. Human Resource Constraints: A small business might struggle to grow due to a shortage of skilled employees or the inability to afford additional hires.
5. Infrastructure Constraints: A city's transportation system might be limited by the capacity of its roads, leading to congestion and delays during peak hours.
6. Technological Constraints: A software development team might face limitations in the capabilities of their programming language or development tools, affecting the features and performance of their product.
7. Natural Resource Constraints: An agricultural community might face water shortages during a drought, limiting crop yields and affecting livelihoods.
8. Regulatory Constraints: A pharmaceutical company might face restrictions on the use of certain chemicals or substances in their products, impacting their ability to manufacture and sell them.

In all these examples, the success or completion of a task or project is hindered by the limited availability of one or more essential resources. Managing resource constraints effectively often requires careful planning, prioritization, and sometimes creative problem-solving.

6.5. What is the difference between duration and work effort?

Duration and work effort are two distinct concepts commonly used in project management to measure and manage tasks. Duration is Business/Calendar Elapsed Days with no correlation to the number of persons or their effort involved. Work effort is person effort with no correlation to the number of calendar days.

For example: A one-day task for someone working 50 percent of their time will have two duration days. Two persons working full-time on a one-day task will show one duration day but a two-work day effort. Here is the difference between the two, along with examples:

1. Duration:
    a. Duration refers to the total amount of time it takes to complete a task or activity.
    b. It is measured in units of time, such as hours, days, weeks, or months.
    c. Duration does not consider the intensity or effort put into the task; it simply measures the elapsed time from the start to the completion of the task.
    d. Duration is often depicted on project schedules and timelines.
    e. Duration can be affected by factors such as resource availability, dependencies, and constraints.

    Example: Painting a room might have a duration of 3 days. Regardless of the effort or number of people involved, it will take 3 days to complete the task.
2. Work Effort:
    a. Work effort refers to the amount of labor or work required to complete a task.
    b. It is measured in units of work, such as person-hours or person-days.
    c. Work effort considers the intensity and effort exerted by individuals or teams to complete the task.
    d. It takes into account factors such as skills, productivity, and efficiency of the people performing the work.
    e. Work effort may vary depending on resource availability, skill level, and the complexity of the task.

    Example: Writing a research report might require 40 person-hours of work. This means that one person working alone would take 40 hours to complete the report, but if two people work together, they might finish it in 20 hours.

In summary, duration focuses on the total time taken to complete a task, while work effort focuses on the amount of labor or work required to accomplish the task. Understanding both concepts is essential for effective project planning and resource allocation.

6.6. What is a network diagram? What are the different kinds of network diagrams and their usage?

A network diagram is a visual representation of a network's structure, connections, and relationships between various components. It is a valuable tool in fields like computer networking, project management, and system architecture. Network diagrams help in understanding the layout of a network, identifying its components, and visualizing how data flows between them.

Here are some common types of network diagrams and their usage:

1. Network Topology Diagrams: These diagrams illustrate the physical or logical layout of a network. They show how devices such as routers, switches, servers, and endpoints are connected and the paths data takes between them. Network topology diagrams help in troubleshooting network issues, planning expansions, and understanding network architecture.
2. Logical Network Diagrams: Unlike physical topology diagrams, logical network diagrams focus on how data flows through a network regardless of physical location. They represent the network's structure in terms of IP addressing, subnets, VLANs, and routing protocols. Logical network diagrams aid in designing and configuring networks, documenting network policies, and planning security measures.
3. Wireless Network Diagrams: These diagrams depict wireless network infrastructure, including access points, routers, clients, and the connections between them. They help in planning Wi-Fi coverage, optimizing signal strength, and ensuring secure wireless communication.

4. Data Flow Diagrams (DFDs): DFDs illustrate the flow of data within a system or process. They show how data moves through different stages, processes, and storage locations within an organization's information systems. DFDs are used in software development, business analysis, and system design to understand data dependencies and improve system efficiency.
5. Unified Communications (UC) Diagrams: These diagrams depict the integration of various communication technologies like voice, video, instant messaging, and email into a single platform. UC diagrams help in designing unified communication systems, planning infrastructure requirements, and ensuring seamless communication across different channels.
6. Server Rack Diagrams: Server rack diagrams provide a visual representation of how servers, storage devices, and networking equipment are organized within server racks or cabinets. They help in optimizing rack space, planning cooling and power requirements, and documenting hardware configurations.

Each type of network diagram serves specific purposes, whether it is planning, designing, documenting, or troubleshooting network infrastructure and systems. Choosing the right type of diagram depends on the context and the information you want to convey.

6.7. What is a network diagram as relates to projects? Describe, compare and contrast "activity on arrow" network diagram and the "activity on node" network diagram. What are the various logical relationship between the activities?

A network diagram in project management is a graphical representation of the project's activities and their dependencies. It illustrates the sequence of activities, their durations, and the logical relationships between them. This visualization helps project managers and team members understand the flow of work and identify critical paths for the project.

There are two primary types of network diagrams used in project management: Activity on Arrow (AOA) and Activity on Node (AON).

1. Activity on Arrow (AOA):
   a. In AOA diagrams, activities are represented by arrows, and nodes (or circles) represent events or milestones.
   b. The arrows depict activities and are labeled with their respective durations.
   c. Nodes represent the starting and ending points of activities, as well as events such as project milestones.
   d. The arrows indicate the sequence of activities and the direction of the workflow.
2. Activity on Node (AON):
   a. In AON diagrams, activities are represented by nodes (or circles), and arrows represent dependencies between activities.
   b. Nodes represent the activities to be performed, and arrows indicate the dependencies or logical relationships between them.
   c. Unlike AOA diagrams, the nodes in AON diagrams are labeled with activity names and durations, while arrows show the sequence and dependencies.

The main difference between AOA and AON diagrams lies in how they represent activities and dependencies.

1. AOA uses arrows to represent activities and nodes for events, while AON uses nodes for activities and arrows for dependencies.
2. AON diagrams are more commonly used in practice due to their clarity and ease of understanding.

The various logical relationships between activities in project management include:

1. Finish-to-Start (FS): Activity B cannot start until Activity A is finished.
2. Start-to-Start (SS): Activity B cannot start until Activity A starts.
3. Finish-to-Finish (FF): Activity B cannot finish until Activity A finishes.
4. Start-to-Finish (SF): Activity B cannot finish until Activity A starts. (This relationship is less common and often avoided due to its complexity and ambiguity.)

AOA diagrams, as illustrated in Figure 6.7.1, were extensively used in project management before the widespread adoption of personal computers. Traditionally, entire rooms of draftsmen maintained these diagrams with paper and pencils. With the advent of personal computers, AOA diagrams became less common, giving way to AON diagrams. Today, AOA diagrams are rarely used in project management.

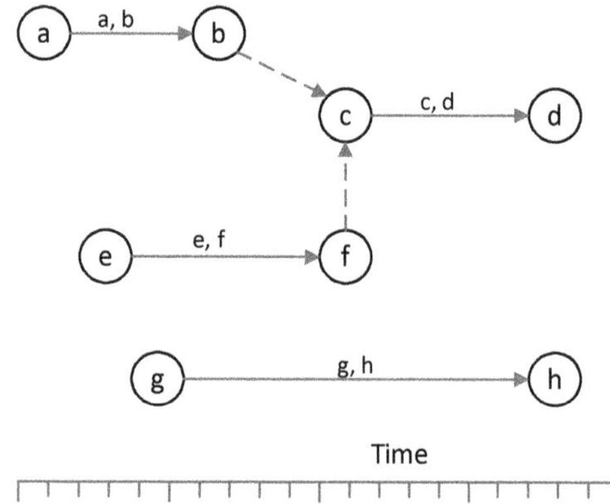

Figure 6.7.1 Activity on Arrow

In AOA diagrams, activities are placed on paper with the tail of the activity arrow at the start date and the head at the planned completion date. Circles at each end of the arrows indicate the beginning and ending events. This method does not always use a time scale, which reduces the need for "dummy" activities but also limits the graphical representation of durations, start dates, and finish dates.

Activity numbering in AOA consists of letters representing the beginning and ending events, separated by a comma. For instance, activity "a, b" is depicted by an arrow with events "a" and "b" at each end. Lowercase letters are traditionally used for event labeling.

When an activity depends on another, the tail of the dependent activity is connected to the head of the independent activity. If multiple activities depend on one, a dummy activity (a dotted or dashed arrow with zero duration) can be used.

In AON network diagrams, as shown in Figure 6.7.2, activities are written in small boxes (nodes), with arrows connecting these boxes to indicate logical relationships between activities. Circles connected by arrows denote AOA diagrams, while boxes connected by arrows denote AON diagrams.

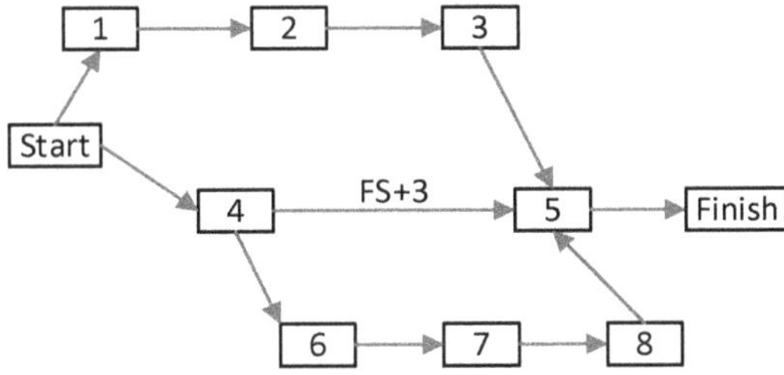

Figure 6.7.2 Activity on Node

In AON diagrams, activities are sequentially numbered. The independent activity number is called the predecessor, and the dependent activity number is the successor, with each activity having a unique number. Arrows show the logical relationships, with the most common being the "finish-start" relationship. This default relationship means the predecessor must finish before the successor can start and is often implied rather than shown explicitly.

Other relationships include "start-start" and "finish-finish." In a start-start relationship, the predecessor must start before the successor can start. In a finish-finish relationship, the predecessor must finish before the successor can finish. For example, in book writing, editing can start once some text is written but can only finish once the entire book is written.

The "start-finish" relationship is rarely used and is typically represented differently in project management software due to its unusual nature. Examples of this relationship are hard to find.

In addition to logical relationships, offsets such as "leads" and "lags" can be used. A lead is a negative offset, and a lag is a positive offset, explicitly shown in the diagram. These are illustrated in the relationship between activity 4 and activity 5 in Figure 6.7.2.

Network diagrams can optionally include special activities to mark the project's start and finish, shown as milestones with zero duration. These are useful for projects with multiple initial activities or concluding activities without successors. By assigning the start activity as the predecessor to initial activities and the finish activity as the successor to concluding activities, the project's start and finish are easily identifiable.

Understanding these relationships helps in determining the sequence of activities and managing dependencies effectively in a project.

6.8. What are the early start, early finish, late start, and late finish dates of a project schedule?

In project management, particularly in the context of the Critical Path Method (CPM), the early start (ES), early finish (EF), late start (LS), and late finish (LF) dates are essential for understanding the timing and flexibility of project activities. Here is a breakdown of each term and how they are calculated:

1. Early Start (ES): The earliest time an activity can begin without delaying the project. It is determined by the earliest finish time of its predecessor activities.
2. Early Finish (EF): The earliest time an activity can be completed. It is calculated as:
   EF = ES + Duration
   where the duration is the time required to complete the activity.
3. Late Finish (LF): The latest time an activity can be completed without delaying the project. It is determined by the latest start time of its successor activities.
4. Late Start (LS): The latest time an activity can begin without delaying the project. It is calculated

as:
LS = LF - Duration

Steps to Calculate ES, EF, LS, and LF

1. Forward Pass (for ES and EF):
    a. Start at the project start date and move forward through the network diagram.
    b. For the initial activities, the ES is typically set to 0 (or the project start date).
    c. For each subsequent activity, ES is the maximum EF of all its immediate predecessor activities.
    d. EF is then calculated as:
       EF = ES + Duration
2. Backward Pass (for LS and LF):
    a. Start at the project end date (or the maximum EF of the final activities) and move backward through the network diagram.
    b. For the final activities, LF is typically set to the project end date (or the maximum EF).
    c. For each preceding activity, LF is the minimum LS of all its immediate successor activities.
    d. LS is then calculated as:
       LS = LF - Duration

Example Calculation. Let us consider a simple project with three activities A, B, and C:

1. Activity A: Duration 3 days
2. Activity B: Duration 2 days, starts after A
3. Activity C: Duration 4 days, starts after B

Forward Pass:

1. Activity A:
    a. ES(A) = 0 (start of the project)
    b. EF(A) = ES(A) + Duration(A) = 0 + 3 = 3
2. Activity B:
    a. ES(B) = EF(A) = 3
    b. EF(B) = ES(B) + Duration(B) = 3 + 2 = 5
3. Activity C:
    a. ES(C) = EF(B) = 5
    b. EF(C) = ES(C) + Duration(C) = 5 + 4 = 9

Backward Pass:

1. Activity C:
    a. LF(C) = 9 (project end date, as there are no successors)
    b. LS(C) = LF(C) - Duration(C) = 9 - 4 = 5
2. Activity B:
    a. LF(B) = LS(C) = 5
    b. LS(B) = LF(B) - Duration(B) = 5 - 2 = 3
3. Activity A:
    a. LF(A) = LS(B) = 3
    b. LS(A) = LF(A) - Duration(A) = 3 - 3 = 0

Thus, the dates for each activity are:

1. Activity A: ES = 0, EF = 3, LS = 0, LF = 3
2. Activity B: ES = 3, EF = 5, LS = 3, LF = 5
3. Activity C: ES = 5, EF = 9, LS = 5, LF = 9

These calculations help project managers identify the critical path (the sequence of activities that determines the project duration) and the float (the amount of time an activity can be delayed without delaying the project). The activities on the critical path will have zero float, meaning their ES = LS and EF = LF.

6.9. How do I make a project schedule?

Creating a project schedule involves several steps. Here is a basic outline to guide you through the process:

1. Define the Project Scope: Clearly define the project's objectives, deliverables, and any constraints or limitations.
2. Break Down the Work: Decompose the project into smaller tasks or activities. Make sure each task is manageable and clearly defined.
3. Sequence the Tasks: Determine the order in which tasks need to be completed. Some tasks may be dependent on others, while some can be done in parallel.
4. Estimate Task Durations: Estimate the time required to complete each task. Consider factors like resources, dependencies, and potential risks.
5. Allocate Resources: Assign resources (e.g., people, equipment) to each task based on availability and skill set.
6. Create a Timeline: Use a project management tool or software to create a timeline or Gantt chart. Plot each task along the timeline based on its start and end dates.
7. Identify Milestones: Define key milestones or checkpoints in the project schedule. These are important events or deliverables that mark significant progress.
8. Consider Constraints: Take into account any constraints such as deadlines, budget limitations, or resource constraints.
9. Account for Contingencies: Build in buffer time or contingency plans to accommodate unexpected delays or issues.
10. Review and Finalize: Review the project schedule with stakeholders to ensure alignment with expectations and constraints. Make any necessary adjustments or revisions.
11. Monitor and Update: Once the project is underway, regularly monitor progress against the schedule and update it as needed to reflect any changes or deviations.

Remember, flexibility is key in project scheduling. Plans may need to be adjusted as the project progresses, so be prepared to adapt as necessary

6.10. What is float or slack in a project schedule? What are the different kinds of float? How do you calculate various floats? What concerns can arise when using various floats? Clarify using examples.

In project management, float, also known as slack, refers to the amount of time a task can be delayed without causing a delay to subsequent dependent tasks or the project's overall completion date. Float is a crucial concept in scheduling as it allows project managers to identify flexibility within the project timeline and manage resources effectively.

There are primarily three types of float:

1. Total Float (TF): Total float is the amount of time a task can be delayed without delaying the project's completion date. It represents the flexibility available within the entire project schedule. Total float is calculated as the difference between the late finish date of the activity and its early finish date, or the late start date and the early start date, whichever gives the lowest value.
   Total Float = Late Finish - Early Finish OR Late Start - Early Start

2. Free Float (FF): Free float is the amount of time a task can be delayed without delaying the start of any of its successor tasks. It measures the flexibility within a specific path of activities. Free float is calculated as the difference between the early start date of the successor task and the early finish date of the current task.
   Free Float = Early Start of Successor - Early Finish of Task
3. Project Float: Project float, also known as path float or terminal float, is the total amount of time a project can be delayed without delaying the externally imposed project completion date, such as a contractual deadline. It is calculated by identifying the difference between the externally imposed completion date and the project's critical path duration.
   Project Float = Externally Imposed Completion Date - Critical Path Duration

Concerns can arise when using floats:

1. Dependency and Risk Management: While float provides flexibility, relying too heavily on it can lead to underestimating dependencies and risks. For instance, assuming there is enough total float might result in neglecting potential delays that could impact the critical path.
2. Resource Allocation: Over-reliance on float might lead to inefficient resource allocation. For example, if a task has significant float, resources might be allocated elsewhere prematurely, resulting in resource shortages when unexpected delays occur.
3. Contractual Obligations: In projects with contractual deadlines, project float needs to be carefully managed. Failure to deliver on time despite having project float can lead to contractual penalties or damaged client relationships.

Let us illustrate these concerns with an example: Imagine a construction project where pouring concrete for the foundation has a total float of 5 days. The project manager, seeing this float, decides to delay ordering the concrete materials to conserve resources. However, unexpected weather conditions cause a 3-day delay in pouring the concrete. Despite having total float, the delay impacts the critical path, leading to an overall project delay. This situation highlights the importance of considering external factors and dependencies, rather than solely relying on float.

6.11. What is a Gantt chart?

A Gantt chart is a popular project management tool used to visualize the schedule of tasks in a project. It provides a graphical representation of a project timeline, displaying the start and finish dates of individual tasks or activities. Named after its creator, Henry Gantt, a Gantt chart typically consists of horizontal bars representing each task or activity, with the length of the bar indicating the duration of the task. These bars are arranged along a timeline, usually horizontal, which represents the overall project duration.

Each bar symbol within it holds distinct significance; for instance, critical tasks are differentiated by their bar symbol and/or color from non-critical ones, and summary tasks stand out with unique symbols.

A Gantt chart serves as a potent tool for visually presenting a project's schedule. Typically, it illustrates the breakdown of work, total duration required for tasks, and the percentage of completion. While it does not directly display the level of effort and is not solely effective for planning purposes, it can be integrated with other reporting tools to provide comprehensive project planning information. Moreover, modern Gantt charts often feature functionality to identify task relationships and dynamically adjust task attributes.

Gantt chart has become a cornerstone of project management reporting, enduring over a century, and transitioning from hand-drawn charts to digital formats ubiquitous in project management software. Its simplicity lies in a calendar along the horizontal axis and a task list along the vertical axis. Each task is represented by a bar spanning from its start date to its end date, inclusive of non-working days and any interruptions, providing a visual depiction of task durations.

The Gantt chart is invaluable for visualizing schedules, indicating when tasks commence and conclude, as well as highlighting activities in progress on any given day. Simultaneous resource requirements are readily apparent when vertical lines intersect activities. By coupling it with a resource histogram, resource utilization and scheduling can be analyzed simultaneously.

However, for comprehensive analysis of logical interdependencies between tasks, the network diagram is preferred over the Gantt chart, especially in complex schedules with numerous activities where logical connections become convoluted. Nevertheless, the Gantt chart accommodates annotations for detailed information on each activity.

Milestones, represented by symbols like diamonds or stars, can be incorporated into the Gantt chart to denote significant events with zero duration. Additionally, summary activities can be visually distinguished to prevent confusion with scheduled tasks.

Progress on activities can be indicated within the bars using proportional length, offering a visual representation of completion status. Moreover, legends can be utilized to denote various activity states such as critical, completed, or in progress.

Comparative analysis between baseline schedules and the current schedule is facilitated by plotting them on the same calendar scale within the Gantt chart, allowing for easy identification of deviations.

Overall, Gantt charts are widely used because they offer a clear and easy-to-understand visualization of project schedules. They help project managers and team members track progress, identify dependencies between tasks, allocate resources effectively, and manage timelines more efficiently. Additionally, Gantt charts can be used to communicate project plans and timelines to stakeholders, providing a comprehensive overview of the project's progress and milestones.

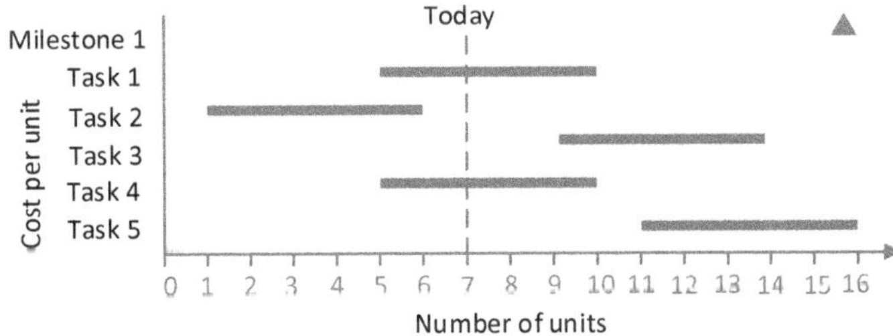

Figure 6.11.1 Gantt chart

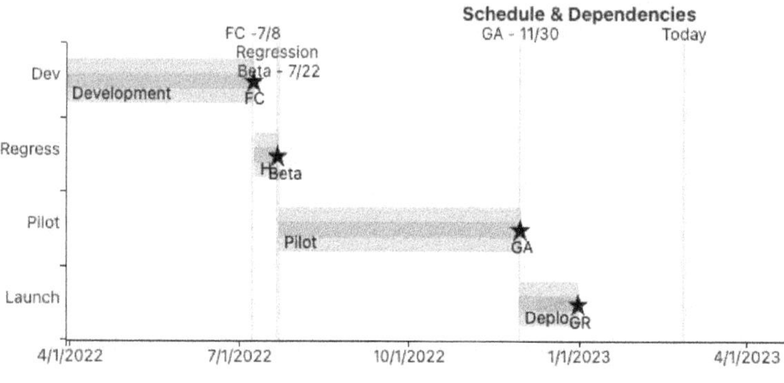

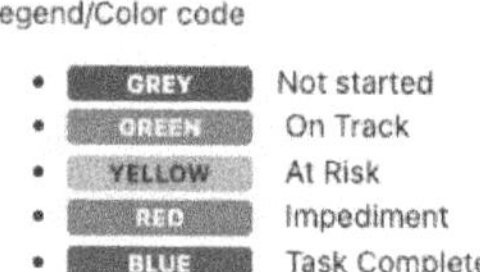

Figure 6.11.2 Gantt chart

6.12. What is a critical path?

In project management, the critical path is the sequence of tasks or activities that determines the shortest possible duration to complete a project. These are the tasks that have zero slack or float, meaning any delay in these tasks will directly delay the entire project.

Here is a breakdown of the concept:

1. Tasks on the Critical Path: These are the essential activities that must be completed on time for the whole project to stay on schedule. If any of these tasks are delayed, the project's completion date will also be delayed.
2. Slack or Float: This is the amount of time that a task can be delayed without causing a delay to subsequent tasks or the project completion date. Tasks on the critical path have zero slack.
3. Critical Path Method (CPM): This is a project management technique used to determine the critical path. By mapping out all the tasks, estimating their duration, and identifying dependencies, you can calculate the longest sequence of dependent tasks (the critical path) and the shortest time to complete the project.
4. Adjustments: If you need to shorten the project timeline, focus on tasks within the critical path by either compressing them (e.g., by adding more resources) or by overlapping tasks that can be done simultaneously (fast-tracking).

Understanding the critical path is crucial for effective project scheduling, resource allocation, and ensuring timely project completion.

6.13. What is the critical path method? How is it used in projects?

The Critical Path Method (CPM) is a project management technique used to identify the longest sequence of dependent activities in a project schedule. It helps project managers determine the shortest possible duration for completing a project.

Here is how it works:

1. Identifying tasks: First, all the tasks necessary to complete the project are identified. These tasks should be well-defined and have clear dependencies.

2. Determining dependencies: Each task is then analyzed to determine its dependencies on other tasks. Some tasks can only start once others are completed, while some can happen concurrently.
3. Estimating durations: For each task, estimates are made for how long it will take to complete. This can be done in terms of hours, days, weeks, etc., depending on the granularity of the project.
4. Constructing the network diagram: Using the information gathered in steps 1-3, a network diagram is constructed. This diagram represents the sequence of tasks and their dependencies.
5. Calculating the critical path: Once the network diagram is constructed, the critical path is determined. The critical path is the longest path through the network, meaning it represents the sequence of tasks that will take the longest time to complete. Any delay in tasks on the critical path will directly affect the project's overall duration.
6. Managing the critical path: Project managers focus their attention on the tasks on the critical path because these are the tasks that, if delayed, will delay the entire project. They may allocate additional resources, adjust schedules, or take other actions to ensure that tasks on the critical path are completed on time.

Overall, the Critical Path Method provides project managers with a clear understanding of which tasks are most critical to the project's timeline, allowing them to prioritize their efforts and resources effectively.

6.14. How do you manage critical path in projects?

Managing the critical path in a project is essential for ensuring that it stays on track and meets its deadlines. Here is a step-by-step guide:

1. Identify Tasks: List all the tasks required to complete the project, along with their dependencies. Tasks that directly affect the project's completion time are critical.
2. Estimate Durations: Estimate the time it will take to complete each task. Be realistic and consider factors like resources, expertise, and potential risks.
3. Define Dependencies: Determine which tasks are dependent on others. Some tasks cannot start until previous ones are completed, creating a sequential order.
4. Construct Network Diagram: Create a network diagram or flowchart that shows the sequence of tasks and their dependencies. This diagram helps visualize the critical path.
5. Calculate Early Start and Early Finish Times: Starting from the first task, calculate the earliest possible start and finish times for each task based on dependencies and durations.
6. Calculate Late Start and Late Finish Times: Starting from the last task, calculate the latest possible start and finish times to avoid delaying the project's completion.
7. Identify Slack or Float: Slack or float refers to the amount of time a task can be delayed without affecting the project's overall timeline. Tasks on the critical path have zero slack.
8. Focus on Critical Path: The critical path consists of tasks with zero slack. These tasks determine the minimum duration required to complete the project. Focus on managing and monitoring these tasks closely.
9. Monitor Progress: Regularly track the progress of tasks on the critical path. Identify any delays or issues that could impact the project's timeline and take corrective actions promptly.
10. Manage Resources: Ensure that resources are allocated effectively to critical path tasks to prevent bottlenecks. Allocate additional resources if necessary to keep critical path tasks on schedule.
11. Risk Management: Identify potential risks that could impact critical path tasks and develop mitigation strategies to minimize their impact on the project's timeline.
12. Communicate Effectively: Keep stakeholders informed about the project's progress, especially regarding critical path tasks and any changes to the schedule. Effective communication helps manage expectations and ensures everyone is aligned.

By following these steps, you can effectively manage the critical path in projects and increase the likelihood of delivering them on time.

6.15. What is PERT?

The Program Evaluation and Review Technique (PERT) is a project management tool used to schedule, organize, and coordinate tasks within a project. PERT was developed in the late 1950s by the U.S. Navy for the Polaris missile project and later adopted by the private sector for various projects.

The PERT method involves the following steps:

1. Identify Tasks: Break down the project into specific tasks or activities required to complete it.
2. Sequence Tasks: Determine the order in which tasks must be completed. Some tasks may be dependent on the completion of others, while some can be performed simultaneously.
3. Estimate Time: Estimate the time required to complete each task. PERT typically uses three time estimates for each task: optimistic time (the shortest time the task might take), pessimistic time (the longest time), and most likely time (the best estimate).
4. Calculate Expected Time: Use a weighted average of the optimistic, pessimistic, and most likely time estimates to calculate the expected time for each task. This is often calculated using the formula: (optimistic time + 4 × most likely time + pessimistic time) / 6.
5. Determine Critical Path: Identify the sequence of tasks that determines the overall duration of the project. The critical path is the longest path through the project network and represents the minimum time required to complete the project.
6. Schedule: Develop a project schedule based on the estimated times for each task and the critical path. This helps in coordinating activities and allocating resources effectively.

PERT, depicted in a network diagram, serves as a visual representation of the sequential relationships among tasks in a project.

It employs a statistical methodology for scheduling projects, particularly useful when uncertainties exist regarding task durations. PERT aims to estimate project completion times by statistically analyzing uncertain task durations, providing a range of values along with their associated probabilities.

For each activity in PERT analysis, three durations are estimated: optimistic, pessimistic, and most likely. These values are then used to calculate the activity's expected duration and standard deviation. The expected duration is determined by a formula considering the optimistic, pessimistic, and most likely durations, while the standard deviation is calculated based on the range between optimistic and pessimistic durations.

These approximations enable the prediction of project completion dates and the likelihood of completion within a given timeframe. For instance, if the expected project completion is forecasted for January 10 with a standard deviation of four days, there is a 95 percent probability that the project will finish between January 2 and January 18.

PERT is particularly valuable when uncertainty surrounds activity durations. The probability distribution of expected project completion dates typically skews to the right, reflecting the tendency for delays to accumulate as projects progress.

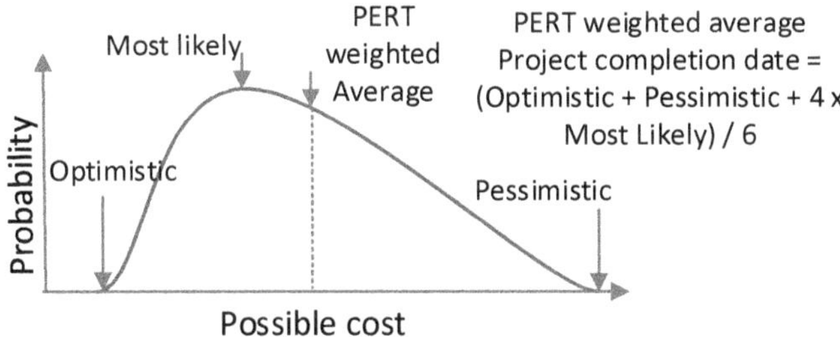

Figure 6.15.1 Skewed Probability Distribution

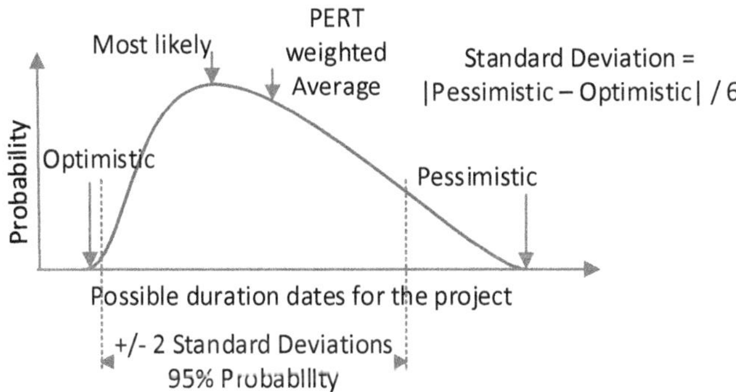

Figure 6.15.2 Skewed Probability Distribution

Figure 6.15.2 illustrates the span of values, which extends two standard deviations in either direction from the PERT weighted average. Standard deviation, always positive, denotes the deviation from the anticipated value. In PERT, it signifies the deviation measured from the PERT weighted average.

The standard deviation represents the range of values around the PERT weighted average. In PERT, this deviation is crucial for determining the likelihood of project completion within specific timeframes. It is particularly pertinent for identifying potential late completions, with a focus on scenarios exceeding the PERT weighted average plus two standard deviations.

However, PERT analysis faces challenges when the critical path of a project changes during execution. Traditional calculations assume fixed durations based on expected values, potentially leading to discrepancies if actual durations vary. To address this, Monte Carlo simulation - a computerized approach - is employed to model various duration scenarios, ensuring a more robust analysis of project completion probabilities.

PERT is particularly useful for complex projects with many interdependent tasks and uncertainties in task durations. It provides a visual representation of the project timeline and helps project managers identify areas where resources may need to be allocated more effectively to ensure timely completion.

6.16. What is a milestone chart?

A milestone chart is a project management tool that provides a visual representation of significant events or achievements within a project. Milestones are critical points or events that indicate progress in the project timeline, such as the completion of key tasks, the achievement of major project phases, or the delivery of important deliverables.

Key Features of a Milestone Chart:

1. Timeline Representation: The chart typically displays a timeline, with milestones marked at specific points along this timeline.
2. Important Dates: Each milestone corresponds to a significant date by which a specific objective should be completed.
3. Visual Clarity: It uses symbols, such as diamonds or dots, to represent milestones, making it easy to see at a glance the major events and their sequence.
4. Progress Tracking: Helps in tracking the progress of the project by indicating which milestones have been reached and which are upcoming.
5. Communication Tool: Provides a clear and concise way to communicate project status to stakeholders, team members, and clients.

Benefits of Using a Milestone Chart:

1. Enhanced Planning: Helps in breaking down the project into manageable sections, making it easier to plan and allocate resources effectively.
2. Focus on Key Deliverables: Keeps the team focused on achieving critical tasks that are essential for project success.
3. Improved Monitoring and Control: Facilitates monitoring of project progress and ensures timely identification of any deviations from the plan.
4. Stakeholder Engagement: Provides a straightforward way to update stakeholders on the project's progress and major achievements.

Example of a Milestone Chart: Imagine a software development project with the following milestones:

1. Project Kickoff: January 1, 2026
2. Requirements Gathering Complete: February 15, 2026
3. Design Phase Complete: March 31, 2026
4. Prototype Release: May 15, 2026
5. Beta Testing Start: June 30, 2026
6. Final Release: August 15, 2026

These milestones would be marked along a timeline in the milestone chart, allowing anyone viewing the chart to quickly understand the project's key phases and their scheduled completion dates.

In summary, a milestone chart is a valuable tool in project management for visualizing and tracking significant events, ensuring better planning, control, and communication throughout the project lifecycle.

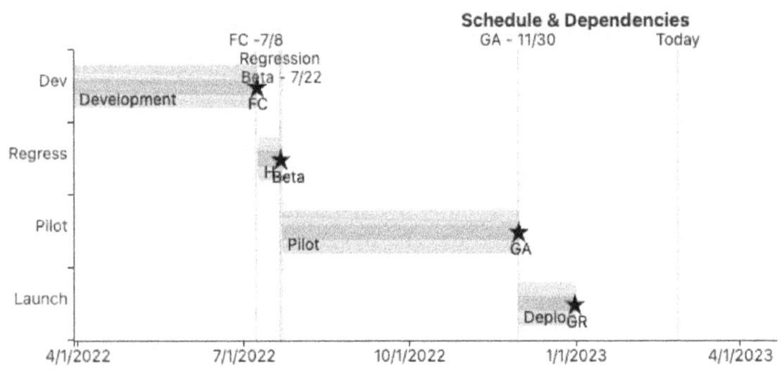

Legend/Color code

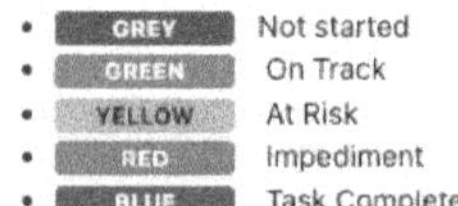

Figure 6.16.1 Milestone Chart

6.17. What is a summary or hammock activity?

A summary or hammock activity in project management is a high-level task that encompasses and summarizes a group of related activities or tasks within a project. Here are key aspects of a summary or hammock activity:

1. Overview Role: It provides an overview of the combined duration and progress of the activities it includes, allowing project managers to monitor and report on several tasks collectively rather than individually.
2. Flexibility in Scope: The specific tasks that fall under a hammock activity can vary, and it may span multiple phases or parts of a project. This makes it adaptable for different reporting and management needs.
3. Start and End Dates: The start date of a hammock activity is typically aligned with the start of the earliest included task, and its end date matches the end of the latest included task. This dynamic nature helps in accurately reflecting the timeline of the encompassed activities.
4. Simplified Reporting: Using a hammock activity simplifies project schedules and reports by collapsing multiple detailed activities into one higher-level task. This is particularly useful in complex projects where detailed task management can become overwhelming.
5. Resource Management: It aids in resource management by giving a broad view of resource allocation and usage over the period covered by the hammock activity.
6. Not a Replacement for Detailed Planning: While it helps in summarizing, it is not a substitute for detailed planning and control of individual tasks. Detailed tracking and management of the underlying tasks are still necessary for effective project execution.

In summary, a hammock activity serves as a summarizing tool in project management, providing a high-level view of multiple related tasks to simplify scheduling, reporting, and resource management.

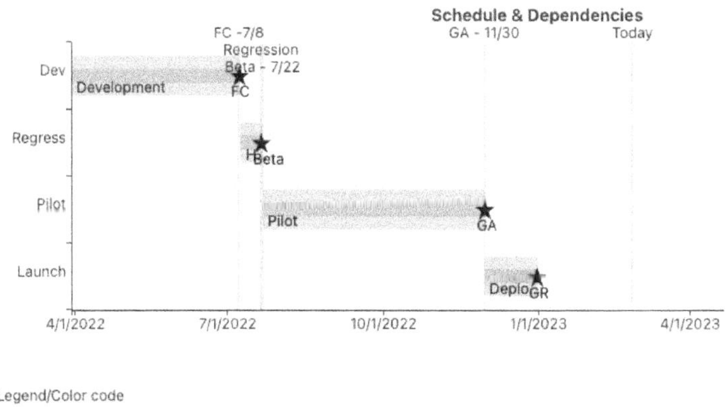

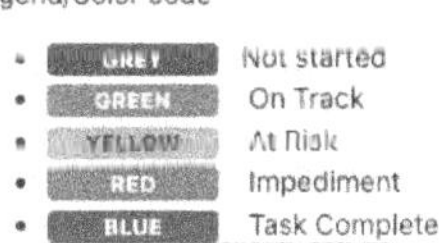

Figure 6.17.1 Activity Chart

6.18. What is a resource histogram?

A resource histogram is a graphical representation that shows the distribution and allocation of resources, such as personnel or equipment, over a period of time in a project. It is a type of bar chart where the x-axis typically represents time (e.g., days, weeks, months) and the y-axis represents the quantity of resources required or used.

Key Features of a Resource Histogram:

1. Time-Based Representation: The horizontal axis (x-axis) usually represents the timeline of the project. This can be broken down into appropriate units such as days, weeks, or months, depending on the duration and granularity needed for the project.
2. Resource Allocation: The vertical axis (y-axis) represents the amount of resources allocated or needed. This could be the number of people, hours worked, or units of equipment.
3. Bars Indicating Usage: Each bar on the histogram represents the resource usage for a specific time period. The height of the bar indicates the amount of resources used during that period.
4. Identifying Peaks and Valleys: The histogram helps identify periods of high and low resource usage. Peaks indicate periods where resource demand is high, which can signal potential over-allocation or the need for additional resources. Valleys indicate periods of low resource demand, which might represent opportunities for resource reallocation.
5. Resource Leveling: By visualizing resource usage over time, project managers can identify imbalances and make adjustments to ensure that resources are used efficiently and effectively. This process is known as resource leveling.
6. Planning and Forecasting: Resource histograms are useful tools in the planning phase of a project, allowing project managers to forecast resource needs and ensure that the necessary resources are available at the right times.

Benefits of Using a Resource Histogram:

1. Improved Resource Management: Helps in managing and optimizing the use of resources throughout the project lifecycle.
2. Enhanced Visibility: Provides a clear and concise visual representation of resource allocation, making it easier to spot trends and issues.
3. Better Planning: Assists in planning for resource needs and identifying potential bottlenecks or periods of underutilization.
4. Informed Decision-Making: Enables project managers to make informed decisions about resource allocation, balancing workloads, and addressing potential resource shortages or surpluses.

Example of a Resource Histogram:
Imagine a project that spans six months and involves various tasks that require different numbers of team members at different times. A resource histogram for this project might show:

1. January: 5 team members needed
2. February: 10 team members needed
3. March: 8 team members needed
4. April: 15 team members needed (peak period)
5. May: 7 team members needed
6. June: 5 team members needed (back to initial level)

This histogram allows the project manager to see that April requires the most resources and plan accordingly, possibly by reallocating resources from months with lower demand.

In summary, a resource histogram is a valuable project management tool that aids in the effective planning, monitoring, and management of resources throughout a project's duration.

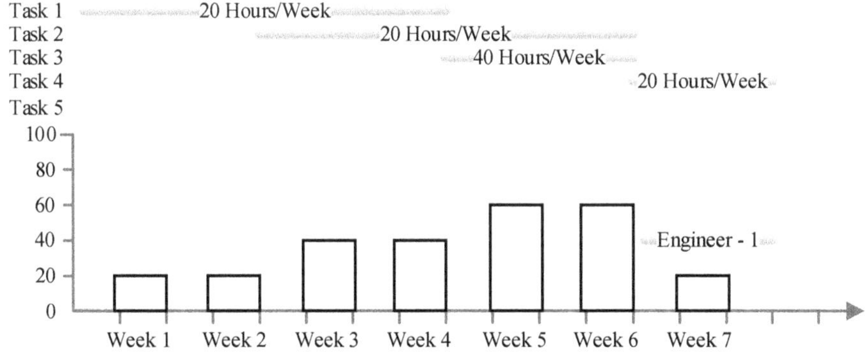

Figure 6.18.1 Resource Histogram with Gantt chart

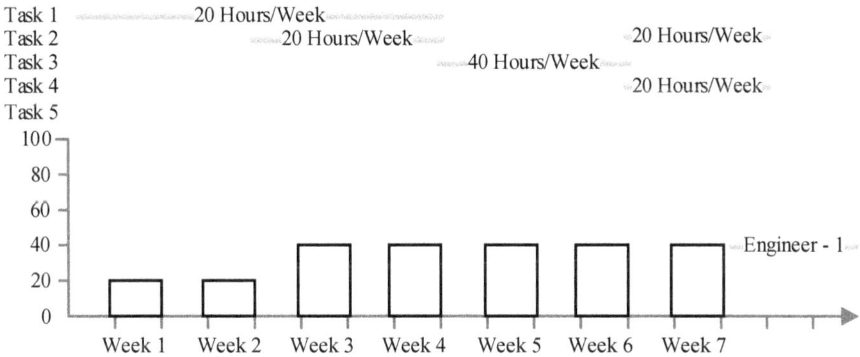

Figure 6.18.2 Over-allocation of Resource Resolved

6.19. What is crashing and fast-tracking a project schedule?

Crashing and fast-tracking are two techniques used in project management to accelerate project schedules and ensure timely completion of project tasks.

Crashing is a technique used to shorten the project schedule by adding additional resources to critical path activities without changing the project scope. The goal is to achieve the maximum schedule compression at the least incremental cost. Here is how it works:

1. Identify Critical Path Activities: Determine which activities are on the critical path, as these directly impact the project completion date.
2. Analyze Costs and Benefits: Assess the cost of adding resources versus the benefit of reducing the schedule. This might include adding more labor, equipment, or overtime work.
3. Implement Resource Allocation: Allocate the necessary additional resources to the identified critical path activities to reduce their duration.
4. Monitor and Adjust: Continuously monitor the progress and adjust resources as necessary to ensure the desired schedule reduction is achieved.

Advantages:

1. Can significantly reduce project duration.
2. Helps meet tight deadlines or recover from delays.

Disadvantages:

1. Increases project costs due to additional resources.
2. May lead to diminishing returns if resources are not used efficiently.
3. Potentially higher risk of resource-related issues such as burnout.

Fast-tracking involves performing tasks in parallel that were originally planned to be done in sequence. This approach can overlap project phases or activities that would typically be done sequentially.

1. Identify Activities for Overlap: Determine which sequential activities can be overlapped. These are usually dependent activities where starting one before completing the other would not result in significant risk.
2. Analyze Risks and Dependencies: Evaluate the potential risks and dependencies of performing these activities in parallel. Ensure that the overlap would not compromise the quality or outcome.
3. Reschedule Overlapping Tasks: Adjust the project schedule to reflect the new sequence of activities.
4. Monitor and Adjust: Keep a close watch on the progress to manage any issues arising from the changes and make necessary adjustments.

Advantages:

1. Reduces the overall project timeline without additional costs.
2. Can be a good solution for projects with high schedule risks.

Disadvantages:

1. Increases risk of rework if parallel activities lead to conflicts or errors.
2. Requires meticulous coordination and communication among teams.
3. Potentially higher stress and resource strain due to overlapping tasks.

Comparison

1. Objective: Both techniques aim to shorten the project duration but use different methods - crashing adds resources while fast-tracking changes the task sequence.
2. Cost: Crashing usually increases project costs due to additional resources, whereas fast-tracking may not incur direct additional costs but can increase indirect costs due to risks and potential rework.
3. Risk: Fast-tracking generally carries higher risk due to overlapping tasks, which can lead to errors and rework, while crashing increases cost-related risks.

As we can see in Figure 6.19.1, the cost of reducing the schedule will increase more and more rapidly as we take more and more days from the schedule.

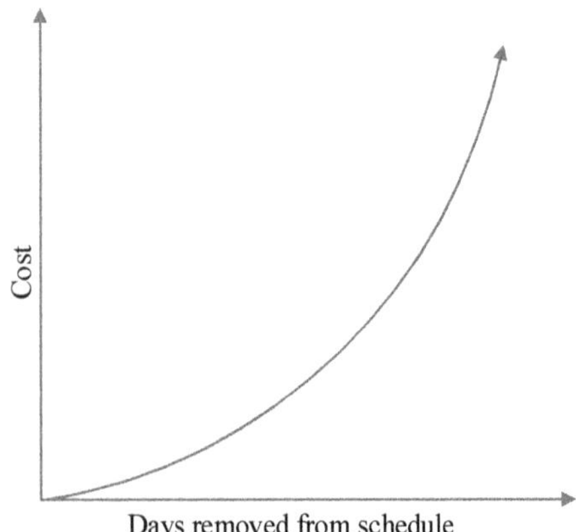

Figure 6.19.1 The Cost of Reducing Schedules

Both crashing and fast-tracking are effective methods for compressing project schedules but should be used carefully considering the project's specific context, resources, and constraints.

6.20. What is a buffered schedule?

A buffered schedule in project management refers to a timeline that includes additional time allowances, known as buffers, to account for potential delays and uncertainties in the project. These buffers provide a cushion against unexpected events that could disrupt the project's progress, ensuring that the overall project remains on track even if certain tasks take longer than anticipated.

There are several types of buffers that can be included in a buffered schedule:

1. Project Buffer: This is added at the end of the project timeline to absorb any delays that occur throughout the project. It ensures that the final delivery date can still be met even if some tasks take longer than planned.
2. Feeding Buffers: These are placed at the points where non-critical tasks (tasks not on the critical path) feed into critical path tasks. They protect the critical path from delays in these feeder tasks, helping to ensure that the critical path remains on schedule.
3. Resource Buffers: These are used to ensure that critical resources (such as key personnel or equipment) are available when needed, avoiding delays due to resource constraints.

The concept of buffered schedules is a key element in methodologies like Critical Chain Project Management (CCPM), which emphasizes the importance of managing uncertainties and resource dependencies to keep projects on track.

By incorporating buffers, project managers can create more realistic schedules, better manage risks, and increase the likelihood of completing projects on time and within budget.

A buffered schedule includes added free float to ensure reliability. This involves inserting planned delays between the end of one activity and the start of its dependent activity. Buffering non-critical path activities is ineffective since the project's completion date hinges on the critical path.

Figures 6.20.1 and 6.20.2 illustrate a project initially set to finish on June 30, with a stakeholder promise date of July 30, showing how buffering adjusts the schedule.

Buffer time is determined by the difference between the promised completion date and the project's late finish date. Distribution of buffer time can follow various schemes, with Goldratt's critical chain method being popular.

Projects often face unrealistic deadlines due to stakeholders' past experiences with delays. These stakeholders push for early completion dates to account for potential delays, believing this strategy will yield earlier actual completion. However, this expectation often perpetuates delays.

Project schedules frequently miss deadlines due to relying on "most likely" activity durations. The distribution of potential completion dates often shows a higher probability of finishing later than the most likely date, as shown in Figures 6.20.3 and 6.20.4. Project managers must evaluate if a 50% probability of lateness is acceptable.

To buffer a schedule, it is essential to justify the added time to stakeholders and management, emphasizing the high probability of late delivery without it.

For example, if a project promises delivery in 200 days but aims for over 95% reliability, calculate expected value (EV) and standard deviation (SD). If optimistic and pessimistic delivery dates are 190 and 220 days, respectively:

1. $EV = (190 + 4 \times 200 + 220) / 6 = 202$ days
2. $SD = (220 - 190) / 6 = 5$ days

A 95% reliable promise date would be:

1. Promise Date $= 202 + 2 \times 5 = 212$ days

Decide where to add the 10-day buffer. Distributing it among critical path activities is more efficient than placing it at the project's end, avoiding the need for constant rescheduling.

Buffer non-critical path activities as needed, using risk analysis to prioritize. Early buffering allows for learning and adjustment. Goldratt suggests scheduling activities with large float later in the project to reduce risks.

Resource criticality also affects buffer distribution; scarce resources require buffered predecessor activities to ensure availability.

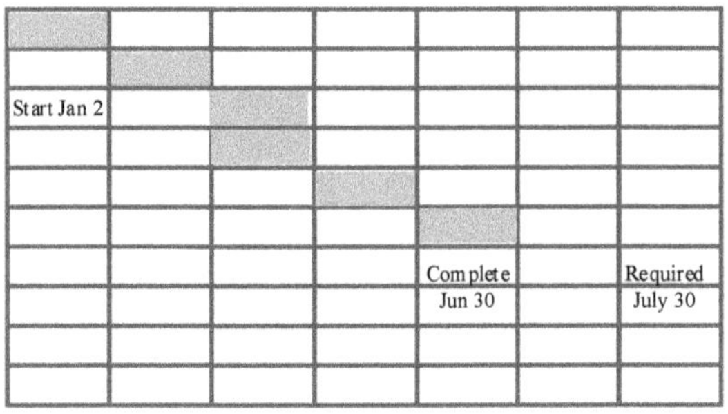

Start Jan 2
Complete Jun 30
Required July 30

Figure 6.20.1 Schedule without Contingency

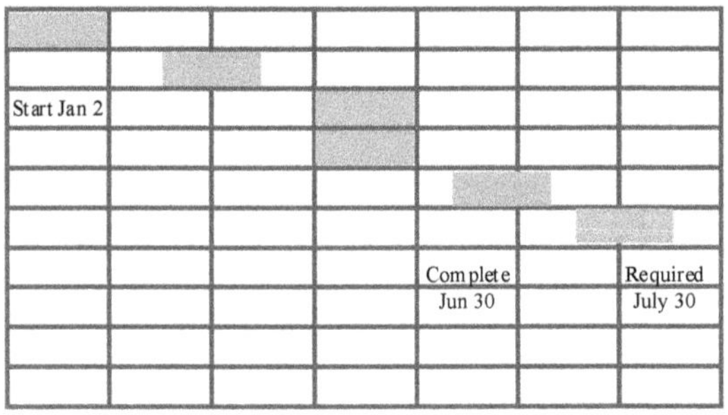

Start Jan 2
Complete Jun 30
Required July 30

Figure 6.20.2 Schedule with Buffer

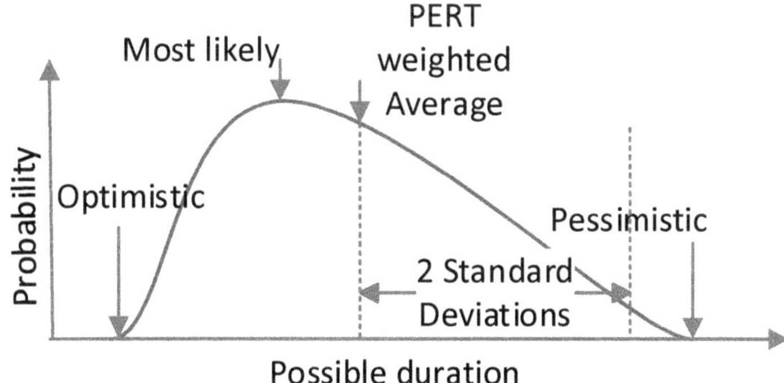

Figure 6.20.3 Probability of Promise Dates

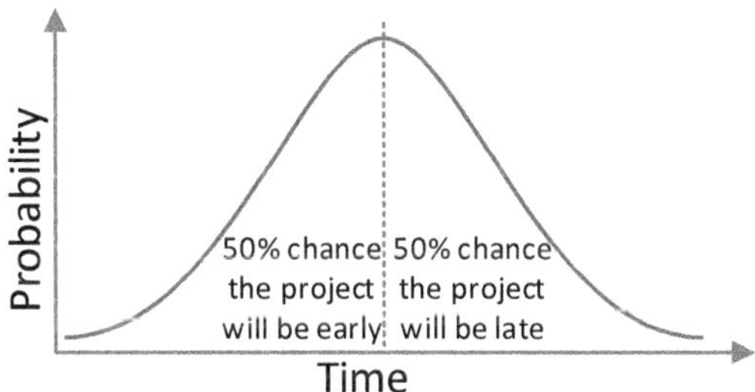

Figure 6.20.4 Will the Project be late?

6.21. What is the Monte Carlo process? What and where are its applications specifically in project management?

The Monte Carlo process, or Monte Carlo method, is a statistical technique that involves using random sampling and statistical modeling to estimate mathematical functions and simulate the behavior of various systems. It is particularly useful for understanding the impact of risk and uncertainty in prediction and forecasting models.

Key Steps in the Monte Carlo Process

1. Define a Model: Establish a mathematical model of the system or process being studied.
2. Input Distribution: Determine the probability distribution of the input variables. These distributions reflect the uncertainty and variability of these inputs.
3. Random Sampling: Use random sampling techniques to generate a large number of possible scenarios for the input variables.
4. Simulate Outcomes: Run the model for each set of generated input values to simulate outcomes.
5. Analyze Results: Aggregate and analyze the results to understand the range and likelihood of different outcomes.

Applications in Project Management: In project management, the Monte Carlo method is applied primarily for risk assessment, schedule analysis, and cost estimation. Here are some specific applications:

1. Risk Analysis
    a. Identifying Risks: Helps in identifying and quantifying potential risks and their impacts on the project.
    b. Probability of Success: Assesses the likelihood of meeting project goals (e.g., deadlines, budget).

    c. Risk Mitigation: Provides insights into how different risk mitigation strategies might affect project outcomes.
2. Schedule Analysis
    a. Project Scheduling: Estimates the time required to complete a project by considering uncertainties in task durations.
    b. Critical Path Analysis: Identifies the probability of delays in critical paths and helps in contingency planning.
    c. Completion Dates: Predicts a range of possible completion dates rather than a single deterministic date.
3. Cost Estimation
    a. Budget Forecasting: Predicts the total project cost by taking into account the variability in cost estimates.
    b. Cost Overruns: Assesses the likelihood and impact of cost overruns.
    c. Resource Allocation: Optimizes resource allocation under uncertainty to minimize costs.

Practical Example in Project Management: Suppose a project manager is planning a construction project with various uncertain factors like labor costs, material availability, and weather conditions. Using the Monte Carlo method, the manager can:

1. Define the Model: Create a project plan with tasks, durations, dependencies, costs, and resources.
2. Input Distribution: Identify the uncertain variables (e.g., labor costs, task durations) and assign probability distributions to these variables based on historical data or expert judgment.
3. Random Sampling: Generate thousands of scenarios using random values from these distributions.
4. Simulate Outcomes: Run the project model for each scenario to see how the project timeline and cost change under different conditions.
5. Analyze Results: Determine the probability of completing the project on time and within budget, and identify critical risks that need mitigation.

Several software tools and project management platforms incorporate Monte Carlo simulations, including:

1. Microsoft Project with add-ons like RiskyProject.
2. Primavera.
3. Crystal Ball (by Oracle).
4. @RISK (by Palisade Corporation).

By applying the Monte Carlo method, project managers can make more informed decisions, better manage risks, and increase the likelihood of successful project outcomes.

7. Project Control

Project Control encompasses the systematic management and regulation of a project's progress, resources, and activities to ensure alignment with predefined objectives and constraints. It involves continuous monitoring of various project elements, such as schedule, cost, quality, and scope, to identify deviations from the plan and take corrective actions when necessary. By effectively managing risks, controlling costs, monitoring schedules, and ensuring quality standards, project control facilitates the successful delivery of projects within the specified timeframes and budgets while meeting stakeholders' expectations. It is a dynamic process that requires proactive decision-making, effective communication, and diligent oversight throughout the project lifecycle to achieve desired outcomes.

7.1. What is Project Control?

Project Control refers to the process of managing and regulating various aspects of a project to ensure that it progresses according to plan. It involves monitoring, tracking, and adjusting different project elements to achieve specific objectives within constraints such as time, cost, quality, and scope. Key components of project control include:

1. Monitoring Progress: Regularly assessing the status of tasks, milestones, and overall project progress to identify any deviations from the plan.
2. Identifying Variances: Analyzing discrepancies between planned and actual performance to understand the reasons behind them and take corrective actions if necessary.
3. Cost Control: Managing project expenditures to ensure they stay within budgetary constraints. This involves tracking expenses, forecasting costs, and implementing cost-saving measures when possible.
4. Schedule Control: Monitoring the project schedule to ensure tasks are completed on time and adjusting timelines as needed to accommodate changes or delays.
5. Quality Control: Implementing processes to ensure that project deliverables meet predefined quality standards. This involves regular inspections, testing, and adherence to quality management practices.
6. Risk Management: Identifying potential risks that could affect the project and implementing strategies to mitigate or respond to them effectively.
7. Communication and Reporting: Keeping stakeholders informed about project progress, issues, and changes through regular communication and detailed reporting.

Overall, project control is essential for ensuring that projects are delivered successfully, meeting stakeholders' expectations while staying within the constraints of time, budget, and scope.

7.2. Why do you need to establish controls?

You Cannot Manage What You Cannot Control. Establishing controls for projects is essential for several reasons:

1. Monitoring Progress: Controls allow you to track the progress of the project in terms of timelines, budget, and quality. By having controls in place, project managers can identify deviations from the plan early on and take corrective actions to ensure the project stays on track.
2. Risk Management: Controls help in identifying and managing risks associated with the project. By having controls such as risk assessment mechanisms, project managers can proactively identify potential risks and implement strategies to mitigate them, reducing the likelihood of negative impacts on the project.
3. Resource Allocation: Controls enable effective allocation and utilization of resources such as manpower, materials, and finances. By monitoring resource usage through controls, project managers can ensure that resources are being used efficiently and effectively, optimizing the project's performance.
4. Quality Assurance: Controls play a crucial role in ensuring the quality of deliverables throughout

the project lifecycle. By implementing quality control measures, project managers can ensure that the project meets the specified quality standards and requirements, ultimately satisfying the stakeholders' expectations.

5. Communication and Reporting: Controls facilitate communication and reporting within the project team and with stakeholders. By having control mechanisms in place, project managers can provide regular updates on the project's progress, highlight any issues or concerns, and facilitate informed decision-making by stakeholders.
6. Compliance: Controls help ensure that the project adheres to relevant laws, regulations, and organizational policies. By implementing controls for compliance, project managers can mitigate legal and regulatory risks, ensuring that the project operates within the boundaries of applicable laws and regulations.

Overall, establishing controls for projects is crucial for ensuring successful project delivery by effectively managing risks, resources, quality, communication, and compliance throughout the project lifecycle.

7.3. Which project control functions need the most improvement?

The project control functions that typically need the most improvement vary depending on the specific project and its circumstances. However, some common areas where improvement is often needed include:

1. Communication: Effective communication is crucial for project success. Improvements may be needed in ensuring that all stakeholders are kept informed about project progress, changes, and issues.
2. Risk Management: Identifying and managing risks effectively can help prevent project delays and cost overruns. Improvements may be needed in conducting thorough risk assessments, developing mitigation strategies, and monitoring risks throughout the project lifecycle.
3. Scope Management: Changes in project scope can lead to scope creep, which can negatively impact project timelines and budgets. Improvements may be needed in defining and controlling the project scope to ensure that it remains aligned with project objectives.
4. Cost Control: Keeping project costs within budget is essential for project success. Improvements may be needed in accurately estimating costs, tracking expenses, and implementing cost-saving measures.
5. Schedule Management: Adhering to project schedules is important for meeting deadlines and delivering results on time. Improvements may be needed in developing realistic schedules, monitoring progress against the schedule, and implementing schedule adjustments as needed.
6. Quality Management: Ensuring that project deliverables meet quality standards is essential for meeting client expectations and achieving project objectives. Improvements may be needed in implementing quality assurance processes and conducting regular quality checks.
7. Resource Management: Optimizing the use of resources, including personnel, materials, and equipment, is crucial for project efficiency. Improvements may be needed in resource allocation, scheduling, and utilization.

By identifying specific areas where improvement is needed and implementing targeted strategies to address them, project teams can enhance their control functions and increase the likelihood of project success.

Based on a survey by Project Management Institute, here is the list in the decreasing order:

1. Managing issue, risk, and change
2. Educating the project team on proper project management processes
3. Estimating project costs
4. Developing project schedule and work breakdown structure
5. Managing critical path to ensure that schedules are met

6. Tracking or analyzing project costs
7. Documenting and delivering project status information
8. Facilitating and/or oversee project planning and control sessions

7.4. Why sometimes staying the course seems better option when your project is in trouble?

Staying the course when your project is in trouble can seem like the better option for a few reasons:

1. Commitment to Vision: Often, projects face difficulties because they are pushing boundaries or trying something new. Staying the course demonstrates a commitment to the original vision despite challenges, which can be inspiring to the team and stakeholders.
2. Consistency: Abrupt changes in direction can create confusion and instability. Sticking to the original plan provides a sense of consistency and reliability, which can be reassuring to those involved.
3. Learning Opportunity: Challenges are opportunities for growth and learning. By staying the course, you give yourself and your team the chance to overcome obstacles, learn from mistakes, and emerge stronger and more resilient.
4. Resource Investment: Changing course mid-project can be costly in terms of time, money, and other resources. Sometimes, it is more prudent to continue with the current plan and try to mitigate issues rather than starting over from scratch.
5. Potential for Recovery: Even when a project is in trouble, there is often still a chance for recovery. By staying the course and working through the challenges, you maintain the possibility of turning things around and achieving success.

However, it is essential to balance the decision to stay the course with a realistic assessment of the situation. Sometimes, persistence can lead to further problems if the underlying issues are not addressed. It is crucial to regularly evaluate the project's progress, adapt as necessary, and be willing to change course if staying on the current path is not viable.

7.5. What are some of the decisions a project manager must make as part of project control?

Project control involves various decisions that project managers must make to ensure the project stays on track and meets its objectives. Some of these decisions include:

1. Resource Allocation: Deciding how to allocate resources such as budget, manpower, equipment, and materials to different tasks and activities within the project.
2. Schedule Management: Making decisions about scheduling activities, setting milestones, and managing timelines to ensure that the project progresses according to the plan.
3. Risk Management: Identifying potential risks to the project and making decisions about how to mitigate, transfer, accept, or avoid these risks to minimize their impact on project objectives.
4. Quality Control: Deciding on quality standards, establishing quality assurance processes, and making decisions about corrective actions to maintain or improve the quality of project deliverables.
5. Communication: Deciding on communication channels, frequency, and methods to ensure effective communication among project team members, stakeholders, and other relevant parties.
6. Scope Management: Making decisions about changes to project scope, assessing the impact of scope changes on project objectives, and deciding whether to approve or reject change requests.
7. Budget Management: Making decisions about budget allocations, tracking project expenses, identifying cost variances, and taking corrective actions to ensure that the project stays within budget.
8. Issue Resolution: Identifying project issues and making decisions about how to address them

effectively to minimize their impact on project progress and objectives.

9. Procurement Management: Making decisions about selecting vendors, negotiating contracts, managing supplier relationships, and ensuring that procurement activities align with project objectives and budget constraints.
10. Stakeholder Management: Making decisions about how to engage and manage stakeholders effectively to gain their support, address their concerns, and keep them informed about project progress and changes.
11. Performance Measurement: Making decisions about how to measure project performance, select key performance indicators (KPIs), and analyze performance data to identify areas for improvement and make informed decisions.

These decisions are critical for maintaining control over the project and ensuring its successful completion within the defined constraints of time, cost, scope, quality, and resources.

7.6. What are the benefits of project control? Why do it?

Project control offers several benefits that are essential for successful project management:

1. Maintaining Schedule Adherence: Project control helps in monitoring and controlling the project schedule, ensuring that tasks are completed on time. This prevents delays and ensures timely delivery of the project.
2. Cost Management: By closely monitoring project expenses and resources, project control helps in controlling costs and avoiding budget overruns. It allows project managers to make adjustments to stay within budget constraints.
3. Quality Assurance: Project control involves monitoring the quality of work throughout the project lifecycle. By implementing quality control measures, project managers can ensure that deliverables meet the required standards and specifications.
4. Risk Management: Effective project control involves identifying and managing risks proactively. By assessing potential risks and implementing mitigation strategies, project managers can minimize the impact of unforeseen events on project outcomes.
5. Resource Allocation: Project control helps in optimizing resource allocation by tracking resource utilization and identifying areas where resources may be underutilized or overallocated. This ensures efficient use of resources throughout the project.
6. Stakeholder Communication: Project control facilitates effective communication with stakeholders by providing timely updates on project progress, issues, and risks. This helps in maintaining stakeholder satisfaction and managing expectations.
7. Decision Making: By providing accurate and up-to-date information about project performance, project control enables informed decision making. Project managers can use this information to make adjustments to the project plan and address emerging issues promptly.

Overall, project control is essential for ensuring that projects are completed successfully, within budget, and meeting quality standards, while also keeping stakeholders informed and engaged throughout the process.

7.7. What are the various project control processes and how to formalize these project control processes?

Project control processes are essential for ensuring that a project stays on track, meets its objectives, stays within budget, and adheres to the planned schedule. Here are some common project control processes:

1. Scope Management: This involves defining and controlling what is and is not included in the project. It ensures that the project stays focused on its objectives.
2. Schedule Management: This process involves developing, maintaining, and controlling the

project schedule. It includes activities like creating a project timeline, tracking progress, and adjusting schedules as needed.

3. Cost Management: This involves estimating, budgeting, and controlling costs throughout the project lifecycle. It ensures that the project stays within its budget constraints.
4. Quality Management: This process involves ensuring that project deliverables meet the specified quality standards. It includes activities like quality planning, quality assurance, and quality control.
5. Risk Management: This involves identifying, assessing, and managing risks that could impact the project's success. It includes activities like risk identification, risk analysis, risk response planning, and risk monitoring.
6. Communication Management: This process involves ensuring that stakeholders are adequately informed about the project's progress, status, and any issues or changes. It includes activities like stakeholder communication planning, information distribution, and performance reporting.
7. Change Management: This involves managing changes to the project scope, schedule, budget, or other aspects. It includes activities like change identification, change evaluation, change control, and change communication.

To formalize project control processes, follow these steps:

1. Document Processes: Create formal documentation outlining each project control process, including roles, responsibilities, procedures, and tools.
2. Establish Standards: Define standards and guidelines for each process to ensure consistency and quality across projects.
3. Implement Tools: Utilize project management tools and software to facilitate project control processes. These tools can help with scheduling, budgeting, risk management, and communication.
4. Training and Education: Provide training and education to project team members on project control processes to ensure they understand their roles and responsibilities.
5. Continuous Improvement: Regularly review and assess project control processes to identify areas for improvement and implement changes as needed.
6. Monitoring and Reporting: Continuously monitor project performance against predefined metrics and report progress, issues, and changes to stakeholders regularly.
7. Adaptability: Be flexible and adaptable to changes in project requirements, environment, or stakeholders' needs, and adjust control processes accordingly.

By formalizing project control processes, organizations can improve project success rates, minimize risks, and ensure efficient project delivery.

7.8. What does Project Control Officer mean? What are its roles and responsibilities? Why do we need this role?

A Project Control Officer (PCO) plays a crucial role in project management, particularly in large-scale projects or programs. Their primary responsibility is to ensure effective governance, control, and coordination of various project activities to achieve project objectives within scope, time, and budget constraints. Here is a breakdown of their roles and responsibilities:

1. Governance and Compliance: PCOs ensure that projects adhere to organizational policies, procedures, and standards. They facilitate compliance with regulatory requirements and industry best practices.
2. Planning and Scheduling: They assist in developing project plans, schedules, and resource allocation strategies. PCOs help in defining project milestones, tasks, and dependencies to ensure a clear roadmap for project execution.
3. Monitoring and Reporting: PCOs track project progress against established plans and milestones.

They gather data, analyze project metrics, and prepare regular progress reports for stakeholders. This includes identifying risks, issues, and deviations from the plan and proposing corrective actions.

4. Risk Management: PCOs identify, assess, and mitigate project risks throughout the project lifecycle. They work with project teams to develop risk mitigation strategies and contingency plans to minimize the impact of potential threats.
5. Financial Management: PCOs manage project budgets, expenses, and financial reporting. They track costs, monitor budget variances, and ensure that financial resources are allocated effectively to support project activities.
6. Stakeholder Management: PCOs facilitate communication and collaboration among project stakeholders, including team members, sponsors, clients, and external partners. They ensure that stakeholders are informed about project progress, issues, and decisions in a timely manner.
7. Change Control: PCOs manage changes to project scope, requirements, and deliverables. They assess change requests, evaluate their impact on the project, and implement appropriate change control procedures to minimize scope creep and ensure alignment with project objectives.
8. Documentation and Knowledge Management: PCOs maintain project documentation, including plans, reports, meeting minutes, and other relevant artifacts. They establish document control processes and ensure that project information is organized, accessible, and up-to-date for future reference.

The need for a Project Control Officer arises from the complexity and scale of modern projects. As projects become larger and more intricate, effective control and coordination become increasingly challenging. PCOs provide the necessary expertise and support to project managers and teams to navigate these complexities, mitigate risks, and ensure successful project delivery. Their proactive approach to governance, monitoring, and problem-solving helps to keep projects on track and aligned with organizational goals.

7.9. What are some of the tips for keeping IT projects under control?

Keeping IT projects under control requires careful planning, effective communication, and proactive management. Here are some tips to help:

1. Define Clear Objectives: Ensure everyone involved understands the project's goals, scope, and desired outcomes from the beginning.
2. Create a Detailed Plan: Develop a comprehensive project plan outlining tasks, timelines, resources, and milestones. Break down the project into manageable phases or sprints.
3. Allocate Resources Wisely: Ensure you have the necessary resources, including skilled personnel, budget, and technology infrastructure, to support the project's requirements.
4. Risk Management: Identify potential risks and develop strategies to mitigate them. Regularly assess risks throughout the project lifecycle and adjust plans accordingly.
5. Effective Communication: Establish open and transparent communication channels among team members, stakeholders, and project sponsors. Regularly update all stakeholders on the project's progress, challenges, and achievements.
6. Set Realistic Deadlines: Avoid setting overly ambitious deadlines that may lead to rushed work or burnout. Set realistic timelines based on careful estimation of task durations and resource availability.
7. Monitor Progress: Continuously monitor the project's progress against the plan. Use project management tools and metrics to track tasks, timelines, budget, and quality metrics.
8. Adaptability: Be prepared to adapt to changes in requirements, priorities, or circumstances. Agile methodologies can be particularly useful for managing iterative and evolving IT projects.
9. Quality Assurance: Implement robust quality assurance processes to ensure that deliverables meet the required standards and specifications. Conduct regular testing and reviews to identify and

address issues early.

10. Stakeholder Engagement: Engage stakeholders throughout the project lifecycle to gather feedback, address concerns, and ensure alignment with their expectations.
11. Document Everything: Maintain detailed documentation of project plans, requirements, decisions, and changes. This documentation serves as a valuable reference and ensures continuity if team members change.
12. Learn from Experience: Conduct post-project reviews to evaluate what worked well and what could be improved. Use lessons learned to inform future projects and refine project management processes.

By following these tips, you can increase the likelihood of keeping IT projects on track, within budget, and delivering the desired results.

7.10. What are some of the steps to regaining project control if the project with issues or high priorities goes out of control?

Regaining control of a project that has gone off track or encountered significant issues requires a systematic approach. Here are some steps to consider:

1. Assess the Situation: Understand the extent of the issues. Identify the root causes, whether they are related to scope creep, resource constraints, communication breakdowns, etc.
2. Realign Objectives: Review the project's objectives and ensure they are still relevant and achievable. If necessary, adjust them to reflect the current situation and priorities.
3. Communicate Transparently: Keep all stakeholders informed about the challenges the project is facing and the steps being taken to address them. Transparency fosters trust and encourages collaboration in finding solutions.
4. Prioritize Tasks: Identify critical tasks and prioritize them based on their impact on project success. Focus on completing these tasks first to regain momentum.
5. Allocate Resources Wisely: Ensure that resources, including human resources, time, and budget, are allocated effectively to address the most pressing issues. Consider reallocating resources from less critical areas if needed.
6. Implement Change Management: If significant changes are required to bring the project back on track, implement a structured change management process. This involves assessing the impacts of the changes, communicating them to stakeholders, and managing resistance.
7. Strengthen Project Controls: Enhance monitoring and control mechanisms to prevent similar issues from occurring in the future. This may involve implementing stricter project management processes, improving risk management practices, or enhancing quality assurance measures.
8. Empower the Team: Provide support and empower the project team to take ownership of their tasks and contribute actively to problem-solving efforts. Encourage collaboration and innovation to overcome challenges.
9. Seek External Support: If necessary, seek assistance from external experts or consultants who have experience in resolving similar project issues. Their fresh perspective and expertise can offer valuable insights and solutions.
10. Review and Learn: Conduct a thorough post-mortem review once the project is back on track to analyze what went wrong and identify lessons learned. Use this feedback to improve project management practices and avoid similar issues in future projects.

7.11. How much control and reporting do we need in project management? To make a success of the project control processes, what are the key objectives a project manager needs to achieve?

Control and reporting are crucial aspects of project management, ensuring that projects stay on track, meet objectives, and deliver desired outcomes. The level of control and reporting required depends on the complexity and scale of the project, as well as organizational requirements and stakeholder expectations. Here are some key considerations:

1. Scope Management: Control over project scope ensures that the project stays within its defined boundaries. This involves identifying and managing changes to the scope, preventing scope creep, and ensuring that deliverables meet agreed-upon requirements.
2. Schedule Management: Project managers need to establish and maintain project schedules, monitoring progress against timelines, identifying potential delays, and taking corrective action to keep the project on schedule.
3. Cost Management: Controlling project costs involves tracking expenses, managing budgets, and ensuring that the project remains financially viable. This includes identifying cost variances, managing resource allocations, and optimizing spending to maximize value.
4. Quality Management: Maintaining control over project quality involves defining quality standards, monitoring deliverables for adherence to those standards, and implementing quality assurance and quality control processes to ensure that the final product meets quality requirements.
5. Risk Management: Project managers need to identify, assess, and mitigate risks throughout the project lifecycle. This includes developing risk management plans, monitoring risk triggers, and implementing response strategies to minimize the impact of potential threats.
6. Communication Management: Effective communication is essential for project success. Project managers must establish clear communication channels, facilitate regular updates, and progress reports, and ensure that stakeholders are informed and engaged throughout the project.
7. Resource Management: Project managers need to effectively manage project resources, including personnel, equipment, and materials. This involves resource allocation, scheduling, and monitoring resource utilization to ensure that project requirements are met efficiently.
8. Stakeholder Management: Managing stakeholder expectations and relationships is crucial for project success. Project managers need to identify key stakeholders, understand their interests and concerns, and engage with them effectively to build support and address any issues or conflicts that may arise.

Key objectives for project managers to achieve success in project control processes include:

1. Ensuring that project objectives and requirements are clearly defined and understood by all stakeholders.
2. Establishing baseline plans for scope, schedule, cost, quality, and other project parameters.
3. Monitoring project performance against baselines and identifying variances or deviations.
4. Taking timely corrective action to address issues, risks, or changes that may impact project outcomes.
5. Communicating regularly with stakeholders to provide updates on project status, progress, and any changes or challenges.
6. Documenting project activities, decisions, and outcomes to provide a record of project performance and facilitate lessons learned for future projects.

By achieving these objectives, project managers can effectively control and report on project progress, mitigate risks, and ensure successful project delivery.

7.12. Why are project communications so important?

Project communications are crucial for several reasons:

1. Alignment: Effective communication ensures that all stakeholders, including team members, clients, sponsors, and other relevant parties, are on the same page regarding project goals, timelines, and expectations. It aligns everyone's understanding and commitment to the project's

objectives.
2. Clarity: Clear communication helps in conveying instructions, requirements, and updates accurately. It reduces the likelihood of misunderstandings, errors, and rework, thus enhancing overall project efficiency.
3. Risk Management: Good communication facilitates the identification and mitigation of risks. Team members can promptly report issues, concerns, or deviations from the plan, allowing for timely intervention and resolution.
4. Decision Making: Effective communication provides stakeholders with the necessary information to make informed decisions. It ensures that decisions are based on accurate data, stakeholder input, and project objectives, leading to better outcomes.
5. Stakeholder Engagement: Regular and transparent communication fosters positive relationships with stakeholders. It keeps them engaged and informed about project progress, which can increase their confidence and support for the project.
6. Conflict Resolution: Open communication channels enable the early detection and resolution of conflicts within the team or with stakeholders. Addressing conflicts promptly prevents them from escalating and disrupting project progress.
7. Performance Monitoring: Communication allows for the monitoring of project performance against established metrics and targets. It enables the identification of deviations from the plan and facilitates corrective actions to keep the project on track.

In summary, project communications are vital for ensuring coordination, clarity, risk management, decision making, stakeholder engagement, conflict resolution, and performance monitoring throughout the project lifecycle.

7.13. How do you control change requests in a waterfall project?

In a waterfall project management approach, change requests refer to modifications or additions to the project scope, requirements, or other project-related factors that were originally defined in the project's initial planning phase. The waterfall model is characterized by its sequential and linear phases, which include requirements gathering, design, implementation, testing, and deployment.

Managing change requests in a waterfall project requires a structured process to ensure that changes are evaluated, approved, and implemented in a controlled manner. Here is a step-by-step guide on how to control change requests in a waterfall project:

1. Establish a Change Control Board (CCB): A Change Control Board (CCB) should be formed, consisting of key stakeholders, project managers, and technical experts. The CCB is responsible for reviewing, approving, or rejecting change requests.
2. Document Change Request Process: Define and document the process for submitting, reviewing, and implementing change requests. This process should be communicated clearly to all project stakeholders.
3. Change Request Submission: Stakeholders who identify a need for change should submit a formal change request. This request should include:
    a. A detailed description of the change.
    b. The rationale for the change.
    c. Impact analysis (on scope, schedule, cost, quality, and resources).
    d. Any alternatives considered.
4. Initial Evaluation: The project manager or a designated team member performs an initial evaluation of the change request to determine its feasibility and alignment with project goals.
5. Impact Analysis: Conduct a thorough impact analysis to assess how the change will affect various project elements:
    a. Scope: Will the change expand or reduce the project scope?

    b. Schedule: How will the change impact the project timeline?
    c. Cost: What are the financial implications of the change?
    d. Quality: Will the change affect the quality of the final deliverable?
    e. Resources: Are additional resources needed?
6. Review by CCB: The CCB reviews the change request and the associated impact analysis. They evaluate:
    a. The necessity and benefits of the change.
    b. The feasibility of implementing the change.
    c. The impact on project constraints (scope, time, cost, quality).
7. Decision Making: The CCB decides to approve, reject, or request modifications to the change request. The decision should be documented and communicated to all relevant stakeholders.
8. Update Project Documents: If the change request is approved, update the following project documents:
    a. Project Plan: Reflect changes in scope, schedule, cost, and resources.
    b. Requirements Document: Adjust requirements based on the approved changes.
    c. Project Schedule: Update timelines and milestones.
    d. Budget: Modify budget estimates to include the costs associated with the change.
9. Implementation Planning: Create a detailed implementation plan for the approved change. This plan should include:
    a. Specific tasks and activities required.
    b. Assigned responsibilities.
    c. Updated timelines.
    d. Communication plan to inform all stakeholders about the changes.
10. Execution and Monitoring: Execute the change according to the implementation plan. Monitor the change to ensure it is integrated smoothly and does not negatively impact the project. Regularly update the CCB and stakeholders on the progress.
11. Review and Close Change Request: After implementing the change, conduct a review to ensure it meets the expected outcomes and objectives. Close the change request formally by documenting the completion and updating all relevant records.
12. Lessons Learned: Document lessons learned from the change request process and integrate these insights into future change management practices to improve efficiency and effectiveness.

By following these steps, a waterfall project can maintain control over changes, ensuring they are managed in a structured and methodical manner that minimizes disruptions and maintains project integrity.

8. Risk Management

During periods of crisis, be it induced by economic downturns, market pressures, or other triggers, companies must refine their operational strategies to not just weather the storm but to emerge stronger. The essence of effective crisis management lies in establishing robust processes, leveraging analytical tools for proactive issue detection, and fostering seamless communication across all channels. The goal is to mitigate the turbulence inherent in crises and ensure organizational stability.

Today's projects contend with tighter deadlines, heightened technical complexities, and often insufficient resources compared to the past. Nonetheless, there exist specific methodologies to navigate project risks and preemptively address potential hurdles. Learn practical approaches for navigating challenging projects and adapt these techniques to your unique project requirements.

Implementing a software risk management process establishes a systematic approach to embedding risk mitigation within your software development lifecycle(s). It sheds light on the intricacies, business risks (both for developers and end-users), and technological uncertainties. Armed with insights into risks, organizations can allocate resources judiciously and make informed decisions regarding product development. This framework sets the baseline for risk management while allowing for customized procedures tailored to individual contexts.

The practice of project risk management yields several invaluable benefits:

1. Enhances the likelihood of project success.
2. Acknowledges and forecasts potential uncertainties.
3. Facilitates sound decision-making, leading to improved business outcomes.
4. Cultivates a culture of creativity and innovation.
5. Enables better resource allocation and reduces unnecessary overheads, fostering a sharper focus on project benefits.
6. Provides senior management with a clear understanding of project dynamics and the hurdles to be overcome.

8.1. Why projects fail?

Projects can fail for a multitude of reasons, and understanding these reasons is crucial for improving project management practices. Here are some of the most frequently cited reasons for project failure:

1. Poor Planning:
    a. Lack of a clear project plan or roadmap.
    b. Inadequate scope definition and unclear objectives.
    c. Insufficient resources and time allocation.
2. Unclear Requirements:
    a. Misunderstanding or miscommunication of stakeholder requirements.
    b. Scope creep due to continuous changes in requirements.
3. Lack of Stakeholder Engagement:
    a. Inadequate involvement of key stakeholders.
    b. Poor communication and collaboration among stakeholders.
4. Ineffective Communication:
    a. Breakdown in communication channels.
    b. Failure to keep stakeholders informed about project progress and changes.
5. Inadequate Risk Management:
    a. Failure to identify potential risks early.
    b. Lack of risk mitigation strategies and contingency plans.
6. Poor Project Management Practices:
    a. Lack of experienced and skilled project managers.
    b. Inadequate project management methodologies and tools.
7. Resource Mismanagement:

    a. Insufficient allocation of resources (human, financial, or technological).
    b. Overloading team members or lack of necessary skills within the team.
8. Technological Challenges:
    a. Technological issues or failures.
    b. Incompatibility of new systems with existing ones.
9. External Factors:
    a. Regulatory changes or compliance issues.
    b. Market changes or economic downturns.
    c. Natural disasters or unforeseen events.
10. Poor Quality Control:
    a. Inadequate testing and quality assurance processes.
    b. Deliverables that do not meet the required standards or expectations.
11. Lack of Executive Support:
    a. Insufficient backing and support from senior management.
    b. Misalignment between project goals and organizational objectives.
12. Unrealistic Expectations:
    a. Setting goals and timelines that are not feasible.
    b. Over-ambitious project scope and deliverables.
13. Resistance to Change:
    a. Organizational resistance to new processes or systems.
    b. Cultural issues and reluctance to adopt change.
14. Financial Issues:
    a. Budget overruns and financial mismanagement.
    b. Inadequate funding and cost estimation errors.
15. Failure to Adapt:
    a. Inflexibility in adapting to changes and unforeseen challenges.
    b. Rigidity in project management processes and lack of innovation.

You can view these reasons for failure through a number of prisms, and with a 'governance' hat on we could identify this aspect in most of them, however, we can see themes of:
1. lack of leadership
2. lack of engagement (with senior sponsors, stakeholders, supply chain)
3. lack of team integration
4. lack of skills.

Addressing these common reasons for project failure involves implementing robust project management practices, improving communication, engaging stakeholders effectively, and ensuring flexibility and adaptability throughout the project lifecycle. By focusing on these areas, organizations can enhance their chances of project success.

8.2. Why should you manage risk?

The delivery of each project involves costs influenced by three primary constraints: Time, Quality, and Resources. Changes in these parameters can impact the project's scope and, consequently, its delivery. To minimize uncertainties in project delivery, such as delays, budget overruns, or cancellations, an organization must be well-prepared to handle risks. Being equipped to manage these risks can significantly reduce setbacks, if not avoid them entirely. Adopting proactive and practical risk management strategies is essential in achieving this goal.

Managing risk in a project is crucial for several reasons:
1. Mitigate Potential Losses: By identifying and addressing risks proactively, you can reduce the

likelihood and impact of negative events that could result in significant losses. Risk management allows you to implement strategies and actions to minimize or eliminate potential problems before they escalate.

2. Enhance Project Success: Effective risk management improves the overall chances of project success. By understanding the potential risks involved, you can develop contingency plans, allocate resources appropriately, and make informed decisions throughout the project lifecycle. This increases the likelihood of achieving project objectives on time, within budget, and with the desired quality.
3. Stakeholder Satisfaction: Managing risks demonstrates your commitment to delivering a successful project. Stakeholders, including clients, customers, investors, and team members, appreciate the proactive approach to risk management. It instills confidence in your ability to handle challenges and increases their trust in the project's outcomes.
4. Resource Optimization: Risk management helps in optimizing the allocation of resources. By identifying potential risks early on, you can allocate resources such as time, budget, and personnel to address those risks effectively. This prevents unnecessary wastage and ensures that resources are utilized efficiently towards risk mitigation efforts.
5. Decision Making: Risk management provides valuable insights that aid decision-making processes. When risks are identified and assessed, you have a better understanding of the potential consequences associated with different choices. This enables you to make informed decisions, considering both the potential rewards and the risks involved.
6. Early Problem Detection: Risk management allows you to detect potential issues at an early stage. By actively monitoring and assessing risks throughout the project, you can identify warning signs and take corrective actions promptly. This helps in preventing risks from escalating into major problems that could derail the project.
7. Continuous Improvement: Risk management is an iterative process that fosters continuous improvement. By documenting and analyzing risks encountered in current and past projects, you can identify trends, common pitfalls, and areas for improvement. This knowledge can be leveraged to enhance future projects and establish best practices within your organization.

In summary, managing risk in a project is essential for minimizing losses, increasing the chances of success, satisfying stakeholders, optimizing resource allocation, facilitating decision-making, detecting problems early, and promoting continuous improvement. It is a proactive approach that enhances project outcomes and overall project management effectiveness

8.3. What does risk management involve? Or What activities does an organization practicing risk management performs?

An organization practicing risk management engages in several key activities to identify, assess, mitigate, and monitor risks across various aspects of its operations. Some of these activities include:

1. Risk Identification: Identify and record risks in risk register. Identifying potential risks that could affect the organization's objectives, projects, or processes. This involves understanding internal and external factors that may pose threats or opportunities.
2. Risk Assessment: Evaluating the likelihood and potential impact of identified risks. Determine the consequences that can happen if risk occur This step helps prioritize risks based on their significance and the organization's tolerance for them.
3. Risk Mitigation: Developing strategies and measures to reduce the probability or impact of identified risks. This could involve implementing controls, transferring risks through insurance, or avoiding certain activities altogether. If it is not viable to avoid it, identify strategies to reduce the impact.
4. Risk Monitoring: Continuously monitoring the effectiveness of risk management measures and reassessing risks as circumstances change. This ensures that the organization remains proactive in

addressing emerging threats and opportunities.

5. Risk Communication: Facilitating open communication channels regarding risks throughout the organization. This involves sharing information about risks, their potential impacts, and the strategies in place to manage them.
6. Risk Reporting: Providing regular reports to stakeholders, including management, investors, regulators, and other relevant parties, on the organization's risk exposure, mitigation efforts, and overall risk posture.
7. Compliance Management: Ensuring that the organization adheres to relevant laws, regulations, and industry standards related to risk management. This includes implementing controls to mitigate legal and regulatory risks.
8. Crisis Preparedness and Response: Developing plans and procedures to effectively respond to crises or unexpected events. This may involve conducting simulations, training staff, and establishing crisis management teams. Assign resources in accordance with risk response plan.
9. Risk Culture Promotion: Fostering a risk-aware culture within the organization, where employees understand their roles and responsibilities in managing risks and feel empowered to raise concerns or propose improvements.
10. Continuous Improvement: Regularly reviewing and refining the organization's risk management processes and practices based on lessons learned, feedback, and changes in the business environment. This ensures that risk management remains effective and adaptable over time.

8.4. What are some of the tips to manage project risks?

Managing project risks effectively is crucial for the success of any project. Here are some key tips for managing project risks:

1. Identify Risks Early and Continually
    a. Risk Identification Workshops: Conduct sessions with stakeholders to brainstorm potential risks.
    b. Historical Data Analysis: Review previous projects to identify common risks.
    c. Regular Reviews: Continuously monitor the project environment to identify new risks.
2. Assess and Prioritize Risks
    a. Risk Assessment Matrix: Evaluate the likelihood and impact of each risk to prioritize them.
    b. Quantitative Analysis: Use techniques like Monte Carlo simulation for a more detailed risk analysis.
    c. Qualitative Analysis: Categorize risks based on their potential impact and likelihood.
3. Develop Risk Mitigation Strategies
    a. Avoidance: Change project plans to eliminate the risk.
    b. Mitigation: Implement actions to reduce the likelihood or impact of the risk.
    c. Transfer: Shift the risk to a third party, such as through insurance or outsourcing.
    d. Acceptance: Acknowledge the risk and prepare contingency plans.
4. Create a Risk Management Plan
    a. Documentation: Clearly document all identified risks, their assessments, and planned responses.
    b. Assign Responsibilities: Ensure each risk has an owner who is responsible for monitoring and managing it.
    c. Contingency Plans: Develop specific plans for high-priority risks.
5. Monitor and Review Risks Regularly
    a. Risk Registers: Maintain an up-to-date list of risks, including their status and any changes.
    b. Regular Meetings: Hold periodic risk review meetings with the project team and stakeholders.

    c. Indicators and Metrics: Use key risk indicators (KRIs) to monitor risk levels and trigger action.
6. Communicate Effectively
    a. Stakeholder Engagement: Keep all relevant stakeholders informed about risks and their management.
    b. Transparent Reporting: Use clear and concise reporting formats to communicate risk status.
    c. Feedback Mechanisms: Establish channels for stakeholders to provide input and feedback on risks.
7. Utilize Risk Management Tools
    a. Software: Use project management software with built-in risk management features.
    b. Templates and Checklists: Leverage existing templates for risk assessment and mitigation planning.
    c. Decision Support Systems: Employ tools that help in analyzing and prioritizing risks.
8. Build a Risk-Aware Culture
    a. Training: Provide risk management training for the project team.
    b. Leadership Support: Ensure that project leadership supports and prioritizes risk management.
    c. Learning from Experience: Encourage a culture of learning from past projects to improve future risk management.
9. Incorporate Flexibility
    a. Adaptive Planning: Be ready to adjust plans as new risks are identified or existing risks change.
    b. Reserves: Include time and budget reserves to accommodate unforeseen risks.
10. Engage with Experts
    a. Consultants: Work with risk management experts for specialized advice.
    b. Industry Insights: Stay informed about risk trends and best practices in your industry.

By following these tips, project managers can effectively identify, assess, and mitigate risks, thereby increasing the likelihood of project success.

8.5. How does project management help the company better manage risk?

It is a critical component of the way we address change management and risk management. For example, we recently completed a large project with a regular customer that had a new manager who was not very good at planning. He fed his business requirements to my team, but his planning and monitoring were inefficient. As a result, the requirements kept changing, which made it difficult to manage the project.

Internally, our project manager highlighted this as an ongoing risk on the project, and we kept a close watch on him, tracking the changes and their impact on our ability to deliver. Eventually, when the project began to suffer, we went to the project steering committee to resolve the problem. Rather than making it a personal issue about the manager, we addressed it as a change-management issue. Because we had the documentation of the requirement changes that had occurred, we were able to justify our concerns and make joint decisions to resolve the problem and get the project back on track.

Project management plays a crucial role in helping companies better manage risk in several ways:

1. Risk Identification: Project managers are responsible for identifying potential risks that may arise during the course of a project. This involves analyzing various aspects of the project such as scope, resources, timelines, and external factors to pinpoint potential threats.
2. Risk Assessment: Once risks are identified, project managers assess the likelihood and potential impact of each risk on the project's objectives. This assessment helps prioritize risks based on

their severity and the degree of impact they could have on project outcomes.

3. Risk Mitigation Planning: Project managers develop strategies and action plans to mitigate identified risks. This may involve implementing preventive measures to reduce the likelihood of risk occurrence or contingency plans to minimize the impact if a risk does materialize.
4. Monitoring and Control: Throughout the project lifecycle, project managers continuously monitor and control risk factors to ensure they remain within acceptable limits. This involves tracking key performance indicators, regularly assessing risk status, and implementing adjustments as necessary.
5. Communication and Stakeholder Engagement: Effective communication is essential for managing risk. Project managers keep stakeholders informed about potential risks, mitigation strategies, and any changes to the risk landscape. Engaging stakeholders in risk management processes fosters collaboration and ensures alignment with project objectives.
6. Adaptability and Flexibility: Project management frameworks often incorporate principles of adaptability and flexibility, allowing teams to respond quickly to changing risk scenarios. Agile methodologies, for example, emphasize iterative development and frequent reassessment of priorities, which can help teams address emerging risks in a timely manner.
7. Documentation and Lessons Learned: Project managers maintain thorough documentation of risk management activities, including risk registers, mitigation plans, and post-project evaluations. This documentation serves as a valuable resource for future projects, enabling teams to learn from past experiences and refine risk management processes over time.

By employing these strategies and techniques, project management helps companies proactively identify, assess, mitigate, and monitor risks, ultimately enhancing their ability to achieve project objectives and minimize potential disruptions.

8.6. Do you plan to produce a risk management plan? And how often do you intend to update the plan?

A risk management plan is developed at the beginning of the project's planning phase to ensure that contingencies are incorporated into the project schedule and cost estimate. This plan should be revised and updated as additional information becomes available throughout the project's lifecycle.

The frequency of updating a risk management plan depends on various factors, including the nature of the project or organization, the level of risks involved, and any changes in the external or internal environment. Typically, risk management plans are reviewed and updated regularly to ensure they remain relevant and effective. It is common for organizations to conduct periodic reviews, such as weekly, monthly, quarterly, or annually, to reassess risks, evaluate the effectiveness of existing risk mitigation strategies, and make necessary adjustments to the plan.

Additionally, risk management plans may also need to be updated whenever significant changes occur within the project or organization, such as changes in objectives, stakeholders, regulations, technologies, or external market conditions. It is important to maintain an ongoing process of risk identification, assessment, and mitigation to adapt to evolving circumstances and minimize potential impacts.

Remember that developing and updating a risk management plan is a dynamic and iterative process, aiming to proactively address potential risks and ensure the successful execution of a project or the resilience of an organization.

8.7. What is the best time to manage risks in your project?

Whether you are launching your project or well into it, one has to be always proactive in identifying and mitigating risks headed your way. A risk brainstorming session should occur early in project planning.

The best time to manage risks in a project is throughout its entire lifecycle, from initiation to closure. Effective risk management is an ongoing process that should be integrated into all stages of project planning and execution. However, there are certain key moments in a project where risk management activities are particularly important:

1. Project Initiation: Identify risks early on during project initiation. This involves conducting a thorough analysis of the project's objectives, scope, stakeholders, and constraints. By identifying potential risks at the beginning, you can develop strategies to mitigate or address them proactively.
2. Planning Phase: Risk management activities should be an integral part of the project planning process. During this phase, perform a comprehensive risk assessment to identify and analyze potential risks, including their impact and likelihood. Develop risk response strategies, contingency plans, and mitigation measures.
3. Ongoing Monitoring: Continuously monitor the project's progress and the external environment to identify any emerging risks. Regularly review and update the risk register to ensure that it reflects the current state of the project. Monitor key performance indicators (KPIs) and conduct risk assessments at regular intervals to proactively address any new risks that may arise.
4. Milestones and Decision Points: Pay particular attention to risk management at project milestones, decision points, or critical stages. These junctures often involve significant changes or important choices that can have a substantial impact on the project's success. Evaluate risks and reassess the effectiveness of risk mitigation strategies to ensure they remain appropriate and effective.
5. Change Management: Whenever there are changes in project scope, objectives, resources, or other critical factors, conduct a thorough analysis of the associated risks. Determine how these changes might affect existing risks or introduce new ones, and adjust risk management strategies accordingly.
6. Project Closure: As the project nears completion, conduct a final risk assessment to identify any remaining risks or potential issues that could affect the project's successful closure. Take necessary steps to address these risks and ensure a smooth transition to post-project activities.

Remember, risk management is an ongoing process that requires continuous attention and adaptation throughout the project's lifecycle. By actively managing risks at each stage, you can enhance the project's chances of success and minimize the negative impacts of unforeseen events.

8.8. How do you approach risk management? How does formal risk analysis and risk management can help you?

Risk management is a structured approach to identifying, assessing, and mitigating risks that could potentially impact the achievement of objectives. Here is how we approach risk management:

1. Risk Identification
   a. Brainstorming: Gather a diverse team to brainstorm potential risks.
   b. Historical Data: Analyze past projects or similar scenarios to identify common risks.
   c. Expert Judgment: Consult with experts to identify less obvious risks.
   d. Checklists: Use risk checklists tailored to the specific industry or project.
2. Risk Assessment
   a. Qualitative Analysis: Evaluate risks based on their likelihood and impact using a risk matrix.
   b. Quantitative Analysis: Use numerical methods such as Monte Carlo simulations, decision trees, or sensitivity analysis to quantify risks.
3. Risk Prioritization

   a. Risk Matrix: Categorize risks based on their severity and likelihood to prioritize them.
   b. Risk Appetite: Consider the organization's risk tolerance to prioritize risks accordingly.
4. Risk Mitigation Strategies
   a. Avoidance: Change the project plan to eliminate the risk.
   b. Mitigation: Implement measures to reduce the likelihood or impact of the risk.
   c. Transfer: Shift the risk to a third party (e.g., insurance, outsourcing).
   d. Acceptance: Acknowledge the risk and plan for contingencies if it occurs.
5. Risk Monitoring and Review
   a. Regular Reviews: Schedule regular risk reviews to monitor the status of identified risks and identify new risks.
   b. Risk Audits: Conduct periodic risk audits to ensure compliance with the risk management plan.
   c. Feedback Loops: Incorporate lessons learned from past projects into the risk management process.
6. Communication and Documentation
   a. Risk Register: Maintain a detailed risk register that documents all identified risks, assessments, and mitigation plans.
   b. Stakeholder Communication: Ensure regular communication with stakeholders about risk status and changes.

How Formal Risk Analysis and Risk Management Help
1. Proactive Identification of Risks: Formal processes ensure that risks are identified early, allowing for proactive management rather than reactive firefighting.
2. Improved Decision Making: Quantitative risk analysis provides data-driven insights that inform better decision-making, balancing risks against potential rewards.
3. Resource Allocation: Prioritizing risks helps in the effective allocation of resources to the most critical areas, ensuring that time and money are spent where they are most needed.
4. Enhanced Project Outcomes: By managing risks systematically, projects are more likely to stay on schedule, within budget, and meet quality standards.
5. Stakeholder Confidence: A formal risk management process demonstrates due diligence and competence, increasing stakeholder confidence and support.
6. Regulatory Compliance: Many industries require formal risk management processes to comply with regulations and standards, thereby avoiding legal and financial penalties.
7. Continuous Improvement: Documenting risks and their outcomes allows organizations to learn from past experiences, continuously improving their risk management practices.

Risk management can be approached as, in the decreasing order of importance:
1. Likelihood and consequences of occurrence
2. Organized assessment and control of project threats
3. Both positive and negative variations to plan
4. Difference between means and ends.

Overall, formal risk analysis and risk management provide a structured and systematic approach to dealing with uncertainty, enhancing the likelihood of achieving organizational objectives and project success.

8.9. What is a project risk? What are its effects, whether positive or negative, on the prospects of achieving project objectives?

A project risk is any uncertain event or condition that, if it occurs, can have a positive or negative effect on a project's objectives. These objectives can include scope, schedule, cost, quality, and overall project performance. Understanding and managing project risks is a critical aspect of project management to ensure successful project completion.

Negative Effects of Project Risks (Threats)

1. Delays in Schedule: Risks such as resource shortages, technical failures, or unforeseen challenges can lead to delays, causing the project to miss deadlines.
2. Cost Overruns: Unexpected expenses from issues like procurement delays, scope changes, or regulatory changes can increase project costs beyond the planned budget.
3. Quality Issues: Risks related to poor quality materials, inadequate testing, or insufficient stakeholder involvement can lead to defects and low-quality outputs.
4. Scope Creep: Uncontrolled changes or continuous addition of features can lead to scope creep, impacting the project's timeline, budget, and resources.
5. Resource Constraints: Unavailability of key resources (personnel, equipment, materials) can halt or slow down project progress.
6. Stakeholder Dissatisfaction: Poor risk management can lead to unmet expectations, reduced trust, and dissatisfaction among stakeholders.

Positive Effects of Project Risks (Opportunities)

1. Cost Savings: Identifying and leveraging cost-saving opportunities, such as bulk purchasing discounts or process efficiencies, can reduce project costs.
2. Time Savings: Streamlining processes or adopting more efficient methodologies can result in completing the project ahead of schedule.
3. Improved Quality: Implementing innovative solutions or adopting best practices can enhance the quality of the project's deliverables.
4. Increased Scope: Discovering additional needs or beneficial features can add value to the project, enhancing its outcomes.
5. Enhanced Stakeholder Satisfaction: Proactively managing risks and communicating effectively can lead to higher stakeholder confidence and satisfaction.

To effectively manage project risks, project managers typically follow these steps:

1. Risk Identification: Identifying potential risks that could affect the project.
2. Risk Assessment: Evaluating the likelihood and impact of each identified risk.
3. Risk Prioritization: Prioritizing risks based on their potential impact and likelihood of occurrence.
4. Risk Mitigation: Developing strategies to minimize the negative impact or enhance the positive impact of risks.
5. Risk Monitoring and Control: Continuously monitoring risks and implementing mitigation strategies as needed.

By systematically identifying, assessing, and managing risks, project managers can minimize the adverse effects of threats and maximize the benefits of opportunities, thereby increasing the likelihood of achieving project objectives successfully.

8.10. How can I detect risks?

Detecting risks is a precondition for managing them. Research shows that many risks known to team members or others involved in a project remain unknown to the decision makers. This could potentially result in a project disaster. Talking to people involved in the project is one of the most effective means to discover risks. Reading relevant documents is another one, as some risks are written down in (project) documents within and outside the company.

Risk detection raises the question of "is something a risk or not"? A risk fulfills the following conditions:

1. Occurrence is uncertain: a risk may or may not happen. The chance of occurrence is a number between 0 and 1.
2. Project objectives are affected: the project goals are at stake if a risk occurs. If the effects on a project are non-existent, there is no risk.

8.11. How should we analyze risks?

Risk analysis aims at understanding the fundamentals of a risk. The insights gained provide a solid basis to find responses and initiate tasks. If you want to analyze risks use a generic approach first, and then focus in depth on the issues that are of most interest. A good start is to describe risks, their causes, and effects. Complex, time consuming quantitative analyses are a last resort.

Analyzing project risks involves a systematic process to identify, evaluate, and prioritize potential risks that could impact the project's success. Here is a comprehensive approach to analyze project risks:

1. Risk Identification
    a. Brainstorming Sessions: Engage the project team and stakeholders in brainstorming sessions to identify potential risks.
    b. Checklists: Use standardized checklists based on previous projects or industry standards to ensure no common risks are overlooked.
    c. SWOT Analysis: Conduct a SWOT analysis to identify internal and external factors that could pose risks.
    d. Expert Judgment: Consult with experts or experienced team members to identify risks based on their knowledge and past experiences.
    e. Documentation Review: Review project documents such as plans, contracts, and specifications to identify potential risks.
2. Risk Categorization
    a. Internal vs. External Risks: Classify risks based on whether they originate within the project or from external sources.
    b. Technical, Managerial, Commercial, and External: Categorize risks into different areas such as technical (e.g., technology failure), managerial (e.g., resource allocation), commercial (e.g., vendor issues), and external (e.g., regulatory changes).
3. Risk Analysis
    a. Qualitative Analysis:
        i. Probability and Impact Assessment: Evaluate the likelihood of each risk occurring and its potential impact on the project. This is often done using a risk matrix.
        ii. Risk Ranking: Rank risks based on their severity, combining both probability and impact. Risk = probability of event x cost of event
        iii. Risk Urgency Assessment: Determine how quickly a response is needed for each risk.
    b. Quantitative Analysis:
        i. Monte Carlo Simulation: Use statistical methods to model the probability of different outcomes.
        ii. Sensitivity Analysis: Assess how variations in project parameters affect risk outcomes.
        iii. Expected Monetary Value (EMV): Calculate the financial impact of risks by multiplying the probability of each risk by its cost impact.
        iv. Decision Tree Analysis: Use decision trees to evaluate the implications of different risk scenarios and their potential outcomes.
4. Risk Prioritization
    a. Risk Matrix: Use a risk matrix to plot risks based on their probability and impact, helping

to prioritize which risks need immediate attention.
    b. Risk Score: Assign scores to each risk based on qualitative and quantitative analysis to facilitate prioritization.
5. Risk Response Planning
    a. Risk Avoidance: Change the project plan to eliminate the risk.
    b. Risk Mitigation: Implement measures to reduce the probability or impact of the risk.
    c. Risk Transfer: Transfer the risk to a third party, such as through insurance or outsourcing.
    d. Risk Acceptance: Acknowledge the risk and decide to accept it without taking any action unless it occurs.
6. Risk Monitoring and Control
    a. Regular Reviews: Conduct regular risk reviews and update the risk register.
    b. Key Risk Indicators (KRIs): Establish KRIs to monitor potential risk triggers.
    c. Contingency Planning: Develop contingency plans for high-priority risks to ensure quick response if they occur.
    d. Risk Audits: Periodically audit risk management processes and controls to ensure they are effective.
7. Documentation and Reporting
    a. Risk Register: Maintain a detailed risk register documenting all identified risks, their analysis, response plans, and current status.
    b. Risk Reports: Regularly report on risk status to stakeholders, highlighting critical risks and actions taken.

Tools and Techniques
1. Risk Management Software: Utilize specialized software for risk identification, analysis, and tracking.
2. Workshops and Meetings: Facilitate workshops and regular meetings to discuss and review risks.
3. Surveys and Questionnaires: Collect input from stakeholders through surveys and questionnaires to identify and assess risks.

By following this structured approach, project managers can effectively analyze and manage risks, increasing the likelihood of project success and minimizing potential negative impacts.

8.12. How should we prioritize risks?

Prioritizing project risks is essential for effective risk management. Given the potentially vast number of risks, it is impossible to address them all simultaneously, necessitating the establishment of priorities. Risks with the greatest impact on the project should be prioritized highest. These are identified by their risk class, which can range from catastrophic to minor for threats, and from superb to negligible for opportunities. Additional criteria influencing prioritization include the frequency of risk occurrences, the nature of their effects, and the tools and resources available to the project team. Prioritization can also occur at the levels of effects, responses, and causes, always starting with those that have the highest impact.

Here is a structured approach you can follow:
1. Risk Identification: Begin by identifying all potential risks associated with your project. This can be done through brainstorming sessions, historical data analysis, expert interviews, and risk checklists.
2. Risk Assessment: Once you have identified potential risks, assess each one based on its probability of occurring and the impact it would have on your project objectives. You can use qualitative (e.g., low, medium, high) or quantitative (numerical scales) methods for this assessment.

3. Risk Analysis: Analyze each risk to understand its root causes, potential triggers, and potential consequences. This step helps in gaining a deeper understanding of the risks and devising appropriate response strategies.
4. Risk Prioritization Techniques:
    a. Risk Matrix: Plot risks on a matrix based on their likelihood and impact. Risks falling in the high likelihood-high impact quadrant should be prioritized.
    b. Risk Scoring: Assign numerical scores to risks based on predefined criteria such as probability, impact, exposure, etc. Calculate a risk score by multiplying probability and impact scores. Rank risks based on their scores.
    c. Risk Categorization: Categorize risks based on their nature (e.g., technical, financial, operational) and prioritize within each category based on their severity.
    d. Expert Judgment: Involve project team members and subject matter experts to collectively prioritize risks based on their knowledge and experience.
5. Risk Response Planning: Develop response plans for prioritized risks. For high-priority risks, focus on proactive strategies such as risk avoidance, mitigation, or transfer. For lower-priority risks, consider contingency plans or acceptance strategies.
6. Continuous Monitoring: Monitor identified risks throughout the project lifecycle. Update risk assessments periodically, especially when significant changes occur in project scope, schedule, or resources.
7. Communication and Documentation: Communicate prioritized risks and their response plans to stakeholders. Maintain a risk register documenting all identified risks, their prioritization rationale, and corresponding response strategies.

By following these steps, you can effectively prioritize project risks and allocate resources for risk management activities accordingly, thereby enhancing the project's likelihood of success.

8.13. What is a risk class?

A risk class refers to a category or grouping of risks based on certain characteristics or criteria. These classes help in organizing, prioritizing, and managing risks more effectively within a project. Risk classes can be defined based on factors such as the source of risk, the impact on the project, the probability of occurrence, or the type of consequences.

The risk class represents the expected impact of a risk on the project, determined by two main criteria:
1. Likelihood of occurrence: How likely is the risk to happen?
2. Risk effect: What will be the impact if the risk occurs?

As both the likelihood and impact increase, the risk class also rises. For risks with negative impacts, the risk class ranges from low to fatal. For risks with positive impacts, the range is from minor opportunity to great opportunity. A third criterion sometimes considered is the project team's ability to influence the risk. When the team has little control over a risk, it poses a greater threat to the project.

Common Risk Classes in Project Management:
1. Technical Risks: Related to technology and the technical aspects of the project, such as software or hardware failures, technical complexities, and integration issues.
2. Financial Risks: Pertaining to financial aspects, including budget overruns, cost escalations, and funding shortages.
3. Operational Risks: Concerns with day-to-day operations, including process inefficiencies, resource unavailability, and logistical challenges.
4. Strategic Risks: Linked to strategic decisions and external factors, such as market changes, competition, and regulatory changes.

5. Compliance Risks: Related to legal and regulatory requirements, such as violations of laws, regulations, or standards.
6. Environmental Risks: Associated with environmental factors and natural events, such as earthquakes, floods, and other natural disasters.
7. Human Resources Risks: Involving personnel issues, such as staff turnover, lack of skilled resources, and labor disputes.
8. Reputational Risks: Risks that can affect the organization's reputation and stakeholder trust, including public relations issues and negative media coverage.

Using Risk Classes in Project Risk Management:

1. Identification: Classifying risks into predefined classes helps in systematically identifying potential risks. It ensures a comprehensive assessment by considering all possible sources and types of risks.
2. Assessment and Prioritization: By grouping risks into classes, project managers can assess and prioritize them more effectively. For example, technical risks might be assessed differently compared to financial risks based on their specific criteria and impact on the project.
3. Analysis: Risk classes allow for more targeted analysis. For example, a detailed analysis can be performed on financial risks using financial models, while technical risks might be analyzed using engineering simulations or technical reviews.
4. Mitigation Strategies: Different risk classes may require different mitigation strategies. By categorizing risks, appropriate and specialized mitigation plans can be developed. For example, operational risks may need process improvements, while compliance risks may need strict adherence to regulations and policies.
5. Monitoring and Control: Grouping risks into classes helps in setting up specific monitoring and control mechanisms for each class. For instance, technical risks might be monitored through regular technical reviews, while financial risks could be tracked through budget reports and financial audits.
6. Communication and Reporting: Using risk classes facilitates clearer communication and reporting. Stakeholders can better understand the nature and implications of various risks when they are organized into classes. It also helps in creating more structured and focused risk reports.
7. Resource Allocation: Allocating resources for risk management becomes more efficient with risk classes. Resources can be assigned based on the risk class's impact and likelihood, ensuring that critical risks receive adequate attention and resources.
8. Continuous Improvement: Analyzing risks within their classes over time can provide insights into trends and patterns, leading to continuous improvement in risk management practices.

Example: Consider a software development project. The project manager can categorize risks as follows:

1. Technical Risks: Software bugs, integration issues, technology changes.
2. Financial Risks: Budget overruns, cost misestimations.
3. Operational Risks: Delays in delivery, resource unavailability.
4. Human Resources Risks: Key personnel leaving, skill shortages.

By classifying these risks, the project manager can develop specific mitigation strategies such as:

1. Conducting regular code reviews and testing (Technical Risks).
2. Monitoring budget and expenditure closely (Financial Risks).
3. Ensuring backup resources and contingency plans (Operational Risks).
4. Implementing staff retention and training programs (Human Resources Risks).

This structured approach enhances the project's risk management efficiency and effectiveness.

8.14. What is the essence of risk management?

Why should a company invest effort in managing project risks? Project managers are often stretched thin as it is, and adding another task may seem like unnecessary stress. However, the rationale is straightforward: effective risk management yields significant returns. Project risk management fundamentally aims to mitigate threats and capitalize on opportunities, ultimately leading to reduced costs and increased revenues. Additionally, it can expedite time-to-market and elevate the quality of project outcomes.

The essence of risk management is the systematic process of identifying, assessing, and mitigating risks in order to minimize potential losses or negative impacts and maximize opportunities. It involves understanding and analyzing risks, making informed decisions, and implementing appropriate strategies to manage or control those risks within an organization or project.

At its core, risk management aims to strike a balance between taking risks to achieve goals and objectives and avoiding or mitigating risks that could hinder success. The essence of risk management can be summarized in the following key points:

1. Identification: Recognizing and understanding potential risks and their sources, both internal and external to the organization or project. This involves evaluating various factors such as financial, operational, legal, reputational, and strategic risks.
2. Assessment: Evaluating the likelihood and potential impact of identified risks. This step helps prioritize risks based on their significance and enables the allocation of resources to manage them effectively.
3. Mitigation: Developing and implementing risk mitigation strategies to reduce the likelihood or impact of identified risks. This may involve avoiding, transferring, accepting, or controlling risks through preventive measures, contingency plans, insurance, contracts, diversification, or other risk treatment options.
4. Monitoring: Continuously monitoring and reviewing risks to ensure that mitigation strategies remain effective and relevant. Regular assessments and updates are necessary as risks can change over time due to internal or external factors.
5. Communication: Establishing effective communication channels to share risk information across all levels of an organization or project. This facilitates awareness, understanding, and collaboration among stakeholders, enabling informed decision-making and prompt response to emerging risks.
6. Adaptation: Being flexible and adaptive to changing circumstances and emerging risks. Risk management is an ongoing process that requires periodic reassessment and adjustment of strategies to address new or evolving risks effectively.

By embracing these principles, organizations can proactively identify and manage risks, enhance decision-making processes, protect assets, and optimize opportunities for success. The essence of risk management lies in fostering a culture that recognizes the importance of risk awareness, informed decision-making, and continuous improvement to achieve desired outcomes while minimizing potential harm.

8.15. What role do project partners have in managing project risks?

Projects often involve collaboration among employees spanning various departments and even different companies. Such collaborations introduce risks that transcend organizational boundaries, necessitating careful consideration of ownership issues. When external partners are part of the equation, contracting becomes crucial. Determining who is responsible for managing risks and bearing the consequences thereof becomes paramount. Often, risks are shared among contracting parties, mirroring the principles of many insurance agreements.

Project partners play a crucial role in managing project risks. Here are some ways in which project partners contribute to risk management:

1. Risk Identification: Project partners bring diverse perspectives, expertise, and experience to the project, which can aid in identifying potential risks. They contribute by actively participating in risk identification activities such as brainstorming sessions, workshops, and risk assessment exercises.
2. Risk Assessment: Partners provide valuable input during the risk assessment process. They help evaluate the likelihood and impact of identified risks based on their domain knowledge and insights. Their contributions assist in prioritizing risks and determining appropriate mitigation strategies.
3. Mitigation Planning: Project partners collaborate with the project team to develop mitigation plans for identified risks. They contribute by suggesting alternative approaches, proposing risk response strategies, and recommending specific actions to reduce or eliminate risks. Their involvement helps ensure a comprehensive and well-rounded mitigation plan.
4. Risk Monitoring: Partners actively participate in the ongoing monitoring of project risks. They assist in tracking the effectiveness of mitigation measures, identifying emerging risks, and evaluating changes in the risk landscape. By providing timely updates and feedback, they help maintain a vigilant approach to risk management throughout the project lifecycle.
5. Risk Sharing: Depending on the project structure and agreements, project partners may also share the responsibility of managing specific risks. This can involve allocating resources, establishing risk-sharing mechanisms, or implementing contractual provisions to address and mitigate potential risks that fall within their scope of expertise or influence.
6. Knowledge Sharing: Project partners bring their unique industry insights, best practices, and lessons learned from previous projects. They share their knowledge and experience, enabling the project team to benefit from a broader perspective on risk management. This collaboration enhances the project's ability to proactively address risks and make informed decisions.
7. Stakeholder Engagement: Project partners often have established relationships with various stakeholders. They can help manage risks associated with stakeholder expectations, communication, and engagement. By leveraging their networks and influence, partners contribute to building strong relationships, resolving conflicts, and ensuring stakeholders' interests are appropriately addressed.

In summary, project partners play an active and collaborative role in managing project risks. Their contributions throughout the risk management process, from identification to mitigation and monitoring, enhance the project team's ability to proactively address risks and increase the chances of project success.

8.16. What are the things you do to get projects back on track?

When a project is off track, there are several steps you can take to get it back on course. Here are some actions you can consider:

1. Assess the current situation: Begin by understanding the project's current status, including its objectives, timelines, deliverables, and resources. Identify the specific areas where the project is falling behind or facing challenges.
2. Identify the root causes: Investigate the reasons behind the project's deviation from the original plan. Look for any gaps in planning, resource allocation, communication, or unforeseen obstacles that might have contributed to the setback.
3. Realign objectives and priorities: Review the project's objectives and goals in light of the current situation. Determine if any adjustments or reprioritization are necessary. Ensure that the team has a clear understanding of the revised objectives and what needs to be achieved.
4. Communicate with stakeholders: Engage in open and transparent communication with project stakeholders, including team members, clients, and sponsors. Inform them about the current

challenges, the steps being taken to address them, and any changes in timelines or deliverables.

5. Review and revise the project plan: Evaluate the existing project plan and make necessary modifications to accommodate the current circumstances. Break down the remaining tasks into manageable milestones and establish realistic deadlines. Ensure that the plan aligns with the project's updated objectives.
6. Allocate and optimize resources: Evaluate the availability and allocation of resources required for the project's successful completion. Consider whether additional resources are necessary or if existing resources can be reallocated to address critical areas. Optimize resource allocation to enhance efficiency and productivity.
7. Enhance team collaboration: Foster effective teamwork and collaboration among project team members. Encourage open communication, promote a problem-solving mindset, and facilitate knowledge sharing. Regularly monitor progress and provide support to team members who may require assistance.
8. Monitor and track progress: Implement a robust project monitoring system to track progress against the revised plan. Use appropriate project management tools and techniques to ensure that tasks are completed on time and within budget. Identify potential risks or bottlenecks early on and take proactive measures to mitigate them.
9. Adjust and adapt as necessary: Stay flexible and adaptable throughout the project recovery process. Be prepared to make further adjustments and refinements as new information or challenges emerge. Continuously evaluate the effectiveness of the recovery efforts and make necessary course corrections.
10. Learn from the experience: Once the project is back on track, conduct a post-mortem analysis to identify lessons learned. Evaluate what went wrong, how it was addressed, and what could be done differently in the future to avoid similar setbacks. Document these insights to improve future project management processes.

Remember, every project is unique, and the specific actions required to get it back on track may vary. It is essential to tailor your approach based on the project's characteristics and the challenges it is facing.

8.17. Your team is primarily junior-level people and you are behind schedule with a drop-dead deliverable date. What would you do?

When you are facing a scenario where your team, composed mainly of junior-level members, is behind schedule with a critical deliverable looming, here are steps you could consider:

1. Assess the Situation: Start by understanding why the team is behind schedule. Is it due to unforeseen challenges, lack of skill, or mismanagement of time and resources?
2. Communicate Clearly: Be transparent with your team about the situation. Let them know the importance of the deliverable, the urgency of catching up, and the potential consequences of not meeting the deadline.
3. Prioritize Tasks: Identify the most critical tasks that need to be completed to meet the deadline. Focus on these tasks first to ensure essential elements are delivered on time.
4. Provide Support and Guidance: Offer support and guidance to junior team members. They may need additional resources, training, or mentorship to overcome challenges and work more efficiently.
5. Encourage Collaboration: Foster a collaborative environment where team members can support each other, share knowledge, and work together to solve problems.
6. Consider Adjusting the Scope: If the deadline is non-negotiable and it becomes apparent that the original scope is unrealistic given the resources and time available, consider negotiating with stakeholders to adjust the scope or deliver the project in phases.
7. Motivate and Inspire: Keep morale high by acknowledging the team's efforts, celebrating small wins, and reminding them of the importance of their work.

8. Lead by Example: Demonstrate a strong work ethic and dedication to meeting the deadline. Show your team that you are willing to roll up your sleeves and help out wherever necessary.
9. Monitor Progress Closely: Keep a close eye on the team's progress and intervene if necessary to address any issues or roadblocks that may arise.
10. Evaluate and Learn: After the project is completed, take the time to evaluate what went well and what could be improved. Use this feedback to learn from the experience and make adjustments for future projects.

By following these steps, you can effectively manage a team of junior-level members and navigate through challenges to deliver the required project on time.

8.18. Describe a time when you had a difficult situation working with a vendor or another peer. What was your approach to resolve the issues while maintaining a positive relationship?

To respond effectively to the interview question about handling a difficult situation with a vendor or peer while maintaining a positive relationship, use the STAR method (Situation, Task, Action, Result). Here is a structured example:

Situation
Begin by describing the context of the situation.
"In my previous role as a project manager, we had a critical project deadline, and a key vendor was consistently missing delivery dates for essential components. This was causing significant delays in our project timeline."
Task
Explain your responsibility in the situation.
"My responsibility was to ensure the project stayed on track and to address any issues with the vendor to get the deliveries back on schedule."
Action
Detail the steps you took to resolve the issue.
"I initiated a meeting with the vendor to discuss the delays. I made sure to approach the conversation with a focus on collaboration rather than confrontation. I asked for their perspective on the delays to understand any underlying issues they were facing. It turned out they were having internal resource allocation problems. We then worked together to create a revised delivery schedule that was realistic for both parties. I also set up regular check-ins to monitor progress and ensure open communication."
Result
Conclude with the outcome of your actions.
"As a result, the vendor was able to meet the revised deadlines, and we completed the project on time. Moreover, by handling the situation diplomatically, we maintained a positive working relationship with the vendor, which proved beneficial for future collaborations."

Key Points to Emphasize:

1. Empathy and Understanding: Show that you tried to understand the vendor's or peer's perspective.
2. Collaboration and Communication: Highlight how you emphasized working together and kept communication lines open.
3. Problem-Solving: Demonstrate your ability to find practical solutions that benefit both parties.
4. Positive Outcome: Focus on the successful resolution and the maintenance of a good relationship.

This approach not only answers the question directly but also showcases your interpersonal skills, problem-solving abilities, and capacity to handle challenging situations effectively.

8.19. When managing a project, when do you know the project is off-track?

Very few (if any) projects fail to hit their expected completion date without prior clues that something is amiss. There are generally two clues that you have a distressed project:

1. Failure to meet milestones on time
2. Changing project requirements.

So, let us examine each in more details. The failure to meet milestones could have several root causes:

1. First, it is the team estimating the time it takes to accomplish various tasks may have been over optimistic (in some cases that is intentional, as you are "downplaying the effort" to get a contract or greenlight, if internal)
2. You might have hit a technical challenge. That happens, especially with new technologies. There is a learning curve, and sometimes its steep! Breakthroughs are notoriously hard to schedule.
3. Your team could be multitasking, in that team members have to stop to work on something else.
4. Conversely, another project is tying up a key resource because they have a problem, and guess what, now you do as well.

The good news is that a successful project can still be late. The changing project requirements is an entirely different issue, but is still a red flag. In fact, nearly all failed projects (defined as never delivering a product) involved important missing requirements, or changes made well after the project was launched.

1. Adding requirements, or scope creep, will add to the projects timeline as well as introduce additional technical risks. If you are fortunate, with the new requirement will come extra time, but that does not always occur (and thus, this point would migrate to the first list!).
2. Missing requirements are similar, but are defined as requirements that should have been part of the original plan.

The biggest problem with "scope creep" is its often senior management adding these new requirements, which makes any offers to politely decline dangerous to one's career. It is one of those damned if you do situations.

Yes, you can document the addition as well as an estimate of the extra effort, but good luck with that. The irony is that organizations prone to do this are also prone to underestimate the time to do the original project scope.

8.20. How to spot a failing project before it becomes a famous failure?

Identifying a failing project early can save time, resources, and reputations. Here are some key signs and strategies to spot a failing project before it becomes a famous failure:

Signs of a Failing Project

1. Lack of Clear Objectives and Scope Creep:
   a. Ambiguous Goals: If the project objectives are not well-defined or keep changing, it can lead to confusion and misalignment.
   b. Scope Creep: Uncontrolled changes or continuous addition of features beyond the original plan can derail the project.
2. Poor Planning and Estimation:
   a. Inaccurate Time and Cost Estimates: Overly optimistic timelines and budgets that do not account for risks and contingencies.
   b. No Detailed Plan: Absence of a detailed project plan with clear milestones and deliverables.
3. Inadequate Resources and Skills:

   a. Lack of Skilled Team Members: Team members lacking the necessary skills or experience for the project.
   b. Insufficient Resources: Not enough people, equipment, or funds to meet project demands.
4. Poor Communication and Collaboration:
   a. Communication Breakdowns: Ineffective communication among team members, stakeholders, and management.
   b. Siloed Work: Teams working in isolation without proper collaboration and integration.
5. Low Morale and High Turnover:
   a. Decreased Motivation: Team members show signs of burnout, disengagement, or lack of enthusiasm.
   b. High Turnover: Frequent changes in team composition due to resignations or reassignments.
6. Missed Deadlines and Deliverables:
   a. Consistent Delays: Regularly missing deadlines and milestones without clear reasons or plans to get back on track.
   b. Incomplete Deliverables: Deliverables that do not meet quality standards or are incomplete.
7. Inconsistent Stakeholder Engagement:
   a. Stakeholder Disinterest: Stakeholders are not actively involved or show declining interest in the project.
   b. Conflicting Priorities: Stakeholders have different or conflicting priorities, causing confusion and delays.
8. Risk Management Failures:
   a. Ignored Risks: Known risks are not being addressed or mitigated.
   b. Unanticipated Problems: Regular emergence of unexpected issues without contingency plans.

Strategies to Identify and Address Potential Failures

1. Regular Progress Reviews:
   a. Conduct frequent status meetings to review progress, identify issues, and adjust plans accordingly.
   b. Use project management tools to track progress against milestones and deliverables.
2. Effective Communication Channels:
   a. Establish clear communication channels and protocols to ensure information flows smoothly among all parties.
   b. Encourage open and honest communication to surface issues early.
3. Stakeholder Involvement:
   a. Ensure stakeholders are regularly updated and involved in key decisions.
   b. Align stakeholder expectations with project goals through regular reviews and feedback sessions.
4. Robust Risk Management:
   a. Develop a comprehensive risk management plan, identifying potential risks and mitigation strategies.
   b. Regularly review and update the risk management plan to address new risks as they arise.
5. Resource Management:
   a. Ensure adequate allocation of resources and address resource gaps promptly.
   b. Provide training and support to team members to build necessary skills and capabilities.
6. Scope Control:
   a. Implement strict change control processes to manage scope changes and prevent scope creep.
   b. Clearly define and communicate project scope from the beginning and get buy-in from all

stakeholders.

7. Quality Assurance:
    a. Establish quality assurance processes to ensure deliverables meet the required standards.
    b. Conduct regular reviews and testing to catch issues early.
8. Performance Metrics:
    a. Define and monitor key performance indicators (KPIs) to gauge project health.
    b. Use KPIs to identify trends and potential problems before they escalate.

By paying attention to these signs and implementing proactive strategies, project managers can spot potential failures early and take corrective actions to steer the project back on track.

8.21. What are the steps to saving troubled projects?

Saving a troubled project involves several critical steps aimed at identifying issues, creating a recovery plan, and implementing corrective actions. Here are the steps to save a troubled project:

1. Identify and Assess Problems
    a. Conduct a Project Review: Analyze the project's current status, including scope, budget, timeline, and quality.
    b. Engage Stakeholders: Communicate with all stakeholders to understand their perspectives and concerns.
    c. Root Cause Analysis: Determine the underlying causes of the problems using techniques such as the 5 Whys or fishbone diagrams.
2. Reassess Project Objectives
    a. Review Project Goals: Ensure the project goals are still valid and align with organizational objectives.
    b. Reprioritize Requirements: Identify which project requirements are critical and which can be modified or deferred.
3. Develop a Recovery Plan
    a. Set Clear Objectives: Define what success looks like for the recovery effort.
    b. Create an Action Plan: Develop a detailed plan that addresses the identified issues, including specific tasks, responsible parties, and deadlines.
    c. Risk Management: Update the risk management plan to address new or previously unidentified risks.
4. Secure Resources
    a. Reallocate Resources: Ensure the project has the necessary resources, which may include additional personnel, budget adjustments, or new tools.
    b. Stakeholder Buy-In: Gain commitment from key stakeholders to support the recovery plan.
5. Implement the Recovery Plan
    a. Execute Corrective Actions: Implement the tasks and strategies outlined in the recovery plan.
    b. Monitor Progress: Establish metrics and monitoring processes to track the implementation of corrective actions.
6. Communicate Regularly
    a. Frequent Updates: Keep all stakeholders informed about progress, changes, and any new issues.
    b. Transparent Reporting: Provide honest and transparent updates to build trust and manage expectations.
7. Adjust as Necessary
    a. Iterative Review: Regularly review progress and make adjustments to the recovery plan as needed.

   b. Flexibility: Be prepared to pivot strategies if certain approaches are not yielding the desired results.
8. Document Lessons Learned
   a. Post-Mortem Analysis: After the project is back on track or completed, conduct a thorough review to identify what went wrong and what was done to fix it.
   b. Knowledge Sharing: Document the lessons learned and share them within the organization to improve future project management practices.

Key Points to Remember
1. Stakeholder Engagement: Keep stakeholders engaged and informed throughout the recovery process.
2. Prioritize Communication: Clear and consistent communication is crucial for managing expectations and maintaining support.
3. Focus on Root Causes: Addressing symptoms without tackling root causes will only provide temporary fixes.
4. Be Realistic: Set achievable goals and timelines to avoid further disappointment and setbacks.

By following these steps, project managers can systematically address issues and steer troubled projects back to a successful path.

8.22. What is risk management?

Risk management is the process of identifying, assessing, prioritizing, and mitigating risks to minimize their impact on an organization's objectives. It involves systematically analyzing potential threats and opportunities, determining the likelihood of occurrence and the potential impact, and then developing strategies to either avoid, reduce, transfer, or accept the risks.

Here is a detailed breakdown of the components of risk management and some examples to illustrate each:
1. Risk Identification: This involves identifying all possible risks that could affect an organization's objectives. Risks can come from various sources such as internal processes, external events, technology, regulations, and market conditions. For example:
   a. Operational Risk: Errors in processes, system failures, or human errors.
   b. Financial Risk: Market volatility, credit risk, or liquidity issues.
   c. Compliance Risk: Violation of laws, regulations, or industry standards.
   d. Strategic Risk: Changes in market dynamics, competitive pressures, or technological advancements.
   e. Reputation Risk: Negative publicity, customer complaints, or brand damage.
2. Risk Assessment: After identifying risks, the next step is to assess their likelihood and potential impact. This is usually done through qualitative or quantitative analysis. Qualitative analysis involves ranking risks based on subjective criteria such as high, medium, or low, while quantitative analysis involves assigning numerical values to the likelihood and impact of risks. For example:
   a. Likelihood: Probability of a risk event occurring (e.g., high, medium, low).
   b. Impact: Severity of the consequences if the risk event occurs (e.g., financial loss, reputation damage).
   c. Risk Matrix: Using a risk matrix to assess and prioritize risks based on their likelihood and impact.
3. Risk Prioritization: Once risks are assessed, they are prioritized based on their significance to the organization's objectives. Risks with higher likelihood and impact are usually given higher priority for mitigation efforts. For example:

    a. Critical Risks: Risks that have a high likelihood and high impact on business objectives.
    b. Moderate Risks: Risks that have either high likelihood or high impact but not both.
    c. Low Risks: Risks with low likelihood and impact, which may be monitored rather than actively managed.
4. Risk Mitigation Strategies: After prioritizing risks, organizations develop and implement strategies to mitigate or manage them effectively. These strategies can include:
    a. Risk Avoidance: Eliminating the activity or process that poses the risk.
    b. Risk Reduction: Implementing controls or safeguards to decrease the likelihood or impact of the risk.
    c. Risk Transfer: Transferring the risk to another party through insurance, contracts, or outsourcing.
    d. Risk Acceptance: Acknowledging the risk and its potential consequences without taking any specific action.
    e. Contingency Planning: Developing plans to respond effectively if the risk event occurs.
5. Monitoring and Review: Risk management is an ongoing process that requires regular monitoring and review to ensure that the identified risks are effectively managed and new risks are promptly addressed. This involves:
    a. Monitoring Key Risk Indicators (KRIs): Tracking indicators that signal changes in risk levels.
    b. Periodic Risk Assessments: Conducting regular assessments to update risk profiles and adjust mitigation strategies as needed.
    c. Learning from Incidents: Analyzing past incidents or near-misses to improve risk management practices.

Overall, effective risk management enables organizations to proactively identify and address potential threats, seize opportunities, and enhance their resilience in a dynamic business environment.

8.23. What are the basic steps in risk management?

Risk management typically involves several steps to identify, assess, mitigate, and monitor risks. Here are the basic steps along with tasks or activities performed in each:

1. Risk Identification:
    a. Task/Activity: Identify potential risks that could impact the project, business, or organization.
    b. Deliverables: Risk register, which documents identified risks along with their descriptions.
2. Risk Assessment:
    a. Task/Activity: Evaluate the likelihood and impact of each identified risk.
    b. Deliverables: Risk assessment matrix or heat map, which ranks risks based on their severity.
3. Risk Mitigation Planning:
    a. Task/Activity: Develop strategies to reduce or eliminate the impact of identified risks.
    b. Deliverables: Risk mitigation plan, which outlines actions to be taken to address each risk.
4. Risk Response Implementation:
    a. Task/Activity: Execute the planned strategies to mitigate or manage the identified risks.
    b. Deliverables: Implemented risk responses, which may include changes to processes, allocation of resources, or contingency plans.
5. Risk Monitoring and Control:
    a. Task/Activity: Regularly monitor identified risks and their associated mitigation strategies.

    b. Deliverables: Risk status reports, which provide updates on the current status of risks and any changes in their likelihood or impact.
6. Risk Communication:
    a. Task/Activity: Share risk information with relevant stakeholders to keep them informed.
    b. Deliverables: Risk communication plan, which outlines how and when risk information will be shared with stakeholders.
7. Risk Review and Evaluation:
    a. Task/Activity: Periodically review the effectiveness of risk management strategies and adjust as necessary.
    b. Deliverables: Lessons learned documentation, which captures insights gained from managing risks and identifies areas for improvement in future projects.

These steps are often cyclical, with risk management being an ongoing process throughout the life of a project or within an organization. Each step contributes to the overall goal of identifying, assessing, and managing risks to minimize their impact on objectives.

8.24. What is risk identification? What areas of the project should be recognized where the risks can occur? What process and/or techniques you should follow for risk identification?

Risk identification is the process of determining risks that could potentially prevent the project from achieving its objectives. It involves recognizing uncertainties, events, or conditions that may have a negative or positive impact on the project. The goal of risk identification is to document these risks and understand their possible effects, which helps in planning and developing strategies to manage them effectively.

Risks can occur in various areas of a project, including but not limited to:
1. Scope: Unclear or changing project requirements, scope creep.
2. Time/Schedule: Delays in project timelines, unrealistic deadlines.
3. Cost: Budget overruns, cost estimation errors, funding issues.
4. Quality: Non-compliance with quality standards, defects in deliverables.
5. Resources: Availability of personnel, equipment, and materials.
6. Stakeholders: Conflicting interests, lack of stakeholder support.
7. Technology: Technology failures, integration issues, technical complexity.
8. Legal/Regulatory: Compliance with laws and regulations, legal liabilities.
9. Environmental: Natural disasters, environmental impacts.
10. Operational: Process inefficiencies, operational disruptions.
11. Market: Market volatility, changes in customer preferences.

Effective risk identification requires a structured approach and the use of various techniques. The process typically involves the following steps:
1. Preparation:
    a. Establish the context by understanding the project goals, scope, and environment.
    b. Gather relevant documents and information.
2. Identification:
    a. Use different techniques to identify potential risks.
3. Documentation:
    a. Record identified risks in a risk register or log with details such as risk description, impact, and probability.
4. Review:
    a. Continuously review and update the risk register as the project progresses.

Techniques for Risk Identification

1. Brainstorming:
    a. Involves a group of people generating ideas about potential risks without immediate critique.
    b. Encourages creative thinking and can uncover a wide range of risks.
2. Delphi Technique:
    a. Uses a panel of experts who anonymously submit risks and then review and refine them through multiple rounds.
    b. Helps in achieving a consensus on significant risks.
3. SWOT Analysis:
    a. Examines internal strengths and weaknesses, as well as external opportunities and threats.
    b. Helps in identifying both positive and negative risks.
4. Checklist Analysis:
    a. Utilizes pre-defined checklists of potential risks based on past projects and industry standards.
    b. Ensures that common risks are not overlooked.
5. Expert Judgment:
    a. Leverages the knowledge and experience of experts to identify risks.
    b. Useful when specialized knowledge is required to foresee potential issues.
6. Root Cause Analysis:
    a. Identifies underlying causes of potential risks.
    b. Helps in understanding and addressing the source of risks rather than just symptoms.
7. Interviewing:
    a. Conducts structured interviews with project stakeholders and team members.
    b. Gathers insights and perspectives on possible risks.
8. Assumption Analysis:
    a. Examines the assumptions made during the project planning.
    b. Identifies risks that could arise if assumptions are incorrect.
9. Diagramming Techniques:
    a. Includes tools like fishbone diagrams (Ishikawa), flowcharts, and influence diagrams to visually map out potential risks.
    b. Helps in understanding relationships and dependencies among risks.
10. Documentation Reviews:
    a. Reviews project documents such as plans, contracts, and requirements.
    b. Identifies risks based on documented information.

By employing a combination of these techniques, project managers can ensure a comprehensive identification of risks, which is crucial for proactive risk management and increasing the likelihood of project success.

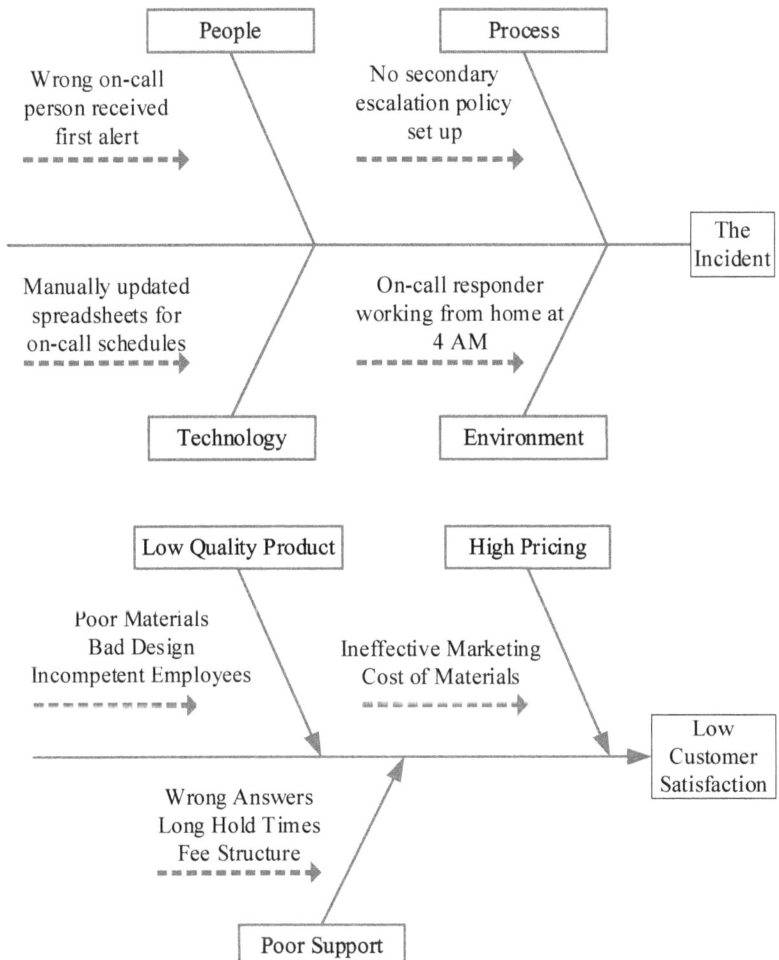

Figure 8.24.1 Cause-and-effect diagrams

8.25. What is risk quantification?

Risk quantification is the process of assigning numerical values to the various risks identified in a project, business operation, or any other endeavor. It involves assessing the likelihood of each risk occurring and estimating the potential impact it could have. By quantifying risks, decision-makers can prioritize them based on their potential severity and likelihood, allowing for more informed risk management strategies.

Risk quantification in project management involves assessing and assigning numerical values to various aspects of risks associated with a project. It is a process of assigning a quantitative value to the probability and impact of identified risks. Here is how it generally works:

1. Identifying Risks: The first step is to identify potential risks that could impact the project's objectives. These risks could be related to budget, schedule, resources, technology, stakeholders, etc.
2. Qualitative Assessment: Initially, risks are often assessed qualitatively, using techniques like risk brainstorming, risk checklists, or risk breakdown structures. This helps in understanding the nature and characteristics of risks.
3. Quantitative Assessment: Once risks are identified and understood qualitatively, the next step is to quantify them. This involves assigning numerical values to parameters such as:
    a. Probability: What is the likelihood of a risk event occurring?
    b. Impact: If the risk event occurs, what will be the extent of its impact on project objectives

(e.g., cost, schedule, quality)?
    c. Exposure: Multiplying the probability and impact gives the overall exposure of a risk, indicating its significance to the project.
4. Risk Prioritization: After quantification, risks are prioritized based on their exposure levels. Risks with higher exposure, i.e., those with higher probability and impact, are given more attention because they pose a greater threat to the project's success.
5. Mitigation Planning: Based on the quantified risks, mitigation strategies are developed to either reduce the probability of occurrence, minimize the impact, or both. These strategies aim to manage and control risks within acceptable thresholds.
6. Continuous Monitoring: Risk quantification is not a one-time activity. Throughout the project lifecycle, risks should be continuously monitored and re-evaluated. New risks may emerge, and the probability and impact of existing risks may change, requiring adjustments to mitigation strategies.

Examples of risk quantification include:

1. Financial Risk: In finance, risk quantification involves calculating the potential losses associated with investment decisions. This could include estimating the probability of market downturns, currency fluctuations, or default by borrowers.
2. Project Management: In project management, risk quantification involves assessing the likelihood and potential impact of various project risks such as budget overruns, delays in delivery, or technical failures. For instance, a project manager might assign a monetary value to the risk of a supplier failing to deliver materials on time.
3. Healthcare: In healthcare, risk quantification could involve assessing the probability and impact of adverse events such as medical errors, patient falls, or hospital-acquired infections. This could help healthcare organizations allocate resources more effectively to mitigate these risks and improve patient safety.
4. Cybersecurity: In cybersecurity, risk quantification involves estimating the likelihood and potential impact of cyber threats such as data breaches, malware infections, or denial-of-service attacks. This could help organizations prioritize security measures and investments based on the most significant risks to their systems and data.
5. Insurance: In the insurance industry, risk quantification is fundamental to setting premiums and determining coverage limits. Actuaries use statistical models to quantify the risks associated with insuring individuals or assets against various perils such as accidents, natural disasters, or illnesses.

Table 8.25.1: Risk Qualitative Evaluation Table

Probability	Impact		
	High	Medium	Low
High	High	High	Low
Medium	High	Medium	Low
Low	Medium	Medium	Low

In each of these examples, risk quantification enables stakeholders to make informed decisions by providing a quantitative understanding of the potential risks involved.

By quantifying risks, project managers can make informed decisions about how to allocate resources, prioritize activities, and manage uncertainties effectively, thereby increasing the likelihood of project success.

8.26. What are few statistical techniques for risk quantification?

Risk quantification is essential in many fields such as finance, insurance, project management, and engineering. Here are a few statistical techniques commonly used for risk quantification:

1. Value at Risk (VaR)
    a. Description: Measures the potential loss in value of a portfolio over a defined period for a given confidence interval.
    b. Usage: Widely used in finance to estimate the maximum potential loss over a specified time frame.
2. Conditional Value at Risk (CVaR)
    a. Description: Also known as Expected Shortfall, it considers the average loss exceeding the VaR.
    b. Usage: Provides a more comprehensive risk assessment by focusing on the tail-end of the loss distribution.
3. Monte Carlo Simulation
    a. Description: Uses random sampling and statistical modeling to estimate the probability of different outcomes.
    b. Usage: Applicable across various domains to simulate complex systems and assess risk under uncertainty.
4. Stress Testing
    a. Description: Evaluates the impact of extreme but plausible adverse conditions on a portfolio or system.
    b. Usage: Often used in banking and finance to ensure resilience under severe economic scenarios.
5. Scenario Analysis
    a. Description: Involves assessing the potential outcomes by analyzing various possible future events or scenarios.
    b. Usage: Useful in strategic planning and decision-making to understand potential risks under different assumptions.
6. Regression Analysis
    a. Description: Assesses the relationship between a dependent variable and one or more independent variables.
    b. Usage: Helps identify risk factors and predict the impact of these factors on outcomes.
7. Credit Scoring Models
    a. Description: Quantifies the likelihood of a borrower defaulting on a loan.
    b. Usage: Extensively used in banking and finance to assess credit risk.
8. GARCH (Generalized Autoregressive Conditional Heteroskedasticity)
    a. Description: Models time-series data where there is volatility clustering.
    b. Usage: Used in finance to forecast volatility and assess risk in asset prices.
9. Extreme Value Theory (EVT)
    a. Description: Focuses on the statistical behavior of the extreme deviations from the median of probability distributions.
    b. Usage: Useful in assessing the risk of rare events, such as natural disasters or financial crises.
10. Risk Matrices
    a. Description: A grid that maps the probability of risks occurring against their impact.
    b. Usage: Commonly used in project management and engineering for visualizing and prioritizing risks.
11. Bayesian Networks
    a. Description: Uses Bayesian inference to compute the probability of outcomes based on prior knowledge.
    b. Usage: Suitable for modeling complex systems and understanding the probabilistic relationships between variables.

12. Actuarial Methods
    a. Description: Uses statistical and mathematical techniques to assess risk in insurance and finance.
    b. Usage: Includes techniques like mortality tables and loss distributions to quantify risk in insurance.

These techniques can be used individually or in combination to provide a comprehensive risk assessment tailored to specific needs and contexts.

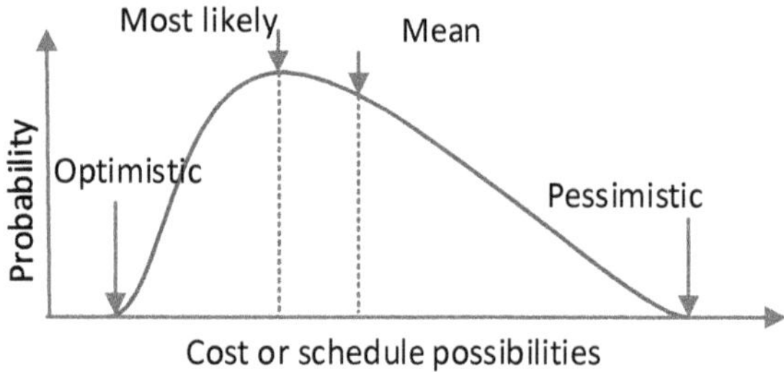

Figure 8.26.1 Typical Probability Distribution for Cost and Schedule Risk

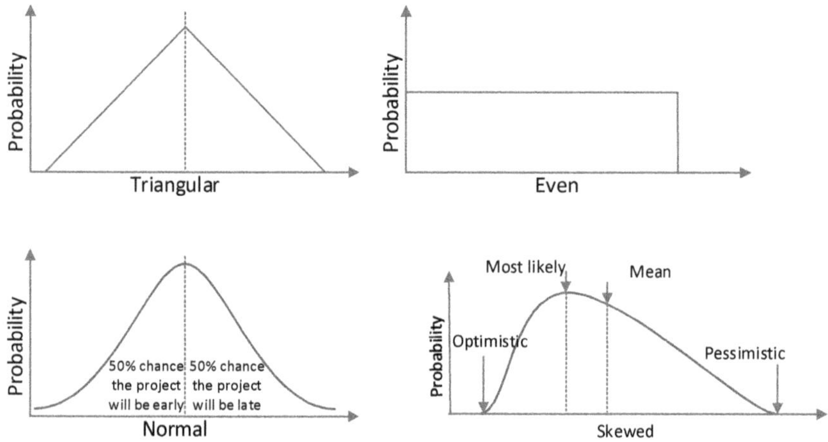

Figure 8.26.2 Probability Distributions

8.27. What is risk tolerance?

Risk tolerance refers to an individual's or an organization's ability and willingness to withstand fluctuations in the value of their investments or to endure potential losses in pursuit of greater returns. It is essentially a measure of how much risk someone is comfortable taking on in their investment portfolio. Factors influencing risk tolerance include financial goals, time horizon, investment knowledge, income stability, and emotional temperament. Generally, people with a higher risk tolerance are more inclined to invest in assets with greater volatility, such as stocks, while those with lower risk tolerance tend to favor more stable investments like bonds or cash equivalents. Understanding your risk tolerance is crucial for constructing a well-suited investment strategy that aligns with your financial objectives and psychological comfort level.

Risk tolerance can vary significantly among individuals and organizations due to a variety of factors, including:

1. Personal or Organizational Goals and Objectives: Individuals and organizations have different goals and objectives, which can influence their willingness to take on risk. For example, a young entrepreneur might be more willing to take risks to pursue rapid growth, while a retiree might prioritize capital preservation.
2. Time Horizon: Time horizon refers to the length of time an individual or organization plans to hold an investment or pursue a particular goal. Those with longer time horizons may be more willing to tolerate short-term fluctuations in exchange for potentially higher long-term returns.
3. Financial Situation: Individuals and organizations with greater financial resources may be more willing to take on risk, as they have the ability to absorb potential losses. Conversely, those with limited resources may have a lower risk tolerance.
4. Experience and Knowledge: Past experiences and level of financial literacy can influence risk tolerance. Individuals or organizations with more experience and knowledge may be more comfortable taking on risk, as they have a better understanding of potential outcomes and how to manage them.
5. Psychological Factors: Psychological factors such as fear, greed, and overconfidence can play a significant role in risk tolerance. Some individuals may have a natural inclination towards risk-taking, while others may be more risk-averse.
6. Regulatory and Legal Constraints: Organizations, particularly financial institutions, may be subject to regulatory and legal constraints that dictate the level of risk they can take on. These constraints may be imposed by government agencies or industry regulators.
7. Culture and Values: Cultural and organizational values can also influence risk tolerance. For example, a culture that values innovation and entrepreneurship may encourage risk-taking, while a conservative culture may prioritize stability and caution.

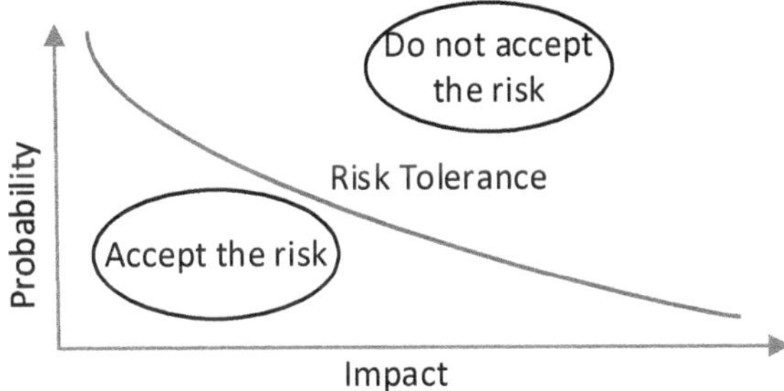

Figure 8.27.1 Risk Tolerance

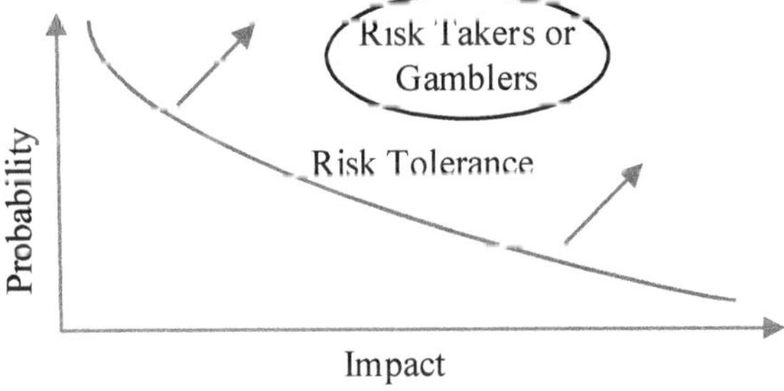

Figure 8.27.2 Risk Tolerance: Gamblers

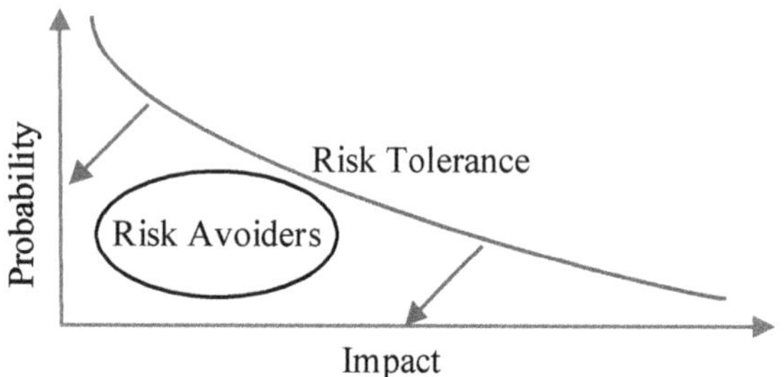

Figure 8.27.3 Risk Tolerance: Avoiders

Overall, risk tolerance is a highly individualized and nuanced concept that is influenced by a wide range of factors. Understanding these factors is crucial for making informed decisions about investment strategies and risk management.

8.28. What are risk response strategies?

Risk response strategies are actions taken to address potential threats to a project or organization. Here are the various risk response strategies commonly used:

1. Avoidance: This strategy involves eliminating the risk by avoiding the situation that gives rise to the risk altogether. For example, if a project involves a high-risk activity, the project team might decide to not pursue that activity.
2. Mitigation: Mitigation aims to reduce the probability or impact of a risk. This can involve implementing preventive measures or contingency plans to lessen the likelihood or severity of the risk if it occurs.
3. Transfer: Risk transfer involves shifting the impact of a risk to a third party, typically through contracts, insurance, or outsourcing. For example, purchasing insurance can transfer the financial risk associated with a particular event to an insurance company.
4. Acceptance: Sometimes, it is neither practical nor possible to avoid, mitigate, or transfer a risk. In such cases, organizations may choose to accept the risk. This can be done actively, by making a conscious decision to accept the consequences if the risk occurs, or passively, by simply acknowledging the risk without taking any specific action.
5. Exploitation: In certain situations, risks can present opportunities for gain. Exploitation involves taking advantage of these opportunities to achieve objectives that might not otherwise be possible. For example, a company might exploit a market risk by entering a new market with high potential for growth.
6. Sharing: Sharing involves collaborating with others to jointly address a risk. This can involve forming partnerships, alliances, or consortia to collectively manage risks that affect multiple parties.

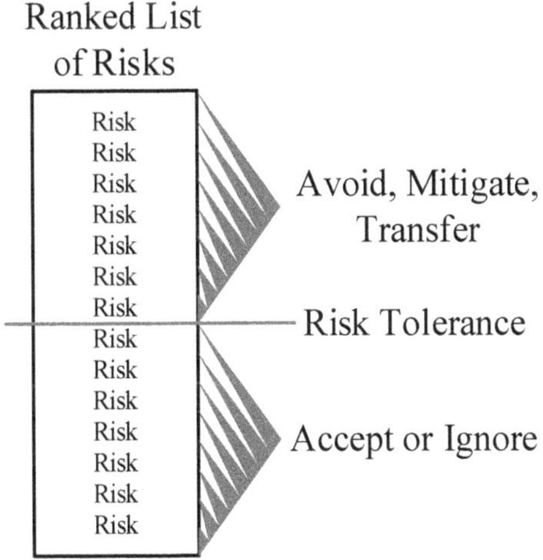

Figure 8.28.1 Risk Strategy

These strategies can be used individually or in combination, depending on the nature of the risks and the specific circumstances of the project or organization.

8.29. What is risk control?

Risk control refers to the process of implementing measures to mitigate or manage risks effectively within an organization or a specific context. It involves identifying potential risks, analyzing their impact and likelihood, and then taking actions to reduce or eliminate those risks to an acceptable level.

Risk control can take various forms, including:

1. Preventive Measures: These are actions taken to prevent risks from occurring in the first place. This might include implementing safety protocols, conducting regular maintenance checks, or providing training to employees.
2. Detective Measures: These measures are aimed at identifying risks as soon as possible after they occur. Examples include monitoring systems, conducting audits, or employing surveillance mechanisms.
3. Corrective Measures: Once a risk is identified, corrective measures are taken to minimize its impact. This could involve implementing backup systems, initiating emergency response procedures, or making necessary changes to prevent similar incidents in the future.
4. Transference of Risk: Sometimes, organizations may transfer their risks to third parties, such as insurance companies, through mechanisms like insurance policies or contractual agreements.
5. Acceptance of Risk: In some cases, organizations may choose to accept certain risks if the cost of mitigating them outweighs the potential impact. However, even in such cases, risk control measures may still be implemented to minimize the consequences.

Overall, risk control is an essential component of risk management, helping organizations to protect their assets, resources, and reputation while maximizing opportunities for success.

8.30. How to spot your weakest link in your project team?

Identifying the weakest link in a project team is crucial for ensuring the overall efficiency and success of the project. Here are some strategies to help spot the weakest link:

1. Performance Metrics
    a. Track Progress: Monitor individual contributions against project milestones and

deadlines.

   b. Quality of Work: Evaluate the accuracy, thoroughness, and consistency of each team member's output.
2. Feedback and Reviews
   a. Peer Reviews: Implement regular peer reviews where team members can provide feedback on each other's work.
   b. 360-Degree Feedback: Use feedback from managers, peers, and subordinates to get a comprehensive view of performance.
3. Communication Patterns
   a. Responsiveness: Observe the response time and communication effectiveness of each team member.
   b. Clarity and Conciseness: Check for clarity and conciseness in communication, both written and verbal.
4. Engagement and Initiative
   a. Participation in Meetings: Note who actively participates in meetings and contributes ideas.
   b. Proactiveness: Identify who takes initiative in solving problems or offering solutions.
5. Collaboration and Team Dynamics
   a. Team Interactions: Observe interactions during team activities. Look for any signs of conflict or lack of cooperation.
   b. Dependability: Assess how often team members rely on each other and who might be failing to deliver on commitments.
6. Adaptability and Learning
   a. Openness to Feedback: See how individuals respond to constructive criticism and their willingness to improve.
   b. Learning and Development: Monitor the efforts team members put into learning new skills or adapting to changes.
7. Stress and Workload Management
   a. Stress Levels: Watch for signs of stress or burnout, which can affect performance.
   b. Time Management: Evaluate how effectively team members manage their time and handle their workload.
8. Project Management Tools
   a. Task Tracking Systems: Use project management software to track task completion rates and identify any bottlenecks.
   b. Analytics and Reports: Utilize data analytics to generate reports on individual performance metrics.
9. Observations and One-on-Ones
   a. Direct Observation: Spend time observing how team members work and interact.
   b. One-on-One Meetings: Conduct regular one-on-one meetings to discuss performance, challenges, and areas for improvement.
10. Root Cause Analysis
    a. Identify Patterns: Look for recurring issues or patterns that point to a particular individual or role.
    b. Analyze Causes: Perform a root cause analysis to determine if problems stem from a lack of skills, motivation, resources, or other factors.

By systematically applying these strategies, you can identify the weakest link in your project team and take appropriate steps to address the issue, whether through training, support, or reallocation of responsibilities.

8.31. What are some of the tips for handling your weak link in your project team?

Handling a weak link in a project team can be challenging but is crucial for the success of the project. Here are some tips to effectively address this issue:

1. Identify the Root Cause:
    a. Assess if the issue is due to skill gaps, lack of motivation, personal problems, or misunderstandings.
    b. Conduct one-on-one meetings to understand their perspective and challenges.
2. Provide Support and Training:
    a. Offer additional training or resources to help them improve their skills.
    b. Assign a mentor or a more experienced team member to guide them.
3. Set Clear Expectations:
    a. Clearly define roles, responsibilities, and performance expectations.
    b. Provide specific, measurable, achievable, relevant, and time-bound (SMART) goals.
4. Regular Feedback and Communication:
    a. Schedule regular check-ins to provide constructive feedback and monitor progress.
    b. Encourage open communication and create a supportive environment where they feel comfortable discussing issues.
5. Leverage Their Strengths:
    a. Identify their strengths and assign tasks that align with those strengths.
    b. Reallocate tasks within the team to balance out weaknesses and leverage collective strengths.
6. Foster Team Collaboration:
    a. Promote teamwork and collaboration to create a support system within the team.
    b. Encourage more experienced team members to assist and share knowledge with the weaker link.
7. Motivate and Engage:
    a. Recognize and reward improvements and contributions to boost morale.
    b. Engage them in decision-making processes to increase their sense of ownership and accountability.
8. Monitor and Document Performance:
    a. Keep detailed records of performance issues and improvement efforts.
    b. Use these records for performance reviews and if necessary, for making decisions about their future in the team.
9. Consider Reassignment or Role Adjustment:
    a. If improvement is not evident, consider reassigning them to a different role that better fits their skills.
    b. In some cases, it might be necessary to replace them to maintain the overall performance of the team.
10. Seek External Assistance:
    a. Involve HR or professional development coaches if internal efforts are not yielding results.
    b. Sometimes an external perspective can provide new solutions and strategies.

By addressing the issue with a balanced approach that combines support, accountability, and strategic adjustments, you can help the weak link improve and contribute more effectively to the project team.

8.32. How do risk management approaches correlate with the other parts of project management methodology?

Risk management is an integral part of project management methodology, and its approaches correlate closely with other aspects of project management. Here is how they intertwine:

1. Integration Management: Risk management is integrated into the overall project management

plan. Risk identification, analysis, response planning, and monitoring are part of the project management process groups.

2. Scope Management: Risks can impact project scope. Changes in scope can introduce new risks or affect the probability and impact of existing risks. Therefore, scope management and risk management processes often overlap.
3. Time Management: Risks can affect project schedules. Time buffers may be added to accommodate potential delays due to risks. Additionally, risk response planning might involve schedule adjustments to mitigate potential impacts.
4. Cost Management: Risks can impact project costs. Contingency reserves are set aside to cover the cost of responding to identified risks. The cost of risk mitigation measures is also considered in project budgets.
5. Quality Management: Risks can impact project quality. Identifying and mitigating risks that could affect the quality of deliverables is essential for ensuring project success.
6. Human Resource Management: Risks related to team members' availability, skills, or motivation can impact project performance. Managing these risks involves human resource planning, training, and motivation strategies.
7. Communication Management: Effective communication is crucial for managing risks. Stakeholders need to be informed about potential risks, their impacts, and the planned responses. Regular communication ensures that everyone is aware of the project's risk status.
8. Procurement Management: Risks related to vendors, suppliers, or subcontractors can impact project outcomes. Procurement processes include risk assessment and management activities, such as evaluating vendors' capabilities and negotiating contracts with risk-sharing provisions.

In summary, risk management is tightly integrated with other parts of project management methodology. It is not a standalone process but rather a pervasive aspect that influences and is influenced by various project management processes.

8.33. What are the most common mistakes to avoid which lead to project failure?

Project failures often result from a variety of mistakes, many of which are preventable with proper planning, communication, and execution. Here are some of the most common mistakes to avoid:

1. Poor Planning and Estimation:
    a. Inadequate Scope Definition: Failing to clearly define the project scope can lead to misunderstandings and scope creep.
    b. Unrealistic Deadlines: Setting deadlines without a realistic assessment of the work involved and the resources available can lead to rushed, poor-quality work.
    c. Underestimating Costs: Not accurately estimating costs can lead to budget overruns.
2. Lack of Clear Objectives and Goals:
    a. Ambiguous Goals: If project goals are not clearly defined and understood by all stakeholders, it can lead to misaligned efforts and priorities.
    b. Changing Objectives: Frequently changing goals can confuse team members and derail progress.
3. Ineffective Communication:
    a. Poor Stakeholder Engagement: Not keeping stakeholders informed and involved can lead to dissatisfaction and misaligned expectations.
    b. Lack of Regular Updates: Failing to provide regular updates to the team and stakeholders can result in a lack of awareness about project status and potential issues.
4. Inadequate Risk Management:
    a. Ignoring Risks: Not identifying and planning for potential risks can leave the project vulnerable to unforeseen problems.
    b. Poor Risk Response: Having inadequate contingency plans can exacerbate issues when

risks materialize.

5. Resource Mismanagement:
    a. Overloading Team Members: Assigning too much work to team members can lead to burnout and decreased productivity.
    b. Insufficient Resources: Not allocating enough resources (time, budget, personnel) can hinder project progress.
6. Lack of Leadership and Governance:
    a. Ineffective Project Leadership: Poor leadership can result in lack of direction, motivation, and conflict resolution within the team.
    b. Weak Governance Structure: Inadequate governance can lead to lack of oversight and accountability.
7. Failure to Adapt:
    a. Resistance to Change: Not being flexible and adaptable to changing circumstances can cause the project to become irrelevant or obsolete.
    b. Ignoring Feedback: Not taking feedback from team members and stakeholders into account can result in persistent issues and missed opportunities for improvement.
8. Inadequate Quality Management:
    a. Skipping Quality Checks: Not performing regular quality checks can lead to defects and rework.
    b. Poor Documentation: Lack of proper documentation can cause misunderstandings and miscommunication among team members.
9. Misalignment with Business Objectives:
    a. Not Aligning with Business Goals: Projects that do not support the overall business objectives may fail to deliver value, leading to their cancellation or failure.
10. Technological Missteps:
    a. Choosing Inappropriate Technology: Selecting technology that is not suited for the project's needs can lead to integration issues and inefficiencies.
    b. Lack of Technical Expertise: Insufficient technical skills within the team can result in implementation challenges and errors.

Avoiding these common mistakes requires diligent planning, effective communication, proactive risk management, and strong leadership. By addressing these areas, the likelihood of project success increases significantly.

8.34. If a project has more than one critical path, which critical path should the project manager focus on and why?

A critical path is the longest sequence of events in a project. Any delays in this path will delay the entire project. It is entirely possible that you have two paths that have the same duration. If that occurs, you then need to consider your risks. You can end up with two critical paths if you improve the original plan or if an issue comes up during the project. Remember that plans are living documents, and often change.

Which of these two have the greatest likelihood of insuring some delay? The one with the highest risk is the one you should focus on. But keep in mind that just because you have greater risk does not mean that issue will occur. It is just more likely to. So, do not put all your eggs in one bucket. Even if you focus more attention to one part of the project, you still need to monitor all other parts as well. An unexpected event could turn your shortest path in your plan to your new longest one.

When a project has more than one critical path, the project manager should focus on all critical paths equally. Here is why:

1. Equal Impact on Project Completion: Each critical path has activities that directly impact the

project's overall completion date. Any delay in activities on any critical path will delay the entire project. Hence, all critical paths need attention to ensure that none of them experience delays.

2. Resource Allocation: Critical paths often compete for the same resources. By monitoring all critical paths, the project manager can ensure that resources are allocated effectively and conflicts are minimized.
3. Risk Management: Multiple critical paths indicate a higher risk profile for the project. Any delay or issue in any critical path can jeopardize the project's success. Focusing on all critical paths helps in identifying and mitigating risks across the project comprehensively.
4. Balanced Attention: Neglecting any critical path could lead to unanticipated delays. By balancing attention across all critical paths, the project manager ensures that all parts of the project receive the necessary oversight and support.

In summary, when a project has more than one critical path, the project manager should give equal focus to all critical paths to ensure timely project completion, efficient resource utilization, effective risk management, and balanced oversight.

8.35. What options do managers have when a project cannot be completed on time?

There are two different kinds of "on time". If you have a game that has to be completed on September 15, so that the ad buy can occur, so that it can be in stores for Christmas, or if you are updating the lander software for a Mars mission and you are going to arrive on Mars orbit at 2214 on April 13, that is one kind of "on time." It is a milestone you cannot miss or the whole project will be wrecked. As a manager, what you do is estimate the whole software project in advance, do all the most unknown parts first, build in slack time for contingencies, and hire enough staff to get the job done and then some. If the project cannot be completed in time, you are basically screwed. It is possible your game can still sell some copies next year, but your orbiter is going to die in an $800 million fireball. So do not do that. Bosses think every project is like this, but they are not.

The second kind of "on time" is where a director wants the project done in Q1 because they want a revenue boost, because some other division is under-performing. And by the way, although March 31 is, technically speaking, in Q1, if you finish on March 31, your director will still be angry at you. This kind of on time has nothing at all to do with the project. Your director does not care how many person-hours you have estimated for your project. He does not care if your headcount is inadequate. He wants what he wants and he thinks it is your job to give it to him.

As a manager, it is your job to stand between the director's demands and your team's ability to deliver. If you are lucky, you got to do all the same scheduling, add slack time, and hire staff as for the other project. But usually, the director's demands are arbitrary. Your best hope is frequent and early communication that the goal is not achievable, that you have ten gallons of features and a five-gallon bucket of staff. I have had success with bringing a list of features and per-feature estimates to a meeting of director-level folks and asking them to prioritize the features, drawing a line across the whiteboard where your staff resources end. During each meeting, you ask the directors if the project still makes sense to them, if they should cancel the project, reduce the feature list, or extend the deadline.

Some organizations embrace the uncertainty of schedules, and refuse to schedule. Instead, you bring working software with whatever features are complete to each director-level meeting, and ask them if they would like to release it.

Some organizations like Facebook or Amazon have projects under continuous development. These organizations pick a line of business where schedules do not matter (except around Christmas). Teams release incrementally, and there is not any such thing as a due date.

Here are some things that can help.

1. Co-locate staff together to facilitate communication.
2. At the start of the project, get automated builds and automated tests going, and make sure staff takes testing seriously. Get a bug database running and making sure QA and marketing post bugs. You may have to teach them how to write a bug report so all bugs are not called, "It is broken!"
3. Ask the team what the project could do to make progress faster. Professional developers are really smart. There will be several good ideas specific to your project.
4. Stay on top of hiring. It is the most important thing you do as a team, because it is the only thing that adds resources to the project.
5. Let senior staff work from home if it makes them more productive.

Here are some things that do not work. As a developer, I have experienced each of these:

1. Fixing your staff with your steely eye and demanding that they give 110% "for the team." If this actually worked, the Superbowl would always have two winning teams. Most developers are working as hard as they can already, out of pride-in-craft. It is magical thinking that people will somehow work harder just because you told them to.
2. Asking staff to work 60+ hour weeks. The first week you will get 50% extra tasks completed, but by week 10 or so it will be down to a few percent. Staff will game the system, coming in late so they can be seen to work late, playing games at their desk because they are too exhausted to code, etc. Staff with outside-of-work commitments like spouses and children will refuse, and if you push them, they will quit, leaving you short-handed.
3. I would like to give a special shout-out for the practice of scheduling mandatory meetings at 8 PM to ensure everyone is working long hours. What sadist thought this up?
4. Offering bonuses for meeting impossible deadlines. Did I mention that developers are really smart? They know if a schedule is achievable or if it is impossible on its face. Your fake bonus just makes them cynical and angry. Only offer bonuses that you actually expect to pay out, or you will kill morale.

8.36. How do you manage business risks through communications?

Managing business risks through communications involves several key strategies:

1. Transparency: Open and honest communication with stakeholders, including employees, investors, customers, and partners, builds trust and credibility. Transparency allows for early identification of potential risks and fosters an environment where problems can be addressed proactively.
2. Regular Updates: Keep stakeholders informed about the status of the business, including any potential risks or challenges that may arise. Regular updates help to manage expectations and mitigate surprises.
3. Clear Channels of Communication: Establish clear channels for communication within the organization, ensuring that relevant information flows freely between different departments and levels of management. This helps to identify risks early and allows for timely decision-making.
4. Risk Assessment and Reporting: Implement processes for identifying, assessing, and reporting on business risks. This may include regular risk assessments, risk registers, and risk reporting mechanisms to ensure that key stakeholders are aware of potential threats to the business.
5. Crisis Communication Plans: Develop comprehensive crisis communication plans that outline how the organization will communicate with stakeholders in the event of a crisis or emergency. These plans should include protocols for rapid communication, designated spokespeople, and clear messaging strategies.
6. Training and Education: Provide training and education to employees on the importance of effective communication in managing business risks. This includes training on how to identify

and report risks, as well as how to communicate effectively during a crisis.

7. Feedback Mechanisms: Establish feedback mechanisms to solicit input from stakeholders on potential risks and areas for improvement. This can include employee surveys, customer feedback mechanisms, and regular stakeholder meetings to discuss concerns and issues.

By implementing these strategies, businesses can effectively manage risks through communication, ensuring that stakeholders are informed, engaged, and prepared to respond to potential challenges.

8.37. What happens if you ignore project communications?

Ignoring project communications can have various negative consequences:

1. Misunderstandings: Ignoring project communications can lead to misunderstandings among team members about project goals, tasks, deadlines, and expectations.
2. Missed Deadlines: If you ignore communications regarding deadlines or changes in project schedules, you might miss important deadlines, which can delay the project and affect its overall success.
3. Decreased Productivity: Ignoring communications can create bottlenecks in workflow and reduce overall productivity as team members might wait for your response or clarification before proceeding with their tasks.
4. Damage to Relationships: Ignoring project communications can damage relationships with team members, stakeholders, or clients, leading to a breakdown in trust and cooperation.
5. Quality Issues: Lack of communication can result in quality issues if team members are not adequately informed about project requirements or changes.
6. Increased Risk: Ignoring project communications can increase the risk of project failure or setbacks as important information or issues may not be addressed in a timely manner.
7. Reputation Damage: Consistently ignoring project communications can damage your reputation as a reliable and responsible team member, which can affect your future opportunities within the organization.

Overall, ignoring project communications can have significant negative impacts on project outcomes, team dynamics, and individual reputation. It is important to stay proactive and responsive in project communication to ensure effective collaboration and project success.

8.38. How do you respond to a question: "Tell me about a time when a project failed and how you recovered?"

When asked about a project failure and subsequent recovery, it is essential to be honest, transparent, and demonstrate your ability to learn and grow from setbacks. Here is a structured response you could use:

"Sure, I would be happy to share. In a previous project, we were tasked with developing a new software application within a tight deadline. Despite our meticulous planning and initial progress, we encountered unforeseen technical challenges midway through the project. This led to significant delays and ultimately jeopardized our ability to deliver on time.

Recognizing the severity of the situation, I immediately convened a meeting with the team to assess the issues and brainstorm potential solutions. We conducted a thorough root cause analysis to understand what went wrong and identified areas where we could improve our approach.

One of the key actions we took was to reallocate resources and adjust our project timeline to accommodate the additional work required to address the technical issues. This meant extending certain deadlines and reallocating team members to focus on troubleshooting and problem-solving.

Additionally, I made a concerted effort to maintain open communication with stakeholders, keeping them informed of the challenges we were facing and the steps we were taking to mitigate them. This helped manage expectations and build trust despite the setbacks.

Ultimately, through perseverance, collaboration, and a willingness to adapt, we were able to overcome the obstacles and successfully deliver the project, albeit slightly behind schedule. However, the experience taught me valuable lessons in resilience, problem-solving, and the importance of effective communication in times of adversity."

This response showcases your ability to handle setbacks, lead a team through challenges, and extract valuable lessons from failure.

8.39. Suppose you are solving a problem but ran into some trouble. You do not have a lot of time and think you can solve it on your own. A friend suggests you work with someone you do not know to help. What are you MOST likely to do?

In such a situation, I would consider a few factors before making a decision:

1. Urgency: If the problem needs to be solved quickly and time is of the essence, I might lean towards working on it myself to ensure a prompt solution.
2. Complexity: If the problem is complex and requires specialized knowledge or skills that I lack, collaborating with someone else, even if I do not know them, could be beneficial. Their unique perspective might lead to insights that I would not have thought of on my own.
3. Trustworthiness: If the friend who suggested the collaboration has a good track record of offering reliable advice, I might give their suggestion more weight. However, if I have doubts about the person's intentions or abilities, I would be cautious.
4. Resources: If the problem requires resources or expertise that I do not have access to, partnering with someone else could help bridge those gaps.
5. Risk and Reward: I would weigh the potential benefits of collaboration against the risks involved. If working with someone unknown carries a significant risk of complicating the situation further, I might be more inclined to handle it on my own.
6. Communication and Compatibility: I would consider whether I have the time and means to effectively communicate with the potential collaborator. Compatibility in work styles, communication methods, and problem-solving approaches can influence the success of the collaboration.

Ultimately, the decision would depend on the specific details of the situation, including the nature of the problem, the time available, and my assessment of my own capabilities and the potential benefits of collaboration.

9. Project Closure

Project closure in project management is the final phase of the project life cycle, where all project activities are completed, and the project is formally closed. This phase involves ensuring that all project deliverables have been completed to the required standards, stakeholders have accepted the final product or service, and all documentation is finalized.

Key steps in project closure include:

1. Final Deliverable Handover: Ensuring that the final product, service, or result is delivered to the client or stakeholders and that they formally accept it.
2. Closure of Contracts: Completing any outstanding contractual obligations, settling any final payments, and formally closing contracts with vendors and partners.
3. Release of Resources: Releasing project resources, including team members, equipment, and budget, so they can be allocated to other projects.
4. Final Project Report: Creating a final report that summarizes the project's performance, lessons learned, and any recommendations for future projects.
5. Post-Implementation Review: Conducting a review to evaluate the project's success, document lessons learned, and assess whether the project met its objectives.
6. Archiving Documentation: Ensuring that all project documents, including plans, reports, and contracts, are archived for future reference.
7. Stakeholder Communication: Communicating the project's closure to all stakeholders, ensuring they are informed of the project's outcome, and gathering feedback.
8. Celebrating Success: Recognizing and celebrating the team's achievements and the successful completion of the project.

By formally closing a project, organizations can ensure that all aspects of the project have been properly completed, documented, and assessed, leading to a smoother transition to operations or the next phase.

9.1. Why project closure phase is important or critical?

Project closure refers to the formal process of finalizing all activities, tasks, and deliverables associated with a project and formally ending it. It is a critical phase in project management that ensures the project is completed successfully, all objectives are met, and all resources are properly released. This phase is important and critical for several reasons:

1. Formal Completion: Project closure signifies the formal end of the project. It ensures that all project activities are completed, and the project is no longer active. This closure helps prevent any additional, unnecessary work from being performed.
2. Client Satisfaction: During project closure, the client or stakeholders are given the opportunity to review the final deliverables and confirm that they meet their expectations. This ensures client satisfaction and reduces the likelihood of post-project disputes.
3. Resource Release: Project closure involves releasing resources, such as team members, equipment, and budget allocations, that were dedicated to the project. This allows resources to be reallocated to other projects or initiatives.
4. Documentation and Lessons Learned: During project closure, documentation is finalized and archived. This documentation serves as a reference for future projects and provides valuable insights for lessons learned. It captures both successful practices and challenges faced during the project, aiding in continuous improvement.
5. Financial Closure: Project closure involves finalizing financial aspects such as budget, expenses, and any outstanding payments. This ensures that all financial obligations are met and accounted for.

6. Risk Mitigation: By formally closing the project, any remaining risks and issues can be identified and addressed. This prevents the project from leaving behind unresolved problems that could impact future activities.
7. Stakeholder Communication: Project closure involves communicating with stakeholders to inform them about the project's completion and outcomes. It provides an opportunity to celebrate achievements and recognize the efforts of the project team.
8. Performance Evaluation: During project closure, the project's success criteria are evaluated against the actual outcomes. This evaluation provides insights into the project's performance, helping organizations understand what went well and what could be improved in future projects.
9. Contractual Closure: For projects involving external vendors or suppliers, closure ensures that all contractual obligations are fulfilled, and contracts are formally closed out.
10. Release of Team Members: Project closure allows team members to be released from their project-specific roles. It provides closure to their involvement and allows them to move on to other projects or tasks.

In essence, project closure ensures that the project is wrapped up in an organized and controlled manner, with all loose ends tied up. It facilitates knowledge transfer, helps organizations learn from their experiences, and provides a smooth transition to future projects or initiatives.

9.2. What are the benefits of project closure?

Project closure is a crucial phase in the project management lifecycle, and it offers several benefits:

1. Formalizing Completion: Closing a project formally acknowledges its completion, ensuring that all project objectives have been met and all deliverables have been produced according to requirements.
2. Resource Release: It allows for the release of project resources, both human and material, for reassignment to other projects or for other purposes within the organization.
3. Lessons Learned: Project closure provides an opportunity to conduct a thorough review of the project, identifying what went well, what did not, and what lessons can be learned for future projects. This helps in improving processes and preventing similar issues in future endeavors.
4. Client Satisfaction: Proper closure involves handing over the project deliverables to the client or stakeholders, ensuring they are satisfied with the results and that their expectations have been met. This can lead to positive relationships and potential future business opportunities.
5. Financial Closure: It allows for the financial closure of the project, including the finalization of budgets, settling of accounts, and closing of contracts. This ensures accurate financial reporting and prevents any ongoing financial commitments related to the project.
6. Legal Closure: Projects often involve legal agreements or contracts. Closing the project ensures that all legal obligations have been fulfilled, contracts have been closed out, and any legal risks associated with the project have been addressed.
7. Team Recognition: Recognizing and celebrating the efforts of the project team members during the closure phase can boost morale and team spirit. It acknowledges their hard work and contributions to the project's success.
8. Organizational Knowledge: Documenting project closure activities, including lessons learned, best practices, and any unique experiences, contributes to organizational knowledge management. This knowledge can be valuable for future projects and can be used to improve project management processes within the organization.

In essence, project closure ensures that the project is formally completed, resources are released efficiently, stakeholders are satisfied, and lessons are learned for future improvement.

9.3. What are the different reasons for premature project closure?

Premature project closure can occur due to various reasons, often stemming from unforeseen circumstances or mismanagement. Here are some common reasons:

1. Budgetary Constraints: If a project exceeds its allocated budget significantly or if funding is suddenly withdrawn, the project may be forced to shut down prematurely.
2. Schedule Delays: Projects that fall significantly behind schedule may face pressure to close prematurely, especially if stakeholders lose confidence in the project's ability to deliver.
3. Scope Creep: Projects may face scope creep, where additional requirements are continuously added without proper evaluation of their impact on resources and timelines. This can lead to project closure if the scope becomes unmanageable.
4. Resource Constraints: Insufficient resources, whether it is human resources, technology, or materials, can lead to project closure if the project cannot proceed without them.
5. Technical Challenges: Projects may encounter unforeseen technical challenges or limitations that make it impractical or impossible to continue.
6. Market Changes: External factors such as changes in market conditions, regulations, or technology trends can make a project obsolete or no longer viable, leading to premature closure.
7. Stakeholder Disagreement: Conflicts among stakeholders regarding project goals, priorities, or execution can lead to a decision to prematurely close the project.
8. Risk Management Issues: Inadequate risk management can lead to project failure. If risks materialize and there are no effective mitigation strategies in place, stakeholders may decide to close the project to minimize further losses.
9. Leadership Changes: Changes in project leadership or key personnel can disrupt project continuity and direction, potentially leading to premature closure.
10. Legal or Compliance Issues: Projects may face legal or compliance issues that cannot be resolved or that pose significant risks to the organization, necessitating project closure.
11. Lack of Stakeholder Support: If key stakeholders, such as clients or sponsors, withdraw their support or lose interest in the project, it may become difficult to justify its continuation.
12. Poor Communication: Inadequate communication within the project team or with stakeholders can lead to misunderstandings, conflicts, and ultimately project closure.
13. Environmental Factors: Natural disasters, political instability, or other external events beyond the project team's control can force premature project closure.
14. Quality Concerns: Persistent quality issues or inability to meet quality standards may lead stakeholders to decide to close the project rather than risk further problems.

Addressing these factors proactively and effectively managing risks can help mitigate the likelihood of premature project closure.

9.4. What sources can be used for identifying lessons learned for a project?

Identifying lessons learned for a project can be a critical aspect of improving future project performance. Here are some sources you can use to gather lessons learned:

1. Project Team Members: Gather input from team members who were directly involved in the project. They can provide insights into what went well, what did not, and what could be improved.
2. Project Documentation: Review project documentation such as project plans, status reports, meeting minutes, and risk registers. These documents can provide valuable insights into the project's progression, challenges faced, and how they were addressed.
3. Stakeholder Feedback: Collect feedback from stakeholders involved in or impacted by the project. This could include clients, sponsors, end-users, and any other relevant parties. Their perspectives can offer valuable insights into their experiences and perceptions of the project.
4. Post-Implementation Review: Conduct a formal post-implementation review (PIR) or post-project evaluation (PPE) session. This involves gathering key stakeholders to discuss the project's

successes, challenges, and areas for improvement in a structured manner.

5. Surveys and Questionnaires: Distribute surveys or questionnaires to project team members and stakeholders to gather feedback on various aspects of the project. This approach can provide anonymous feedback and encourage honest responses.
6. Lessons Learned Workshops: Facilitate workshops or focus groups specifically dedicated to identifying and documenting lessons learned from the project. These sessions can encourage open discussion and collaboration among team members.
7. External Benchmarks: Compare the project's performance with industry standards, best practices, or benchmarks from similar projects. This can help identify areas where the project excelled or fell short compared to external norms.
8. Expert Interviews: Interview subject matter experts or individuals with experience in similar projects to gain additional insights and perspectives on lessons learned.
9. Data Analysis: Analyze project performance data, such as budget variance, schedule adherence, quality metrics, and risk management effectiveness. Data-driven insights can highlight areas for improvement and guide future decision-making.
10. Reflection and Retrospectives: Encourage team members to reflect individually or in group retrospectives on their experiences with the project. This can uncover valuable insights and personal lessons learned.

By leveraging these sources, you can gather comprehensive insights into the project's strengths, weaknesses, and areas for improvement, helping to inform future project planning and execution.

9.5. How do you allocate resources for project closure?

Allocating resources for project closure involves several key steps to ensure that the project is wrapped up effectively and efficiently. Here is a general guideline on how to allocate resources for project closure:

1. Define Closure Objectives and Criteria: Clearly outline the objectives and criteria that need to be met for the project to be considered closed successfully. This could include factors like completion of deliverables, approval from stakeholders, documentation, and financial reconciliation.
2. Identify Remaining Tasks: Review the project plan and any outstanding tasks to identify what still needs to be completed before the project can be closed. This might involve finalizing documentation, conducting final testing, addressing outstanding issues, and completing any remaining administrative tasks.
3. Allocate Personnel: Assign the necessary personnel to complete the remaining tasks. This might involve reassigning team members who have finished their primary tasks to assist in closing activities. Make sure everyone understands their roles and responsibilities during the closure phase.
4. Resource Reassignment: As the project nears its end, some resources may no longer be needed. Evaluate the resource allocation and release any excess resources that can be reassigned to other projects or tasks.
5. Financial Reconciliation: Review the project's financial status to ensure that all expenses are accounted for and properly documented. Allocate resources to finalize any financial reconciliation, such as closing contracts, paying outstanding bills, and ensuring that all budgetary considerations are resolved.
6. Stakeholder Communication: Allocate resources for communicating with stakeholders about the project's closure. This might involve sending project closure reports, conducting final meetings or presentations, and addressing any questions or concerns.
7. Documentation and Knowledge Transfer: Allocate resources to document the project's outcomes, lessons learned, and best practices. This documentation will serve as a valuable resource for future projects and teams. Additionally, ensure that knowledge is transferred to relevant teams or

individuals who might need to maintain or build upon the project's work.

8. Quality Assurance: Allocate resources for quality checks to ensure that all deliverables meet the required standards and criteria outlined in the closure objectives. This might involve conducting final reviews and audits.
9. Risk Management: Consider any potential risks that might arise during the closure process and allocate resources to mitigate them. This could involve addressing potential legal or contractual issues, ensuring data security and privacy, and managing any last-minute challenges.
10. Final Review and Sign-Off: Allocate resources for a final review of all closure activities to ensure that everything is in order. Obtain sign-off from relevant stakeholders to officially close the project.
11. Celebrate and Learn: Allocate some resources for celebrating the successful closure of the project. This could be a small team gathering or a virtual celebration. Also, allocate time for a project review meeting to discuss what went well, what could be improved, and what lessons were learned.

Remember that the specific allocation of resources will depend on the nature and complexity of the project. Flexibility and adaptability are important, as unexpected issues can arise during the closure phase. Proper planning and communication will contribute to a smooth and effective project closure process.

9.6. How do you go about writing a project close-out report?

Writing a project close-out report is crucial for documenting the achievements, lessons learned, and future recommendations from a project. Here is a general guide on how to go about it:

1. Introduction:
    a. Begin with an overview of the project, including its objectives, scope, stakeholders, and duration.
2. Project Summary:
    a. Provide a brief summary of the project's accomplishments, highlighting key milestones, deliverables, and outcomes achieved.
3. Achievements:
    a. Detail the specific achievements of the project, such as meeting deadlines, staying within budget, and fulfilling objectives. Include quantitative data if possible.
4. Challenges and Lessons Learned:
    a. Discuss any challenges or obstacles faced during the project and how they were addressed.
    b. Reflect on lessons learned from both successes and failures. This could include process improvements, communication strategies, or risk management techniques.
5. Stakeholder Feedback:
    a. Include feedback from stakeholders on the project's performance, deliverables, and overall satisfaction. This can provide valuable insights for future projects.
6. Impact Assessment:
    a. Evaluate the project's impact on the organization, stakeholders, and relevant metrics. This could include cost savings, efficiency improvements, or customer satisfaction ratings.
7. Recommendations:
    a. Offer recommendations for future projects based on lessons learned and feedback received. This might include adjustments to processes, resource allocation, or stakeholder engagement strategies.
8. Documentation and Deliverables:
    a. Provide a list of all project documentation and deliverables, including final reports, presentations, and any relevant files or data.
9. Acknowledgments:

a. Acknowledge the contributions of team members, stakeholders, and any external parties who supported the project's success.

10. Conclusion:
    a. Summarize the key points of the report and emphasize the significance of the project's outcomes.
11. Appendices:
    a. Include any additional supporting documents, charts, or data that provide further context or detail.

When writing the report, ensure it is clear, concise, and well-organized. Use headings, bullet points, and visuals to enhance readability. Tailor the content to the specific needs and requirements of your organization and stakeholders. Finally, review the report carefully for accuracy and completeness before distributing it to relevant parties.

9.7. Provide a project closure checklist.

A project closure checklist helps ensure that all necessary tasks and activities are completed before officially closing out a project. Here is a comprehensive checklist:

1. Finalize Deliverables:
    a. Review all project deliverables to ensure they meet the agreed-upon requirements.
    b. Obtain client or stakeholder sign-off on deliverables.
2. Review Budget and Financials:
    a. Verify that all project expenses are accounted for.
    b. Close out financial accounts and ensure all invoices are paid.
3. Document Lessons Learned:
    a. Conduct a project review meeting to discuss what went well, what did not, and areas for improvement.
    b. Document lessons learned for future reference.
4. Archive Project Documentation:
    a. Ensure all project documentation, including plans, reports, and correspondence, is properly archived for future reference.
    b. Organize documents in a logical manner for easy retrieval.
5. Communicate Closure:
    a. Notify stakeholders, team members, and any relevant parties that the project is officially closed.
    b. Provide information on project outcomes, successes, and any next steps.
6. Release Resources:
    a. Release project team members from their project responsibilities.
    b. Return any borrowed equipment or resources to their respective owners.
7. Close Contracts and Agreements:
    a. Review and close any contracts or agreements related to the project.
    b. Ensure all legal obligations are fulfilled.
8. Conduct Final Review:
    a. Perform a final review of project goals and objectives to ensure they have been met.
    b. Address any outstanding issues or concerns.
9. Celebrate Successes:
    a. Recognize and celebrate the achievements of the project team.
    b. Show appreciation for their hard work and dedication.
10. Transition Responsibilities:
    a. Identify any ongoing maintenance or support responsibilities and ensure they are properly transitioned to the appropriate individuals or teams.

    b. Provide necessary training or documentation for ongoing support.
11. Update Stakeholders:
    a. Provide a final project report to stakeholders, summarizing key metrics, achievements, and outcomes.
    b. Solicit feedback from stakeholders for future improvement.
12. Formally Close the Project:
    a. Obtain formal approval to close the project from the project sponsor or relevant authority.
    b. Complete any necessary paperwork or documentation to officially close the project.

By following this checklist, you can ensure that all necessary tasks are completed and that the project is successfully closed in an organized and efficient manner.

10. Project Evaluation

Project evaluation is a systematic process used to assess the effectiveness, efficiency, and impact of a project. It involves collecting and analyzing data on the project's implementation and outcomes to determine whether it has met its objectives. This process includes various types of evaluation, such as formative (ongoing feedback), summative (post-completion assessment), process (implementation examination), outcome (results assessment), and impact (long-term effects). Through methods like surveys, interviews, observations, and document reviews, project evaluation provides valuable insights that help improve decision-making, accountability, and future project design.

The primary benefits of project evaluation are improved decision-making, enhanced accountability to stakeholders, and the promotion of continuous learning and development among project teams. By systematically reviewing and analyzing project data, evaluation identifies strengths and weaknesses, offers actionable recommendations, and ensures that resources are utilized effectively to achieve desired outcomes. This process is crucial for refining project methodologies and enhancing the overall success and sustainability of future projects.

10.1. What is project evaluation?

Project evaluation is a systematic process of assessing a project's effectiveness, efficiency, and impact to determine its success and identify areas for improvement. It involves collecting and analyzing data related to the project's implementation and outcomes. Here are the key components of project evaluation:

1. Purpose: The primary goal of project evaluation is to understand how well a project has met its objectives, to learn from the experiences, and to make informed decisions about future projects.
2. Types of Evaluation:
    a. Formative Evaluation: Conducted during the development and implementation phases to provide ongoing feedback that can improve the project.

b. Summative Evaluation: Conducted after the project is completed to assess its overall impact and effectiveness.
c. Process Evaluation: Focuses on the implementation process, examining whether the project activities were carried out as planned.
d. Outcome Evaluation: Focuses on the results of the project, assessing whether the project met its objectives and what changes occurred as a result.
e. Impact Evaluation: Examines the long-term effects and broader impacts of the project on the community or environment.

3. Steps in Project Evaluation:
   a. Define Objectives: Clearly articulate the goals and objectives of the project.
   b. Develop Evaluation Criteria: Establish the standards and benchmarks against which the project will be evaluated.
   c. Collect Data: Gather quantitative and qualitative data through surveys, interviews, observations, and other methods.
   d. Analyze Data: Interpret the data to understand the project's performance and outcomes.
   e. Report Findings: Compile the results into a report that includes conclusions and recommendations.
   f. Use Findings: Apply the insights gained to improve current and future projects.
4. Methods of Data Collection:
   a. Surveys and questionnaires
   b. Interviews and focus groups
   c. Observations
   d. Document and record reviews
   e. Case studies
5. Benefits of Project Evaluation:
   a. Improved Decision-Making: Provides evidence-based insights to guide future projects.
   b. Accountability: Demonstrates to stakeholders that resources were used effectively.
   c. Learning and Development: Helps project teams learn from their experiences and improve their skills.
   d. Enhanced Project Design: Offers feedback that can be used to refine project plans and methodologies.

Overall, project evaluation is essential for ensuring that projects are effective, efficient, and achieve their intended outcomes. It provides a structured approach to learning from experience and continuously improving project management practices.

10.2. How do you evaluate a project?

Evaluating a project involves assessing its performance, outcomes, and impact against predefined criteria and objectives. Here are the key steps to evaluate a project:

1. Define Objectives and Criteria
   a. Set Clear Goals: Identify the project's primary goals and objectives.
   b. Establish Evaluation Criteria: Develop specific criteria for measuring success, such as scope, time, cost, quality, stakeholder satisfaction, and impact.
2. Collect Data
   a. Quantitative Data: Gather numerical data related to budget, timelines, resource utilization, and performance metrics.
   b. Qualitative Data: Collect feedback from stakeholders, team members, and end-users through surveys, interviews, and observations.
3. Analyze Project Performance
   a. Scope: Evaluate if the project met its defined scope and delivered the intended

deliverables.
   b. Time: Compare planned vs. actual timelines to assess any schedule variances.
   c. Cost: Analyze budget adherence by comparing planned vs. actual expenses.
   d. Quality: Assess the quality of deliverables and whether they meet the specified standards and requirements.
4. Measure Outcomes and Impact
   a. Outcome Achievement: Determine if the project outcomes align with the initial goals and objectives.
   b. Impact Assessment: Evaluate the broader impact of the project on the organization, community, or target audience.
5. Evaluate Stakeholder Satisfaction
   a. Stakeholder Feedback: Gather feedback from key stakeholders to understand their satisfaction with the project's process and results.
   b. Client/End-User Satisfaction: Assess the satisfaction of clients or end-users with the final product or service.
6. Identify Lessons Learned
   a. Successes and Failures: Identify what worked well and what did not.
   b. Areas for Improvement: Highlight areas for improvement in future projects.
7. Prepare an Evaluation Report
   a. Summary of Findings: Provide a comprehensive summary of the evaluation findings.
   b. Recommendations: Offer actionable recommendations for future projects based on the evaluation results.
8. Review and Reflect
   a. Project Team Review: Conduct a review meeting with the project team to discuss the evaluation results.
   b. Adjust Future Practices: Implement changes and improvements in project management practices based on the evaluation insights.

Tools and Techniques
1. Performance Metrics: Use Key Performance Indicators (KPIs) to measure project performance.
2. SWOT Analysis: Analyze the project's strengths, weaknesses, opportunities, and threats.
3. Earned Value Management (EVM): Utilize EVM techniques to measure project performance and progress.
4. Surveys and Questionnaires: Collect qualitative data from stakeholders.
5. Project Management Software: Use tools like MS Project, JIRA, or Trello for tracking and reporting.

Evaluating a project systematically helps ensure that you understand its successes and shortcomings, leading to better planning and execution of future projects.

10.3. What are some of the ways to measure the success of any project?

Measuring the success of a project involves assessing various factors to determine whether the project has met its objectives and delivered the expected benefits. Here are some common ways to measure project success:
1. Completion on Time
   a. Schedule Performance Index (SPI): Measures the efficiency of time utilization.
   b. Adherence to Milestones: Tracks if project milestones were met on the planned dates.
2. Within Budget
   a. Cost Performance Index (CPI): Measures cost efficiency by comparing the budgeted cost of work performed to the actual cost.

   b. Budget Variance: The difference between the budgeted cost and actual cost.
3. Scope and Quality
   a. Requirements Fulfillment: Ensures all project requirements and objectives have been met.
   b. Quality Metrics: Includes defect rates, error rates, and other quality control measures.
   c. User Acceptance Testing (UAT): Feedback from end-users regarding whether the project meets their needs and expectations.
4. Stakeholder Satisfaction
   a. Surveys and Feedback: Collecting feedback from stakeholders, clients, and team members.
   b. Net Promoter Score (NPS): Measures the likelihood of stakeholders to recommend the project's outcomes to others.
5. Performance Indicators
   a. Key Performance Indicators (KPIs): Specific metrics relevant to the project's objectives, such as increase in sales, user engagement, or operational efficiency.
   b. Balanced Scorecard: Measures financial, customer, internal business processes, and learning/growth aspects.
6. Benefit Realization
   a. Return on Investment (ROI): The financial return from the project compared to its cost.
   b. Cost-Benefit Analysis: Comparing the benefits gained from the project to the costs incurred.
   c. Payback Period: The time it takes for the project to repay its initial investment.
7. Risk Management
   a. Risk Register Analysis: Reviewing the effectiveness of risk management processes and the number of risks that were mitigated or avoided.
   b. Issue Resolution Efficiency: Assessing how efficiently issues were resolved during the project.
8. Team Performance
   a. Team Morale and Turnover Rates: Indicating how the project impacted team members.
   b. Productivity Metrics: Measuring output and efficiency of the project team.
9. Customer and Market Impact
   a. Customer Satisfaction: Post-project surveys and interviews with customers.
   b. Market Share: Changes in market share attributable to the project's outcomes.
10. Compliance and Governance
   a. Regulatory Compliance: Ensuring the project meets all legal and regulatory requirements.
   b. Audit Results: Internal or external audits confirming compliance and proper governance.

Each of these measures provides a different perspective on project success. By combining them, project managers and stakeholders can gain a comprehensive understanding of how well the project achieved its goals and delivered value.

10.4. What is the most important success criterion for a project and why?

The most important success criterion for a project in the decreasing order of importance:

1. Achieve total customer satisfaction
2. Achieve the planned scope of work
3. Complete the project within budget
4. Meet schedule commitments.

The most important success criterion for a project can vary depending on the specific nature of the project, its goals, and the stakeholders involved. However, one commonly recognized success criterion is delivering the project within the agreed-upon time, scope, and budget. This is often referred to as the "triple constraint" or the "iron triangle" of project management.

1. Time: Completing a project within the established timeframe is crucial because it ensures that the project aligns with the expectations and requirements of stakeholders. Timeliness is often linked to market demands, business objectives, and the ability to seize opportunities. Delays can result in missed market windows, increased costs, and decreased customer satisfaction.
2. Scope: Delivering the project according to the defined scope is essential for meeting the desired outcomes and objectives. Scope defines the boundaries of the project and outlines the specific features, deliverables, and requirements. Adhering to the agreed-upon scope helps prevent scope creep, where additional, unplanned work is introduced, leading to project delays, increased costs, and potential dissatisfaction among stakeholders.
3. Budget: Staying within the allocated budget is crucial for ensuring the financial viability of a project. Effective cost management ensures that resources are utilized efficiently, expenses are controlled, and financial goals are met. Overspending or uncontrolled budget deviations can lead to financial strain, resource shortages, and even project failure.

While these three criteria are commonly considered as the primary indicators of project success, it is important to note that they do not capture all aspects of success. Other factors, such as stakeholder satisfaction, quality of deliverables, and long-term impacts, should also be considered depending on the project's specific context and objectives. Project success is a multidimensional concept, and the importance of each criterion may vary based on the project and its stakeholders' priorities.

10.5. How do you define project success?

Defining project success involves evaluating several key factors that measure the achievement of the project's objectives and the satisfaction of stakeholders. Here are the main criteria for defining project success:

1. Scope Fulfillment:
   a. The project meets all defined goals and objectives.
   b. All deliverables and requirements specified in the project scope are completed satisfactorily.
2. Timeliness:
   a. The project is completed within the agreed-upon schedule.
   b. Milestones are met according to the timeline set out at the beginning of the project.
3. Budget Adherence:
   a. The project is completed within the allocated budget.
   b. Efficient use of resources to prevent cost overruns.
4. Quality Standards:
   a. Deliverables meet the required quality standards and specifications.
   b. Acceptance criteria are met, ensuring that the outputs are fit for purpose.
5. Stakeholder Satisfaction:
   a. Stakeholders, including clients, sponsors, and team members, are satisfied with the project outcomes.
   b. Effective communication and collaboration throughout the project lifecycle.
6. Resource Management:
   a. Optimal use of human, financial, and material resources.
   b. Team members are utilized effectively and efficiently without burnout.
7. Risk Management:
   a. Identification, assessment, and mitigation of risks throughout the project.
   b. Minimal impact of unforeseen issues on the project's success.
8. Value Addition:

    a. The project adds value to the organization or stakeholders.
    b. Achievement of strategic objectives and benefits realization.
9. Compliance and Governance:
    a. Adherence to relevant laws, regulations, and standards.
    b. Effective governance practices and ethical conduct throughout the project.
10. Sustainability:
    a. Consideration of environmental, social, and economic impacts.
    b. Implementation of sustainable practices where applicable.

Project success is often subjective and may vary depending on the perspectives of different stakeholders. Therefore, it is important to establish clear success criteria at the outset of the project and ensure alignment with all stakeholders. Regular reviews and assessments throughout the project can help ensure that it stays on track to meet these success criteria.

10.6. What are the top ten reasons projects fail or slip in time?

Projects often fail or slip in time for a variety of reasons. Here are ten of the most common factors:

1. Poor Planning and Scheduling: Inadequate planning, unrealistic timelines, and insufficient resource allocation can lead to project delays. Without a clear roadmap, projects can easily veer off track.
2. Scope Creep: Uncontrolled changes or continuous growth in a project's scope can cause delays and overrun budgets. When additional features or requirements are added without proper evaluation, the project timeline extends.
3. Lack of Clear Objectives: When project goals and objectives are not well-defined or understood by all stakeholders, it leads to confusion and misalignment, resulting in delays and inefficiencies.
4. Ineffective Communication: Poor communication among team members, stakeholders, and project managers can cause misunderstandings, missed deadlines, and errors. Effective communication is crucial for coordinating tasks and managing expectations.
5. Inadequate Risk Management: Failing to identify, assess, and mitigate risks can result in unforeseen obstacles that delay the project. Proactive risk management is essential to handle potential issues before they become critical.
6. Resource Constraints: Insufficient resources, such as inadequate staffing, budget limitations, or lack of necessary equipment and materials, can hinder progress and cause delays.
7. Technical Challenges and Issues: Projects involving new or complex technologies can face unexpected technical problems. These issues can delay the project if there is no contingency plan or expertise to address them promptly.
8. Poor Project Management: Ineffective project management practices, including lack of leadership, poor decision-making, and inadequate monitoring and control, can lead to project failures. Strong project management skills are vital for keeping the project on track.
9. Stakeholder Conflicts: Disagreements and conflicts among stakeholders, including clients, team members, and management, can cause delays. Aligning stakeholder interests and managing expectations are crucial for project success.
10. Unrealistic Expectations: Setting goals and deadlines that are not achievable given the resources and time available can lead to inevitable delays and frustration. It is important to set realistic, attainable milestones to maintain project momentum.

Addressing these issues proactively can significantly enhance the likelihood of project success and timely completion.

10.7. What are the top ten project management challenges?

Project management comes with a variety of challenges, some common across industries and others specific to certain projects or contexts. Here are ten of the most prevalent challenges faced by project managers:

1. Scope Creep: This occurs when the project's scope expands beyond what was originally planned, often leading to increased costs, delays, and resource allocation issues.
2. Resource Allocation: Balancing resources such as budget, time, and manpower is often challenging, especially when unexpected demands arise or when resources are limited.
3. Time Management: Meeting deadlines and milestones is crucial in project management. Managing time effectively requires careful planning, scheduling, and monitoring to ensure tasks are completed on time.
4. Communication: Effective communication is essential for keeping stakeholders informed, resolving conflicts, and ensuring everyone is aligned with project goals and objectives.
5. Risk Management: Identifying, assessing, and mitigating risks is a key aspect of project management. Failure to manage risks effectively can lead to project failure or costly setbacks.
6. Stakeholder Management: Projects involve various stakeholders with different interests and expectations. Managing these stakeholders' needs and expectations requires diplomacy, communication skills, and sometimes negotiation.
7. Quality Control: Maintaining quality standards throughout the project lifecycle is essential for meeting customer expectations and ensuring project success. This involves regular quality checks and addressing any issues promptly.
8. Budget Management: Staying within budget is crucial for project success. Monitoring expenses, identifying cost-saving opportunities, and adapting to changes in budget constraints are all part of effective budget management.
9. Team Collaboration: Managing teams with diverse skills, backgrounds, and personalities can be challenging. Fostering collaboration, resolving conflicts, and keeping team members motivated are important aspects of team management.
10. Adapting to Change: Projects rarely go exactly as planned, and changes are often inevitable due to factors such as market conditions, technology advancements, or stakeholder preferences. Project managers must be adaptable and able to adjust plans and strategies accordingly.

Addressing these challenges requires a combination of effective leadership, communication skills, strategic planning, and problem-solving abilities. By proactively identifying and addressing these challenges, project managers can increase the likelihood of project success.

10.8. What are the toughest challenges to the success of customer relationship management projects?

Customer relationship management (CRM) projects can face several challenges that may hinder their success. Here are some of the toughest challenges:

1. Data Quality and Integration: CRM relies heavily on data. Poor data quality or difficulties integrating data from various sources can lead to inaccurate insights and ineffective decision-making.
2. User Adoption: Resistance from employees to adopt new CRM systems or processes can be a significant challenge. Lack of proper training, perceived complexity, or resistance to change can all contribute to low user adoption rates.
3. Lack of Executive Support: Without strong support from top management, CRM projects may struggle to get the necessary resources, funding, and alignment with broader organizational goals.
4. Limited Customer Insights: CRM aims to improve customer relationships by providing insights into customer behavior and preferences. However, limited access to relevant data or inability to extract actionable insights can impede the effectiveness of CRM initiatives.
5. Technology Issues: Issues related to the CRM software itself, such as downtime, bugs, or poor

scalability, can disrupt operations and undermine user confidence in the system.

6. Customization and Flexibility: CRM systems often need to be customized to meet specific business requirements. However, excessive customization can lead to complexity, higher costs, and longer implementation times.
7. Alignment with Business Processes: For CRM to be successful, it must align with existing business processes. Failure to integrate CRM into daily workflows or adapt processes to leverage CRM capabilities can reduce its effectiveness.
8. Security and Privacy Concerns: Handling sensitive customer data requires robust security measures to protect against data breaches or unauthorized access. Compliance with data privacy regulations such as GDPR (General Data Protection Regulation) or CCPA (California Consumer Privacy Act) adds an additional layer of complexity.
9. Measuring ROI: Quantifying the return on investment (ROI) of CRM initiatives can be challenging. It may take time to see tangible results, and attributing improvements solely to CRM efforts can be difficult in complex business environments.
10. Cultural Resistance: Organizational culture plays a significant role in CRM success. Resistance to customer-centric strategies or a lack of customer-focused mindset among employees can undermine CRM efforts.

Addressing these challenges requires a comprehensive approach involving effective leadership, clear communication, adequate resources, and a willingness to adapt and learn from setbacks.

10.9. What are the major issues and challenges you face in implementing business process management?

Business process management (BPM) faces many of the same hurdles as project management, such as issues with stakeholder buy-in, executive commitment and sometimes lack of training. To overcome cultural resistance in organizations, it is recommended that companies pursuing BPM projects consider forming a process improvement team made up of key individuals from each of the functional areas involved in the process.

In the decreasing order of importance:

1. Commitment by top management
2. Program organization and structure
3. Performance objectives aligned to process
4. Certification of process people
5. Process improvement training
6. Functioning of improvement teams
7. Tools, techniques, and methods
8. Stakeholder buy-in
9. Information systems integration.

10.10. What are the top reasons projects succeed in your organization?

In many organizations, including mine, project success often hinges on a combination of factors. Here is a list of reasons projects succeed, ordered by decreasing importance:

1. Clear Objectives and Goals: Projects that have well-defined objectives and goals from the outset tend to succeed more often. When everyone involved understands what they are working towards, it helps maintain focus and alignment throughout the project lifecycle.
2. Effective Communication: Strong communication among team members, stakeholders, and leadership is crucial. It ensures everyone is on the same page, problems are addressed promptly, and changes can be managed smoothly.

3. Skilled and Committed Team: A competent and dedicated team with the right skills and expertise greatly increases the chances of project success. Team members who are motivated and committed to the project's success will go the extra mile to overcome challenges.
4. Risk Management: Successful projects often involve proactive risk management strategies. Identifying potential risks early, developing mitigation plans, and regularly monitoring and addressing risks throughout the project lifecycle can prevent or minimize disruptions.
5. Effective Leadership: Strong leadership provides direction, support, and guidance throughout the project. Leaders who inspire confidence, foster collaboration, and empower team members contribute significantly to project success.
6. Adaptability and Flexibility: Projects rarely go exactly as planned. Those that succeed often demonstrate adaptability and flexibility in response to changing circumstances, requirements, or priorities.
7. Stakeholder Engagement: Engaging stakeholders effectively ensures their needs, expectations, and feedback are considered throughout the project. It builds trust, facilitates decision-making, and increases support for the project's outcomes.
8. Resource Allocation: Adequate resources, including funding, time, and personnel, are essential for project success. Properly allocating and managing resources ensures that the project stays on track and can deliver results within the specified constraints.
9. Quality Assurance: Maintaining high standards of quality throughout the project lifecycle is critical. Implementing robust quality assurance processes helps identify and rectify issues early, preventing costly rework or delays.
10. Continuous Improvement: Projects that emphasize continuous improvement and learning from both successes and failures tend to be more successful in the long run. By incorporating feedback and lessons learned into future projects, organizations can refine their processes and increase their chances of success over time.

While these factors contribute to project success individually, it is often the synergy between them that truly drives successful outcomes.

10.11. What are the dos and do nots for software project success?

Achieving success in software projects involves adhering to best practices and avoiding common pitfalls. Here is a list of dos and do nots for ensuring software project success:

Dos for Software Project Success

1. Clear Requirements and Goals:
    a. Define Requirements: Clearly articulate and document the project requirements.
    b. Set Realistic Goals: Establish achievable and measurable goals for the project.
2. Effective Planning:
    a. Create a Detailed Project Plan: Include timelines, milestones, resource allocation, and risk management.
    b. Use Agile Methodologies: Adapt to changes efficiently with iterative development and continuous feedback.
3. Stakeholder Engagement:
    a. Involve Stakeholders: Ensure continuous communication with stakeholders to align expectations and gather feedback.
    b. Regular Updates: Provide frequent status updates to all stakeholders.
4. Strong Project Management:
    a. Assign a Competent Project Manager: Ensure the project manager has the necessary skills and experience.
    b. Monitor Progress: Regularly track the project's progress against the plan.

5. Skilled Team:
    a. Assemble a Competent Team: Hire team members with the required technical and domain expertise.
    b. Provide Training: Offer ongoing training and professional development.
6. Effective Communication:
    a. Maintain Open Communication Channels: Use tools and practices that facilitate clear and continuous communication.
    b. Hold Regular Meetings: Schedule stand-ups, retrospectives, and other necessary meetings.
7. Quality Assurance:
    a. Implement Testing Procedures: Integrate unit tests, integration tests, and user acceptance testing.
    b. Conduct Code Reviews: Regularly review code to maintain quality and catch issues early.
8. Risk Management:
    a. Identify and Mitigate Risks: Proactively identify potential risks and develop mitigation strategies.
    b. Have a Contingency Plan: Prepare for unexpected issues with a backup plan.
9. User-Centric Design:
    a. Focus on User Experience: Design with the end-user in mind, ensuring the product is intuitive and meets user needs.
    b. Gather User Feedback: Regularly collect and incorporate user feedback into the development process.
10. Continuous Improvement:
    a. Iterate and Improve: Continuously refine and improve the product and processes based on feedback and performance metrics.
    b. Retrospectives: Conduct retrospectives to learn from successes and failures.

Do Nots for Software Project Success
1. Poor Requirement Management:
    a. Avoid Ambiguous Requirements: Do not proceed with vague or incomplete requirements.
    b. Ignore Scope Creep: Do not allow the project scope to expand without proper evaluation and approval.
2. Inadequate Planning:
    a. Skip Planning: Do not start development without a solid project plan.
    b. Ignore Risks: Do not disregard potential risks and assume everything will go as planned.
3. Lack of Stakeholder Involvement:
    a. Exclude Stakeholders: Do not exclude stakeholders from the planning and development process.
    b. Delay Communication: Do not wait until the end of the project to involve stakeholders.
4. Ineffective Project Management:
    a. Micromanage: Do not micromanage the team; trust them to do their jobs.
    b. Neglect Tracking: Do not ignore progress tracking and necessary adjustments.
5. Incompetent Team:
    a. Hire Unqualified Personnel: Do not compromise on the skills and experience of team members.
    b. Neglect Team Morale: Do not ignore the team's morale and well-being.
6. Poor Communication:
    a. Keep Information Siloed: Do not withhold information from team members.
    b. Avoid Feedback: Do not disregard feedback from the team or users.

7. Neglect Quality Assurance:
    a. Skip Testing: Do not skip or minimize the importance of testing.
    b. Ignore Technical Debt: Do not ignore technical debt; address it promptly.
8. Ineffective Risk Management:
    a. Avoid Risk Identification: Do not ignore the identification and assessment of risks.
    b. Lack of Contingency Plans: Do not proceed without contingency plans for potential issues.
9. Ignore User Needs:
    a. Neglect User Experience: Do not ignore the user experience and usability aspects.
    b. Disregard User Feedback: Do not dismiss user feedback and its implications for the product.
10. Resist Change and Improvement:
    a. Avoid Iteration: Do not resist iterative development and continuous improvement.
    b. Ignore Lessons Learned: Do not neglect the lessons learned from previous projects or iterations.

Following these guidelines will help steer software projects towards success by ensuring effective planning, execution, and continuous improvement.

10.12. How to capture lessons learned?

Capturing lessons learned in projects is a crucial part of project management, ensuring that both successes and failures contribute to the organization's collective knowledge and improve future project outcomes. Here is a comprehensive approach to capturing lessons learned effectively:

1. Preparation
    a. Define Objectives: Clearly articulate the purpose of capturing lessons learned. Is it to improve processes, enhance team performance, avoid past mistakes, or all of the above?
    b. Establish a Framework: Set up a standard template or framework that will be used to capture lessons learned. This could include sections for project details, lessons learned, impact, recommendations, and actions taken.
2. During the Project
    a. Ongoing Documentation: Encourage team members to document lessons as they arise throughout the project, not just at the end. This can be done using project management software, shared documents, or dedicated lessons learned tools.
    b. Regular Reviews: Hold regular review meetings (e.g., after each project phase or sprint in agile projects) to discuss and document lessons learned up to that point.
3. Post-Project Review
    a. Conduct a Lessons Learned Meeting: Schedule a formal meeting at the end of the project to review and discuss what was learned. Include the entire project team and, if possible, stakeholders.
        i. Facilitated Session: Consider having a neutral facilitator to guide the discussion, ensuring all voices are heard and the session remains constructive.
        ii. Structured Approach: Use a structured approach like the "4Ls" (Liked, Learned, Lacked, Longed for) or "Start, Stop, Continue" to guide the discussion.
4. Documentation
    a. Record Lessons Learned: Use the predefined template to document the lessons learned during the review meeting. Include specific details like the issue encountered, how it was resolved, and recommendations for future projects.
    b. Categorization: Categorize the lessons learned (e.g., by project phase, type of issue, functional area) to make it easier to search and reference in the future.
5. Analysis and Integration

   a. Analyze Patterns: Look for patterns or recurring themes in the lessons learned across multiple projects. This can help identify systemic issues or best practices.
   b. Integrate into Processes: Update organizational processes, standards, and training materials based on the lessons learned to institutionalize the knowledge gained.
6. Dissemination
   a. Share with the Team: Ensure that the documented lessons learned are shared with the project team and relevant stakeholders. This can be done through email, project management tools, or a shared knowledge base.
   b. Central Repository: Store lessons learned in a central repository that is accessible to all project managers and relevant staff. This could be an internal wiki, a lessons learned database, or a project management system.
7. Continuous Improvement
   a. Feedback Loop: Create a feedback loop where team members can provide input on the usefulness and application of the lessons learned. This helps in refining the process and ensuring continuous improvement.
   b. Regular Updates: Periodically review and update the lessons learned repository to keep it current and relevant.

Tools and Techniques

1. Surveys and Questionnaires: Use surveys to gather feedback from team members and stakeholders about what went well and what could be improved.
2. Interviews and Focus Groups: Conduct one-on-one interviews or focus group discussions to capture in-depth insights and perspectives.
3. After-Action Reviews (AARs): A structured review process used by the military, AARs can be adapted to project management to systematically evaluate what happened, why it happened, and how it can be done better next time.

Capturing lessons learned is an ongoing, systematic process that requires commitment and participation from the entire project team. By embedding this practice into the project lifecycle and organizational culture, you can enhance learning, improve future project performance, and drive continuous improvement.

10.13. When do you complete lessons learned during your project?

Lessons learned are typically completed at various stages throughout the lifecycle of a project, ensuring that valuable insights are captured and utilized to improve future projects. Here are the key points when lessons learned should be documented:

1. Throughout the Project (Ongoing):
   a. Regularly Scheduled Reviews: During project status meetings, sprint reviews (in Agile methodologies), and other regular touchpoints, teams should document lessons as they arise. This ensures that issues and successes are recorded in real time.
   b. After Major Milestones: When significant phases or deliverables are completed, it is beneficial to conduct a review session to capture what was learned during that period. This could be after the completion of a major phase like design, implementation, or testing.
2. End of Major Phases:
   a. End of Planning Phase: Capture insights from the planning process, including what worked well in project scoping, budgeting, and scheduling, and what challenges were faced.
   b. End of Execution Phase: Document lessons from the execution of tasks and activities, including resource management, team dynamics, and communication issues.

3. Project Closure:
    a. Final Project Review: A comprehensive review session, often called a post-mortem or retrospective, is held to evaluate the entire project. This includes reviewing project objectives, deliverables, timelines, budget adherence, and stakeholder satisfaction.
    b. Documentation and Reporting: Compile the lessons learned into a formal document or database that can be referenced for future projects. This final report should include detailed insights on what worked well, what did not, and recommendations for future projects.
4. Post-Project:
    a. Operational Handover: As part of the transition to operations or the client, capture feedback on the handover process and initial operational issues.
    b. Follow-Up Reviews: After some time has passed since project completion, conduct a follow-up review to capture any additional lessons that may have emerged during the stabilization period.

By capturing lessons learned throughout the project lifecycle, teams can ensure continuous improvement and leverage insights for future projects, enhancing overall project management practices and outcomes.

10.14. Tell me about a project that you were involved in that did not go well? What did you learn?

When responding to this interview question, it is important to demonstrate your ability to reflect on challenges and learn from them. Here is a structured approach you could take:

1. Choose the Right Example: Select a project that did not go as planned but still allowed you to gain valuable insights or skills. Make sure it is not too recent or critical to your candidacy for the position.
2. Briefly Describe the Project: Provide context about the project, including its goals, your role, and any relevant details about its scope and challenges.
3. Discuss What Went Wrong: Be honest about the setbacks or issues that arose during the project. This could include anything from miscommunication among team members to unforeseen technical difficulties.
4. Highlight Your Response: Describe the actions you took to address the challenges and try to mitigate the issues. This could involve problem-solving, teamwork, or adapting your approach as the situation evolved.
5. Share What You Learned: This is the most crucial part. Discuss the lessons you gleaned from the experience. Emphasize how it helped you grow both professionally and personally. Talk about any changes you would make in similar situations in the future.
6. Conclude on a Positive Note: Wrap up your response by emphasizing that while the project may not have gone as planned, it provided valuable learning opportunities that have made you a stronger and more capable professional.

Here is an example response:

"Sure, let me tell you about a project I was involved in during my previous role. We were tasked with developing a new software application to streamline our client onboarding process. I was leading the development team responsible for building the user interface.

Unfortunately, we encountered several challenges along the way. There was a lack of clear communication between our team and the stakeholders, which led to misunderstandings about the project requirements. Additionally, we underestimated the complexity of integrating the new application with our existing systems, resulting in delays and technical issues.

However, we quickly realized the importance of regular communication and alignment with stakeholders. We implemented weekly progress meetings and established a more structured feedback process to ensure everyone was on the same page. Additionally, we adopted a more iterative approach to development, allowing us to identify and address issues earlier in the process.

From this experience, I learned the critical importance of effective communication, stakeholder management, and agile development methodologies. I now approach projects with a greater emphasis on collaboration and adaptability, which I believe has made me a more effective team member.

While the project did not go as smoothly as we had hoped, the lessons learned have been invaluable in shaping my approach to project management and problem-solving. I am confident that I can apply these insights to future projects to ensure their success."

Here is another example:

1. Project: The project was to implement the complete automation of port and marine base operations for a major commercial sea port in Asia. It was a three-year project from systems study till implementation. There were four project teams each responsible for one portion of the project - onsite, user interface, back-end, and financial systems. About 35 members were in all the teams. The fourth project team, in Asia, was responsible for system study, end-user coordination, integration, onsite implementation, and support. The lead project manager in Asia was responsible for onsite work, work allocation and coordination of all other project teams.
2. Problem: The project deliverables and milestones not only slipped many times but the quality of deliverables lacked with the result - unsatisfied customer.
3. Lessons learnt: In order to ensure successful timely and quality delivery of the product, we should have diligently followed the software project management and controls, more specifically in multi-location diverse teams, like:
    a. Effectively managing the customer expectations
    b. Risk management
    c. Effective change control
    d. Scope creep
    e. Adopting the phased or staged delivery approach
    f. Effective project monitoring so as to uncover any glaring issues early.

10.15. How do software engineering teams measure their success?

Software engineering teams measure their success through various metrics and indicators that assess both the quality of their work and their ability to deliver value to the business or organization. Some common ways in which software engineering teams measure success include:

1. Delivery Timeliness: Did you do what you said you would do, roughly on time? Meeting deadlines and delivering projects on time is a key indicator of success. This can be measured by comparing estimated delivery dates with actual delivery dates.
2. Quality of Code: Does your code suck? Is it buggy? Is it maintainable? How much technical debt did you add? The quality of code is assessed through code reviews, static code analysis tools, and automated tests. Metrics such as code coverage, code complexity, and adherence to coding standards are often used to evaluate code quality.
3. Bug Fixing Rate: The speed at which bugs are identified, reported, and fixed is an important measure of success. Lowering the time it takes to resolve bugs indicates an improvement in the development process.
4. Customer Satisfaction: Gathering feedback from end-users or customers about the software's usability, reliability, and functionality helps gauge its success in meeting user needs and

expectations.

5. User Adoption: The number of active users or the adoption rate of new features indicates the software's usefulness and relevance to its target audience.
6. Retention Rate: For software products with subscription-based models or recurring usage, the retention rate of customers over time reflects the software's ability to retain users and provide ongoing value.
7. Performance Metrics: Monitoring the software's performance metrics such as response time, uptime, and scalability helps ensure that it meets performance requirements and can handle user load efficiently.
8. Return on Investment (ROI): Did your efforts bring in the money that was expected? You can write all the code and make it beautiful, but if it does not bring in the money, you have failed. Assessing the financial impact of software projects in terms of revenue generated, cost savings, or efficiency improvements helps determine their success from a business perspective.
9. Team Satisfaction and Productivity: Tracking metrics related to team morale, collaboration, and productivity can provide insights into the overall health and effectiveness of the software engineering team.
10. Alignment with Business Goals: Evaluating how well software projects align with the organization's strategic objectives and contribute to its overall mission and vision is essential for measuring their success in the broader context of the business.

By analyzing these metrics regularly and making data-driven decisions, software engineering teams can continuously improve their processes and outcomes, ultimately leading to greater success in delivering high-quality software that meets user needs and business requirements.

10.16. How do you measure your project team's performance?

Measuring the performance of a project team is crucial to evaluate its effectiveness and identify areas for improvement. Here are some common methods and metrics used to measure project team performance:

1. Timeliness: Assess how well the team meets project deadlines and milestones. Measure the actual completion time against planned schedules to identify any delays or bottlenecks.
2. Budget adherence: Evaluate the team's ability to manage project costs within the allocated budget. Compare actual expenditures to the budgeted amounts and analyze any significant variances.
3. Quality of deliverables: Determine the quality of the team's outputs or deliverables. This can be assessed through objective criteria, such as error rates, customer satisfaction surveys, or adherence to predefined quality standards.
4. Scope management: Evaluate how well the team manages project scope. Assess whether they are able to deliver the agreed-upon project scope without significant scope creep or uncontrolled changes.
5. Stakeholder satisfaction: Gather feedback from project stakeholders, including clients, end-users, and management, to assess their satisfaction with the team's performance. This can be done through surveys, interviews, or regular communication channels.
6. Team productivity: Measure the team's productivity by tracking key performance indicators (KPIs) such as tasks completed, work hours, backlog size, or throughput. Analyze trends over time to identify patterns and areas for improvement.
7. Communication and collaboration: Evaluate the effectiveness of communication and collaboration within the team. Assess factors such as responsiveness, clarity of communication, teamwork, and knowledge sharing.
8. Employee satisfaction: Monitor team members' satisfaction and engagement levels through surveys or feedback sessions. High levels of employee satisfaction often correlate with better project performance.

9. Lessons learned: Conduct post-project reviews or retrospectives to identify lessons learned and gather insights from team members. This can help improve future project performance by identifying best practices and areas for growth.

It is important to note that the selection of performance metrics should align with project goals, objectives, and organizational priorities. The specific metrics and methods used may vary based on the nature of the project, industry, and team dynamics.

10.17. What can be the reasons why senior management is not as happy as you expected even when your latest project is nearly on time, under budget, and with scope?

There could be several reasons why senior management might not be as happy as expected, even when a project is nearly on time, under budget, and within scope:

1. Lack of Alignment with Strategic Goals: Despite meeting project objectives, senior management might feel that the project does not align well with the company's broader strategic goals. If the project does not contribute directly to the organization's long-term vision or priorities, they may not see it as a success.
2. Unmet Stakeholder Expectations: While the project might be on time, budget, and scope, it is possible that it does not meet the expectations of key stakeholders, such as customers, investors, or regulatory bodies. If their needs or requirements were not fully addressed, senior management might perceive the project as falling short.
3. Quality Concerns: Even if the project meets its basic objectives, senior management might have concerns about the quality of the deliverables. If there are issues with reliability, performance, or usability, they may worry about the project's long-term viability or its impact on the company's reputation.
4. Communication Breakdown: Senior management might not fully understand the value or significance of the project if there was a breakdown in communication between the project team and senior leadership. If the project's achievements were not effectively communicated or if senior management was not kept informed throughout the process, they may not appreciate its success.
5. Market Changes: External factors, such as shifts in the market or changes in customer preferences, could diminish the perceived success of the project, even if it was executed flawlessly. If the project no longer addresses a relevant need or if the competitive landscape has shifted, senior management might question its value.
6. Organizational Politics: Internal politics or competing priorities within the organization could also influence senior management's perception of the project's success. If there are other initiatives or agendas vying for attention or resources, they might detract from the recognition of the project's accomplishments.
7. Unforeseen Risks: Even if the project was successful in terms of schedule, budget, and scope, senior management might be concerned about unforeseen risks that could impact its long-term success. They may worry about potential future challenges or dependencies that were not adequately addressed during the project's execution.

Addressing these concerns requires effective communication, stakeholder management, and a clear understanding of the organization's strategic priorities. It is important to engage with senior management to understand their perspective and address any underlying issues that may be impacting their happiness with the project's outcomes.

10.18. What can be the possible reasons project teams keeps on putting out one fire after another?

There could be several reasons why project teams find themselves constantly dealing with issues and putting out fires:

1. Poor Planning: Inadequate planning can lead to underestimated timelines, lack of resources, or incomplete requirements, setting the stage for problems down the line.
2. Unclear Objectives: If the project objectives are ambiguous or keep changing, it can cause confusion among team members and lead to frequent rework.
3. Scope Creep: Continuous changes or additions to the project scope without proper evaluation can strain resources and timelines, leading to constant firefighting to meet deadlines.
4. Resource Constraints: Insufficient resources, whether it is manpower, budget, or technology, can result in overburdened team members and increased likelihood of errors and delays.
5. Poor Communication: Ineffective communication channels or lack of transparency can lead to misunderstandings, missed deadlines, and increased chances of errors.
6. Lack of Risk Management: Ignoring potential risks or not having a proper risk management plan in place can leave the project vulnerable to unforeseen challenges.
7. Inadequate Skill Sets: If team members lack the necessary skills or expertise to handle their assigned tasks, it can result in errors, rework, and delays.
8. Stakeholder Issues: Conflicting priorities or demands from stakeholders can disrupt the project flow and force the team to constantly address divergent needs.
9. Technology Failures: Dependence on unreliable or outdated technology can lead to frequent technical glitches, disrupting the project progress.
10. External Factors: Market changes, regulatory issues, or external events beyond the team's control can introduce unexpected challenges that require immediate attention.

Addressing these issues often requires a combination of proactive planning, effective communication, stakeholder management, and risk mitigation strategies to minimize the frequency of firefighting and ensure smoother project execution.

10.19. How do you respond to a question: "Tell me about your most exciting project."

When responding to the question, "Tell me about your most exciting project," follow these steps to create a compelling and professional answer:

1. Choose the Right Project
    a. Select a project that aligns with the skills or experience relevant to the role you are applying for.
    b. Pick one where you played a significant role or made a measurable impact.
2. Provide Context (What and Why)
    a. Briefly describe the project, its purpose, and its goals.
    b. Highlight why it was exciting for you (e.g., learning opportunity, high stakes, or innovative aspects).
3. Explain Your Role (How)
    a. Detail your specific contributions to the project.
    b. Mention challenges you faced and how you overcame them.
4. Highlight Outcomes (Results)
    a. Share measurable results (e.g., metrics, awards, or impact).
    b. Focus on the value your work brought to the team, company, or clients.
5. Connect It Back to the Role
    a. Relate the skills and experience from the project to the position you are applying for.

If I were asked that question, I would likely share some details about a project that really ignited my passion and challenged me to push my boundaries. For instance, I could talk about a time when I worked on developing an AI-driven application that solved a real-world problem, like optimizing energy usage in buildings or improving healthcare diagnostics. I would describe the innovative solutions we implemented, the collaborative process with teammates, and the sense of fulfillment when we achieved tangible results. It is all about conveying enthusiasm and showcasing the impact of the project.

Example Response:
"One of my most exciting projects was leading the redesign of a cloud-based collaboration platform at my previous job. The goal was to improve user engagement by 25% through a more intuitive interface and advanced features.

I collaborated with cross-functional teams, including designers and engineers, and conducted user research to identify pain points. One of the biggest challenges was managing competing stakeholder priorities, which I addressed by facilitating workshops to align on the most impactful features.

Ultimately, the project launched on schedule, exceeded the engagement goal by 30%, and earned recognition from the executive team. It was rewarding because it combined problem-solving, leadership, and user-centered design - skills I am eager to bring to this role."

This structure ensures your response is concise, engaging, and demonstrates your value.

11. Project Management Organization

More organizations are realizing that project management is a fundamental skill for everyone within the company. It is clear that achieving all project goals requires proper organization of people, communication, tasks, and resources. However, the optimal structure for such organization can be less clear. Each company has its own approach to structuring itself and its operations. If three companies performing similar work were compared, it is likely they would each have a distinct organizational structure. Furthermore, all three could be equally successful (or unsuccessful), indicating that there is not necessarily a single best organizational solution.

11.1. Why do organizations do projects?

Organizations undertake projects for a variety of strategic, operational, and financial reasons. Here are some key motivations:

1. Achieving Strategic Goals: Projects help organizations implement their strategic plans. Whether it is entering new markets, developing new products, or expanding operations, projects are essential for executing these high-level objectives.
2. Innovation and Development: Projects often drive innovation. They provide structured approaches to research and development, enabling organizations to create new products, services, or processes that can give them a competitive edge.

3. Improving Efficiency: Many projects aim to improve operational efficiency. By streamlining processes, adopting new technologies, or re-engineering workflows, organizations can reduce costs, increase productivity, and enhance quality.
4. Responding to Market Demands: Projects allow organizations to respond swiftly to changes in the market. Whether it is adapting to regulatory changes, addressing customer needs, or keeping up with industry trends, projects provide the flexibility needed to stay relevant.
5. Compliance and Risk Management: Projects are often undertaken to comply with new regulations or standards, thereby mitigating legal and financial risks. For instance, projects related to data security, environmental sustainability, or workplace safety fall into this category.
6. Resource Optimization: Effective project management can lead to better utilization of resources. By managing time, budget, and human resources more efficiently, organizations can achieve more with less.
7. Customer Satisfaction and Retention: Projects aimed at improving customer service, developing new features, or customizing products can significantly enhance customer satisfaction and loyalty, leading to sustained business growth.
8. Revenue Growth: Projects that result in new or improved products and services can open up new revenue streams. This is critical for long-term financial health and growth.
9. Competitive Advantage: Undertaking projects can help organizations differentiate themselves from competitors. Successful projects can lead to unique offerings or capabilities that are hard to replicate.
10. Cultural and Organizational Change: Projects can drive cultural and organizational changes that align with evolving business environments. For example, projects related to digital transformation can change how an organization operates at a fundamental level.

By structuring efforts as projects, organizations can ensure that these endeavors are well-planned, systematically executed, and rigorously controlled, thereby increasing the likelihood of successful outcomes.

11.2. Why program management office?

Program management offices (PMOs) enhance organizational performance by optimizing the management of projects, thus increasing the capacity to achieve superior results from both planned and ongoing projects. PMOs have become a best practice for most Fortune 500 companies and are now being adopted by organizations of all sizes to efficiently manage their projects.

By implementing a flexible program management framework and institutionalizing project management best practices, organizations can develop a strategic competency that aligns individual project goals with the overall program or organizational mission and business objectives. This involves establishing project and program baselines, developing measurable performance standards, and managing lifecycle activities in ways that are both meaningful and adaptable, allowing experts within the organization the flexibility to respond to changing requirements and technological advancements.

11.3. What are the most significant benefits of creating and maintaining a project management office?

A Program Management Office (PMO) is established within an organization for several critical reasons. Here are some of the key benefits and purposes of having a PMO:

1. Standardization and Consistency:
    a. A PMO helps standardize project management practices across the organization, ensuring consistency in how projects are planned, executed, and monitored.
    b. It provides standardized tools, templates, and methodologies, which can improve

efficiency and reduce errors.

2. Improved Project Success Rates:
    a. By providing oversight and governance, a PMO can help ensure that projects align with organizational goals and are completed on time, within scope, and on budget.
    b. It offers guidance and support to project managers, increasing the likelihood of project success.
3. Resource Management:
    a. A PMO oversees the allocation and utilization of resources across projects, ensuring that resources are used effectively and efficiently.
    b. It helps avoid resource conflicts and ensures that the right skills are available for the right projects.
4. Risk Management:
    a. The PMO plays a crucial role in identifying, assessing, and mitigating risks across projects.
    b. It ensures that risk management practices are followed consistently, reducing the overall risk to the organization.
5. Strategic Alignment:
    a. A PMO ensures that projects are aligned with the organization's strategic objectives.
    b. It helps prioritize projects based on their strategic value and impact, ensuring that resources are invested in the most important initiatives.
6. Performance Monitoring and Reporting:
    a. The PMO monitors project performance and provides regular reports to senior management and stakeholders.
    b. It offers a centralized view of project status, helping to identify issues early and take corrective action.
7. Knowledge Management:
    a. A PMO captures and disseminates lessons learned and best practices from completed projects.
    b. It acts as a repository of project knowledge, which can be used to improve future projects and prevent repeating past mistakes.
8. Enhanced Communication and Collaboration:
    a. The PMO fosters better communication and collaboration among project teams, stakeholders, and management.
    b. It ensures that information flows smoothly and that everyone is informed about project progress and changes.
9. Change Management:
    a. The PMO supports change management processes by helping to manage the impact of changes on projects and the organization.
    b. It ensures that changes are implemented smoothly and with minimal disruption.
10. Governance and Compliance:
    a. A PMO enforces governance policies and ensures that projects comply with regulatory and organizational requirements.
    b. It establishes and maintains project management standards, ensuring compliance with industry best practices.

Overall, a PMO is vital for ensuring that project management practices are robust, effective, and aligned with the strategic goals of the organization. It enhances the organization's ability to deliver projects successfully, manage resources efficiently, and achieve desired outcomes.

11.4. What are the critical elements for a successful project office?

A successful project office, also known as a project management office (PMO), relies on several critical elements to function effectively. These elements may vary depending on the organization's size, culture, and industry, but generally include:

1. Clear Objectives and Alignment: The project office must have a clearly defined purpose and objectives aligned with the organization's strategic goals. It should support project delivery, governance, and performance improvement.
2. Executive Support and Sponsorship: Strong backing from senior leadership is crucial for the project office's credibility, authority, and resource allocation. Executive sponsorship ensures alignment with organizational priorities and provides necessary resources.
3. Skilled Personnel: A competent team with diverse skills in project management, business analysis, and relevant domains is essential. Having experienced professionals who understand the organization's culture and processes ensures effective project oversight and support.
4. Robust Processes and Methodologies: Defined processes, standards, and methodologies for project initiation, planning, execution, monitoring, and closure ensure consistency and efficiency in project delivery. This includes frameworks like PMBOK (Project Management Body of Knowledge), PRINCE2, Agile, or hybrid approaches.
5. Effective Governance Structure: A well-defined governance framework with clear roles, responsibilities, and decision-making authorities ensures accountability and transparency. It facilitates effective communication, issue resolution, and escalation paths.
6. Resource Management: Efficient allocation and utilization of resources, including people, budget, and technology, are vital for project success. The project office should have mechanisms for resource forecasting, allocation, and optimization to meet project demands.
7. Risk Management: Identification, assessment, mitigation, and monitoring of project risks are critical for minimizing disruptions and achieving project objectives. The project office should implement risk management processes and tools to proactively address uncertainties.
8. Performance Measurement and Reporting: Establishing key performance indicators (KPIs) and metrics enables the project office to monitor progress, identify trends, and assess project performance. Regular reporting to stakeholders facilitates informed decision-making and course corrections.
9. Stakeholder Engagement and Communication: Effective communication and engagement with project stakeholders, including sponsors, customers, team members, and vendors, are essential for managing expectations, resolving conflicts, and building trust.
10. Continuous Improvement Culture: Encouraging a culture of learning, feedback, and continuous improvement helps the project office adapt to changing environments, embrace innovation, and enhance its capabilities over time.
11. Flexibility and Adaptability: The project office should be flexible and adaptable to accommodate evolving project requirements, market dynamics, and organizational priorities. It should embrace change and adjust its processes and approaches accordingly.

In summary, the key elements for establishing a successful project office are:

1. Adopting a project management methodology
2. Defining the role of the project manager
3. Training program managers, project managers, sponsors, and team members in their respective roles
4. Implementing a tool to support the project environment
5. Establishing a project office
6. Advancing the project management discipline through advanced training and professional certification

To effectively support project management as an operational function, it is essential to:

1. Recognize that project management is a tool, and

2. Implement organization-wide discipline related to the management and practice of this tool.

By ensuring these critical elements are in place and functioning effectively, a project office can significantly enhance the success rate of projects within an organization.

11.5. What are the pros and cons of outsourcing project management?

Outsourcing project management involves hiring external professionals or firms to oversee and manage projects instead of using in-house resources. Here are the pros and cons of outsourcing project management:

Pros

1. Expertise and Experience:
    a. Access to Specialized Skills: Outsourcing provides access to experienced project managers with specialized skills that may not be available in-house.
    b. Best Practices: External project managers often bring industry best practices and methodologies that can enhance project outcomes.
2. Cost Savings:
    a. Reduced Overhead Costs: Outsourcing can be more cost-effective than hiring full-time staff, especially for short-term projects.
    b. Scalability: Companies can scale their project management resources up or down based on project needs without incurring significant costs.
3. Focus on Core Business:
    a. Resource Allocation: Outsourcing allows internal teams to focus on core business activities rather than being distracted by project management tasks.
    b. Improved Efficiency: By delegating project management, companies can improve overall efficiency and productivity.
4. Flexibility and Agility:
    a. Adaptability: External project managers can quickly adapt to changing project requirements and market conditions.
    b. Access to Global Talent: Companies can leverage global talent pools, gaining insights and expertise from different regions and industries.

Cons

1. Communication Challenges:
    a. Miscommunication: Differences in time zones, languages, and cultures can lead to miscommunication and misunderstandings.
    b. Coordination Issues: Managing remote teams requires effective communication strategies, which can be challenging to implement and maintain.
2. Loss of Control:
    a. Reduced Oversight: Companies may have less control over outsourced project management processes and decisions.
    b. Quality Concerns: Ensuring the quality and consistency of project deliverables can be challenging when relying on external resources.
3. Dependency on External Providers:
    a. Reliability: The success of the project may heavily depend on the reliability and performance of the outsourcing partner.
    b. Vendor Risks: Risks related to the financial stability, business practices, and continuity of the outsourcing provider can impact project success.
4. Security and Confidentiality:
    a. Data Security: Outsourcing can pose risks to data security and confidentiality, especially

if sensitive information is involved.

b. Intellectual Property: Protecting intellectual property and proprietary information can be more challenging when working with external parties.

5. Alignment with Organizational Goals:
    a. Cultural Fit: External project managers may not fully understand or align with the company's culture, values, and strategic objectives.
    b. Prioritization Issues: Outsourced project managers might prioritize their own business interests over the company's project goals.

Outsourcing project management can offer significant advantages in terms of expertise, cost savings, and flexibility. However, it also presents challenges such as communication issues, loss of control, and potential risks related to security and confidentiality. Companies should carefully evaluate these pros and cons, considering their specific needs, resources, and strategic goals before deciding to outsource project management functions.

11.6. What are the differences between functional management and project management?

Functional management and project management are two distinct approaches to organizing work and managing resources within an organization. Here are the key differences between them:

1. Scope of Responsibilities
    a. Functional Management:
        i. Focuses on overseeing a specific functional area or department, such as finance, marketing, human resources, or production.
        ii. Responsibilities are ongoing and include managing day-to-day operations, maintaining standards, and improving processes within the department.
        iii. Emphasis is on efficiency, consistency, and achieving long-term departmental goals.
    b. Project Management:
        i. Centers on managing specific projects that have defined objectives, timelines, and deliverables.
        ii. Responsibilities are temporary and revolve around planning, executing, and closing projects.
        iii. Emphasis is on meeting project goals, deadlines, and budget constraints.
2. Time Horizon
    a. Functional Management:
        i. Long-term focus with ongoing responsibilities.
        ii. Concerned with the continuous performance and growth of the department.
    b. Project Management:
        i. Short-term focus with a fixed project lifecycle.
        ii. Concerned with the successful completion of a specific project within the given timeframe.
3. Goals and Objectives
    a. Functional Management:
        i. Goals are related to improving departmental performance, enhancing productivity, and ensuring the department contributes to the overall strategic objectives of the organization.
        ii. Objectives are often process-oriented and aim at maintaining and enhancing the capabilities of the department.
    b. Project Management:
        i. Goals are specific to the project's outcomes, such as delivering a new product,

implementing a new system, or organizing an event.

ii. Objectives are often result-oriented and aim at achieving the project's deliverables on time and within budget.

4. Authority and Decision-Making
    a. Functional Management:
        i. Managers have formal authority over their department and its employees.
        ii. Decision-making power is typically limited to the scope of their functional area.
    b. Project Management:
        i. Project managers often have limited formal authority and must rely on influence and negotiation to coordinate resources and manage project teams.
        ii. Decision-making is focused on project-related issues and requires collaboration across different departments.
5. Resource Allocation
    a. Functional Management:
        i. Resources are dedicated to the department and used for ongoing operations.
        ii. Resource allocation is stable and managed within the department's budget.
    b. Project Management:
        i. Resources are allocated temporarily for the duration of the project.
        ii. Project managers must often compete for resources with other projects and departments.
6. Skills and Competencies
    a. Functional Management:
        i. Requires deep expertise in a specific functional area.
        ii. Skills focus on managing people, processes, and technologies related to that function.
    b. Project Management:
        i. Requires a broad set of skills, including project planning, risk management, stakeholder communication, and team leadership.
        ii. Skills focus on managing the project lifecycle and ensuring successful project delivery.
7. Organizational Structure
    a. Functional Management:
        i. Operates within a hierarchical structure where each department has a clear chain of command.
        ii. Employees typically report to a functional manager.
    b. Project Management:
        i. Can operate within various organizational structures, such as matrix, projectized, or hybrid.
        ii. Team members may report to both functional managers and project managers, especially in a matrix structure.
8. Performance Metrics
    a. Functional Management:
        i. Performance is measured based on departmental efficiency, productivity, and contribution to overall organizational goals.
        ii. Metrics are often continuous and process-oriented.
    b. Project Management:
        i. Performance is measured based on project success criteria, including on-time delivery, staying within budget, and meeting quality standards.
        ii. Metrics are specific to the project's scope and objectives.

Understanding these differences helps organizations assign appropriate management strategies to different aspects of their operations, ensuring both functional stability and successful project outcomes.

11.7. How should we organize for project management? What all to consider to setup a project organization? What are the different types of project organization, and pros and cons of each type?

Setting up a project organization involves careful consideration of various factors to ensure efficient management and successful project delivery. Here is a breakdown of key aspects to consider and the different types of project organizations:

1. Project Scope and Complexity: Understand the scope and complexity of the project. Larger and more complex projects often require more sophisticated organizational structures.
2. Project Objectives and Goals: Clearly define project objectives and goals to align the organizational structure with the project's specific requirements.
3. Resource Availability and Skill Sets: Assess the availability of resources (human, financial, and technical) and required skill sets for the project. This will influence the choice of organizational structure.
4. Communication Requirements: Consider communication needs within the project team and with external stakeholders. Effective communication is crucial for project success.
5. Decision-Making Processes: Determine decision-making processes within the organization. This includes identifying key decision-makers and establishing communication channels for decision-making.

Now, let us delve into the different types of project organizations:

1. Pure Project Organization (Projectized):
    a. Description: In a pure project organization, resources are assigned exclusively to a single project for its duration. The project manager has full authority over the project team.
    b. Pros:
        i. Clear project focus.
        ii. Fast decision-making.
        iii. Team members develop deep expertise in their project area.
    c. Cons:
        i. Duplication of resources across projects.
        ii. Lack of continuity between projects.
        iii. Potential for conflicts over resource allocation.
2. Functional Organization:
    a. Description: Resources are grouped by their functional specialty (e.g., marketing, engineering) and report to functional managers. Projects are managed within each functional department.
    b. Pros:
        i. Efficient use of resources.
        ii. Clear career paths for employees within their functional areas.
        iii. Specialized expertise.
    c. Cons:
        i. Slow decision-making.
        ii. Lack of project focus.
        iii. Difficulty in prioritizing projects across functions.
3. Matrix Organization:
    a. Description: Matrix organizations blend aspects of both functional and projectized structures. Employees have dual reporting lines: to a project manager and a functional manager.
    b. Pros:

i. Efficient resource utilization.
ii. Clear project focus while maintaining functional expertise.
iii. Flexibility in resource allocation.

c. Cons:
i. Potential for power struggles between project and functional managers.
ii. Complex communication channels.
iii. Role ambiguity for team members.

4. Balanced Organization (Composite or Hybrid):
   a. Description: Balanced organizations seek to balance the advantages of pure project and functional structures. They maintain some permanent functional departments while also forming temporary project teams as needed.
   b. Pros:
      i. Combines the strengths of both projectized and functional structures.
      ii. Offers flexibility in resource allocation.
      iii. Provides continuity between projects.
   c. Cons:
      i. Requires careful coordination between functional and project managers.
      ii. Potential for conflicts over resource allocation.
      iii. May lead to role ambiguity for employees.

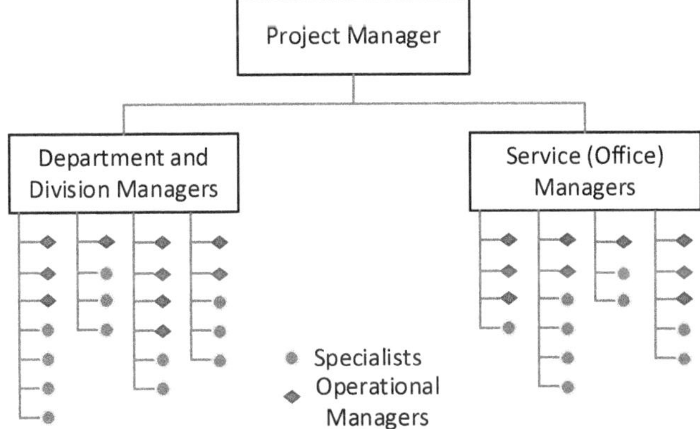

Figure 11.7.1 Project Organization

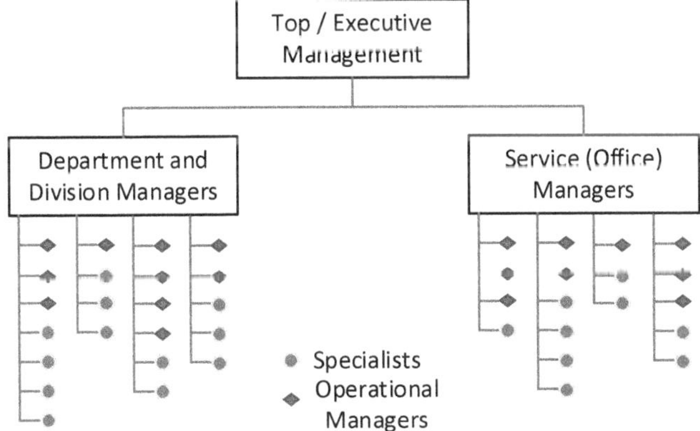

Figure 11.7.2 Functional Organization

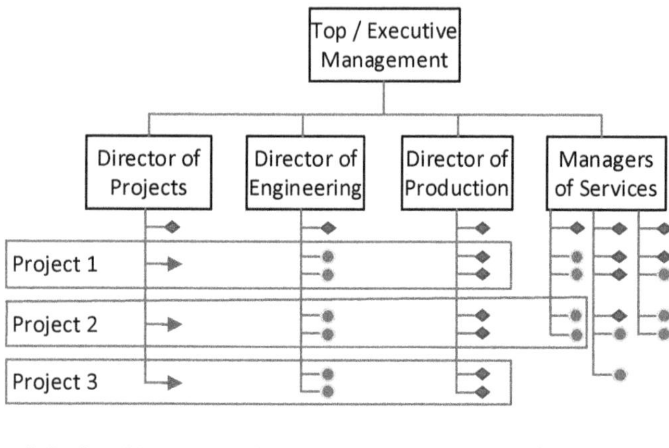

Figure 11.7.3 Matrix Organization

Choosing the right project organization depends on the specific needs and characteristics of the project, as well as the organizational culture and context. It is essential to weigh the pros and cons of each type against the project's requirements to make an informed decision.

11.8. What is a balanced matrix organization? What are the pros and cons of matrix organization comparing other types of organizations?

A balanced matrix organization is a type of organizational structure where there is an equal emphasis on both functional and project management. In a balanced matrix organization, employees have dual reporting relationships: they report to both a functional manager and a project manager. This setup aims to leverage the strengths of both functional and project-based organizational structures.

Key Characteristics of a Balanced Matrix Organization:

1. Dual Authority: Employees report to both a functional manager and a project manager.
2. Shared Resources: Resources (e.g., employees, equipment) are shared across functional and project teams.
3. Collaboration: Functional and project managers need to collaborate and coordinate to achieve organizational goals.
4. Flexibility: It allows the organization to be flexible and dynamic in responding to market changes and project demands.

Pros of a Balanced Matrix Organization:

1. Efficient Resource Utilization: Resources are utilized more effectively as they can be shared across projects.
2. Enhanced Communication: Promotes better communication across different functions and project teams.
3. Flexibility and Adaptability: Can quickly adapt to changes and reallocate resources as needed for different projects.
4. Skill Development: Employees can develop a broader set of skills by working on various projects and with different teams.
5. Focus on Multiple Objectives: Allows the organization to focus on both functional excellence and project delivery simultaneously.

Cons of a Balanced Matrix Organization:

1. Complex Reporting Relationships: Dual reporting can lead to confusion and conflict between

managers.
2. Power Struggles: Potential for power struggles between functional and project managers.
3. Increased Overhead: Managing a matrix organization can require more coordination and administrative effort.
4. Ambiguity in Roles and Responsibilities: Employees may face ambiguity regarding their roles and responsibilities, leading to potential conflicts.
5. Slow Decision-Making: Decision-making can be slower due to the need to get buy-in from multiple managers.

Comparison with Other Types of Organizational Structures:

1. Functional Organization:
    a. Pros: Clear hierarchy, defined roles, and responsibilities; efficient for routine and repetitive tasks; economies of scale within functions.
    b. Cons: Silos can develop, hindering communication and collaboration; less flexibility in responding to market changes; limited career development opportunities across functions.
2. Projectized Organization:
    a. Pros: High focus on project goals; project managers have full authority over resources; clear project accountability; more flexibility and agility.
    b. Cons: Duplication of resources; potential for resource underutilization between projects; less emphasis on functional expertise and development.
3. Matrix Organization:
    a. Pros: Balances the benefits of both functional and projectized structures; promotes resource sharing and cross-functional collaboration; supports multiple and dynamic objectives.
    b. Cons: Complexity in management and reporting; potential for conflicts and power struggles; requires robust processes and strong leadership to be effective.

In summary, a balanced matrix organization aims to take advantage of both functional specialization and project-based flexibility. While it offers several benefits such as improved resource utilization and enhanced communication, it also poses challenges like complex reporting relationships and potential for conflicts. The choice of organizational structure should align with the organization's strategic goals, culture, and operational needs.

11.9. Why would we want to use an unbalanced matrix organization?

An unbalanced matrix organization is a type of matrix organizational structure where the balance of power and influence between project managers and functional managers is deliberately skewed in favor of one over the other. Here are several reasons why an organization might opt for an unbalanced matrix structure:

1. Strategic Priorities: If an organization has strategic priorities that align more closely with either functional excellence or project success, an unbalanced matrix can help ensure that the dominant force in the organization aligns with these priorities. For example, if rapid product development is crucial, project managers might be given more power.
2. Resource Allocation: In cases where resources are scarce or need to be prioritized carefully, an unbalanced matrix can help streamline decision-making and resource allocation. By giving more authority to either functional or project managers, organizations can more effectively direct resources where they are most needed.
3. Flexibility and Agility: An unbalanced matrix can provide greater flexibility and agility by allowing one group to make faster decisions without the need for extensive negotiation or consensus-building. This can be particularly important in dynamic or highly competitive environments.

4. Clearer Accountability: When one side of the matrix has more power, accountability can be clearer. For example, if project managers have more authority, they can be held more directly responsible for project outcomes. Conversely, if functional managers are more powerful, they can be held accountable for maintaining and developing their respective areas of expertise.
5. Specialized Focus: In some industries, it is crucial to maintain a high level of specialized knowledge and expertise within functional areas. An unbalanced matrix can ensure that functional managers have the authority to maintain and develop this expertise without being overly constrained by project demands.
6. Organizational Culture: The culture of an organization might naturally lend itself to one type of authority over the other. For example, a company with a strong history of innovation might favor project managers to drive new initiatives, while a company focused on operational excellence might favor functional managers.
7. Leadership Style: The leadership style and philosophy of top management can influence the choice of an unbalanced matrix. Leaders who value strong project leadership might design an organization to empower project managers more, whereas those who prioritize functional excellence might empower functional managers.
8. Risk Management: In certain industries or situations, it might be necessary to have one side of the matrix take the lead to manage risks more effectively. For instance, in highly regulated industries, functional managers might need more authority to ensure compliance with laws and regulations.

By deliberately skewing the balance of power, an unbalanced matrix organization can be tailored to meet the specific strategic, operational, and cultural needs of the organization. However, it is important for organizations to carefully consider the potential downsides, such as possible conflicts, reduced collaboration, and the risk of demotivation on the less powerful side of the matrix.

11.10. What does move toward matrix management require?

Moving toward matrix management requires several key changes and considerations to ensure successful implementation and operation. Here are the primary requirements:

1. Cultural Change: An organization must embrace a culture that values collaboration, flexibility, and shared responsibility. Employees and managers need to be open to working across traditional functional boundaries.
2. Clear Roles and Responsibilities: There must be a clear definition of roles and responsibilities to avoid confusion and conflicts. This includes clarifying the decision-making authority and accountability of both functional and project managers.
3. Strong Leadership Support: Senior leadership must actively support the matrix structure, demonstrating commitment through resources, policies, and practices that reinforce matrix principles.
4. Effective Communication: Robust communication channels are necessary to facilitate coordination and information sharing among team members who may report to different managers or be located in different parts of the organization.
5. Training and Development: Employees and managers need training to develop the skills required for working in a matrix environment, such as negotiation, conflict resolution, and collaborative problem-solving.
6. Balanced Power Dynamics: There should be a balance of power between project managers and functional managers to ensure that neither side dominates decision-making processes.
7. Performance Management Systems: Implementing performance management systems that recognize and reward contributions from both project and functional perspectives is crucial. This helps to align individual and team goals with the overall objectives of the organization.
8. Resource Allocation Processes: Efficient processes for allocating resources across multiple projects and functional areas are needed to ensure that priorities are managed effectively and

resources are utilized optimally.

9. Conflict Resolution Mechanisms: Mechanisms must be in place to address and resolve conflicts that arise from competing priorities and interests within the matrix structure.
10. Technology and Tools: Investing in technology and tools that support project management, communication, and collaboration can enhance the effectiveness of a matrix management system.

By addressing these requirements, organizations can create an environment where matrix management can thrive, leading to improved flexibility, resource utilization, and project outcomes.

11.11. How do organizations affect the projects and how does project management influence organizations?

Organizations and projects are deeply interconnected, influencing each other in several ways. Understanding this bidirectional relationship is crucial for successful project management and organizational growth. Here is a detailed look at how organizations affect projects and how project management influences organizations:

How Organizations Affect Projects

1. Culture and Values: The organizational culture and values shape the way projects are conceived, executed, and managed. A culture that values innovation will encourage creative project solutions, while a risk-averse culture may focus on maintaining the status quo.
2. Structure and Hierarchy: The organizational structure, whether it is functional, matrix, or projectized, dictates the flow of information, decision-making processes, and resource allocation. In a functional structure, project managers may have less authority, whereas in a projectized structure, they have more control.
3. Resource Availability: Organizations determine the availability of resources such as personnel, budget, and technology. Limited resources can constrain project scope, timelines, and quality.
4. Policies and Procedures: Established policies and procedures provide a framework within which projects must operate. These can include project management methodologies, compliance requirements, and standard operating procedures.
5. Strategic Alignment: Organizations set strategic goals and priorities that influence project selection and prioritization. Projects that align with the organization's strategic objectives are more likely to receive support and funding.
6. Stakeholder Expectations: The expectations and influence of internal and external stakeholders, including executives, employees, customers, and regulatory bodies, shape project goals and deliverables.
7. Change Management: Organizational readiness and ability to handle change can impact project implementation and success. A well-prepared organization will facilitate smoother transitions and adoption of project outcomes.

How Project Management Influences Organizations

1. Achievement of Strategic Goals: Effective project management ensures that projects align with and contribute to the organization's strategic objectives, facilitating growth and competitive advantage.
2. Improved Efficiency and Effectiveness: Project management practices improve resource utilization, streamline processes, and enhance productivity, leading to cost savings and better performance.
3. Innovation and Improvement: Projects often drive innovation and process improvements, introducing new products, services, and technologies that can transform the organization.
4. Risk Management: Project management introduces structured risk management processes, helping organizations identify, assess, and mitigate risks associated with various initiatives.

5. Stakeholder Satisfaction: By effectively managing stakeholder expectations and delivering projects on time, within scope, and on budget, project management enhances stakeholder satisfaction and trust.
6. Capability Development: Project management fosters the development of skills and competencies within the organization. Project teams gain valuable experience and knowledge that can be leveraged in future projects.
7. Change Facilitation: Through structured change management processes, project management helps organizations adapt to change, ensuring that new systems, processes, and structures are effectively integrated.
8. Performance Measurement: Project management provides tools and techniques for monitoring and evaluating project performance, offering insights that can be used for continuous improvement and informed decision-making.
9. Cultural Impact: Successful project management can influence organizational culture by embedding a culture of accountability, excellence, and continuous improvement.
10. Enhanced Communication and Collaboration: Project management fosters better communication and collaboration across different departments and teams, breaking down silos and encouraging a more integrated approach to achieving organizational goals.

The interplay between organizations and project management is dynamic and symbiotic. Organizations provide the environment, resources, and strategic direction that shape project execution. Conversely, effective project management drives organizational success by ensuring that projects deliver value and align with overarching business goals. Recognizing and optimizing this relationship is key to achieving both project and organizational excellence.

11.12. On a multinational project, which factor is most critical to efficient work?

On a multinational project, the most critical factor to efficient work is effective communication. Here are several reasons why:

1. Language Barriers: Different team members may speak different languages, and ensuring clear, concise, and accurate communication is crucial to avoid misunderstandings and errors.
2. Cultural Differences: Team members from different cultures may have varying communication styles, work ethics, and approaches to problem-solving. Recognizing and respecting these differences can enhance collaboration and reduce friction.
3. Time Zones: Multinational teams often work across multiple time zones, which can complicate scheduling and coordination. Effective communication tools and practices can help manage these challenges.
4. Technology and Tools: Using the right communication technologies (e.g., video conferencing, collaborative software) ensures that all team members can participate fully and stay informed, regardless of their location.
5. Clear Documentation: Maintaining clear, detailed, and accessible documentation of project plans, decisions, and updates helps ensure that all team members are aligned and can reference important information as needed.
6. Regular Updates and Meetings: Establishing a routine for regular updates and meetings can help keep the project on track and ensure that any issues are addressed promptly.

By prioritizing effective communication, a multinational project can overcome the challenges associated with diverse teams and geographical dispersion, leading to more efficient and successful outcomes.

11.13. What are the typical delivery execution challenges that haunt the management with a project team setup across geographies?

There are quite a few challenges faced by project team set up across geographies. I have listed out few challenges:

1. The management team and the team members need to be identified at the beginning of the project.
2. Set up of the necessary software, hardware, and networking infrastructure to avoid delay in starting the development work.
3. Assess the quality of the resources and augment where there is a competency gap.
4. Regular interaction with the wide spread team to bring the team on the same page.
5. Ensure explicit delegation and validate assumptions.
6. Understanding the project deliverables explicitly by the team members.
7. Reducing the communication loop to ensure timely deliverables.
8. Facilitate tool driven query resolution, that is, effective tracking of task and development.
9. Manage effort variance constructively - for development work.
10. Not complimenting the team when good work is done.
11. Whether to allow the offshore team to communicate directly with the end-client or stake holders.
12. The offshore teams need to understand the work culture and also, they need to understand what the implications of missing a deadline are.
13. Due to distance, time, and cultural issues, it is imperative that the offshore and onshore team leads get very well acquainted. Ideal instance is a 30-day visit if it is possible. I have had 100 percent success when I have been able to get face time for the offshore team leads and the onshore project teams on a regular basis and for go live.
14. During testing, have the testing team comprise some of the sustaining team whether client or outsourced. This again increases communication and reduces cut over time.
15. Different time zone. I know that everyone should have come across this challenge. Most of team has to stay till another country get to its day. Extended hours to get issue resolved and question answered. This will lead to burn out and need lots of motivation from leads and management to keep the ball rolling.

12. Program Management

Let us acknowledge a reality: hardly anyone deals with just one project. Having multiple projects is the standard rather than the exception, and there are solid reasons for this. Many projects do not warrant a full-time project manager because they are not sizable enough. Relying on just one manager would be impractical. In a multi-project environment, significant work can be accomplished efficiently by streamlining processes and reducing the overhead of project management. Here, you will discover how to identify and effectively manage the unique traits of each situation, how to plan and structure your workload, how to influence individuals who are not under your direct supervision, and ultimately, how to achieve results.

In every industry, the perpetual challenge persists: consistently delivering successful projects. With the increasing number of projects, the demand for adept Project and Program Management escalates. There is mounting pressure to ensure projects align with overarching strategic business objectives, necessitating leadership to steer toward those objectives and secure desired outcomes.

Although program managers and project managers have distinct roles, they share overlapping skill sets. This fosters a synergistic relationship between the two, creating complementary management types who collaborate effectively. It also means that a project manager can aspire to advance to a program manager role.

Program management naturally extends from project management. Projects aim to deliver a unique product or service, whereas a program coordinates a set of related projects to attain benefits beyond what individual projects could achieve. Consequently, skills like leadership, management, mentoring, communication, negotiation, and planning are transferrable.

Communication stands out as a particularly critical skill. At the project level, a manager must grasp how various factors align for or against the project and manage these interfaces accordingly. At the program level, this becomes even more crucial as organizational outcomes carry higher stakes.

Both project and program management share common assets like leadership, negotiation, planning, support provision, change and issue management, risk assessment, and strategic assistance. A proficient project manager, well-versed in navigating organizational dynamics, recognizes the project's place within the broader organizational portfolio. Both roles contribute to organizational development and enhancement, emphasizing resource integration and optimal utilization at various levels.

Program managers must fulfill stakeholder expectations and align with company objectives, necessitating a comprehensive perspective and seamless communication with project managers. Overlooking how projects integrate and contribute to program goals would be detrimental to the organization's interests. Program managers grasp that realizing ROI might span years, underscoring the importance of seeing the big picture.

The collaboration between project management and program management is essential for project completion success. Understanding and attaining both short-term and long-term goals are pivotal for the project's overall impact.

12.1. What is a project team?

A project team is a group of individuals brought together to accomplish a specific project or set of tasks within a defined time frame. The team is typically composed of members with diverse skills and expertise relevant to the project's goals. The primary characteristics and functions of a project team include:

1. Diverse Skill Set: Team members often have different professional backgrounds and expertise, ensuring that all aspects of the project are covered.
2. Clear Objectives: The team works towards specific goals and objectives outlined in the project plan.
3. Defined Roles and Responsibilities: Each team member has a specific role and set of responsibilities to contribute effectively to the project's success.
4. Collaborative Effort: Members work collaboratively, leveraging each other's strengths and compensating for any weaknesses.
5. Temporary Nature: A project team is usually formed for the duration of the project and disbanded upon its completion.
6. Leadership and Coordination: Often led by a project manager or team leader who coordinates

activities, manages resources, and ensures that the project stays on track.

7. Communication: Effective communication is essential for the smooth functioning of the team, involving regular meetings, updates, and feedback loops.
8. Resource Management: Efficient utilization and management of resources, including time, budget, and materials, are crucial for project success.
9. Problem-Solving: The team collaboratively addresses and resolves issues and challenges that arise during the project.

The effectiveness of a project team significantly impacts the success of the project, making team dynamics, leadership, and communication critical factors.

12.2. What is common in a project team?

The success of any project is not attributable to one extraordinary individual. It emerges from the collaborative endeavors of a diverse group of individuals transcending departmental limits. This collective, known as the project team, encompasses individuals with diverse skills, talents, work methodologies, and expertise. For the project team to succeed, it is imperative to share a unified goal, vision, and comprehensive understanding of expectations. Regardless of hierarchical distinctions, these individuals must function seamlessly as a motivated team to realize the business objectives.

In a project team, several common elements typically exist:

1. Shared Goal/Objective: All team members are working towards a common goal or objective. This goal provides direction and purpose to the team's efforts.
2. Roles and Responsibilities: Each team member has specific roles and responsibilities within the project. These roles are usually diverse and complementary, ensuring that all necessary tasks are covered.
3. Communication: Effective communication is vital for project success. Team members need to communicate regularly to share updates, discuss progress, address challenges, and coordinate tasks.
4. Collaboration: Project teams often require collaboration among members. This involves sharing ideas, offering feedback, and working together to solve problems or complete tasks.
5. Diversity: Project teams typically consist of individuals with diverse backgrounds, skills, and expertise. This diversity can lead to creative problem-solving and innovative solutions.
6. Accountability: Each team member is accountable for their contributions to the project. This accountability ensures that everyone pulls their weight and delivers on their commitments.
7. Leadership: While there may be a designated project manager or leader, leadership qualities are often distributed among team members. Leadership can emerge in various forms, such as taking initiative, providing guidance, or motivating others.
8. Adaptability: Projects are often dynamic, with changing requirements, deadlines, and circumstances. Team members need to be adaptable and flexible in response to these changes.
9. Trust: Trust is essential for effective teamwork. Team members must trust each other's abilities, judgment, and commitment to the project.
10. Problem-solving: Projects inevitably encounter challenges or obstacles. Team members need to be adept at problem-solving, whether individually or collaboratively, to overcome these challenges and keep the project on track.

12.3. What is a program?

A program consists of a group of related projects managed together to achieve benefits and control that cannot be obtained by managing them separately. Programs may also include elements of related work that are beyond the scope of the individual projects within the program. These programs are composed of various components, primarily the individual projects, but also the management efforts and infrastructure required to oversee the entire program. Therefore, programs may include aspects such as the management of the program itself, which are outside the scope of the individual projects.

Both programs and projects provide benefits to organizations by enhancing current capabilities or developing new ones. A benefit is an outcome that offers utility to the organization as a result of specific actions and behaviors.

Programs, like projects, help organizations achieve their goals and objectives, often aligning with strategic plans. Some projects within a program can deliver incremental benefits to the organization even before the entire program is completed. For example, an organization-wide process improvement program might consist of multiple projects that each contribute useful benefits along the way.

However, in many programs, all benefits are delivered at the end, with everything coming together simultaneously. This is common in industries such as construction, aerospace, military development, public works, shipbuilding, and similar sectors.

12.4. What is program management?

Program management is the process of managing multiple related projects in a coordinated way to achieve strategic business objectives. It involves overseeing a group of projects that are aligned with the same strategic goals, ensuring they are managed and executed in a way that maximizes their collective benefits and minimizes risks. Here are key aspects of program management:

1. Strategic Alignment: Ensuring that the program's goals are aligned with the overall strategic objectives of the organization. Programs typically address broad, long-term goals and deliver value beyond the sum of individual project outcomes.
2. Governance: Establishing frameworks, policies, and procedures for decision-making, accountability, and management. This includes defining roles and responsibilities, setting up reporting structures, and ensuring compliance with standards.
3. Integration: Coordinating and integrating multiple projects within the program to ensure they work together effectively. This involves managing interdependencies, synchronizing project schedules, and ensuring that the outputs of one project feed seamlessly into others.
4. Benefits Management: Identifying, planning, tracking, and realizing the benefits of the program. This involves defining what constitutes success, measuring performance, and ensuring that the program delivers value to the organization.
5. Stakeholder Management: Engaging with and managing relationships with stakeholders, including sponsors, customers, and team members. Effective communication and managing stakeholder expectations are crucial for program success.
6. Resource Management: Allocating and managing resources across the projects in the program to ensure optimal utilization. This includes managing budgets, human resources, and physical assets.
7. Risk Management: Identifying and managing risks that affect the program as a whole. This includes developing risk mitigation strategies and ensuring that risks are managed proactively across all projects within the program.
8. Performance Monitoring and Control: Continuously monitoring the progress of the program, assessing performance against plans, and implementing corrective actions as needed. This involves tracking key performance indicators (KPIs), reporting progress, and making adjustments to keep the program on track.
9. Change Management: Managing changes within the program to ensure that they are implemented smoothly and effectively. This includes assessing the impact of changes, communicating changes to stakeholders, and updating plans and strategies accordingly.
10. Program Closure: Closing the program in a structured way once the objectives have been

achieved. This involves finalizing all activities, ensuring that all deliverables have been completed, and capturing lessons learned for future programs.

Program management is critical for organizations that undertake complex, interrelated projects as it ensures that these projects are managed in a way that maximizes their collective value and supports the achievement of strategic goals.

12.5. What is project management vs. program management vs. portfolio management?

Project management, program management, and portfolio management are three distinct but interrelated disciplines within the broader field of management. Each has its own focus, objectives, and methodologies. Here is a detailed comparison:

Project Management

1. Focus:
   a. The primary focus of project management is on the successful completion of specific projects. A project is a temporary endeavor with a defined beginning and end, undertaken to create a unique product, service, or result.
2. Objectives:
   a. Deliver the project on time and within budget.
   b. Achieve the project's specific goals and objectives.
   c. Ensure the quality of the deliverables.
3. Key Activities:
   a. Defining project scope.
   b. Developing detailed project plans.
   c. Managing project resources (time, budget, personnel).
   d. Risk management.
   e. Stakeholder communication.
   f. Monitoring and controlling project progress.
4. Tools and Methodologies:
   a. Gantt charts, Work Breakdown Structures (WBS).
   b. Project management software (e.g., Microsoft Project, Asana, Trello).
   c. Agile, Waterfall, PRINCE2, PMBOK (Project Management Body of Knowledge).

Program Management

1. Focus:
   a. Program management involves managing a group of related projects in a coordinated way to obtain benefits and control not available from managing them individually. Programs are often ongoing and can encompass multiple projects that are aligned with broader strategic goals.
2. Objectives:
   a. Achieve strategic business objectives and benefits that would not be realized if the projects were managed independently.
   b. Manage interdependencies and resource conflicts between projects.
   c. Optimize resource allocation across the projects within the program.
3. Key Activities:
   a. Defining the program's scope and objectives.
   b. Coordinating and monitoring project activities within the program.
   c. Managing interdependencies between projects.
   d. Stakeholder communication and management.

    e. Benefits realization management.
    f. Risk management across the program.
4. Tools and Methodologies:
    a. Program roadmaps.
    b. Program management software (e.g., Planview, Microsoft Project Server).
    c. MSP (Managing Successful Programs).

Portfolio Management

1. Focus:
    a. Portfolio management is the centralized management of one or more portfolios, which includes identifying, prioritizing, authorizing, managing, and controlling projects, programs, and other related work to achieve specific strategic business objectives.
2. Objectives:
    a. Align projects and programs with the organization's strategic goals.
    b. Optimize resource allocation and investment across the entire portfolio.
    c. Balance the portfolio in terms of risk, reward, and strategic alignment.
    d. Maximize the value of the portfolio by selecting the right mix of projects and programs.
3. Key Activities:
    a. Strategic planning and alignment.
    b. Portfolio analysis and selection.
    c. Resource allocation and optimization.
    d. Performance measurement and management.
    e. Risk management at the portfolio level.
    f. Stakeholder engagement and communication.
4. Tools and Methodologies:
    a. Portfolio management frameworks (e.g., MoP - Management of Portfolios).
    b. Portfolio management software (e.g., Primavera P6, JIRA Portfolio, Microsoft Project Online).
    c. Decision support tools and techniques (e.g., SWOT analysis, financial metrics).

Summary of Differences

1. Scope: Project management focuses on individual projects, program management focuses on managing related projects, and portfolio management focuses on the strategic alignment and overall value of all projects and programs.
2. Objectives: Project management aims at successful project delivery, program management aims at achieving benefits through coordinated project management, and portfolio management aims at strategic alignment and value maximization.
3. Activities: Project management involves detailed planning and execution of projects, program management involves coordination and oversight of related projects, and portfolio management involves strategic decision-making and resource optimization.

Understanding these distinctions helps organizations effectively allocate resources, manage risks, and achieve strategic objectives.

12.6. How do you matrix manage?

The issue is effectively managing multiple projects and activities simultaneously. How?

1. Start with a plan for each project and itemize needed activities.
2. Manage both end results and leading indicators before the end reached. This prevents a surprise from happening on the back end.
3. Identify projected outcomes before they happen and make adjustments to the plan when

necessary.

4. Stay organized: Stay closely tied to your calendar and do not procrastinate. Never let your email inbox build up. Read and file emails but get through them and schedule time when necessary.
5. Rank each task as A, B, or C. Make sure to get highest-priority tasks completed first.

12.7. How do you manage multiple projects?

Managing multiple projects requires effective organization, prioritization, and communication. Here are some strategies to help manage multiple projects efficiently:

1. Prioritize Tasks and Projects:
    a. Identify Critical Projects: Determine which projects are most critical to your organization's goals.
    b. Rank Tasks by Importance and Urgency: Use methods like the Eisenhower Matrix to categorize tasks.
2. Plan and Set Clear Goals:
    a. Break Down Projects: Divide each project into smaller, manageable tasks.
    b. Set SMART Goals: Ensure goals are Specific, Measurable, Achievable, Relevant, and Time-bound.
3. Create a Master Schedule:
    a. Use a Calendar or Gantt Chart: Visualize deadlines, milestones, and dependencies.
    b. Allocate Time Blocks: Dedicate specific time slots for each project to ensure balanced progress.
4. Utilize Project Management Tools:
    a. Task Management Software: Tools like Trello, Asana, or Jira can help track progress, assign tasks, and set deadlines.
    b. Collaborative Tools: Use tools like Slack or Microsoft Teams for communication and document sharing.
5. Delegate and Collaborate:
    a. Assign Tasks to Team Members: Delegate tasks based on team members' strengths and availability.
    b. Encourage Team Collaboration: Foster a collaborative environment where team members can support each other.
6. Regularly Review Progress:
    a. Hold Regular Meetings: Schedule check-ins or stand-up meetings to review progress and address issues.
    b. Adjust Plans as Needed: Be flexible and adjust timelines or priorities based on project progress and any new developments.
7. Effective Communication:
    a. Keep Stakeholders Informed: Regularly update stakeholders on project status and any changes.
    b. Clear and Concise Communication: Ensure all communications are clear to avoid misunderstandings.
8. Manage Resources Efficiently:
    a. Resource Allocation: Ensure that resources (time, budget, personnel) are allocated effectively across projects.
    b. Monitor Workload: Avoid overloading team members by monitoring their workload and redistributing tasks as needed.
9. Risk Management:
    a. Identify Risks: Anticipate potential risks for each project.
    b. Develop Contingency Plans: Have plans in place to address risks should they arise.
10. Time Management:

a. Use Time Management Techniques: Techniques such as Pomodoro (working in short, focused bursts) can improve productivity.
b. Avoid Multitasking: Focus on completing one task at a time to maintain quality and efficiency.

11. Stay Organized:
    a. Document Everything: Keep detailed records of project plans, timelines, and progress.
    b. Maintain a Clean Workspace: A tidy workspace can help improve focus and efficiency.

By incorporating these strategies, you can manage multiple projects more effectively, ensuring that each project receives the attention it needs and progresses towards successful completion.

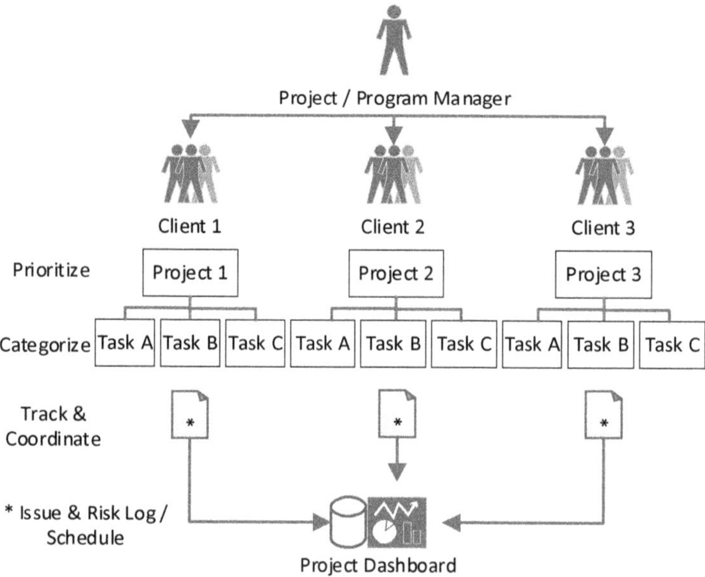

Figure 12.7.1 Process for managing multiple projects

12.8. How would you handle multiple priorities that are all equally urgent?

When faced with multiple priorities that are all equally urgent, it can be challenging to determine the best course of action. Here is a suggested approach to handle such a situation:

1. Assess the scope and impact: Start by evaluating each priority's scope and potential impact on your goals, projects, or responsibilities. Consider the short-term and long-term implications of addressing or neglecting each priority.
2. Seek clarification: If the priorities are coming from different sources or stakeholders, reach out to them for further clarification. Understand the expectations, deadlines, and consequences associated with each priority. This information can help you make better informed decisions.
3. Evaluate available resources: Take stock of the resources at your disposal, including time, manpower, and other necessary tools. Assess how these resources align with the requirements of each priority. Identifying potential gaps in resources will inform your decision-making process.
4. Prioritize based on dependencies: Analyze any dependencies or interrelationships among the priorities. Determine if completing one task is a prerequisite for another. If there are dependencies, consider tackling priorities that enable or unblock the progress of other tasks.
5. Timeboxing: Allocate specific time blocks or windows for each priority based on their urgency and importance. Define clear start and end times for each task. This timeboxing approach ensures that all priorities receive attention while preventing excessive time spent on any single task.

6. Communicate and negotiate: If you are working with a team or collaborating with others, communicate the situation and seek their input. Transparently discuss the urgency and equal importance of the priorities. Collaborative decision-making can help distribute the workload or provide alternative perspectives.
7. Monitor and adapt: Regularly review your progress and adjust your plan accordingly. Assess whether the allocated time for each priority is realistic and adjust as needed. Stay flexible and adapt to changing circumstances or new information that may affect your priorities.
8. Practice self-care: Balancing multiple urgent priorities can be mentally and physically demanding. Take breaks, prioritize self-care, and avoid burnout. Maintain a healthy work-life balance to sustain your productivity and well-being.

Remember, in situations where everything is equally urgent, it may not be possible to tackle all priorities simultaneously. Making conscious decisions, effectively managing expectations, and communicating transparently can help you navigate such circumstances more efficiently.

12.9. How do you manage competing change requests from stakeholders?

Managing competing change requests from stakeholders can be a challenging task, but with proper planning and communication, it can be effectively handled. Here are some steps you can follow to manage competing change requests:

1. Prioritize and evaluate: Start by prioritizing the change requests based on their impact, urgency, and alignment with project goals. Evaluate each request against criteria such as business value, risk, feasibility, and resource availability.
2. Communicate with stakeholders: Engage in open and transparent communication with stakeholders. Inform them about the change request evaluation process and the criteria used to prioritize requests. Set realistic expectations regarding the acceptance and implementation of changes.
3. Facilitate collaboration: Encourage collaboration and dialogue among stakeholders to identify common goals and areas of compromise. Facilitate meetings or workshops where stakeholders can discuss their requests and work towards a mutually agreeable solution.
4. Assess impacts and dependencies: Analyze the impacts of each change request on the project timeline, budget, resources, and other ongoing activities. Identify any dependencies between requests and consider how they may affect one another.
5. Negotiate and find compromises: Work closely with stakeholders to negotiate and find compromises where conflicting change requests can be addressed. Look for alternative solutions or phased implementations that can accommodate multiple requests without jeopardizing the project's success.
6. Align with project objectives: Consider the overarching project objectives and align the change requests with them. Evaluate how each request contributes to the project's success and whether it aligns with the overall vision and strategy.
7. Seek guidance from project sponsors or governance boards: In cases where the competing change requests cannot be resolved at the project level, seek guidance from project sponsors or governance boards. They can provide guidance and make decisions based on the project's priorities and strategic alignment.
8. Document decisions and communicate outcomes: Once decisions are made regarding the change requests, document them clearly and communicate the outcomes to all stakeholders. Ensure everyone understands why certain requests were accepted, rejected, or modified.
9. Monitor and manage changes: Continuously monitor and manage approved changes throughout their implementation. Regularly review the impact of changes on the project and make adjustments as necessary.
10. Learn from the process: After managing competing change requests, reflect on the experience and

identify lessons learned. Use this knowledge to improve change management processes for future projects.

Remember that effective change management involves balancing the needs and expectations of stakeholders while keeping the project's goals and constraints in mind. Open communication, collaboration, and a structured decision-making process are key to successfully managing competing change requests.

12.10. What does managing complex programs involve?

Project management is like juggling three balls: time, cost, and scope. In contrast, managing complex programs is similar to a group of circus performers standing in a circle, each juggling three balls and occasionally exchanging them with one another.

Handling complex programs requires a distinct set of skills, including expertise in integration, scope, time, cost, quality, human resources, communication, risk, and procurement management. The difficulties faced by traditional project managers are magnified in complex programs due to the multitude of variables that are difficult to identify. Without identifying these variables, how can we schedule and control them? How can we estimate their costs? How can we effectively allocate resources across the many components of the program? Program managers must develop and utilize a robust management infrastructure that addresses all these aspects in relation to each other.

Managing complex programs involves a multifaceted approach that integrates various disciplines and techniques to ensure the successful delivery of the program's objectives. Here are the key components involved in managing complex programs:

1. Program Governance:
    a. Establishing clear governance structures and decision-making processes.
    b. Defining roles and responsibilities, and ensuring accountability.
    c. Setting up a program management office (PMO) to oversee the program.
2. Strategic Alignment:
    a. Ensuring the program aligns with organizational goals and strategy.
    b. Continuously evaluating the program's relevance and impact on strategic objectives.
3. Stakeholder Management:
    a. Identifying and analyzing stakeholders' needs and expectations.
    b. Engaging and communicating effectively with stakeholders.
    c. Managing stakeholder relationships and addressing concerns proactively.
4. Scope and Requirements Management:
    a. Defining and managing program scope to ensure it meets objectives.
    b. Gathering, documenting, and validating requirements.
    c. Controlling scope changes through a formal change management process.
5. Planning and Scheduling:
    a. Developing comprehensive program plans that integrate all project plans.
    b. Creating detailed schedules and milestones.
    c. Monitoring and adjusting plans as needed to stay on track.
6. Resource Management
    a. Identifying and allocating the necessary resources (people, technology, budget).
    b. Managing resource constraints and optimizing resource utilization.
    c. Ensuring the availability and capability of resources.
7. Risk Management:
    a. Identifying, assessing, and prioritizing risks.
    b. Developing and implementing risk mitigation strategies.

c. Monitoring and controlling risks throughout the program lifecycle.

8. Quality Management:
   a. Establishing quality standards and metrics.
   b. Implementing processes to ensure quality deliverables.
   c. Conducting regular quality reviews and audits.
9. Financial Management:
   a. Budgeting and financial planning for the program.
   b. Tracking costs and managing financial performance.
   c. Ensuring financial compliance and reporting.
10. Communication Management:
    a. Developing a communication plan to keep stakeholders informed.
    b. Ensuring timely and transparent communication.
    c. Utilizing appropriate communication channels and tools.
11. Change Management:
    a. Managing the impact of changes on the program and stakeholders.
    b. Implementing change management processes and tools.
    c. Supporting stakeholders through transitions and transformations.
12. Performance Measurement and Control:
    a. Establishing key performance indicators (KPIs) and metrics.
    b. Monitoring program progress and performance against objectives.
    c. Implementing corrective actions to address performance issues.
13. Integration Management:
    a. Coordinating and integrating various components of the program.
    b. Ensuring alignment and coherence among projects within the program.
    c. Managing interdependencies and interfaces between projects.
14. Continuous Improvement:
    a. Promoting a culture of continuous improvement and learning.
    b. Conducting post-implementation reviews and lessons learned sessions.
    c. Applying insights to improve future program management practices.

Managing complex programs requires a combination of strategic vision, meticulous planning, effective communication, and rigorous execution. It involves balancing multiple priorities, addressing unforeseen challenges, and ensuring that the program delivers its intended benefits to the organization and its stakeholders.

12.11. How often you should review your project portfolio?

Reviewing your project portfolio is essential to ensure alignment with strategic goals, efficient resource allocation, and timely identification of issues or opportunities. Here are some key guidelines for how often you should review your project portfolio:

1. Regular Reviews (Monthly or Quarterly):
   a. Monthly Reviews: For large, dynamic organizations with numerous ongoing projects, monthly reviews are beneficial. They allow for timely updates on project progress, quick identification of issues, and prompt decision-making.
   b. Quarterly Reviews: Suitable for organizations with a more stable project environment. Quarterly reviews provide a balanced approach, ensuring regular check-ins without being overly frequent.
2. Milestone-Based Reviews:
   a. Conduct reviews at critical project milestones. This approach ensures that significant progress points are evaluated, and necessary adjustments are made before moving on to the next phase.

3. Annual Strategic Review:
    a. An annual review should be conducted to align the project portfolio with the organization's strategic objectives for the upcoming year. This review often coincides with the annual planning and budgeting process.
4. Ad-Hoc Reviews:
    a. Situations may arise that necessitate unscheduled reviews, such as major changes in market conditions, organizational restructuring, or significant issues in key projects. Ad-hoc reviews ensure the portfolio remains responsive to unforeseen circumstances.
5. Post-Project Reviews:
    a. After the completion of major projects, conduct a review to evaluate performance, outcomes, and lessons learned. This helps improve future project planning and execution.

Factors Influencing Review Frequency:
1. Project Complexity and Size: Larger, more complex projects might require more frequent reviews to ensure all aspects are managed effectively.
2. Industry Dynamics: Fast-paced industries may necessitate more frequent reviews to stay competitive and responsive to changes.
3. Resource Availability: The availability of key resources and stakeholders can influence the feasibility of more frequent reviews.
4. Organizational Culture: Some organizations may have a culture that supports continuous monitoring and frequent reviews, while others may prefer less frequent but more in-depth reviews.

Best Practices:
1. Establish a Consistent Schedule: Regularly scheduled reviews help maintain discipline and ensure that reviews are not overlooked.
2. Use Standardized Metrics and KPIs: Consistent metrics and key performance indicators (KPIs) facilitate objective assessment across different projects.
3. Engage Stakeholders: Involve key stakeholders in the review process to ensure comprehensive evaluation and buy-in for any necessary adjustments.
4. Document Outcomes: Keep detailed records of review findings, decisions made, and actions taken to provide a clear audit trail and facilitate continuous improvement.

By adhering to these guidelines, organizations can maintain a healthy, strategically aligned project portfolio that supports their overall objectives and adapts to changing conditions effectively.

12.12. What is the role of a project manager?

The role of a project manager (PM) is critical to the success of any project. A project manager is responsible for planning, executing, and closing projects, ensuring they are completed on time, within budget, and to the required quality standards. Here are the key responsibilities and roles of a project manager:
1. Planning
    a. Define Project Scope: Establish clear and achievable project objectives and deliverables.
    b. Create a Project Plan: Develop a detailed project plan outlining tasks, timelines, resources, and milestones.
    c. Budgeting: Estimate costs and develop a budget that aligns with the project scope and objectives.
    d. Resource Planning: Identify and allocate necessary resources, including team members, equipment, and materials.
2. Organizing

    a. Build the Project Team: Assemble a team with the right skills and experience to complete the project tasks.
    b. Assign Tasks: Delegate responsibilities and tasks to team members based on their expertise.
    c. Develop a Schedule: Create a timeline for project activities and milestones.
3. Leading
    a. Provide Leadership: Guide, motivate, and support the project team to achieve project goals.
    b. Facilitate Communication: Ensure effective communication within the team and with stakeholders.
    c. Problem-Solving: Address and resolve any issues or conflicts that arise during the project.
    d. Stakeholder Management: Maintain relationships with stakeholders, keeping them informed and engaged throughout the project lifecycle.
4. Controlling
    a. Monitor Progress: Track the project's progress against the plan, ensuring it stays on track.
    b. Quality Control: Ensure that project deliverables meet the required quality standards.
    c. Risk Management: Identify potential risks, develop mitigation strategies, and respond to issues as they arise.
    d. Change Management: Manage changes to the project scope, schedule, and costs effectively.
5. Closing
    a. Project Completion: Ensure all project activities are completed and the project objectives are met.
    b. Documentation: Compile project documentation, including reports and final deliverables.
    c. Evaluation: Assess the project's success, gather lessons learned, and document best practices for future projects.
    d. Stakeholder Satisfaction: Ensure stakeholders are satisfied with the project outcomes.

Additional Roles

1. Strategic Alignment: Ensure the project aligns with the organization's strategic goals and objectives.
2. Financial Management: Oversee financial aspects, ensuring efficient use of resources and adherence to the budget.
3. Continuous Improvement: Foster a culture of continuous improvement by integrating feedback and refining processes.

A successful project manager combines technical skills, leadership, and communication abilities to navigate the complexities of project management, balancing the needs of the team, stakeholders, and organizational objectives.

12.13. What is the responsibility of a technical project manager?

Technical project manager (TPM) is someone responsible for seeing that people accomplish a business objective by means of a technical task. This task could be application- or support-related. Both kinds of tasks have a customer or user who must be satisfied and whose expectations must be managed.

The responsibility of a technical project manager is multifaceted, as they play a crucial role in overseeing the successful execution of technical projects within an organization. Here are some key responsibilities:

1. Project Planning: They are responsible for creating project plans, defining project scope, objectives, timelines, and deliverables. This involves breaking down tasks, estimating resource

requirements, and setting milestones.
2. Resource Management: Technical project managers allocate resources effectively, including human resources, budget, and equipment, to ensure the project progresses according to plan.
3. Team Leadership: They lead project teams, providing direction, motivation, and support to team members. This involves fostering a collaborative and productive team environment.
4. Risk Management: Identifying potential risks and developing mitigation strategies to address them is a critical responsibility. They anticipate challenges that may arise during the project lifecycle and take proactive measures to minimize their impact.
5. Stakeholder Communication: Technical project managers facilitate communication between project stakeholders, including clients, team members, and senior management. They ensure stakeholders are kept informed of project progress, changes, and any issues that may arise.
6. Quality Assurance: Ensuring the quality of deliverables is another important aspect of their role. They define quality standards, establish testing processes, and monitor the quality of work throughout the project.
7. Budget Management: They are typically responsible for managing project budgets, tracking expenses, and ensuring that the project remains within budget constraints.
8. Adaptability: Technical project managers must be adaptable and able to pivot quickly in response to changing project requirements, timelines, or resources.
9. Documentation: Maintaining accurate project documentation, including project plans, status reports, and meeting minutes, is essential for tracking progress and ensuring transparency.
10. Continuous Improvement: After project completion, they conduct post-project reviews to evaluate performance, identify lessons learned, and implement improvements for future projects.

Overall, the technical project manager is accountable for the successful planning, execution, and delivery of technical projects, while effectively managing resources, risks, and stakeholder expectations.

12.14. What does upper management look for in a project manager?

Every manager seeks a reliable individual to handle specific business objectives. It is challenging for a manager to relinquish control over tasks they are familiar with to advance up the corporate ladder. Even more difficult is entrusting these responsibilities to someone new. Therefore, it is crucial to demonstrate qualities of trust and dependability. This means not only managing the project effectively but also maintaining open communication with upper management and users. Keeping management informed about both positive and negative developments is essential. However, it is important to exhibit leadership by not presenting every minor detail and problem without offering solution options. If you involve upper management in all decisions, it undermines your role and implies that they are doing your job.

Upper management typically looks for several key qualities and skills in a project manager:
1. Leadership Abilities: Upper management wants a project manager who can effectively lead a team, inspire confidence, and drive projects forward.
2. Communication Skills: Clear and concise communication is crucial for a project manager to convey goals, expectations, and updates to both the team and stakeholders.
3. Strategic Thinking: Upper management seeks project managers who can see the big picture, anticipate challenges, and develop strategic plans to overcome them.
4. Problem-Solving Skills: Project managers should be adept at identifying and resolving issues that arise during a project, ensuring that timelines and deliverables are not compromised.
5. Organizational Skills: Strong organizational skills are essential for managing timelines, resources, and budgets effectively.
6. Adaptability: Projects often face unexpected changes or obstacles, and upper management values project managers who can adapt quickly and find creative solutions.
7. Risk Management: Upper management wants project managers who can assess risks and develop

mitigation strategies to minimize potential negative impacts on the project.

8. Stakeholder Management: Building and maintaining positive relationships with stakeholders is crucial for project success, so upper management looks for project managers who excel in this area.
9. Results-Oriented: Project managers should be focused on achieving results and meeting project objectives within the allocated time and budget.
10. Team Management: The ability to build and motivate a high-performing team is highly valued by upper management. This includes fostering collaboration, resolving conflicts, and providing support and guidance to team members.

Overall, upper management seeks project managers who can effectively plan, execute, and deliver projects while demonstrating strong leadership, communication, and problem-solving skills.

12.15. How important are people management skills for a project manager?

People management skills are critically important for a project manager. These skills encompass a range of abilities that enable a project manager to effectively lead, motivate, and manage a project team to achieve project goals. Here are several reasons why people management skills are essential for a project manager:

1. Team Building and Leadership:
    a. Creating Cohesive Teams: Project managers need to build and maintain strong, cohesive teams. This involves selecting the right team members, understanding their strengths and weaknesses, and fostering a collaborative environment.
    b. Inspiring and Motivating: Effective project managers inspire and motivate their teams, keeping them focused and driven towards the project's objectives. This requires understanding what motivates each team member and leveraging that knowledge to maintain high levels of engagement and productivity.
2. Communication:
    a. Clear Instructions and Feedback: Project managers must communicate clearly and effectively, providing precise instructions and constructive feedback. This ensures that team members understand their roles, responsibilities, and the expectations placed upon them.
    b. Stakeholder Management: Managing relationships with stakeholders is crucial. Project managers need to communicate project progress, challenges, and outcomes to stakeholders, ensuring transparency and alignment.
3. Conflict Resolution:
    a. Mediating Disputes: Conflicts are inevitable in any team setting. Project managers must have the skills to mediate disputes, addressing issues promptly and fairly to maintain team harmony and prevent disruptions to the project.
    b. Problem-Solving: Effective problem-solving skills help project managers address and resolve issues that arise within the team, ensuring that conflicts do not hinder project progress.
4. Delegation and Empowerment:
    a. Effective Delegation: Project managers need to delegate tasks appropriately, ensuring that responsibilities are assigned based on team members' skills and capabilities. Effective delegation helps optimize the team's performance and allows the project manager to focus on higher-level management tasks.
    b. Empowering Team Members: Empowering team members to take ownership of their tasks and make decisions fosters a sense of accountability and boosts morale.
5. Emotional Intelligence:
    a. Understanding Team Dynamics: Emotional intelligence enables project managers to

understand and manage their own emotions, as well as those of their team members. This understanding is crucial for managing stress, maintaining positive team dynamics, and creating a supportive work environment.
   b. Building Trust and Rapport: Establishing trust and rapport with team members is essential for effective teamwork. Project managers with high emotional intelligence are better equipped to build these relationships, leading to increased team cohesion and collaboration.
6. Adaptability and Flexibility:
   a. Adapting to Change: Projects often face changes and unforeseen challenges. Project managers need to be adaptable and flexible, guiding their teams through transitions and ensuring that changes are implemented smoothly.
   b. Maintaining Morale: During periods of change or uncertainty, effective people management helps maintain team morale and ensures continued focus on project objectives.
7. Performance Management:
   a. Setting Expectations and Goals: Clear goal setting and performance expectations are critical for team success. Project managers need to establish and communicate these expectations, monitoring progress and providing support as needed.
   b. Recognition and Reward: Recognizing and rewarding team members' efforts and achievements is vital for maintaining motivation and job satisfaction.

In summary, people management skills are a cornerstone of effective project management. They enable project managers to lead their teams successfully, navigate challenges, and achieve project objectives. Without strong people management skills, even the most well-planned projects can struggle to succeed.

12.16. What characteristic do you value most in project team members?

The most valued characteristic in project team members often depends on the role and project. However, a few universally important traits stand out:

1. Collaboration: The ability to work effectively with others, contributing to team goals while respecting diverse perspectives.
2. Accountability: Taking ownership of their tasks and delivering high-quality work on time.
3. Adaptability: Flexibility to handle changing priorities, unexpected challenges, or shifting project goals.
4. Proactive Communication: Keeping stakeholders informed and addressing concerns or obstacles promptly.
5. Problem-Solving Skills: A willingness to think critically and creatively to overcome challenges.

In project team members, I highly value adaptability. Projects can often take unexpected turns, encounter obstacles, or require changes in direction. Team members who can adapt to shifting priorities, new information, or unforeseen challenges are invaluable. They are able to pivot quickly, maintain productivity, and contribute effectively to finding solutions. Adaptability fosters resilience and innovation, crucial qualities for successful project completion.

12.17. Who are program managers?

Program managers are professionals responsible for overseeing the execution of a set of related projects within an organization. They are tasked with ensuring that these projects align with the organization's goals and objectives, and they work closely with various stakeholders to ensure successful outcomes. Program managers typically have a broad view of the projects they manage, coordinating resources, managing risks, and resolving issues that arise during the course of the program. They play a crucial role in driving the success of complex initiatives by providing strategic direction, managing interdependencies between projects, and facilitating communication among team members. Program managers often have strong leadership, communication, and organizational skills, and they may possess expertise in specific domains relevant to the programs they oversee.

As a program manager, you play a pivotal leadership role in cultivating and enhancing a culture that fosters the success of your project managers.

Program managers (PMs) prioritize customer satisfaction, ensuring that the company's products not only meet but exceed user expectations, empowering them to excel. Additionally, program management offers an opportunity to leverage technical prowess: your strategic technical decisions propel products and features towards fruition.

Collaborating across diverse teams including product marketing and sales, program managers translate customer needs into tangible product features and develop functional specifications. They then drive the implementation process, working closely with key technical stakeholders such as software development, testing, documentation, localization, and technical support.

Typically hailing from a software development background, program managers blend technical expertise with skills in advocacy, empathy, conflict resolution, and an unwavering commitment to project completion.

Program managers fulfill vital functions within the team, including:

1. Spearheading the definition of a compelling product vision
2. Championing the product's vision to stakeholders
3. Guiding the team towards consistent and predictable delivery.

As a Lead/Group Program Manager, you collaborate with various program managers to enhance the company's product management processes and strategies.

12.18. What are the key qualities of a good program manager?

Program managers (PMs) play a vital role in steering product development by crafting detailed product specifications, establishing clear goals, envisioning features, and maintaining technical proficiency with a deep understanding of algorithmic concepts. They excel in communication and project management, serving as the linchpin for software projects. PMs exhibit strong leadership by overseeing project activities, tackling challenges head-on, and ensuring successful project completion while mitigating risks. Their effectiveness lies in their ability to manage customer expectations, devise comprehensive project plans, extract meaningful metrics, troubleshoot issues, and consistently deliver high-quality products.

A good program manager possesses a blend of technical expertise, leadership skills, and strategic vision. Here are some key qualities:

1. Strong Leadership: A program manager should be able to inspire and motivate teams, providing clear direction and guidance while fostering a collaborative and supportive environment.
2. Effective Communication: Clear and concise communication is crucial for ensuring that all stakeholders understand project objectives, milestones, and expectations. This includes both verbal and written communication skills.
3. Strategic Thinking: Program managers need to see the big picture and understand how their projects fit into the broader organizational goals. They should be able to develop strategic plans and make decisions that align with these objectives.
4. Problem-Solving Skills: Projects often encounter obstacles and challenges, and a good program

manager must be adept at identifying problems and finding creative solutions to overcome them.

5. Organizational Skills: With multiple moving parts and stakeholders involved, organization is key. A program manager must be able to keep track of deadlines, resources, and budgets to ensure that projects stay on track.
6. Risk Management: Every project comes with risks, whether they are related to scope, schedule, or budget. A good program manager anticipates potential risks and develops mitigation strategies to minimize their impact.
7. Team Building and Management: Building a strong team is essential for project success. A program manager should be able to assemble the right talent, delegate tasks effectively, and foster a positive team dynamic.
8. Adaptability: Projects rarely go exactly as planned, and a good program manager must be flexible and adaptable in the face of change. They should be able to adjust plans and strategies as needed to accommodate shifting priorities or unexpected developments.
9. Client and Stakeholder Management: Program managers often serve as the primary point of contact for clients and stakeholders. Building and maintaining strong relationships with these parties is crucial for ensuring project success and securing future opportunities.
10. Quality Focus: Delivering a high-quality product or service is paramount. A good program manager should have a keen eye for detail and a commitment to excellence in all aspects of project execution.

By embodying these qualities, a program manager can effectively lead teams and deliver successful outcomes on complex projects.

12.19. What are the responsibilities of a program manager?

The responsibilities of a program manager can vary depending on the organization and the specific nature of the programs they oversee. However, here are some common responsibilities:

1. Program Planning: Developing a comprehensive plan for the program, including defining objectives, scope, deliverables, timelines, and budget.
2. Stakeholder Management: Identifying key stakeholders and establishing effective communication channels to ensure their needs and expectations are understood and addressed throughout the program lifecycle.
3. Resource Management: Allocating and managing resources such as budget, personnel, equipment, and materials to support the program's objectives.
4. Risk Management: Identifying potential risks to the program's success and developing strategies to mitigate or respond to them effectively.
5. Monitoring and Reporting: Regularly monitoring progress against the program plan, tracking key performance indicators, and providing status updates to stakeholders.
6. Issue Resolution: Identifying and resolving issues and conflicts that arise during program execution to ensure that the program stays on track.
7. Quality Management: Ensuring that the deliverables produced by the program meet the required quality standards and specifications.
8. Change Management: Managing changes to the program scope, schedule, or budget, and assessing the impact of those changes on the program's objectives.
9. Coordination and Collaboration: Facilitating collaboration and coordination among various teams, departments, and stakeholders involved in the program.
10. Continuous Improvement: Identifying opportunities for process improvement and implementing best practices to enhance the efficiency and effectiveness of program management processes.
11. Closure and Transition: Ensuring a smooth closure of the program by delivering all agreed-upon deliverables, conducting post-implementation reviews, and transitioning any ongoing activities to the appropriate stakeholders or teams.

Overall, a program manager plays a crucial role in driving the successful delivery of complex programs by providing leadership, direction, and oversight throughout the program lifecycle.

12.20. What are the typical duties of a lead project manager?

The role of a lead program manager often involves overseeing multiple projects that are interconnected or contribute to a common goal. The duties of a lead project manager can vary depending on the organization and the specific project, but typically they involve:

1. Strategic Planning: Developing a strategic vision for the program and aligning it with organizational goals.
2. Program Governance: Establishing governance structures and processes to ensure effective decision-making and accountability within the program.
3. Stakeholder Management: Identifying and engaging stakeholders at various levels, including executives, project managers, team members, and external partners.
4. Resource Management: Allocating resources across projects within the program to optimize efficiency and achieve objectives.
5. Risk Management: Identifying and managing risks that could impact the overall success of the program, including dependencies between projects.
6. Budget Oversight: Managing the program budget, tracking expenses, and ensuring that spending is aligned with priorities and delivers value.
7. Performance Monitoring: Monitoring the performance of individual projects and the program as a whole, tracking key metrics and KPIs to assess progress and identify areas for improvement.
8. Coordination and Integration: Ensuring coordination and integration across projects within the program, including managing dependencies and facilitating communication between project teams.
9. Quality Assurance: Establishing quality standards and processes to ensure that deliverables meet requirements and expectations.
10. Change Management: Managing changes to the program scope, schedule, or resources, and ensuring that stakeholders are informed and aligned.
11. Communication: Providing regular updates to stakeholders on program progress, milestones, risks, and issues, and facilitating communication between project teams and stakeholders.
12. Continuous Improvement: Identifying opportunities for process improvement and implementing best practices to enhance program performance and delivery.

Overall, the role of a lead program manager is to provide leadership, direction, and support to ensure the successful execution of multiple projects within a program, ultimately delivering value to the organization.

12.21. What are some of the things that make a good project manager great?

A good project manager ensures project completion within scope, time, and budget. A great project manager, however, goes beyond these basics. Here are some key attributes and practices that elevate a good project manager to greatness:

1. Exceptional Communication Skills
    a. Clarity and Transparency: Clearly articulates project goals, expectations, and updates.
    b. Active Listening: Understands team members' concerns and feedback.
    c. Stakeholder Management: Effectively communicates with stakeholders to manage expectations and report progress.
2. Leadership and Motivation
    a. Inspires the Team: Motivates team members to achieve their best.

    b. Conflict Resolution: Manages and resolves conflicts efficiently.
    c. Decision-Making: Makes informed and timely decisions.
3. Strategic Vision
    a. Big Picture Thinking: Understands how the project fits into the broader organizational goals.
    b. Goal Setting: Sets clear, achievable, and strategic goals.
4. Adaptability and Flexibility
    a. Agile Mindset: Adapts to changes and can pivot project direction when necessary.
    b. Problem-Solving: Quickly identifies issues and implements effective solutions.
5. Risk Management
    a. Proactive Approach: Anticipates potential risks and develops mitigation strategies.
    b. Risk Assessment: Continuously evaluates risks throughout the project lifecycle.
6. Technical Proficiency
    a. Understanding of Tools and Techniques: Proficient in project management software and methodologies.
    b. Industry Knowledge: Understands the technical aspects of the industry to make informed decisions.
7. Organization and Planning
    a. Detailed Planning: Develops comprehensive project plans with clear timelines and milestones.
    b. Prioritization: Prioritizes tasks effectively to ensure critical deadlines are met.
8. Empathy and Emotional Intelligence
    a. Understanding Team Dynamics: Recognizes and respects individual team member needs and strengths.
    b. Building Relationships: Creates a positive and collaborative team environment.
9. Continuous Improvement
    a. Learning Orientation: Continuously seeks to improve skills and knowledge.
    b. Feedback Utilization: Actively seeks and utilizes feedback to improve project processes and outcomes.
10. Results-Oriented
    a. Focus on Deliverables: Keeps the team focused on achieving the end goals.
    b. Performance Tracking: Regularly monitors progress and performance metrics to ensure alignment with objectives.
11. Client-Centric Approach
    a. Understanding Client Needs: Thoroughly understands and aligns with client requirements and expectations.
    b. Client Satisfaction: Prioritizes client satisfaction through quality deliverables and effective communication.
12. Cultural Awareness
    a. Global Perspective: Manages and respects cultural differences within international teams.
    b. Inclusive Leadership: Promotes diversity and inclusion within the project team.

By embodying these attributes and practices, a project manager can transform from being merely good to truly great, leading projects to success while fostering a positive and productive team environment.

12.22. Describe your program management experience.

It is essential to structure your answer to clearly convey your skills, accomplishments, and relevance to the role. Here is a step-by-step guide for crafting a compelling response:

1. Start with an Overview. Begin with a brief summary of your overall experience in program management. Highlight the duration of your experience and the types of programs you have

managed.

    a. Example: "I have over 7 years of experience managing large-scale programs across various industries, including technology and healthcare. I specialize in coordinating cross-functional teams, ensuring alignment with strategic goals, and delivering results on time and within budget."

2. Highlight Key Responsibilities. Describe your main responsibilities as a program manager, showcasing your ability to handle complex tasks and prioritize effectively.
    a. Example: "In my role, I have been responsible for setting program objectives, defining deliverables, creating detailed project plans, and monitoring progress to ensure alignment with business goals. I also manage budgets, risk assessments, and stakeholder communication."
3. Provide Specific Examples. Share a specific, quantifiable example of a program you managed successfully. Use the STAR (Situation, Task, Action, Result) method to structure your example.
    a. Example: "In my previous role at XYZ Corp, I managed a company-wide digital transformation program. The goal was to integrate new tools to improve team collaboration and efficiency. I coordinated with five departments, developed a phased rollout plan, and managed a $2 million budget. As a result, we increased operational efficiency by 25% within a year and improved employee satisfaction scores by 15%."
4. Showcase Key Skills. Mention skills that align with program management, such as leadership, communication, risk management, and problem-solving.
    a. Example: "I excel at stakeholder engagement, ensuring that everyone from executives to team members is aligned. Additionally, my ability to anticipate risks and adapt plans has been instrumental in achieving program success."
5. Tailor to the Role. Connect your experience to the specific role or company. Show that you understand their goals and how your background aligns with their needs.
    a. Example: "Given your organization's focus on scaling operations, my experience in leading multi-million-dollar programs and driving organizational change would allow me to deliver measurable results."
6. End with Enthusiasm. Conclude by expressing enthusiasm for the opportunity to bring your expertise to the role.
    a. Example: "I am passionate about program management because it allows me to combine strategic thinking with practical execution, and I am excited about the opportunity to contribute to your team's success."

Example: "I have 8 years of program management experience, primarily in the tech and financial sectors. My responsibilities have included defining program goals, aligning cross-functional teams, and ensuring timely delivery within budget. For instance, at ABC Corp, I managed a program to implement a global CRM system, coordinating 10 teams across 3 continents. By setting clear milestones and maintaining open communication, we completed the project 2 months ahead of schedule and under budget by 10%. My strong leadership, problem-solving skills, and ability to manage stakeholder expectations make me confident in my ability to drive impactful results in this role."

12.23. Describe a recent project where you were responsible for managing multiple people or teams. What were some of the key challenges and how did you handle those challenges?

This question highlights the importance of result-oriented leadership. Project managers must focus on delivering results and staying committed to achieving the final objective. Merely identifying issues without actively working to resolve them would not push the project forward. Effective project managers showcase their ability to manage projects by coordinating across multiple teams, overcoming challenges, and successfully achieving the project's goals.

When responding to this interview question, it is essential to structure your answer thoughtfully to showcase your leadership abilities and problem-solving skills. Here is a suggested approach:

1. Introduction to the Project: Start by providing a brief overview of the project you managed, including its scope, objectives, and the teams or people involved. Make sure to highlight its relevance to the position you are interviewing for.
2. Key Responsibilities: Outline your role and responsibilities in managing multiple people or teams. Emphasize your leadership role, decision-making authority, and how you coordinated efforts to achieve project goals.
3. Key Challenges Faced: Identify the main challenges you encountered during the project. These could include issues such as communication barriers, conflicting priorities, resource constraints, or unforeseen obstacles. Be specific and provide examples to illustrate each challenge.
4. How You Handled the Challenges: Describe the strategies and tactics you employed to address each challenge effectively. Highlight any leadership skills, problem-solving techniques, or interpersonal approaches you utilized. If applicable, mention any adjustments or adaptations you made to the project plan or team dynamics.
5. Results and Outcomes: Conclude your response by discussing the results and outcomes achieved despite the challenges. Quantify your success whenever possible, such as meeting deadlines, exceeding targets, or improving team performance. Additionally, reflect on any lessons learned or improvements implemented for future projects.

Here is an example response:

"In my previous role as a project manager at XYZ Company, I was tasked with overseeing the development of a new product line, which involved coordinating multiple teams across different departments. One of the key challenges I faced was managing communication between these teams, as each had their own priorities and workflows.

To address this challenge, I implemented a regular meeting schedule where representatives from each team could provide updates, share insights, and raise any issues or concerns. Additionally, I established a centralized project management platform to streamline collaboration and ensure everyone had access to the latest information and documents.

Another challenge was resource allocation, particularly when unexpected delays or changes arose. In these instances, I practiced adaptability by reallocating resources as needed and renegotiating deadlines with stakeholders to ensure minimal disruption to the project timeline.

Despite these challenges, we were able to successfully launch the new product line ahead of schedule and within budget. The project received positive feedback from both internal stakeholders and customers, with sales exceeding projections by 20%. Moving forward, I have integrated the lessons learned from this experience into my project management approach, emphasizing proactive communication and flexible resource management."

12.24. What is the difference between project manager, program manager, and product manager roles?

The roles of project manager, program manager, and product manager, while overlapping in some ways, have distinct focuses and responsibilities. Here is a detailed comparison of each:

Project Manager

1. Focus:

a. Scope and Deliverables: Ensures specific projects are completed on time, within budget, and meet the defined scope.
b. Timeline and Budget: Manages project schedules, resources, and budgets.
c. Team Coordination: Leads and coordinates project teams, assigns tasks, and tracks progress.
d. Risk Management: Identifies risks and develops mitigation strategies.
e. Stakeholder Communication: Keeps stakeholders informed about project status and changes.

2. Responsibilities:
    a. Defining project objectives and planning project activities.
    b. Scheduling tasks and milestones.
    c. Monitoring project progress and performance.
    d. Managing changes to the project scope, schedule, and costs.
    e. Reporting on project progress to stakeholders and executives.
3. Example:
    a. Overseeing the development of a new website from concept to launch.

Program Manager

1. Focus:
    a. Multiple Projects: Manages a portfolio of related projects that together achieve a strategic objective.
    b. Alignment and Integration: Ensures that individual projects are aligned with the organization's overall goals and strategy.
    c. Resource Management: Allocates resources across projects to optimize efficiency and effectiveness.
    d. Stakeholder Engagement: Manages communication and expectations among various stakeholders at a higher level than project managers.
2. Responsibilities:
    a. Coordinating multiple projects and ensuring they align with the broader business objectives.
    b. Managing dependencies and potential conflicts between projects.
    c. Ensuring that projects collectively meet organizational goals.
    d. Reporting program status and progress to senior management.
    e. Implementing best practices and processes across projects.
3. Example:
    a. Overseeing a series of projects aimed at implementing a new enterprise resource planning (ERP) system across all company departments.

Product Manager

1. Focus:
    a. Product Development and Lifecycle: Responsible for the entire lifecycle of a product, from ideation through development to market release and beyond.
    b. Market and Customer Needs: Ensures the product meets customer needs and market demands.
    c. Strategy and Vision: Develops the product vision, strategy, and roadmap.
    d. Cross-functional Leadership: Works closely with engineering, design, marketing, and sales teams.
2. Responsibilities:
    a. Defining product vision and strategy based on market research and customer feedback.
    b. Creating and managing the product roadmap.
    c. Prioritizing features and enhancements based on business value and customer impact.

d. Collaborating with development teams to ensure timely and high-quality product releases.
e. Analyzing product performance and gathering feedback for continuous improvement.

3. Example:
    a. Managing the development and launch of a new mobile app, including defining features, overseeing design and development, and planning marketing strategies.

Key Differences

1. Scope of Responsibility:
    a. Project Manager: Focuses on specific projects with defined objectives.
    b. Program Manager: Oversees multiple related projects and ensures they align with broader business goals.
    c. Product Manager: Manages the lifecycle and success of a specific product.
2. Strategic vs. Tactical:
    a. Project Manager: Tactical, dealing with the execution of tasks and meeting deadlines.
    b. Program Manager: Strategic and tactical, ensuring project alignment with organizational strategy.
    c. Product Manager: Strategic, focusing on product vision, market needs, and long-term success.
3. Timeframe:
    a. Project Manager: Short-term, project-specific timeframes.
    b. Program Manager: Medium to long-term, depending on the duration of the program.
    c. Product Manager: Long-term, covering the entire product lifecycle.

Each role plays a crucial part in the success of an organization, and their responsibilities often intersect, requiring strong collaboration and communication among them.

12.25. Why do companies need both product managers and product owners?

Product manager or owner plays a vital role in the development and success of a product. Their job is to ensure that the product meets the needs and expectations of customers, and product remains competitive, while also aligning with the overall vision, roadmap, strategy, and goals of the business. It is a challenging and rewarding role but it also requires a unique set of skills and experience.

The truth is, in general, product managers rarely make good product owners. Here is why: If you were to interview the highest-level people at your company (think C-levels, directors, etc.) and ask them "What about our business keeps you up at night?" they are going to describe strategic problems. The reason these people are good at what they do is that they are gazing out at the horizon of business decisions, thinking about such issues as:

1. what are the new markets we should be fighting for?
2. what are new products we should create?
3. how do we hit our revenue targets?

We might call them "40,000-foot people". Now ask the same question of a typical Scrum team member and you will learn they are pretty much tactical thinkers. What worries them:

1. what do we need to do to meet our sprint commitment?
2. what impediments are blocking our ability to deliver?
3. how can we deal with technical debt?

Compared to the 40,000-foot types, Scrum team members are right on the ground - almost completely tactical. In between these two extremes, a good Product Owner is about a "10,000-foot person." Mainly tactical, yes, but with a connection up to the strategic. They can see the big picture well enough to plan intelligently.

A good Product Manager, by contrast, is about a "25,000-foot person." Can they make decisions? Yes. See the bigger picture? You bet. But will they do the "grunt work" of being a Product Owner such as writing user stories, breaking down epics or features, meeting with stakeholders on a regular basis? No.

A good, well-experienced Product Owner can plan about 3 - 6 months out. A good Product Manager can do a 2-year product road map. Such people tend to find the day-to-day work of writing stories and the like to be tedious…so they would not do it.

In smaller companies where titles are inflated (and everyone has to pitch in to get work done) these roles can sometimes be blurred. But in bigger companies, Product Managers neither enjoy nor excel at the Product Owner role.

12.26. How do you distinguish between project management and program management?

Project management and program management are both disciplines within the field of management, but they involve different levels of coordination and scope. Here is how you can distinguish between project management and program management:

1. Definition and Scope:
    a. Project Management: Project management focuses on the planning, execution, and control of specific projects. A project is a temporary endeavor with a defined scope, objectives, and deliverables. Project management deals with managing resources, tasks, timelines, risks, and stakeholders within the project's boundaries.
    b. Program Management: Program management involves coordinating multiple related projects and activities to achieve broader organizational goals. A program consists of a collection of projects and initiatives that are interconnected and contribute to a common strategic objective. Program management involves overseeing the interdependencies, resource allocation, and overall progress of multiple projects within the program.
2. Objectives:
    a. Project Management: The primary objective of project management is to successfully complete the project within the defined constraints of time, budget, and quality. The project manager's focus is on delivering the project's specific outputs or outcomes.
    b. Program Management: Program management aims to achieve strategic objectives and organizational benefits by effectively managing a portfolio of projects. The program manager's focus is on aligning projects within the program to ensure they collectively contribute to the desired outcomes.
3. Scope Management:
    a. Project Management: Project managers are responsible for defining and managing the project's scope. They ensure that the project's deliverables and objectives are well-defined, and any changes to the scope are properly controlled and communicated.
    b. Program Management: Program managers oversee the scope of the entire program, which includes coordinating and balancing the scope of individual projects within the program. They ensure that projects align with the program's strategic objectives and make decisions regarding scope changes that affect multiple projects.
4. Stakeholder Management:
    a. Project Management: Project managers identify and engage with stakeholders who have a direct interest in the project's outcomes. They manage stakeholder expectations,

communicate project progress, and address any concerns specific to the project.
    b. Program Management: Program managers deal with a broader range of stakeholders, including those who are interested in the overall program's success. They focus on stakeholder alignment, managing relationships across multiple projects, and ensuring stakeholder engagement at the program level.
5. Risk Management:
    a. Project Management: Project managers identify, assess, and manage risks that may affect the project's objectives. They develop risk mitigation strategies and contingency plans to minimize the impact of potential risks on the project.
    b. Program Management: Program managers address risks that arise at the program level, such as risks associated with interdependencies between projects, resource allocation, or strategic alignment. They coordinate risk management efforts across projects and implement risk response strategies at the program level.

While project management and program management share some common principles and practices, program management involves a higher level of complexity and coordination due to its focus on managing multiple projects to achieve strategic goals.

12.27. How do project management and program management complement each other? How do you choose between them? How do you learn and improve them?

Project management and program management are both disciplines within the field of management, but they have distinct differences and roles. Here is how they differ, complement each other, and how you can learn and improve in each field:

1. Distinction between Project Management and Program Management:
    a. Project Management: Project management focuses on the planning, execution, and control of a specific project with well-defined objectives, scope, deliverables, and timeline. It involves managing resources, coordinating tasks, monitoring progress, and ensuring the project's successful completion.
    b. Program Management: Program management deals with managing multiple related projects that are aligned with a common strategic goal or objective. It involves coordinating and integrating various projects to achieve overall organizational objectives, managing interdependencies, allocating resources, and optimizing outcomes across the projects.
2. Complementary Nature of Project Management and Program Management:
    a. Project and Program Alignment: Program management ensures that projects within a program are aligned with the organization's strategic goals and objectives.
    b. Resource Management: Program management facilitates the efficient allocation and utilization of resources across multiple projects, enabling optimal utilization and coordination.
    c. Risk Management: Program management helps identify and manage risks and dependencies across projects, minimizing potential impacts on the program's objectives.
    d. Strategic Oversight: Program management provides a holistic view of the organization's initiatives, ensuring that projects contribute to the overall strategic vision.
3. Choosing Between Project Management and Program Management:
    a. Project Management: Choose project management when dealing with a single, standalone project with specific deliverables and timelines.
    b. Program Management: Choose program management when multiple interdependent projects need to be managed to achieve a common strategic objective or when managing a portfolio of projects.
4. Learning and Improving Project Management and Program Management:

a. Education and Training: Seek formal education, certifications, or training programs specific to project management or program management.
b. Experience: Gain hands-on experience by working on projects or programs, gradually increasing your responsibilities and exposure.
c. Professional Networks: Engage with professional organizations, attend conferences, join forums, and connect with experienced project or program managers to learn from their experiences and insights.
d. Continuous Improvement: Reflect on your past projects/programs, identify areas for improvement, seek feedback, and implement lessons learned to refine your skills.

Remember, while project management and program management have distinct roles, they are not mutually exclusive. Many professionals transition from project management to program management as they gain experience and develop broader perspectives on managing multiple projects.

12.28. How to become a program manager?

Becoming a program manager typically involves a combination of education, experience, and skills development. Here is a general roadmap to help you navigate your journey toward becoming a program manager:

1. Education:
    a. Bachelor's Degree: Most program manager positions require a bachelor's degree in a relevant field such as computer science, engineering, business administration, or a related discipline. However, depending on the industry, some employers may accept candidates with degrees in other fields if they have relevant experience.
    b. Master's Degree (Optional): While not always required, having a master's degree in project management, business administration, or a related field can give you a competitive edge and help you develop advanced skills in leadership, communication, and project management methodologies.
2. Gain Relevant Experience:
    a. Project Management Experience: Start by gaining experience in project management roles. This could involve working as a project coordinator, project assistant, or junior project manager to learn the ropes of managing projects, coordinating resources, and working with cross-functional teams.
    b. Industry Experience: Gain experience in the industry you wish to work in as a program manager. Understanding the nuances and challenges of specific industries can be invaluable when managing programs and projects within them.
    c. Leadership Experience: Develop your leadership skills by taking on roles that involve leading teams, managing stakeholders, and making strategic decisions. This could involve leading small projects or initiatives within your current organization or taking on leadership roles in professional or community organizations.
3. Develop Key Skills:
    a. Communication: Strong communication skills are essential for program managers to effectively convey information, facilitate discussions, and negotiate with stakeholders. Work on honing your verbal and written communication skills.
    b. Leadership: Program managers need to inspire and motivate teams, provide direction, and resolve conflicts. Develop your leadership skills by taking on leadership roles, seeking feedback, and continuously learning about leadership best practices.
    c. Strategic Thinking: Program managers must have a strategic mindset and the ability to align program objectives with broader organizational goals. Develop your strategic thinking skills by staying informed about industry trends, analyzing data, and thinking critically about business challenges and opportunities.

   d. Problem-Solving: Program managers encounter complex problems and obstacles that require creative and analytical thinking to solve. Practice problem-solving skills by tackling challenging projects and seeking out opportunities to solve problems within your current role.
   e. Stakeholder Management: Program managers interact with a wide range of stakeholders, including team members, executives, clients, and external partners. Learn how to manage stakeholder expectations, build relationships, and communicate effectively with diverse groups.
4. Obtain Certifications (Optional):
   a. Project Management Professional (PMP): The PMP certification, offered by the Project Management Institute (PMI), is one of the most widely recognized certifications for project managers. While not specifically for program management, it demonstrates expertise in project management principles and practices.
   b. Program Management Professional (PgMP): The PgMP certification, also offered by PMI, is specifically designed for program managers. It validates your ability to oversee multiple projects and align them with organizational objectives.
   c. Other Certifications: Depending on your industry and area of specialization, there may be other relevant certifications you can pursue to enhance your skills and credibility as a program manager.
5. Network and Seek Opportunities:
   a. Networking: Build relationships with professionals in your industry, attend industry events, join professional organizations, and participate in online forums and communities related to program management.
   b. Seek Opportunities: Keep an eye out for opportunities to transition into program management roles within your current organization or explore opportunities with other companies. Consider seeking out mentors who can provide guidance and advice as you progress in your career.
   c. Continuous Learning: Stay updated on industry trends, best practices, and emerging technologies related to program management. Invest in your professional development through workshops, seminars, online courses, and reading relevant books and articles.

Becoming a program manager is a rewarding career path that requires dedication, continuous learning, and a commitment to developing the necessary skills and experience. By following these steps and staying proactive in your career development, you can increase your chances of success in this role.

12.29. How do you plan and conduct an effective program kick-off meeting and a program review meeting?

Planning and conducting effective program kick-off and review meetings are crucial for the success of any project or initiative. Here is a step-by-step guide for both types of meetings:

Program Kick-off Meeting:

1. Define Objectives: Clarify the purpose of the kick-off meeting. Clearly communicate what the program is about, its goals, scope, and expected outcomes.
2. Identify Participants: Determine who should attend the meeting. This usually includes key stakeholders, team members, sponsors, and anyone directly involved in the program.
3. Choose a Date and Time: Schedule the meeting at a time that accommodates the majority of participants. Consider time zones and working hours.
4. Create an Agenda: Outline the topics to be discussed during the meeting. This might include introductions, program overview, roles and responsibilities, milestones, timelines, communication plan, and any other relevant details.

5. Send Invitations: Use a calendar tool to send out invitations with the agenda, date, time, and meeting link. Make sure participants have the necessary materials in advance.
6. Prepare Materials: Gather any materials, presentations, or documents that need to be shared during the meeting. Ensure they are organized and easy to access.
7. Facilitate the Meeting:
    a. Start with introductions to ensure everyone knows each other.
    b. Present the program overview, goals, and expected outcomes.
    c. Discuss roles and responsibilities of team members and stakeholders.
    d. Present the program timeline, milestones, and deliverables.
    e. Share the communication plan, including how updates will be provided and how feedback will be collected.
    f. Allow time for questions and open discussions.
8. Set Expectations: Clearly communicate next steps, assignments, and any follow-up actions. Make sure everyone understands their roles and responsibilities moving forward.
9. Document Meeting Minutes: Assign someone to take notes during the meeting. These minutes should capture key decisions, action items, and any other relevant discussions.
10. Follow-Up: After the meeting, distribute the meeting minutes, presentation materials, and any other relevant documents to all participants. Ensure everyone is on the same page and has access to the information discussed.

Program Review Meeting:

1. Define Objectives: Clarify the purpose of the review meeting. Are you assessing progress, identifying challenges, or evaluating outcomes? Define what you aim to achieve.
2. Identify Participants: Similar to the kick-off meeting, determine who needs to attend the review meeting. This often includes project managers, team leads, stakeholders, and relevant subject matter experts.
3. Choose a Date and Time: Schedule the review meeting well in advance, allowing participants to prepare and attend.
4. Create an Agenda: Outline the topics for discussion. This might include progress updates, challenges encountered, achievements, risks, and any adjustments to the plan.
5. Send Invitations: Send out invitations with the agenda and meeting details. Ensure that all necessary parties are included.
6. Gather Progress Reports: Collect progress reports or updates from various team members and stakeholders. These reports will be used to guide the discussion during the meeting.
7. Facilitate the Meeting:
    a. Start by reviewing the original goals and objectives of the program.
    b. Present a summary of progress made since the last meeting.
    c. Discuss achievements, milestones reached, and successful outcomes.
    d. Address any challenges, roadblocks, or risks that have arisen.
    e. Analyze whether the program is on track and meeting its goals.
    f. Brainstorm potential solutions for any identified issues.
8. Review Metrics and Data: If relevant, present data and metrics that indicate the program's performance and impact. This could include financial data, key performance indicators (KPIs), and other relevant measurements.
9. Discuss Lessons Learned: Encourage open discussions about what went well and what could be improved. This fosters a culture of continuous improvement.
10. Make Decisions and Set Action Items: Based on the discussions, make decisions about any necessary course corrections, changes to the plan, or adjustments in resource allocation. Assign action items to specific individuals.
11. Document Meeting Minutes: As with the kick-off meeting, document the key points, decisions, action items, and any other relevant details discussed during the review meeting.

12. Follow-Up: Distribute the meeting minutes and relevant materials to participants. Ensure that action items are tracked and followed up on in subsequent meetings.

Both kick-off and review meetings play a crucial role in effective program management. They set the tone, keep stakeholders informed, and provide a platform for collaboration and decision-making. By following these steps, you can ensure that these meetings are productive and contribute to the success of your program.

13. Framework, Methodology, and Process

Aim for Success, Not for Perfection.

Let us delve into the concepts of framework, methodology, and process, and understand how they differ from each other.

1. Framework
    a. A framework is a broad structure or a set of guidelines used to develop something or solve a problem. It provides a foundational structure but is flexible enough to allow for adjustments and adaptations based on specific needs.
    b. Characteristics:
        i. High-level, conceptual structure
        ii. Offers guidelines and best practices
        iii. Typically not prescriptive; allows for customization
        iv. Can be industry-specific or general
    c. Example: In software development, a framework like Angular provides a structure for building web applications, offering tools and libraries while allowing developers to adapt it to their specific project requirements.
2. Methodology
    a. A methodology is a system of practices, techniques, procedures, and rules used by those who work in a discipline. It provides a comprehensive set of guidelines and principles that can be systematically followed to ensure consistent and efficient results.
    b. Characteristics:
        i. More detailed than a framework
        ii. Prescriptive, outlining specific steps and procedures
        iii. Focused on a particular field or discipline
        iv. Aims to provide consistency and reliability
    c. Example: Agile methodology in project management provides a specific approach to managing and executing projects, including principles like iterative development, collaboration, and flexibility to change.

3. Process
    a. A process is a series of steps or actions taken to achieve a particular end. It is the practical implementation of a methodology or framework, detailing the exact sequence of activities to produce a desired outcome.
    b. Characteristics:
        i. Detailed and specific steps or actions
        ii. Sequential and often linear
        iii. Designed to produce a specific result
        iv. Can be repetitive and standardized
    c. Example: In software development, the process of Continuous Integration (CI) includes specific steps like code commit, automated testing, and integration into the main branch, aiming to improve code quality and reduce integration issues.

Differences

1. Level of Detail:
    a. Framework: High-level, conceptual.
    b. Methodology: Detailed, systematic guidelines.
    c. Process: Highly detailed, specific steps.
2. Flexibility:
    a. Framework: Flexible, adaptable to different needs.
    b. Methodology: Structured, but allows some flexibility.
    c. Process: Least flexible, often strictly defined.
3. Purpose:
    a. Framework: Provides a foundational structure.
    b. Methodology: Offers a systematic approach to achieve consistency and efficiency.
    c. Process: Details the exact sequence of actions to produce an outcome.
4. Application:
    a. Framework: Broad, can be applied in various contexts.
    b. Methodology: Discipline-specific, used within a particular field.
    c. Process: Specific to tasks and activities within a methodology or framework.

Summary

1. Frameworks offer a conceptual structure and guidelines, adaptable to various situations.
2. Methodologies provide a comprehensive set of principles and steps to follow, aimed at achieving consistency and reliability.
3. Processes outline the exact, detailed steps needed to accomplish specific tasks, focusing on execution and outcome.

13.1. What do you mean by best practice?

"Best practice" refers to a way, method or technique that has been widely accepted as superior to all other known methods or techniques for achieving a particular outcome or goal. In various fields such as business, medicine, education, or technology, best practices are established based on research, experience, and consensus among experts. They are considered to be the most effective and efficient ways of accomplishing tasks, solving problems, or delivering services. Best practices are often documented and shared within industries or communities to guide others in achieving similar success. A lesson learned from one area of a business that can be passed on to another area of the business or between businesses.

"Best practices" in project management refer to proven methods, techniques, or processes that are widely accepted as producing superior results in project execution. These practices are developed through experience and continuous improvement efforts within the project management community. Here are a few examples:

1. Clear Project Scope Definition: Clearly defining project scope ensures that all stakeholders understand what is included (and excluded) from the project. This helps in preventing scope creep and ensures that resources are utilized efficiently.
2. Effective Communication Plans: Establishing clear communication channels and protocols ensures that information flows smoothly among team members, stakeholders, and project sponsors. This includes regular status updates, progress reports, and issue resolution mechanisms.
3. Risk Management: Identifying, assessing, and mitigating risks throughout the project lifecycle is crucial for minimizing potential negative impacts on project objectives. This involves proactive risk identification, risk analysis, and the development of contingency plans.
4. Stakeholder Engagement: Engaging stakeholders throughout the project ensures that their expectations are managed, and their input is considered. This involves regular communication, feedback mechanisms, and addressing concerns in a timely manner.
5. Resource Allocation and Management: Efficiently allocating and managing resources, including human resources, budget, and materials, is essential for completing projects on time and within budget. This may involve resource leveling, resource allocation tools, and regular monitoring of resource utilization.
6. Change Management: Implementing a structured change management process helps in managing changes to project scope, schedule, and budget. This involves assessing the impact of changes, obtaining approvals, and communicating changes to relevant stakeholders.
7. Quality Assurance and Control: Implementing quality assurance processes ensures that project deliverables meet the required standards and specifications. Quality control measures involve monitoring and verifying the quality of work throughout the project lifecycle.
8. Project Closure Procedures: Properly closing out a project involves documenting lessons learned, conducting post-project reviews, and transitioning deliverables to the appropriate stakeholders. This helps in capturing knowledge for future projects and ensuring a smooth transition to operations or subsequent phases.

These best practices help project managers and teams deliver successful projects by providing guidance on how to effectively plan, execute, monitor, and control project activities.

13.2. What is brainstorming?

Brainstorming is a creative problem-solving technique where individuals or groups generate a wide range of ideas and solutions to a particular problem or challenge. The main goal of brainstorming is to encourage free thinking and produce as many ideas as possible without judgment or criticism. It is commonly used in various fields such as business, education, and design to foster innovation and creativity.

Here are some key aspects of brainstorming:

1. Quantity over Quality: During brainstorming, the focus is on generating a large number of ideas. The more ideas produced, the higher the chance of finding effective solutions.
2. No Judgment: All ideas, no matter how unusual or unconventional, are welcomed and encouraged. Criticism or evaluation of ideas is deferred until after the brainstorming session.
3. Building on Ideas: Participants are encouraged to build on each other's ideas, combining or improving them to create more refined or innovative solutions.
4. Encouraging Creativity: Brainstorming aims to remove barriers to creative thinking, allowing participants to think outside the box and come up with novel ideas.
5. Facilitation: A facilitator often guides the brainstorming session, helping to keep the discussion focused and ensuring that all participants contribute.

After the brainstorming session, the ideas are typically reviewed, analyzed, and prioritized to identify the most feasible and effective solutions.

13.3. What is a methodology?

A methodology is a systematic set of principles, rules, and methods used in a particular discipline or field to conduct research, solve problems, or achieve specific objectives. It provides a structured approach to carry out tasks, ensuring consistency, reliability, and validity in the outcomes. Methodologies can vary widely depending on the discipline or context in which they are applied, such as scientific research, project management, software development, or social sciences.

In essence, a methodology outlines the "how" of accomplishing tasks, including the tools, techniques, and processes involved. It often includes guidelines on data collection, analysis, and interpretation, ensuring that the work is conducted in a replicable and credible manner.

A methodology is defined as a set of repeatable processes that include project-specific methods, rules, and guidelines aimed at creating quality application systems that are both manageable and valuable to the organization. It is a well-structured, organized, and systematic approach for achieving a broad objective. These methodologies outline the necessary steps, tasks, roles, objectives, and deliverables required for the successful implementation of any system.

The key concept here is "repeatable process" - executing projects consistently in the same manner. In essence, a methodology serves as a roadmap guiding you to your desired outcome. By outlining a repeatable set of processes and procedures for building systems, a methodology enhances value and productivity within organizations.

Today, methodologies are increasingly integrating with project management techniques, process management methods, and other frameworks, providing a comprehensive approach to tackling many of the challenges in application development.

In project management, a methodology is a structured approach that outlines the processes, techniques, tools, and best practices used to manage a project effectively from initiation to completion. It serves as a framework to guide project managers and teams in planning, executing, and closing projects, ensuring that they meet their goals, stay on schedule, and adhere to budget constraints.

A project management methodology typically includes:

1. Phases: The stages of the project lifecycle, such as initiation, planning, execution, monitoring and controlling, and closing.
2. Processes: Specific actions or steps that need to be taken in each phase, like defining project scope, creating a project schedule, managing risks, and conducting quality assurance.
3. Tools and Techniques: Methods and instruments used to carry out the processes, such as Gantt charts, critical path analysis, risk management matrices, and communication plans.
4. Roles and Responsibilities: Clear definitions of who is responsible for various aspects of the project, including stakeholders, project managers, team members, and sponsors.
5. Deliverables: The specific outputs or products that must be completed and delivered at the end of each phase or the entire project.

Some of the most commonly used project management methodologies include:

1. Waterfall: A linear, sequential approach where each phase must be completed before moving on to the next.
2. Agile: An iterative and flexible approach that focuses on continuous improvement and customer

feedback.
3. Scrum: A specific form of Agile, emphasizing short sprints, daily stand-ups, and regular reviews.
4. PRINCE2: A process-based approach that provides detailed guidelines and templates for every phase of the project.
5. Lean: Focuses on maximizing value by eliminating waste and improving efficiency.

The choice of methodology depends on the nature of the project, the industry, the team's expertise, and the specific goals and constraints of the project.

13.4. Why use a methodology?

Using a methodology in project management provides several key benefits that enhance the likelihood of a project's success. Here is why it is important:

1. Structured Approach: A methodology offers a systematic and organized way to plan, execute, and complete projects. This structure helps ensure that all aspects of the project are considered and managed properly.
2. Consistency: By following a methodology, project managers can apply the same processes across different projects, leading to more predictable outcomes. This consistency helps in setting expectations and delivering results that meet stakeholder needs.
3. Improved Communication: Methodologies often come with defined processes and terminologies, which enhance communication among team members and stakeholders. Everyone knows what to expect and how to proceed at each stage.
4. Risk Management: A good methodology includes steps for identifying, analyzing, and mitigating risks. This proactive approach to risk management can prevent problems before they arise or minimize their impact.
5. Resource Management: Methodologies help in planning and allocating resources efficiently, ensuring that the project is completed within the given constraints of time, budget, and scope.
6. Accountability and Control: Methodologies often include checkpoints, reviews, and reporting mechanisms, which create accountability and allow for better control over the project. This makes it easier to track progress and make necessary adjustments.
7. Quality Assurance: Following a methodology helps ensure that quality is built into every stage of the project, leading to better deliverables that meet or exceed stakeholder expectations.
8. Learning and Improvement: Many methodologies incorporate lessons learned and continuous improvement processes, which help teams to refine their approach and avoid repeating mistakes in future projects.
9. Alignment with Business Goals: Methodologies often tie the project's objectives to broader business goals, ensuring that the project delivers value to the organization.

By using a project management methodology, project managers and teams can work more efficiently, manage risks better, and achieve higher-quality outcomes, ultimately contributing to the success of the project and the organization as a whole.

13.5. What is a process?

A process is a sequence of steps, actions, changes, or functions that lead to a desired outcome, such as digestion or obtaining a driver's license. The effectiveness of processes is influenced by several factors, including:

1. The personnel who operate the processes
2. The materials used as inputs, including information
3. The machines or equipment involved in executing, monitoring, or measuring the process
4. The methods employed, including criteria and documentation used throughout the process

5. The work environment

Understanding the interaction and impact of these factors is crucial in the study of processes.

13.6. What is a procedure?

In the realm of computer science and programming, a procedure refers to a sequence of instructions or actions that perform a specific task. Procedures are often grouped together under a single name, making it easier to manage and reuse code. They are commonly known as functions, methods, subroutines, or routines depending on the programming language.

Procedures typically accept input parameters, process them, and may produce output. They encapsulate a set of actions that can be called upon multiple times within a program without having to rewrite the code each time. This not only promotes code reusability but also enhances readability and maintainability.

In a broader context, procedures can also refer to a series of steps or protocols followed to accomplish a particular task or goal in various fields, not just limited to computing. For instance, in medical contexts, a procedure might refer to a set of steps for performing surgery or administering medication.

13.7. What is a technique?

A defined systematic procedure employed by a human resource to perform an activity to produce a product, result or deliver a service, and that may employ one or more tools.

A technique is a method or procedure used to accomplish a particular task or to achieve a specific goal. In various fields such as science, art, sports, and technology, techniques are developed and refined to improve efficiency, effectiveness, and quality of outcomes. Techniques can range from simple procedures to complex methodologies, and they often involve a set of steps or actions performed in a systematic manner. For example, in cooking, chopping vegetables with a particular knife grip can be considered a technique, while in martial arts, executing a specific sequence of movements to perform a kick is a technique. Overall, techniques are fundamental tools used to achieve desired results across different domains.

13.8. What is the difference between method, methodology, technique and standard?

A method is a specific way of accomplishing something, such as a particular technique for cooking vegetables. It refers to the distinct approach you take to complete a task, often used in routine activities. Essentially, a method is a systematic process for doing something, typically in a step-by-step manner. Methodology, on the other hand, is the framework or process used to define these methods.

A process is the overall manner in which something is done, encompassing the entire activity from start to finish.

A technique is a specialized procedure or skill employed to complete a specific task, usually in predictable situations, like solving a long division problem.

An approach refers to the manner in which you handle or treat a situation. Consistent approaches are necessary in experiments to ensure reproducibility of results.

A strategy is a planned course of action designed to navigate through a situation, often involving preparation and foresight. Strategies are typically employed in new or challenging situations, such as devising a strategy to win a game.

A standard is a documented specification that establishes a common language and precise criteria, intended for consistent use as a rule, guideline, or definition. At its core, a standard is an agreed-upon, repeatable way of doing something, applied across various materials, products, methods, and services. Standards simplify life and enhance the reliability and effectiveness of many goods and services we use daily. They are developed through the collective expertise of producers, sellers, buyers, users, and regulators related to a particular material, product, process, or service.

Standards are voluntary and do not impose regulations, although laws may reference specific standards, making adherence mandatory. For example, the standard for the physical characteristics and format of credit cards is defined by BS EN ISO/IEC 7810:1996. Compliance with this standard ensures global usability. Standards are the result of collaborative efforts by committees comprising manufacturers, users, research organizations, government departments, and consumers, continually evolving to meet societal and technological demands.

In Programming:

1. Method: In programming, a method is a function associated with a class definition in object-oriented programming (OOP). Once an instance of the class is created, the method is bound to that instance and cannot be used separately from it, unlike standalone functions.
2. Technique: This refers to the manner of using methods, functions, and code commands to achieve the desired outcome when the code is executed.

Example: To calculate a user's age, one technique might involve writing a function to prompt for the date of birth, subtracting it from today's date (using a method from the date class), and then outputting the result. Here, methods are the specific code commands for input, processing, and output, while the technique encompasses the overall approach. Alternatively, a different technique might simply involve asking the user for their age directly.

In Computer Animation:

1. Method: A method in computer animation is a specific tool or procedure used to create an element of the artwork. For instance, to model a cylinder in 3D, one could either extrude a circle into a cylindrical shape or revolve a straight line around a central axis. The latter method offers more control over the cylinder's silhouette, making it preferable for complex shapes like a wine glass or beer bottle.
2. Technique: This is a broader set of methods used to create the illusion of motion in a scene. For example, to animate a wine glass breaking, one technique could involve modeling the broken pieces and then animating them coming together (to be played in reverse). A better technique might involve using the revolve method mentioned earlier, splitting the finished model, and key-framing the pieces to move apart. Another approach could use a simulation to generate and animate the breaking pieces automatically.

13.9. What is a life cycle and why do you need one?

A life cycle in the context of systems, software, or product development refers to the series of stages or phases that a project, product, or system goes through from its inception to its retirement. Each phase has specific activities, objectives, and deliverables that contribute to the overall project or product.

Types of Life Cycles

1. Development Life Cycle: Focuses on the creation and evolution of a product or system. Commonly includes phases such as:

   a. Requirements Gathering: Identifying the needs and constraints.
   b. Design: Creating the architecture and detailed design.
   c. Implementation: Developing the actual product.
   d. Testing: Ensuring the product meets the required standards.
   e. Deployment: Releasing the product to users.
   f. Maintenance: Updating and fixing the product over time.
2. Maintenance Life Cycle: Concentrates on the activities necessary to keep a system or product functional after it has been deployed. This includes:
   a. Corrective Maintenance: Fixing defects or bugs.
   b. Adaptive Maintenance: Modifying the system to cope with changes in the environment.
   c. Perfective Maintenance: Enhancing performance or adding new features.
   d. Preventive Maintenance: Improving the system to prevent future problems.

Why You Need a Life Cycle

1. Structured Approach: A life cycle provides a structured approach to managing complex projects, ensuring that nothing is overlooked.
2. Improved Planning: By breaking down the process into phases, you can plan resources, time, and costs more effectively.
3. Risk Management: Identifying and addressing risks at each stage can help avoid costly mistakes later.
4. Quality Assurance: Defined stages with clear deliverables allow for better quality control and testing.
5. Stakeholder Communication: A life cycle makes it easier to communicate progress, expectations, and changes to stakeholders.
6. Continuous Improvement: By following a life cycle, teams can learn from each phase and improve processes for future projects.

In summary, a life cycle provides a roadmap for the development and maintenance of a system or product, helping to ensure that the final outcome is of high quality, delivered on time, and meets the needs of stakeholders.

13.10. Where does prototyping fit in to the project life cycle?

Prototyping fits in throughout the project, particularly during the initial phases, - because seeing is believing. Prototyping is a good vehicle for verifying functionality, business rules, and data requirements with the users as well as for testing performance. Be careful, however, that prototypes do not become quick-and-dirty production applications. Production prototypes are notorious for requiring high maintenance. Here is an overview of where prototyping typically plays a role:

1. Initiation Phase
   a. Idea Generation and Conceptualization: During this phase, prototypes can be used to explore different concepts and ideas. It helps in visualizing what the final product might look like and assessing feasibility.
2. Planning Phase
   a. Requirements Gathering and Analysis: Prototypes help stakeholders and the project team understand the requirements better. They serve as a tangible representation of the product, facilitating discussions and refining requirements.
3. Design Phase
   a. Design and Architecture: Prototyping is crucial in the design phase to create mock-ups, wireframes, or even interactive models. This allows designers and developers to experiment with different layouts, user interfaces, and interactions before finalizing the design.

   b. Validation of Design Concepts: Prototypes are tested with users to validate design concepts. Feedback from these tests informs the design decisions and helps in making necessary adjustments.
4. Execution Phase
   a. Development and Iteration: During development, prototypes may be used to create minimum viable products (MVPs) or beta versions. These prototypes are tested, and feedback is used to iterate and improve the product.
   b. User Testing and Feedback: Prototypes are crucial for gathering user feedback early and often. This feedback loop ensures that the product evolves in line with user expectations and requirements.
5. Monitoring and Controlling Phase
   a. Continuous Improvement: Even during this phase, prototypes can be used to test new features or changes before full implementation. This helps in mitigating risks and ensuring that any modifications are beneficial.
6. Closing Phase
   a. While prototyping is less common in the closing phase, any lessons learned from the prototyping process are documented and used for future projects. This phase focuses more on final deliverables and project closure.

Benefits of Prototyping in the Project Life Cycle

1. Risk Reduction: By testing ideas early, prototypes help in identifying and mitigating potential issues.
2. Improved Communication: Prototypes provide a visual and functional representation of the product, enhancing communication among stakeholders.
3. User-Centered Design: Prototyping ensures that user feedback is incorporated, leading to a product that meets user needs and expectations.
4. Cost and Time Efficiency: Early identification of issues and iterative development reduce the risk of costly changes later in the project.

Types of Prototyping

1. Low-Fidelity Prototyping: Simple sketches or wireframes used in the early stages to explore ideas.
2. High-Fidelity Prototyping: More detailed and interactive prototypes that closely resemble the final product, used in later stages for detailed feedback and testing.

In summary, prototyping is an integral part of the project life cycle, particularly in the initiation, planning, and design phases, but it also plays a role during development and even monitoring and controlling. It helps in refining ideas, gathering feedback, and ensuring that the final product meets user expectations and requirements.

13.11. How does object-oriented development differ in project management techniques from traditional development?

Object-oriented development (OOD) and traditional development (often associated with procedural or structured development) differ in project management techniques due to their distinct approaches to software design, coding, and maintenance.

Object-oriented projects typically require smaller, less aggressive teams. What truly matters are the skills and roles of each team member. Individuals may need to take on different roles during various phases of the project, making it essential for them to be honest about their strengths and weaknesses. The key roles, which may be filled by one or more people, include:

1. Architect - responsible for the system's overall structure.
2. Abstractionist - focused on defining classes and class categories.
3. Application Engineer - tasked with implementing and assembling the classes and managing the interactions between them.

Just like in traditional development, individuals are not interchangeable. Software development is fundamentally a human endeavor, and even the most talented team cannot successfully complete the simplest project if they cannot collaborate effectively toward a shared goal.

Here is how they differ:

1. Project Planning and Estimation
   a. Traditional Development: Project planning in traditional development is often linear and follows a Waterfall approach, where the project is broken down into phases like requirements gathering, design, coding, testing, and maintenance. Estimations are made based on each phase, and the project moves sequentially through them.
   b. Object-Oriented Development: OOD is more iterative and incremental, often aligning with Agile methodologies. Projects are planned around iterations or sprints, where small, functional units of the software are designed, developed, and tested in cycles. Estimations are based on user stories or features, allowing for more flexibility and adjustment as the project progresses.
2. Design and Architecture
   a. Traditional Development: Emphasizes a top-down approach with a focus on functional decomposition. The system is designed around processes and data flow diagrams, with a clear separation between data and functions.
   b. Object-Oriented Development: Focuses on modeling real-world entities and their interactions. The design is centered around objects, which encapsulate both data and behaviors. This leads to the use of class diagrams, inheritance hierarchies, and relationships like aggregation and composition in the design phase.
3. Team Structure and Roles
   a. Traditional Development: Roles are often more rigid, with clear distinctions between analysts, designers, developers, and testers. The flow of work is sequential, with each role working on a specific phase.
   b. Object-Oriented Development: Teams are typically cross-functional, with roles that overlap. Developers may work closely with analysts and testers throughout the project, especially in Agile environments where collaboration and communication are key.
4. Development and Coding
   a. Traditional Development: Coding is done in a procedural manner, focusing on functions or procedures that operate on data structures. The development process is usually less modular, and changes can be more difficult to manage because of tight coupling between functions and data.
   b. Object-Oriented Development: Emphasizes modularity through the use of objects and classes. Code is organized around objects, making it easier to manage changes, reuse components, and extend the system. OOD encourages practices like encapsulation, inheritance, and polymorphism, which affect how code is structured and maintained.
5. Testing and Quality Assurance
   a. Traditional Development: Testing is often done after the entire system has been developed, which can lead to the discovery of defects late in the project. This approach can result in longer testing phases and higher costs for fixing issues.
   b. Object-Oriented Development: Testing is integrated throughout the development process. Unit testing, integration testing, and even Test-Driven Development (TDD) are common practices in OOD, where testing is done at the class or object level. This allows for

continuous feedback and quicker identification of issues.

6. Project Management Methodologies
    a. Traditional Development: Often aligns with Waterfall or V-Model methodologies, which are more rigid and sequential. The focus is on completing each phase before moving to the next, with extensive documentation and formal review processes.
    b. Object-Oriented Development: Typically aligns with Agile or Iterative methodologies, where the focus is on delivering small, functional increments of the software. Project management is more adaptive, with regular reviews, sprint planning, and retrospective meetings to continuously improve the process.
7. Change Management
    a. Traditional Development: Changes are often more difficult to manage due to the linear nature of the process. Late-stage changes can be costly and time-consuming.
    b. Object-Oriented Development: OOD is more adaptable to change, with its modular and iterative nature. Changes can be more easily incorporated into the project, often being accommodated within the next iteration or sprint.
8. Maintenance
    a. Traditional Development: Maintenance can be challenging due to the tight coupling between functions and data. Changes to one part of the system can have unintended consequences in other areas.
    b. Object-Oriented Development: Maintenance is generally easier because of the modular design. Objects and classes can be modified or extended without affecting other parts of the system, and code reuse is common.

In summary, object-oriented development tends to be more flexible, modular, and iterative compared to traditional development, which is more linear and phase-driven. These differences influence project management techniques, with OOD often aligning better with modern, Agile methodologies.

13.12. What is the P-CMM?

The P-CMM (People Capability Maturity Model) is a framework that helps organizations improve the management and development of their workforce. It is based on the Capability Maturity Model (CMM) used in software development but focuses on the processes and practices related to human resources and workforce development.

Here are the key aspects of P-CMM:

1. Maturity Levels: P-CMM defines five levels of maturity that describe the evolutionary stages of an organization's workforce practices:
    a. Level 1: Initial - Workforce practices are inconsistent and depend on individual managers. There is little formal HR structure.
    b. Level 2: Managed - Basic policies for workforce management are in place. There is more consistency in how people are treated.
    c. Level 3: Defined - Workforce practices are standardized and documented across the organization.
    d. Level 4: Predictable - Workforce capabilities are measured, and the organization can predict performance based on these measurements.
    e. Level 5: Optimizing - Continuous improvement of workforce practices is emphasized, and the organization focuses on developing the potential of its workforce.
2. Key Process Areas (KPAs): At each maturity level, there are specific process areas that organizations need to focus on to move to the next level. For example, at Level 2, key process areas might include workforce planning, performance management, and training.
3. Goals and Practices: Each KPA has specific goals that need to be achieved and practices that

guide how to reach those goals.

4. Implementation: P-CMM provides a roadmap for organizations to assess their current workforce practices, identify areas for improvement, and implement changes to progress through the maturity levels.

The P-CMM is widely used in industries where human resources and talent management are critical to success, such as IT, consulting, and finance. By following P-CMM, organizations can develop a more capable and motivated workforce, leading to better performance and competitiveness.

13.13. What is standard deviation?

Standard deviation is a measure of the amount of variation or dispersion in a set of values. It quantifies how much the values in a data set deviate, on average, from the mean (average) of the data set. In simpler terms, it tells you how spread out the numbers in your data set are.

Calculation of Standard Deviation

1. The standard deviation is calculated using the following steps:
2. Find the Mean: Calculate the mean (average) of the data set.
3. Subtract the Mean: Subtract the mean from each data point to find the deviation of each data point from the mean.
4. Square the Deviations: Square each of these deviations to eliminate negative values.
5. Find the Average of Squared Deviations: Calculate the mean of these squared deviations. This value is called the variance.
6. Take the Square Root: Finally, take the square root of the variance to get the standard deviation.

$$\sigma = \sqrt{\frac{1}{N}\sum_{i=1}^{N}(x_i - \mu)^2}$$

Where:
σ is the standard deviation
N is the number of data points
x_i represents each data point
μ is the mean of the data set

Applications of Standard Deviation: Standard deviation is widely used in various fields for different purposes:

1. Finance:
   a. Used to measure the risk or volatility of an investment. A higher standard deviation indicates more risk because the returns on the investment are more spread out from the average return.
2. Quality Control:
   a. In manufacturing, standard deviation helps determine whether a process is consistent and stable. Lower standard deviation indicates a more consistent process.
3. Statistics:
   a. Used in inferential statistics to make conclusions about a population based on sample data.
   b. It is also crucial in the calculation of confidence intervals and hypothesis testing.
4. Psychology and Education:
   a. Helps in understanding the variability in test scores or behavioral measurements. It provides insight into how much variation exists in individuals' performances or traits.
5. Weather and Climate Studies:

   a. Helps in understanding the variability in weather patterns, such as temperature and rainfall.
6. Sports:
   a. Used to assess the consistency of athletes' performances. A lower standard deviation in performance scores indicates higher consistency.

Practical Example - Imagine you have the test scores of a class of students: Scores: 70, 80, 90, 100, 60
To find the standard deviation:
1. Mean: (70+80+90+100+60)/5=80
2. Deviations from Mean: -10, 0, 10, 20, -20
3. Squared Deviations: 100, 0, 100, 400, 400
4. Variance: (100+0+100+400+400)/5=200
5. Standard Deviation: Sq Rt of 200≈14.14

This standard deviation indicates how much the students' scores vary around the mean score of 80.

13.14. What is segmentation?

Segmentation involves dividing a large group into smaller, logical categories for easier analysis. Common examples include segmenting customers, data sets, or markets. For instance, you might gather data on the causes of defects in a process and display this information using a Pareto chart. A Pareto chart is a type of bar graph where the lengths of the bars represent frequency or cost (in terms of time or money) and are arranged from the longest bars on the left to the shortest on the right. This arrangement visually highlights which issues are most significant. The chart might show, for example, that Type A defects account for 50%, Type B defects for 30%, and Type C defects for 20%. This is one way to segment the data for clearer insights.

Segmentation, in a broad context, refers to the process of dividing something into distinct parts or sections. Depending on the field of study or industry, segmentation can have different specific meanings:
1. Market Segmentation: In marketing, segmentation is the process of dividing a broad consumer or business market into sub-groups of consumers (known as segments) based on some type of shared characteristics. These characteristics can include demographics, psychographics, behavior, and geographical locations. The goal is to tailor marketing efforts to specific segments to more effectively meet their needs and increase profitability.
2. Image Segmentation: In computer vision and image processing, segmentation refers to the process of partitioning a digital image into multiple segments (sets of pixels) to simplify or change the representation of an image into something more meaningful and easier to analyze. It is often used to locate objects and boundaries (lines, curves, etc.) in images.
3. Network Segmentation: In cybersecurity, segmentation involves dividing a computer network into smaller parts, or segments, to improve security and manageability. By isolating parts of the network, organizations can control the flow of traffic between segments and limit the spread of cyber threats.
4. Genomic Segmentation: In genomics, segmentation can refer to the process of dividing a DNA sequence into regions with similar properties, such as similar gene expression levels or chromosomal locations.
5. Segmentation in Psychology: In cognitive psychology, segmentation refers to the process of dividing a continuous stream of behavior, thoughts, or experiences into discrete, meaningful units.

Each of these contexts uses segmentation to break down a complex whole into more manageable or analyzable parts.

13.15. What is a flowchart?

A flowchart is a visual diagram that represents a sequence of steps or decisions needed to perform a process or solve a problem. It uses various symbols to denote different types of actions or decisions, connected by arrows that indicate the flow of the process. Flowcharts are commonly used in programming, business process modeling, and project management to clearly outline procedures, workflows, or algorithms.

Common Symbols in a Flowchart:

1. Oval: Represents the start or end of a process.
2. Rectangle: Denotes a process or action step.
3. Diamond: Indicates a decision point, where the flow can branch based on different outcomes.
4. Parallelogram: Represents input or output (e.g., data entry, displaying results).
5. Arrow: Shows the direction of the flow from one step to another.

Example of Flowchart Use:

1. In Business: To outline the steps of a customer service process.
2. In Programming: To visualize the logic of an algorithm.
3. In Project Management: To map out the steps in a project timeline.

Flowcharts help in understanding and communicating complex processes in a clear and straightforward way.

13.16. Define metrics.

A business metric is a measurable indicator that companies use to track, monitor, and evaluate the performance of various business processes. The primary purpose of business metrics is to provide insight into an organization's progress toward achieving specific long- and short-term goals.

To effectively utilize business metrics, it is crucial to gather input from key stakeholders to identify which metrics are most relevant to their areas of business. Some organizations even incorporate these metrics into their mission statements, requiring alignment and commitment across all levels of the company. Others may integrate them into their routine operations.

Business metrics play a vital role in helping a company achieve its strategic and financial objectives. They enable business owners and managers to make informed decisions and evaluate the efficiency of their operations. Additionally, metrics address the specific concerns of stakeholders.

By quantifying business insights, metrics allow managers to develop and refine strategies to improve business outcomes.

However, business metrics are meaningless without context; companies interpret metrics through the lens of existing benchmarks, practices, and goals. When used strategically, metrics can enhance business practices, drive progress toward objectives, and optimize performance.

The term "metric" refers to a method of measurement, often used within organizations to assess quality levels. In this context, a metric is a consistent and repeatable way to measure the size and complexity of a project. Metrics are calculated using various methods throughout a project's lifecycle. Some widely used methods include:

1. Function Point Analysis (Allan Albrecht)
2. Bang Method (Tom DeMarco)

3. Weighted Average
4. Lines of Code (LOC).

13.17. What are KPI measurement techniques?

A Key Performance Indicator (KPI) is a quantifiable measure that reflects how well a company is achieving its critical business goals. Organizations rely on KPIs to assess their progress toward specific targets. These indicators provide insight into a company's effectiveness in reaching its objectives and can be applied across various industries, departments, or individual tasks. KPIs are monitored over a designated time frame and are compared to previous performance metrics or established standards.

Without the establishment and monitoring of appropriate KPIs, companies would lack clarity on their performance. They might believe they are successful, but what type of success are they achieving? And how does it compare to expectations? While companies may know which metrics are trackable, the challenge lies in identifying which ones are most crucial. With KPIs in place, you can set realistic goals, develop strategies to achieve them, assess your progress, and eventually maintain a historical record of your business's performance.

Key performance indicators are vital tools for assessing the health and effectiveness of a company and its employees. Each KPI is a metric that, when positive, indicates the company is on the right track. For instance, new revenue from sales might serve as a KPI to gauge the performance of a sales team. However, determining which KPIs are essential for your business can be challenging. Consider the following approaches:

1. Define Success Collectively: To measure staff performance effectively, the team must first agree on what "success" means. For example, if you are leading a sales team, clear goals such as "closing three deals per week" must be established. This clarity is crucial for holding the team accountable and tracking the KPI.
2. Identify Data Sources for Measurement: Once the team understands the definition of success, the next step is to identify a reliable data source to measure progress. This could be a CRM system or a simple internal spreadsheet updated regularly. The key is to have data in a documented form that everyone can access, ensuring transparency in tracking progress towards your goals.
3. Regularly Share Updates and Address Obstacles: Effective KPIs are updated frequently. Their purpose is to indicate whether the team is on track, allowing managers to make necessary adjustments and guide the team towards success. Consider sharing weekly written status updates so everyone is informed about plans, progress, and any challenges team members face.
4. Make KPI Measurement Visible and Transparent: Performance indicators should not be reviewed only during monthly staff meetings. They need to be examined frequently (often daily) to quickly identify and address issues. Whether through automated systems or manual processes, there should be a consistent approach to reporting KPIs to the team.
5. Take Action When Performance is Lacking: Even the most well-defined and accessible KPIs are ineffective if the team does not act when performance is below expectations. Managers must hold the team accountable to a certain performance level, using KPIs as a tool to do so. A critical aspect of effective KPI management is taking action based on the measured results.

Key Performance Indicators (KPIs) are measurable values that demonstrate how effectively an organization is achieving key business objectives. To measure KPIs, several techniques can be employed depending on the type of KPI and the data available. Here are some common KPI measurement techniques:

1. Quantitative Analysis
    a. Direct Measurement: Using numerical data to directly measure performance against a specific target (e.g., sales numbers, revenue, or customer retention rates).

b. Percentage Calculation: Measuring KPIs as a percentage of a whole, such as the percentage of sales growth or customer satisfaction rates.
c. Ratios: Calculating ratios like the profit margin, return on investment (ROI), or customer acquisition cost (CAC).

2. Qualitative Analysis
   a. Surveys and Feedback: Gathering customer or employee feedback through surveys, interviews, or focus groups to assess satisfaction, engagement, or other non-quantifiable metrics.
   b. Observational Techniques: Monitoring and recording behavioral patterns or processes to measure performance, such as time taken to complete tasks or adherence to procedures.
3. Benchmarking
   a. Internal Benchmarking: Comparing current performance against past performance within the organization to measure improvement over time.
   b. External Benchmarking: Comparing performance against industry standards or competitors to assess where the organization stands relative to others.
4. Dashboards and Scorecards
   a. Performance Dashboards: Visual tools that provide real-time data on various KPIs, often with interactive features that allow for in-depth analysis.
   b. Balanced Scorecards: A strategic planning tool that tracks KPIs across different perspectives, such as financial, customer, internal process, and learning and growth.
5. Trend Analysis
   a. Historical Data Comparison: Analyzing trends over time to identify patterns, anomalies, or changes in performance.
   b. Forecasting: Using past data to predict future performance and set KPI targets.
6. Statistical Methods
   a. Regression Analysis: Identifying relationships between variables to understand how different factors influence a KPI.
   b. Variance Analysis: Comparing actual performance to targets or budgets to identify deviations and their causes.
7. Operational Analysis
   a. Process Metrics: Measuring the efficiency and effectiveness of processes, such as cycle time, error rates, or production yields.
   b. Capacity Utilization: Assessing how well resources (like labor or equipment) are being used in relation to their maximum capacity.
8. Financial Analysis
   a. Financial Ratios: Calculating financial ratios such as liquidity ratios, profitability ratios, and leverage ratios to measure financial health.
   b. Cost-Benefit Analysis: Evaluating the cost-effectiveness of initiatives by comparing the benefits derived from them against their costs.
9. Goal Setting and Tracking
   a. SMART Goals: Setting Specific, Measurable, Achievable, Relevant, and Time-bound goals and tracking progress against them.
   b. Milestone Tracking: Monitoring the achievement of specific milestones that lead up to the overall KPI target.
10. Root Cause Analysis
    a. Fishbone Diagrams: Identifying potential causes of performance issues by breaking down the factors that contribute to the problem.
    b. 5 Whys: Repeatedly asking "why" to drill down into the underlying cause of a KPI's underperformance.

Each technique can be used alone or in combination with others, depending on the complexity and nature of the KPI being measured.

13.18. What are some of the most useful program management techniques and frameworks that you would recommend?

Program management involves overseeing multiple related projects to ensure that they align with organizational goals and objectives. There are several program management techniques and frameworks that are widely used and recommended in the industry to effectively plan, execute, and control complex programs. Here are some useful program management techniques and frameworks:

1. Agile Methodology: Agile is a popular framework for managing projects, emphasizing flexibility, collaboration, and incremental delivery. Agile methodologies such as Scrum, Kanban, and Lean provide tools and practices for iterative development and continuous improvement.
2. Waterfall Methodology: While not as flexible as Agile, the Waterfall methodology is still widely used, especially in industries with strict regulatory requirements or highly predictable projects. It involves a sequential approach to project management, with distinct phases such as requirements gathering, design, implementation, testing, and deployment.
3. Scaled Agile Framework (SAFe): SAFe is a framework for scaling Agile practices to large organizations. It provides guidance on coordinating Agile teams, managing dependencies, and aligning work with strategic goals.
4. ITIL (Information Technology Infrastructure Library): ITIL provides a framework for IT service management, focusing on aligning IT services with the needs of the business. It is particularly relevant for organizations that rely heavily on IT infrastructure and services.
5. PRINCE2 (Projects in Controlled Environments): PRINCE2 is a structured project management methodology that divides projects into manageable stages and emphasizes clear roles and responsibilities. It provides a framework for effective project governance and control.
6. PMI's Program Management Professional (PgMP) Certification: Offered by the Project Management Institute (PMI), the PgMP certification is designed for experienced program managers. It covers advanced program management concepts and best practices, providing a comprehensive framework for managing complex programs.
7. PMO (Project Management Office): Establishing a PMO within an organization can help standardize project management practices, provide governance, and oversight, and support continuous improvement. PMOs can range from providing project support services to actively managing portfolios of projects and programs.
8. Critical Chain Project Management (CCPM): CCPM is a project management approach that focuses on identifying and managing project constraints to improve project performance. It emphasizes the importance of resource management and buffer management to reduce project delays and improve delivery times.
9. Earned Value Management (EVM): EVM is a project management technique for measuring project performance and progress objectively. It integrates project scope, schedule, and cost to provide insights into project health and forecast future performance.
10. Lean Six Sigma: Lean Six Sigma combines Lean principles for process improvement with Six Sigma methodologies for reducing defects and variability. It provides a structured approach to optimizing processes and reducing waste in program management.
11. Risk Management: Effective risk management is essential for program success. Techniques such as risk identification, assessment, mitigation, and monitoring help program managers anticipate and address potential issues before they escalate into problems.
12. Hybrid Approaches: Many organizations create custom hybrid approaches by combining elements of different frameworks to suit their specific needs.

The choice of technique or framework depends on factors such as the nature of the program, the organization's culture, the team's experience, and the specific project requirements. It is often beneficial to tailor and adapt these techniques to fit the unique context of the program you're managing.

13.19. What project management framework is best for leadership?

The best project management framework for leadership depends on the nature of the project, the organization, and the leadership style. However, here are a few frameworks that are often considered effective for leaders:

1. Agile
    a. Best For: Projects requiring flexibility, rapid iteration, and frequent stakeholder engagement.
    b. Why It is Effective for Leadership: Agile promotes collaboration, adaptability, and continuous improvement, which are key traits for strong leadership. Leaders can quickly respond to changes and guide their teams through iterative cycles, ensuring that the project aligns with evolving needs.
2. Scrum
    a. Best For: Complex projects with a need for rapid delivery and iterative progress.
    b. Why It is Effective for Leadership: Scrum emphasizes accountability, transparency, and continuous feedback. Leaders in Scrum environments can focus on removing obstacles for their teams, empowering team members, and ensuring that the project delivers value consistently.
3. Waterfall
    a. Best For: Projects with well-defined requirements and a clear, linear process.
    b. Why It is Effective for Leadership: Waterfall provides a structured approach, allowing leaders to plan thoroughly and set clear expectations. This framework is particularly effective in environments where changes are minimal, and there is a need for strict adherence to schedules and budgets.
4. PRINCE2 (Projects IN Controlled Environments)
    a. Best For: Large-scale projects or those in highly regulated environments.
    b. Why It is Effective for Leadership: PRINCE2 provides a comprehensive and detailed framework that emphasizes organization, control, and risk management. Leaders using PRINCE2 can maintain tight control over the project while ensuring that all aspects are thoroughly managed.
5. Lean
    a. Best For: Projects focused on maximizing value by eliminating waste.
    b. Why It is Effective for Leadership: Lean encourages leaders to streamline processes, reduce inefficiencies, and focus on value creation. This framework fosters a culture of continuous improvement and encourages leaders to be proactive in problem-solving.
6. Hybrid Models (e.g., Agile-Waterfall)
    a. Best For: Projects that require the flexibility of Agile with the structure of Waterfall.
    b. Why It i Effective for Leadership: Hybrid models allow leaders to tailor their approach based on the project's specific needs, combining the strengths of different frameworks to best suit the team and objectives.
7. OKR (Objectives and Key Results)
    a. Best For: Aligning project goals with organizational objectives.
    b. Why It is Effective for Leadership: OKRs help leaders focus on the most critical outcomes, aligning team efforts with broader business goals. This framework encourages strategic thinking and accountability.
8. Kanban
    a. Best For: Projects needing continuous delivery without overloading team members.
    b. Why It is Effective for Leadership: Kanban allows leaders to visualize workflow, identify bottlenecks, and ensure that work progresses smoothly. It promotes a balanced workload

and continuous delivery of tasks.

Leadership effectiveness in project management often depends not just on the chosen framework but also on the leader's ability to communicate, motivate, and align the team with the project's goals. Choosing a framework that aligns with the organization's culture and the project’s needs is essential.

Getting a diverse group of busy executives to adopt the same project management approach can be challenging. Each leader has their own preferred way of working, and convincing them to align with a unified approach, let alone a specific tool, is not easy. With that in mind, consider the following:

1. Keep It Simple: The simpler the system, the better. Avoid buzzwords and complex systems that require leaders to change their workflow or learn a new interface. While it may seem old-fashioned, many teams find that a shared spreadsheet works best. It may lack advanced reporting and metrics, but it is something everyone will actually use.
2. Focus on Objectives (MBOs): No matter what method you choose, success hinges on defining clear objectives and tracking progress toward them. In a cross-functional executive team, data sources for tracking success will vary widely (e.g., CRM, marketing automation systems, individual knowledge). The key is ensuring that every leader understands the goals and how success will be measured. If they are top performers, they will collaborate to achieve those goals.
3. Document Status Updates: Whether you are using a simple spreadsheet or a comprehensive project management tool, progress needs to be documented. Sometimes this will be done automatically by the different systems in use. Well-resourced companies may employ business intelligence (BI) tools to visualize this data.
4. Allow Leaders Flexibility: Recognize that it is difficult to impose a single project management system across a cross-functional leadership team. Each leader may have their preferred methods, so it is wise to give them the freedom to manage their work in their own way, without micromanaging. As long as communication is standardized (e.g., through weekly meetings and updates), the specific execution methodology can be left to each leader’s discretion.
5. Ensure Accountability: Whatever approach is taken; leaders must be held accountable for making progress and delivering results. Tools and methods can vary, but as long as progress is tracked in writing and the CEO reviews it at least weekly to provide feedback, accountability will be maintained.

13.20. How can you manage agile vs waterfall projects more efficiently?

Managing Agile and Waterfall projects efficiently requires a nuanced approach, as these methodologies are fundamentally different in their structures, processes, and expectations. Here are some strategies to manage both effectively:

1. Understanding the Key Differences:
    a. Waterfall:
        i. Sequential phases (Requirement → Design → Implementation → Testing → Deployment).
        ii. Fixed scope, budget, and timeline.
        iii. Detailed documentation and upfront planning.
    b. Agile:
        i. Iterative, incremental development.
        ii. Flexible scope; priorities can change.
        iii. Continuous feedback and collaboration.
2. Selecting the Right Methodology:
    a. Project Nature:
        i. Use Waterfall for projects with clear, well-defined requirements and where changes are unlikely.

    ii. Opt for Agile when the project scope is dynamic, or if rapid delivery of partial functionality is beneficial.
b. Stakeholder Engagement:
    i. Waterfall works well with stakeholders who prefer detailed upfront planning and limited involvement during the execution phase.
    ii. Agile suits stakeholders who are willing to engage regularly and adapt to evolving requirements.

3. Combining Agile and Waterfall (Hybrid Approach):
   a. Phased Approach: Use Waterfall for high-level planning and Agile for execution. For example, use Waterfall for initial requirement gathering and Agile for the development phase.
   b. Parallel Tracks: Use Waterfall for one part of the project (e.g., infrastructure setup) and Agile for another (e.g., software development).
   c. Agile-Waterfall Integration: Use Agile sprints for iterative development within each Waterfall phase, especially in projects where certain deliverables are better suited to Waterfall but require ongoing flexibility.
4. Team Management:
   a. Skillset Alignment:
      i. Ensure team members are skilled in the specific methodology being used.
      ii. For hybrid projects, provide cross-training or use dedicated teams for different phases.
   b. Communication and Collaboration:
      i. Use Agile's communication tools (like daily stand-ups, retrospectives) to keep teams aligned.
      ii. Ensure that Waterfall teams have access to clear, structured documentation and that they understand the project timeline and milestones.
5. Project Tracking and Reporting:
   a. Agile Tools: Use Agile project management tools (like Jira, Trello) for tracking sprints, user stories, and tasks.
   b. Waterfall Tools: Use Gantt charts or project management software (like Microsoft Project) for detailed timelines and milestone tracking.
   c. Hybrid Reporting: Develop a reporting mechanism that aligns with both methodologies, like using burndown charts for Agile and milestone tracking for Waterfall, with regular updates to stakeholders.
6. Risk Management:
   a. Waterfall: Focus on upfront risk identification and mitigation planning. Revisit risks at each phase gate.
   b. Agile: Manage risks through continuous iteration and feedback loops, adjusting priorities as new risks emerge.
   c. Hybrid: Use Waterfall for broad risk management and Agile for responding to risks that emerge during development.
7. Adaptability and Continuous Improvement:
   a. Regularly evaluate the project's progress and methodology effectiveness.
   b. For Agile, hold retrospectives after each sprint to learn and adapt.
   c. In Waterfall, use post-milestone reviews to assess progress and refine future phases.
   d. In hybrid models, have periodic assessments to ensure that the balance between Agile and Waterfall is still appropriate for the project.
8. Stakeholder Management:
   a. Waterfall: Ensure stakeholders are aligned with the project scope, timeline, and deliverables from the outset.
   b. Agile: Keep stakeholders engaged with regular updates, demos, and feedback sessions.

    c. Hybrid: Tailor communication to suit the stakeholder's preference - detailed for Waterfall phases and iterative for Agile phases.

By applying these strategies, you can manage Agile and Waterfall projects more efficiently, ensuring that each project's unique needs are met while maintaining overall alignment with business goals.

13.21. Compare and contrast SAFe with Agile Scrum.

SAFe (Scaled Agile Framework) and Agile Scrum are both methodologies used to manage and execute work in a flexible, iterative, and collaborative way. However, they operate at different levels of scale and have distinct structures, making them suitable for different organizational contexts. Below is a comparison and contrast of the two:

1. Purpose and Scope:
    a. Agile Scrum:
        i. Purpose: Scrum is a framework designed for small teams (typically 5-9 members) to manage and control complex product development in an iterative manner.
        ii. Scope: It is primarily focused on individual teams. It does not prescribe how multiple teams should coordinate their work when working on the same product.
    b. SAFe (Scaled Agile Framework):
        i. Purpose: SAFe is a framework that scales Agile practices across large organizations with multiple teams working on a shared product or portfolio.
        ii. Scope: It addresses work at multiple levels - Team, Program, Large Solution, and Portfolio - and includes guidance for coordinating large groups of Agile teams.
2. Structure:
    a. Agile Scrum:
        i. Key Roles: Product Owner, Scrum Master, Development Team.
        ii. Ceremonies: Sprint Planning, Daily Standup (Daily Scrum), Sprint Review, and Sprint Retrospective.
        iii. Artifacts: Product Backlog, Sprint Backlog, Increment.
        iv. Sprint Duration: Typically 2-4 weeks.
    b. SAFe:
        i. Key Roles: Includes roles from Scrum but adds others such as Release Train Engineer (RTE), Product Management, System Architect/Engineer, and Business Owners.
        ii. Ceremonies: In addition to Scrum ceremonies, SAFe introduces ceremonies like Program Increment (PI) Planning, System Demo, Inspect and Adapt, and more.
        iii. Artifacts: Includes Scrum artifacts and adds Program Backlog, Solution Backlog, PI Objectives, and others.
        iv. Program Increment (PI) Duration: Typically 8-12 weeks, consisting of multiple Sprints.
3. Implementation:
    a. Agile Scrum:
        i. Adoption: Scrum is easier to adopt for single teams or smaller organizations. It requires less overhead and is more lightweight.
        ii. Flexibility: Teams have more freedom to adjust practices as needed without the constraints of coordinating with many other teams.
    b. SAFe:
        i. Adoption: SAFe is more complex and requires more investment in training, tools, and change management. It's better suited for larger enterprises.
        ii. Coordination: SAFe provides detailed guidance on aligning work across multiple

teams, including synchronization of Sprints and alignment with strategic goals.

4. Focus:
   a. Agile Scrum:
      i. Focus: Team-level productivity, delivering working increments of product every Sprint, and continuous improvement at the team level.
      ii. Decision-Making: Typically decentralized within the team. Product Owners have strong influence on priorities.
   b. SAFe:
      i. Focus: Aligning the work of multiple teams with the organization's broader objectives. SAFe emphasizes collaboration, alignment, and transparency across the enterprise.
      ii. Decision-Making: More hierarchical, with decisions being made at various levels (Team, Program, Solution, Portfolio).
5. Framework Complexity:
   a. Agile Scrum:
      i. Complexity: Scrum is relatively simple, with clear roles and practices. It's easy for teams to understand and implement quickly.
   b. SAFe:
      i. Complexity: SAFe is more complex and structured, with multiple levels and roles. It requires comprehensive understanding and buy-in from the entire organization.
6. Training and Certification:
   a. Agile Scrum:
      i. Training: Many certifications are available (e.g., Certified ScrumMaster (CSM), Professional Scrum Master (PSM)).
      ii. Focus: Primarily on the Scrum framework and its application within teams.
   b. SAFe:
      i. Training: Requires more extensive training, such as SAFe Agilist (SA), SAFe Program Consultant (SPC), and others, to understand the full framework.
      ii. Focus: Training is broader, covering not just Agile practices, but also how to scale Agile across large enterprises.
7. Usage Context:
   a. Agile Scrum:
      i. Best Suited For: Small to medium-sized teams that work independently on products or features. It is ideal for organizations looking to implement Agile without a heavy framework.
   b. SAFe:
      i. Best Suited For: Large organizations with multiple teams working on interconnected projects. It is particularly useful when there is a need for consistent alignment across large programs and portfolios.

Summary:
1. Agile Scrum is simpler, more focused on individual teams, and is generally easier to implement, making it ideal for smaller organizations or single teams.
2. SAFe provides a structured, scalable framework designed to bring multiple Agile teams together under a single, unified process, making it suitable for large enterprises aiming to scale Agile across the organization.

13.22. Project Issues and Risks Template

Project Issues

Issue Date	Issue	Impact (if not resolved)	Action Plan	Status	Target Close Date	Actual Close Date

Project Risks

Risk	Likelihood	Impact (if not resolved)	Mitigation Plan	Status	Owner

Likelihood - Low, Medium, High
Impact - Low, Medium, High - Time, Money, Quality, Customer Satisfaction
Status - Open, Closed

www.ingramcontent.com/pod-product-compliance
Ingram Content Group UK Ltd.
Pitfield, Milton Keynes, MK11 3LW, UK
UKHW061830190726
13853UKWH00009B/2534

9 798890 021748